An Introduction to Reformed Dogmatics

D1604431

An Introduction to Reformed Dogmatics

Auguste Lecerf

Translated by
André Schlemmer

Preface by
S. Leigh-Hunt

Baker Book House
Grand Rapids, Michigan

PHOTOLITHOPRINTED BY CUSHING - MALLOY, INC.
ANN ARBOR, MICHIGAN, UNITED STATES OF AMERICA

TRANSLATOR'S NOTE

This work originally appeared in two volumes under the title *Introduction à la Dogmatique Réformée*: Premier Cahier, *De la Nature de la Connaissance Religieuse* (302 pages, 1931); Second Cahier, *Du Fondement et de la Spécification de la Connaissance Religieuse* (262 pages, 1938); both published by Editions Je Sers, Paris. The author's lamented death in 1943 prevented him from completing the volumes on Reformed Dogmatics which he had in contemplation.

The position adopted in this *Introduction*, and indeed throughout all Dr. Lecerf's later work, is that of authentic or classical Calvinism confronted by and fully cognizant of the various thought movements of the day. Kuyper and Bavinck are his mentors rather than Barth, who is referred to only twice and then merely in such courteous and general terms as *le génial restaurateur de la théologie réformatrice* (11.2).

Part I discusses the nature of religious knowledge. The author maintains that Calvinism has no place for natural theology but only for a theology based on faith in divine revelation (1.2–4). Modern philosophical views are examined in some detail, and Cartesian rationalism, Baconian empiricism and Kantian idealism are shown to be inadequate as foundations for a Christian theory of knowledge. The philosophy which, in his view, accords best with the facts of the case, is a moderate, critical and transcendental realism for which support is drawn from McCosh (1.8), Vollenhoven, Dooyeweerd and the neo-thomists (11.3).

The second part is concerned with the concept of apologetics in Calvinism, with the relation of the latter to philosophy and, in the concluding chapters, with dogmatics directly considered. Lecerf rejects Barth's view that the doctrine of total depravity excludes reasoning about spiritual matters. On the contrary, faith is the beginning of truly normal thought. Regeneration involves the restoration of the reason which, however, is not autonomous but dependent on God as its supreme guarantor. "The faith remains the faith. But it can assume a scientific form in dogmatics proper, and it contains the psychological and intellectual conditions for the elaboration of a specifically Christian philosophy" (11.2 *ad fin.*).

5

The Christian philosopher finds himself in the position of a student who knows the solution of a problem in mathematics or physics but must show the reasoning processes required in order to reach it. The solution in this case is that God is the universal creator. The so-called "proofs" of His existence are in reality arguments, explanatory propositions, testimonies, rather than proofs in the technical sense of the term. The dogmas of revelation are necessary for the Christian philosopher who, *pace* Bertrand Russell, does not cease to be a philosopher because he accepts them. (Might not Russell himself be disregarded as an epistemologist for paying some attention to common sense as well as to critical analysis in constructing a philosophical conception of the external world?) The real task of the Christian philosopher is to work out the necessary relation between the supreme legislator and His creatures, and in pursuance of this end he will not hesitate to use what is sound in the work of pagan philosophers, recognizing it as the effect of common grace (11.3).

Finally, having considered the relevant objections, Lecerf shows why dogmatics must be theistic (11.4), orthodox (11.7) and Protestant (11.8). In a chapter on the formal and external principle of the Reformed Faith (11.9) the Church doctrine of biblical inspiration and consequent inerrancy is defended against the criticism of the 19th century and after. Objections are dealt with in detail, particular reference being made by the author to the radical views of his former professor Auguste Sabatier. In discussing the canon of the New Testament, the testimony of the Spirit to and through the Church receives due emphasis (11.10). The same Spirit witnesses in the New Testament to the Palestinian canon of the Old Testament (11.11). Chapter 12 defines the Calvinistic attitude towards Church unity, a subject of deep interest to the author who by precept and example sought at all times to give it practical expression. The concluding chapters show that the formal authority of Scripture is a first principle of theology (11.13) and that Christian theology must be Calvinistic and Reformed (11.14).

Footnotes in square brackets have been added by the translator. Quotations from Calvin's *Institutes of the Christian Religion* (*Institutio Christianae religionis*) are indicated as follows : e.g. *Inst.* I, i. 1 signifying Book I, chapter i, section 1, respectively, the references being to the definitive edition of 1559, unless otherwise specified. Grateful thanks are due to Dr. André Schlemmer and the Rev. John W. Wenham for reading the proofs and making valuable suggestions. S.L.-H.

PREFACE

In 1930 a visitor knocked at Professor Lecerf's door and introduced himself with these words: "Some friends of mine, hearing that I was passing through Paris, have advised me to come and see you. M. Lecerf is a unique personality, they say, he is in fact the last of the Calvinists and when he dies the type will be extinct. So whatever happens, do not fail to pay him a visit."

When God called his servant home in 1943, he had seen the divine blessing upon his labours. Far from being the sole defender of a lost cause, he had become the leader of a living movement, which was rapidly and irresistibly reversing all the positions of the once prevalent modernism. Practically all the young people coming out of the Theological Faculties of France and Geneva were declaring themselves Calvinists. The Reformed Church of France was returning to its traditional standpoint and those who might be described as "survivors" were certainly not those who shared the faith of Auguste Lecerf.

He was not, of course, the sole originator of the movement in question. The grace of God had been at work throughout the world. Every branch of Reformed Christendom was being affected by a theological revival which had its sources in Holland and France. In French-speaking countries first place must be given to Emile Doumergue with his monumental biography *Jean Calvin: Les hommes et les choses de son temps.* Later came Jean de Saussure's *A l'Ecole de Calvin*, the work of Jean Cadier and his group, and the influence of Pierre Maury, translator of Karl Barth and Professor Lecerf's successor in the chair of Dogmatics at Paris. But Lecerf was, by common consent, the most eminent representative of Calvinism in Calvin's native land.

To him came students for their graduation theses, delegates to the synods for their reports, persons of every rank for spiritual direction, all certain of gaining valuable information from his vast store of learning, of finding sure advice in his spiritual wisdom and of receiving an attentive welcome from his friendly heart. His thought was always clear, vigorous and distinct, his culture in many spheres immense: theology, philosophy and linguistics were subjects which he could justly call his own. An expert in Hebrew, Greek and Latin, he spoke English like a native and read several other languages with ease. His appearance might have suggested austerity, with his fine features, pale complexion and thin lips. Whether in the pulpit or in private conversation, no one spoke of God with greater solemnity, expounded his thought with greater authority or defended his faith with greater clarity of expression.

Although there was something of the grand seigneur about his bearing, no one could have been more simple, more friendly or more finely comprehensive in his personal dealings. A terrible judge in regard to ideas, he was full of charity in regard to persons; but, holding in horror all display of sentiment and all mere emotionalism, his good nature was often veiled by a malicious sense of humour.

His faith was clearly the work of efficacious grace: there was nothing in his family or ancestry to predispose him to his vocation. Born in London on 18 September, 1872, his earliest days were spent in an atmosphere entirely detached from Christianity, that of the "Communards" who had fled from France after the suppression of their movement in the previous year. Occasionally his mother, a British subject of Italian descent, would pronounce the name of God but that was all. One day when about twelve years of age, walking alone he looked in through the open door of a Protestant church. It was the hour of Sabbath school and the teacher was exhorting the children to consecrate their lives to the service of God. "If there is only one here", he said, "who responds to this appeal, I shall thank God that it was not made in vain." The boy was impressed by the idea that he might be that one, but the thought soon passed from his mind.

Some time afterwards the purchase of a New Testament and the reading in particular of the Epistle to the Romans, together with some first-hand knowledge of the modern Roman Church gained during a period at a school at Angers conducted by a religious order, convinced him that the Gospel was true and that its doctrines were those held by the Reformed Churches.

One day while browsing over the bookstalls on the banks of the Seine in Paris, he noticed a second-hand copy of Calvin's *Institution de la religion Chrétienne*. He began to turn over the pages and at once felt within himself the solemn impact of truth. The volume was purchased and eagerly perused, and he read and re-read it from that moment until the day of his death.

His vocation was decided. Despite family opposition, at the

8

age of 17 he was baptized and made his first communion at the Church of the *Saint-Esprit* in Paris, entered the theological seminary and later studied in the Faculty of Theology there. Despite the extreme Liberalism of his professors, of whom Auguste Sabatier was the most eminent, he completed his course at the age of 23 after presenting a definitely Calvinistic thesis on *Determinism and Responsibility in the Calvinistic system.*

There followed 19 years of arduous parochial labours in rural Normandy, succeeded by five years of war with the army, after which Lecerf settled in Paris in order to study, teach and write; but the work he was obliged to undertake left little time or energy for personal achievement. However, he began to give a free course on Reformed dogmatics in the Theological Faculty of Paris, which was soon attended by most of the students. Yet it was only in 1932 that he was appointed lecturer, and not until 1938 that he became professor. He was 60 and 66 respectively when he succeeded in publishing the two parts of the present work. His health had been affected by the material and moral conditions of enemy occupation. He always proclaimed his certainty of final victory, which he did not live to see as he died on 1 September 1943.

Dr. Lecerf's busy life of preaching and teaching did not permit of much leisure for purely literary effort. Some of his best theological articles and papers lie buried in the reports of proceedings of the various International Calvinistic Congresses in which he took part and in the *Bulletin* of the Société Calviniste de France which he founded in 1926. It was under the auspices of this society that he published in 1934 the edition of the *Catéchisme de Genève* in modern French to which reference is made throughout these pages.

That his work remains unfinished is due to his doctrinal isolation and to the difficult conditions in which he had to labour during most of his career. It was his intention eventually to write a complete treatise on *Reformed Dogmatics*, to which the present volume forms but the *Introduction*. From the unpublished manuscripts of his lectures one can envisage what would have been the value of such a treatise. But, anxious to revise his work before publication and confident that God would raise up someone to complete it, he withheld his notes from the press.

Nevertheless, the present *Introduction* sufficiently indicates the extent of his erudition, the suppleness and strength of his mind, the depth and clarity of his thought and, above all, the power of his faith. One of its outstanding features is the care

PREFACE

which the author has exercised in clearing the ground for
Reformed dogmatics, first removing one by one all the concepts
standing in the way. Reading these pages, one is impressed with
the importance attached to refuting the philosophical systems,
religious theories and confessional doctrines whose *a priori*
assumptions exclude the principles of Reformed Christianity.
In order to achieve this result, the author has taken pains to
assess correctly ideas and systems in conflict with his own and to
do them full justice. Thus he begins with a critique of the
theories of knowledge which are opposed to the idea that
religious knowledge can be a true knowledge of a real object; he
then continues with a critique of psychological, historical
(sociological) and rational explanations of religion, showing that
it is faith alone which forms the basis of true religion. He
concludes with a critique of the religious doctrines which
contradict or limit submission to the truth revealed in the
sacred Scriptures, whether by reason of their method of appre-
hending religious truth (symbolofideism, Bergsonism), in
virtue of their doctrine of God (deism, pantheism), or by their
criterion of Christian religious truth (immanentism, liberalism,
Roman Catholicism, Melanchthonian Lutheranism and Wesleyan Arminianism).

This does not mean that the contents of the book are exclusively or even principally polemical. On the contrary, it
contains a wealth of positive ideas and penetrating views,
original, finely differentiated and suggestive. It lays the
foundations for a firm and solid school of thought. The reader
will find in it, everywhere expressed with abundant verve and
spirit, in terse, vivid and concise language, the basis, methods and
characteristics of the Christian Faith (apart, of course, from its
content which must be sought in Holy Scripture for Christian life
and in dogmatics for systematic thought). Through the medium
of this intellectual discipline, we behold afresh the flame which
forged the iron faith of our fathers, valiant for truth, witnesses of
Jesus Christ. Beholding, we give glory to God that—at a time
when all that constituted the power and *raison d'être* of the
Churches of His Word seemed to be passing away—He was
pleased to raise up and sustain by His sovereign grace, among
the cohort of restorers of our Faith: Auguste Lecerf.

ANDRÉ SCHLEMMER, M.D. (Paris)
Vice-President, Société Calviniste de France

10

CONTENTS

CONTENTS

PART ONE

THE NATURE OF RELIGIOUS KNOWLEDGE

CHAPTER I

PRELIMINARY CONSIDERATIONS

Broadly speaking, the task which confronted the Reformers of the sixteenth century was twofold. They had, first, to resist the invasion of the Church by the pagan spirit; and, secondly, to restore to the believer the joy of salvation by Christ. Their watchwords were, on the one hand, *soli Deo gloria*; and, on the other, *sola fide*, the justification of the sinner by means of faith alone. Lutheranism was largely preoccupied with the question of individual salvation: Calvin and the Swiss Reformers subordinated a legitimate concern with salvation to the restoration of a sense of the sovereign independence and exclusive authority of God. Thus Calvinism developed a stricter conception of the formal authority of Scripture and of the rôle assigned to predestination in devotion, a more spiritual conception of the sacraments, a doctrine of the Incarnation which takes sufficient account of the human element in the person of Christ, and a more radical reform in worship. Reformed dogmatics, as distinct from other forms of orthodox Protestantism, is that system which draws its inspiration from this theocentric viewpoint.

A methodological introduction to such a system is not only conceivable but has been actually realized. Its object is to find a place for Reformed dogmatics among the theological disciplines. Equally conceivable is an historical introduction tracing the development of Reformed theology, the causes of its deviations and restorations, and the progress which it has made.

But the character of these introductions, and of the conclusions to which they lead, will obviously depend on the answer that one previously gives to the question: what is Reformed dogmatics? Is the religion of which it is the scientific expression the result of a divine revelation, or is it rather the product of the spontaneous activity of the human mind?

It is precisely to questions of this sort that a canonical introduction[1] to Reformed dogmatics must address itself. This introduction must thus precede the methodological and historical

[1] *Vide* Appendix I, p. 387.

introductions. It will be necessary in the first place to show why there must be dogmatic theology and not merely philosophical speculations drawn only from psychological and historical sources. It will be necessary further to show why a system of dogmatics with scientific pretensions must be Christian, and not Jewish or Mohammedan; Protestant, and not Roman or Greek; Reformed, and not Lutheran or individualistic.

From the scientific point of view, it is not sufficient for the theologian to declare that he adopts the principles which he lays down because he believes them to be true. The fact that he believes them to be such, justifies his position morally, but this is merely an individual accident: it is not a scientific necessity. The fact that in studying the faith he starts from one point of view rather than from another is not necessarily an individual accident, but in order to make this clear a canonical discipline is needed to elucidate the nature and the value of the principles underlying his system of dogmatics.

We have endeavoured to give our work the character of a canonical discipline, and that in a more thorough sense than previous writers, such as Bavinck, who approximate most closely to the ideal at which we aim.

In *The Foundations of Belief*, A. J. Balfour attempted an introduction to dogmatics, but succeeded only in sketching the first part of his subject, which shows why God must be considered as the *principium essendi* of religion. W. P. Paterson, in his treatise on *The Rule of Faith* (London, 1912) compares various rules of faith, concluding in favour of a type of Ritschlian Protestantism, strongly tinged by Calvinistic influences: he imagines himself to have treated "of that which ordinarily forms the subject matter of introductions to dogmatics", but in reality he has merely sketched the second part of the canonical introduction and has confined himself to assuming that man must be religious and Christian.

H. Bavinck, in the introductory part of his work on Reformed dogmatics, that veritable *summa* of contemporary Calvinism, goes much farther. He gives an outline of the principles of knowledge, general as well as religious, and propounds a theory of the principles of orthodox Protestantism, without showing, however, why this system of dogmatics must be specifically Reformed. In maintaining the same ground as Bavinck, we have tried, in our way and according to our principles, to blend the matter of the works of Balfour and Paterson above mentioned, and thus to provide a sound canonical introduction to dogmatic theology.

The method we have adopted is as follows. We begin by explaining the idea of a canonical introduction and the principles which, from a confessional point of view, distinguish Reformed dogmatics. Next we proceed to a discussion of the nature of knowledge in general, reviewing the systems proposed and concluding in favour of a moderate critical realism. The study of this knowledge, particularly in the light of its object, which is religious knowledge, presupposes clear views as to the nature of religion, its universality and persistence, and this forms the subject-matter of the following chapters.

The remainder of Part I deals with religious knowledge, showing that it has a real object and content. It is here that we shall indicate the philosophical position which renders logically possible the construction of a theory of religious knowledge taking into account the fact of this knowledge. In this way, our opposition to the theories which deviate from the traditions of Reformed theology will be clearly defined from the start. Having reduced the "proofs" of the existence of God to their true proportions, we shall then endeavour to show that He is indeed the *principium essendi* of religion and the real author of religious knowledge. With this object in view, we shall trace the origin, and suggest a critique, of the objections raised by realism, idealism and the protagonists of systematic doubt. In conclusion, an attempt will be made to reconcile the necessity which proceeds from certainty, with liberty in the act of faith.

Part II will show that it is necessary scientifically to specify religious certitude as culminating in Reformed dogma, determined by the external principle of Scripture, supreme source and rule of faith, and by the internal principle of *soli Deo gloria*.

A complete bibliography of the subject would require a large volume to itself. Information regarding the works to which special reference is made will be found in the footnotes to the pages which treat of them. The list which follows includes only those works which have been of special assistance in building up the theoretical construction of Part 1.

For the methodological discussions after Calvin we have drawn inspiration chiefly from Abraham Kuyper, *Encyclopedie der Heilige Godgeleerdheit*, 3 vols., Kampen, 1908 (the third volume), and from H. Bavinck, *Gereformeerde dogmatiek*, 3 vols., Kampen, 1918 (the first volume). The first volume of each of these works treats of the principles and of the position of Calvinism in relation to philosophy and particular sciences.

For the building up of the realist theory of knowledge we have consulted: Augustine, *Contra academicos, Soliloquia*; Aquinas,[1] *Summa Theol.*, 1 qu. I, qu. 77–88; Zanchius,[2] the first Calvinist schoolman, *Opera*, III, 636 ff. and Calvin, *Inst.*, I, xv; among moderns, J. McCosh, *Psychology: the Cognitive Powers*, London, 1886; *Realistic Philosophy defended in a Philosophical Series*, 2 vols., London, 1887 (McCosh was a Calvinistic theologian as well as a philosopher); Liberatore, *Die Erkenntnistheorie des h. Thomas von Aquin*, Maienz, 1861; H. Bavinck, *Geref. Dog.*, I, 224 ff. *Christelyke Wereldbeschouwing*, Kampen, 1904.

Traité élémentaire de philosophie, by the professors of the Institut Supérieur de Philosophie of the University of Louvain, Louvain, 1922; J. Maréchal, S. J., *Le point de départ de la métaphysique*, more particularly Part V, *Le thomisme devant la philosophie critique*, Louvain and Paris, 1926; E. Gilson, *Le thomisme: Introduction au système de saint Thomas d'Aquin*, Strasbourg, 1920; R. Kremer, *Le néoréalisme américain*, Louvain, 1926; *La théorie 'de la connaissance chez les néoréalistes anglais*, Louvain, 1928; Parodi, *La Philosophie contemporaine en France*, Paris, 1919.

On scientific matters, notably on the theory of evolution: A. S. Eddington, *La nature du monde physique*, translation by G. Cros, Paris, 1929; Albert Fleischman, *Der Entwikelungsgedanke in der Gegenwärtigen Natur u. Geist. Wissenschaft*, Leipzig, 1922; L. Vialleton, *Morphologie générale . . . Critique morphologique du Transformisme*, Douin, 1924; *L'Illusion transformiste*, Paris, 1929.

On the nature and origin of religion, among older writers: Aquinas, *Summa Theol.*, II, 2 qu. 81; Calvin, *Inst.*, I, i–v, x–xii; *Opera*, passim; the second catechism contains the elements of a philosophy of religion, especially in its first two sections; Ursinus, *Heidelberg Catechism*, qu. 94–103; Zanchius, *De natura Dei, De operibus Dei*, II, III; Hornbeek, *Theol. Pract.* IX, vi–viii. Among moderns: Abraham Kuyper, *E voto Dordraceno*, 4 vols., Kampen, especially on questions 94–100 of the Heidelberg Catechism; Bavinck, *Geref. Dog.*, I, 238 ff.; II, 1–73; H. Visser, *De Oorsprong der Religie*, Utrecht, 1904; Mgr. Le Roy, *La religion des primitifs*, Paris, 1909; P. W. Schmidt, *Der Ursprung der Gottesidee* I, Münster, J. W. 1926; A. Lang, *The Making of Religion*, London, 1909; Sertillanges, *Les sources de*

---

[1] [Thomas Aquinas (1226–74), the Angelic Doctor, who taught at Paris, Cologne, Rome, Bologna, and Naples, applied the Aristotelian philosophy as a whole to theology. His *Summa theologica* and his *Summa contra gentiles* may be taken as affording the best representation of his teaching.]
[2] [Girolamo Zanchi (1516–90), Italian Reformer.]

la croyance en Dieu, Paris, 1906; Xavier Moisant, *Dieu: L'expérience en métaphysique*, Paris, 1907.

McCosh, *The Intuition of the Mind Inductively Investigated*, London, 1860; Hobson, "English Theistic Thought at the Close of the 19th Century", *Presbyterian and Reformed Review*, Oct. 1901, 509–559; H. H. Kuyper, *Evolutie of Revelatie*, 1903; Marc Boegner, *Dieu, l'éternel tourment des hommes*, Clamart, 1929.

CHAPTER 2

THE IDEA OF AN INTRODUCTION TO DOGMATICS

In Protestant circles it is commonly admitted that faith and knowledge have each a distinct sphere. Religion, confounded with religiosity, should be solely an "affair of the heart". Its exclusive domain should be that of sentiment. It should add nothing to our knowledge, the rôle of extending our knowledge having devolved on science.

Now, it is certain that Reformed Christianity, as a social, traditional, and historical fact, presents itself as the depository of a revelation which does not visualize the heart except through the intelligence. It attaches value to emotion and enthusiasm only in so far as these sentiments are provoked by religious truth, recognized as such, by a divine promise, the meaning of which has been grasped and the divine character of which has been verified intellectually. No doubt, as Calvin's well-known aphorism declares, the seat of religious knowledge is the heart rather than the head. But, in order that it may descend into the heart and set the will in motion, it must in the first place be received in the mind and understood by it.

Thus, even in so far as it has been assimilated by the individual and has become subjective, religion is not purely an affair of sentiment, still less of sentimentalism. To our knowledge of sensorial and rational origin, it adds supra-sensorial and supra-rational knowledge, concerning that which God wills that we should think of Him, in order that we may glorify Him and find in Him our happiness and our "unique consolation in life and death".

The organ which grasps religious truth must be normally that which we call religiosity, or religious consciousness, that is to say, the intelligent sensibility of man, orientated towards God. This sensibility must be considered above all as a representative faculty; or better, to adopt the phraseology of the philosopher Wolff, as a "presentative faculty", but this faculty has been gravely injured by sin: it requires to be regenerated and restored. It then takes the name of virtual faith. This latter is pure receptivity, aptness to recognize the divine reality, in the scholastic sense of stable disposition. Faith in act is religious knowledge grasped and possessed by the subject.

In a general sense, it may be said that for Rome faith is a pure and simple intellectual adhesion to the teaching of the infallible Church. The Reformers profoundly modified this conception. Calvin, for example, declares faith in act to be "a certain and firm knowledge of the love of God towards us, according to which, by His Gospel, He declares Himself to be our Father and Saviour by means of Jesus Christ."[1] Here, faith has for its object no longer the Church but God and His promises. It rests on the Word of God. It is no longer an intellectual state, pure and simple. It is as inseparable from the confidence of the heart as the sun is from its heat or its light.[2] It has an object which it grasps intellectually: God, His love; Christ, His redemptive work. It is a knowledge of these things, founded on the authority of God, speaking in and through the Scriptures. The act of adhesion of the will follows and does not precede the knowledge, for it is the latter which conditions it. By the aid of a *Deus dixit* our Reformer criticizes the doctrinal system of Rome, and in the Word of God, which is for him the Bible, he seeks out all the materials for his theological edifice.

It follows that while a theology which will not take into consideration this fact and which imagines itself capable of building on a different foundation may claim the title of Protestant, it places itself historically outside the current of the Reformation. A new principle demands a new name. The title inscribed at the head of this work indicates our standpoint: the formal external principle and the supreme rule before which we bow. The canonical books of Holy Scripture are, for us, in the sense in which they were for our fathers, the source and the rule of faith. "We believe that the Word contained in these books has proceeded from God, from whom alone they derive their authority and not from men. And because it is the rule of all truth, containing all that is necessary for the service of God and for our salvation, it is not permissible for men, nor even for angels, to add to it, diminish or change it; whence it follows that neither antiquity, nor customs, nor the multitude, nor human wisdom; nor judgments, nor sentences, nor edicts, nor decrees, nor councils, nor visions, nor miracles, ought to be opposed to this Holy Scripture but, on the contrary, all things ought to be examined, regulated and reformed in accordance with it."[3] The principle, which is for religion the principle of all revision,

---

[1] *Geneva Catechism*, XVIII.
[2] Calvin, *Opera*, II, 183 ff.
[3] *Confessio Gallicana* or *Confession of La Rochelle*, 1559, art. v.

is itself irrevisable: it is the *inconcussum*. To replace it by another is, from the intellectual point of view, not simply to reform the ancient religion, but to pass from one religion to another. Now we intend to live and die in the faith for which our martyrs suffered and died, because we believe it to be true. We can do no other. We are bound by a power which we perceive to be the power of God.

The idea that one might dream of re-establishing in all its vigour the formal principle laid down by the Reformer of our Church will probably be envisaged with amazement by those who imagine that this principle is discredited scientifically. We ask such to suspend judgment until the moment when we shall be in a position to study the relations between the doctrine of inspiration and the claims of science.

Since it is our declared intention to reaffirm Calvinism in the scientific sphere, we can have no objection in principle to textual criticism, nor to literary criticism of the documents of revelation, provided it is conducted with a strict regard for facts. But we consider that theological subjectivism has taken the wrong direction by following the line of least resistance. Instead of progressively narrowing the fact of inspiration, restricting it first to the ideas, then to the things, then to the persons, and finally to their religious emotions, the means of effecting a fundamenta¹ reconciliation between dogma and the findings of science should be sought in a more supple, organic and vital conception of plenary inspiration itself. This is what we hope to do at a later stage of the present work, and it will be for our readers to judge whether we succeed or not.

Scripture is the unique source of religious knowledge. Faith does not derive this knowledge from itself but is merely the receptive organ which takes cognisance of it (*fides qua creditur*). By extension, the term faith may denote the religious truth itself to which the believer adheres (*fides quae creditur*), that which is believed.

It is of the highest importance to observe that in religious language, as distinct from current speech, to believe does not signify to maintain as true something which one recognizes as merely possible but does not know effectively. In the two senses of the term, religious faith signifies the supreme certitude: the faith of the subject who believes excludes the doubt of adherence and repels the doubt of temptation. The faith which is believed, that is to say, the objects of the faith, the dogmas, whether directly, in virtue of their intrinsic force, or indirectly, in virtue of a testimony the authority for which has the same intrinsic force, are capable of claiming our adhesion legitimately. The subject who believes is psychologically conscious of being affected by an object to the constraint of which his judgment submits: it is only by adhesion that faith becomes a free act.

From the epistemological point of view, it will suffice, strictly speaking, to notice two moments in the concept of faith. First, a receptive moment: the judgment (representative and intelligent sensibility) is put into active receptivity through contact with divine realities. This is the moment of intuition and of intellection. Second, a dynamic moment: the will adheres and the heart confides. This moment is determined by efficacious grace. It is the act of faith properly so called: the succession of these two moments involves as a necessary consequence a knowledge distinguished by the repose of the intelligence in the certainty of divine faith.

The first of these moments implies that God knows himself perfectly (*theologia archetypica*): that according to the analogical method, he is capable of communicating this knowledge to creatures endowed with intelligence, in particular, to man (*theologia ectypica*). Our early theologians also designated this mode of religious knowledge by the expression *theologia viatorum*, the theology of the wayfarer. After glorification in heaven this knowledge will become a knowledge of possession by the perfect realization of the promises. This will then be the theology *beatorum*. The religious thought of Christ, the supreme teacher and prophet of mankind, was described as a theology of the personal union of the divine human nature (*theologia unionis*). The second moment implies that the believing reason is capable of receiving a revelation communicated in human language and of systematizing the ectypic knowledge so acquired.

Dogmatics is nothing less than science, that is to say, the genetic and synthetic exposition of realities of which faith has only a spontaneous knowledge, certain indeed, but scarcely, if at all, organized. Reduced to these proportions, however, dogmatics would be no more than an incomplete science. Every discipline sufficiently elaborated must be taken as itself the object of its researches and must reflect on its own methods, principles and origins. It is not sufficient for the theorist to introduce precision and order into its facts: he should be able to give an account of the route which he has followed in arriving at them. Every order of science has a corresponding philosophy. It is to meet this need that introductions and prolegomena to dogmatics are attempted, as well as philosophies of religion or of belief, when they are the philosophies of believers.

Reformed theology itself, which became Cartesian in the 17th century, and thus formally rationalistic, while remaining all the while materially orthodox, has been particularly fruitful in treatises of natural theology. These treatises have generally been little else but thinly disguised essays on the philosophy of religion. Natural theology is considered in them as an autonomous discipline, constituted solely by the resources of the light of nature and leading to the living God, the author of positive revelation. The function of revelation begins, once this truth has been acquired. Properly considered, however, this manner of procedure is incompatible with certain doctrines which possess a vital importance for the Reformed religion, for example, the doctrine of total corruption.

Moreover Calvin, Peter Martyr and the first Calvinistic divines make the certitude and exactitude of the results obtained by the light of nature to depend on the very principle of dogmatics. This is one of the most happily original aspects of primitive Reformed theology. Recent Calvinistic theologians like Boehl, Kuyper and Bavinck, have returned to the primitive conception which Voetius still maintained in the 17th century. With this fundamental conception we associate ourselves.

The introduction to the study of dogmas is a philosophy of faith through the faith. It thus constitutes not the final chapter of a metaphysics but the first part of dogmatics itself. It is only by justifying its principles and methods scientifically that religion and theology, the science of religion, can escape from the debasing servitude to which Durkheim, the leader of the sociological school, would reduce them when he writes: "Actually religion does not know itself. If does not know of what it is made, nor to what need it corresponds. Far from being in a position to make law and science, it is itself the object of science."[1]

Religious thought is bound, therefore, to show that it has an answer to questions concerning the nature, objects and objective certitude of religion. It must perform this duty if it does not wish to deliver the keys of the fortress into the hands of the satellites of the man of the totem. For such a task the religious

---

[1] E. Durkheim, *Les formes élémentaires de la vie religieuse*, 1912, p. 615. [Emile Durkheim (1858–1917), French sociological positivist, stresses "the group mind" which for him is the point of reference for all human knowledge. The group mind has an impersonal, non-subjective character that is superior to the individual mind and acts as a directive force for the individual agents that comprise society.]

man alone is qualified, precisely for the reason which disqualifies him in the eyes of Durkheim who declares that "No one ought to study religion while taking into account his own experience of the religious life".[1] We maintain, on the contrary, that since he is religious, in him religion not only can live but can take cognizance of itself and become, for him who lives, the object of immediate observation. He knows it at first hand. Thus, to the paradoxical affirmation of Durkheim, we oppose the view that a personal knowledge of the matter and the processes of a discipline is the indispensable condition of framing a philosophy for it. No one would confide to a mathematician, limited by his branch of knowledge, the task of elaborating a philosophy of history. It would be presumptuous for a blind man to argue about a colour scheme with a man who can see. In this connexion, Aristotle's dictum cited by Höffding[2] at the head of the first chapter of his *Philosophy of Religion* is most apt: οὐκ ἔστιν λύειν ἀγνοῦντα τὸν δεσμόν. ("Only he who knows how can untie the bond.")

But it may be objected that religious thought in analysing the content of the faith and endeavouring to synthesize its own intellections, is not occupying itself with the religious problem properly so called. The problems with which it is occupied are connected with inner life of religion. In Höffding's view, Religion itself can never become a problem; it must be accepted as a starting-point which admits of no doubt.[3]

He is mistaken in this, however, for religious thought does occupy itself with the problems of which he himself treats. It is certainly true that the starting-point differs from his. Moreover, the religious problem appears under another aspect. The position of a believer confronted with a person who denies God or doubts His existence is analogous to that of a philosopher, convinced of the existence of other men, who finds himself at grips with a solipsist idealist. In the latter case, the problem would consist, not in proving the existence of other men, which is impossible, but in making the solipsist understand how we can be certain of it and how this certitude must legitimately take rank

---

[1] *Règles de la méthode sociologique,* p. 43.
[2] [Harald Höffding (1843–1931), Danish philosopher at the University of Copenhagen, author of texts in psychology, history of philosophy and the philosophy of religion. He held that the world of reality as a whole is unknowable, although we may believe that conscious experience and its unity afford the best keys to unlock the metaphysical riddle. His system of thought is classified on the positive side as a cautious idealistic monism (his own term is "critical monism"). Principal publications: *Philosophy of Religion* (1901); *Kierkegaard; Rousseau; History of Modern Philosophy*].
[3] *Op. cit.,* p. 1.

in science. Another problem would be the investigation of the proper method of showing the illegitimacy of the doubt which the solipsist entertains with regard to the objective existence of the external world.

In order to arrive at a religious problem we have simply to transpose the question, and to envisage the doubt relative to the existence of God. Höffding takes for granted that his religious doubt is legitimate, for the sole reason that it is possible and real. The existence of honest doubters, intellectually normal, is certainly a problem to be considered by religious thought and one which it must endeavour to solve. The believer views the religious problem in a different light from Höffding: he does not ask, for example, what is to replace religion in order to save supreme values, when it has disappeared. He knows that it is irreplaceable and can tell the reason why. As a philosopher, Höffding should know that there are pseudo-problems. One of the tasks of a philosophy of religion, conceived from the viewpoint of faith, is to determine the proper methods for eliminating these pseudo-problems.

If the introduction to dogmatics is regulated by the same principles as dogmatics proper, it nevertheless follows a different method of exposition. The method of dogmatics proper is genetic and synthetic. Proceeding from the data of revelation, it formulates the dogmas, the mysteries of the faith, places in evidence the internal opposition implied by the encounter between the infinite and the finite, between God and the creature: then it endeavours to determine the organic bond which exists between the mysteries and thus to form a synthesis. The introduction to dogmatics is concerned with tracing facts and dogmas to the principles from which the synthetic exposition proceeds. Its method is analytical. But, in the same sense as dogmatics, it is a science of faith by faith. It would make no attempt to guide the seeker's feet towards its principle, if it had not already discovered that principle on its own account. Anselm's *credo ut intelligam* has a value for it in the same way as for the science to which it is the introduction.[1]

In both cases, it is a question of understanding what one knows already by faith. In dogmatics proper, the purpose is to discover the organic bond which makes real the unity of the body of Christian doctrine: in the introduction to dogmatics, what is proposed for consideration is the nature and foundation

[1] [Anselm (1033–1109), O.S.B., born at Aosta, Archbishop of Canterbury from 1093 till his death; noted for his ontological argument to prove the existence of God; author of *Monologion, Proslogion, De Veritate,* and *Cur Deus Homo?* His theology and general philosophy are Augustinian.]

of religious knowledge itself. Only the dogmas which have a direct relation with the epistemological problem enter into discussion here, and these are studied only from the angle of formal religious knowledge. It is our business to show that they have a meaning intelligible for us; that they are not mere formulas empty of all content assimilable by thought.

CHAPTER 3

THE INTERNAL CRITERIA OF RELIGIOUS TRUTH

Certain works, like Jurieu's *L'analyse de la foi et le vrai système de l'Église*; Leibnitz' *Conformité de la foi et de la raison*; Newman's *Grammar of Assent*; Balfour's *Foundations of Belief*; Sabatier's *L'esquisse d'une philosophie de la religion*; Franck's *System der christlichen Wahrheit*; and many others, all written in a spirit of faith, but from extremely different points of view prove that the mind of believers is by no means closed to the questions which form the subject of the philosophy of religion. Höffding is in error when he maintains the contrary.

What then shall be the criterion of religious truth? There are three sources to which we may have recourse in order to establish a religious knowledge capable of leading to the God of positive revelation, namely, speculative reason; practical reason, with its categorical imperative; and sentiment. These three methods of establishing religious knowledge or religious life give us three criteria of religious truth. Assuming that one of these points of view is adopted, the internal mark of religious truth will be its rational character, its harmonious relation to the moral law, or the satisfaction that it gives to the sentiments or even to sentimentality.

We shall have to return to these three methods and pass judgment on them. Meanwhile, we shall show, first, that the employment of these methods proceeds from a philosophy of belief which may be the philosophy of a believer; and, secondly, why Calvinistic theology is obliged by the internal logic of its system to create another method proceeding from a more specifically religious conception.

I. SPECULATIVE REASON

Thomism distinguishes between religious truths demonstrable by reason, e.g. the existence of God, liberty, immortality, and others which are certified to us only by the authority of the Church. In this way, the existence of God can be demonstrated by the aid of *a posteriori* proofs. The credibility of a natural revelation and of the institution of the infallible magisterium of the Church can be established in the next place equally by reasoning.[1] Hence natural religion, founded on ontological science, is or can become the preamble to supernatural religion founded on the faith.[2] The existence of God, says Cardinal Mercier, is not an object of faith.[3] Is there at the foundation of these assertions a philosophy of belief to which we can subscribe?

If, with Höffding, we understand by philosophy of religion, religion studied objectively from the standpoint of doubt, free enquiry and independent research about the Church, there can be no question that the term is used correctly. It shows us what we can learn by the free enquiry of the reason and why this free enquiry must give place, at a given moment in the process of thought, to submission of the reason to the decree of the Church. In any case, this philosophy starts with the idea of a discussion conducted solely according to the principles of logic. By its very name the absolute fideism of Hermes and Bautain[4] must stand condemned. It rests on rationalist premises, on an exact notion of ideogony.

When, with Aquinas, it rejects the proof of the existence of God *a simultaneo*, declaring that He cannot be known except by *a posteriori* reasoning, starting with creatures, it reveals itself as an anti-innatist rationalism. It owes its inspiration to Aristotelianism.

When it appeals, with Anselm, to the proof *a simultaneo*, it is Platonist innatism which serves as a starting-point. According to this view, unaided reason becomes the source of the fundamental knowledge of religion; of the knowledge of God. The idea of God is impressed on man at birth and he discovers it in his mind as soon as the latter opens itself to reflexion. This is the method followed, after Anselm, by Descartes, Malebranche, Gioberti and the ontological school among Catholics: by Leibnitz, Guélincx, Heydan, among the Protestants, to mention only a few names.

---

[1] "Rational conclusions provide certain proofs of the existence of God, the spiritual nature of the soul and the liberty of the will" (Pontifical decree, June 11, 1855). Höffding himself quotes this decision (*op. cit.*, p. 357), which adds that, as faith presupposes a revelation, no appeal can be made to it in discussions with atheists and deists.

[2] *Conc. Vatic.*, sess. III, cap. iii; Thomas Aquinas, *Summa Theol.* I, qu. 2, art. 2; *Contra gentiles*, I, x–xiii.

[3] *Traité élémentaire de philosophie*, vol. II, p. 22: "The existence of God cannot be made the object of an act of divine faith"; cf. pp. 23, 28.

[4] [L. E. M. Bautain (1796–1867) in his *Philosophie du christianisme* attempted to justify the teachings of Christianity by the theory that all knowledge rests upon premises accepted by faith. The premises of religion are to be found in the tradition of the Synagogue and the Church, which tradition needs no rational criticism because it is self-critical.]

27

But, whatever way it may be, what is presented to us is merely an attempt to explain psychologically the nature and origin of subjective religion, and the certainty of its supreme object. It is the answer to the capital question set by that part of the science of religions which Goblet d'Alviela would call "heirosophy", and which is usually designated "the philosophy of religion". Is religious thought valid for the scientific mind? What relation can it have with intellectual activity?

Although they arrive at different results, because they start from different or opposite premises, the Spinozas, the Schellings, and the Hegels, can make no more of it than this. Believing that they have discovered the method of arriving at religious certainty—within the limits of natural religion—they find themselves simultaneously in possession of the criterion. This internal criterion is the conformity of religious affirmation to the demands of speculative thought. In natural religion, that which presents no internal opposition, that which can be demonstrated, is true.

We accept as our starting-point neither religious certitude nor the criterion which speculative reason presents to us. We cannot consent to make the affirmations of the faith rest on fallible reasonings. Experience proves that philosophers have not even been able to agree as to the value of the classical "proofs" of the existence of God. Metaphysical arguments require delicate handling. It is very difficult to assure oneself that one has not committed a slight error in formulation from the start. The cleverest technicians may be mistaken. The question whether the ontological proof is the most peremptory of proofs, or a miserable sophistry, is one which is disputed, and will be disputed for a long time to come. This explains why one never can arrive at a firm conclusion by force of argument alone. Calvin had already noticed this. These so-called "proofs" are in turn cried up or discredited. Even amongst the most recent theologians, they are now declared to be without value after a searching criticism (Boehl, Wichelhaus); now left to the appreciation of each individual mind (Charles Hodge); now denied dialectical validity, while utilized nevertheless as valuable indications provided for the human mind in search of God (Bavinck). Attitudes so diverse among specialists whose theism and Calvinistic orthodoxy are above suspicion make us think that Hodge was not wrong when he relegated to the subjective judgment of each individual the task of appreciating the validity of the "proofs" in question. They are, or are not, conclusive according to the philosophical premises that one adopts.

They cannot serve as solid foundations for the certainty of divine faith or positive religion. Besides, would it not be to surrender the autonomy of dogmatics, and of the faith itself, to make specifically religious knowledge rest on such a necessarily frail foundation as the certainty of human faith? Finally, if it is admitted that reason is capable of deriving from its own resources a science of God, by the aid of innate ideas or of forms of understanding, without direct contact with the object which reveals itself, this science would not give us God, a living reality, but something vastly different, namely, an idea of God. In this way, one would arrive at nothing better than a revelation of the architectonic faculties of the mind. God would appear as a Being of reason; the Creator created by one who feels he knows Him. Incapable of establishing the certainty of religious knowledge, speculative reason is also incapable of giving us the criterion of this truth.

It is true that an internal contradiction is a sure sign of error. A contradiction is literally "nonsense". It does not follow from this, however, that religious truth must be circumscribed within the limits of reason. A complex idea, the elements of which cannot be co-ordinated in a manner satisfactory to reason, is not necessarily an error: far from it. In order to know that there is a contradiction, it is necessary that these elements should themselves be clearly known. Now there are truths which lay hold of the understanding, and which appear in opposition to others, because they are known only formally, incompletely, and by analogy.

A religious doctrine supposes always, under certain aspects, the encounter of the infinite God with the finite, the creature. Now the infinite is not knowable except as supra-rational, incomprehensible. On the other hand, the creature itself is not knowable to us except in an inadequate manner. A religious affirmation then implies necessarily an internal opposition, a mysterious element.

If this element is missing from it, we have a sure sign that a part of the truth has been eliminated. The contradiction is above and beyond the reason which judges it. But mystery is the mark which the infinite being has placed on his work, and it judges reason. Mystery is the atmosphere necessary to the religious life, because this life cannot be conceived except as in union with God. The task of theology, then, does not consist in causing the internal oppositions of dogma to disappear, but, on the contrary, in bringing them to the light. All the orthodox confessions of faith qualify their statements with a certain *et tamen,* and nevertheless . . . because they desire to respect all the data of reality. If they were nothing more than products of pure reason, nothing would be easier for them than to avoid all appearance of contradiction, by suppressing one of the terms of the mystery.

It is thus that pantheistic theologies see only God and deny the creature, and that deist and Pelagian theologies, in order to maintain the existence of creatures distinct from God, must needs curtail God and reduce Him to nothing more than a *primus inter pares,* a being, the greatest of all, among beings who are themselves divine.

We conclude that the rôle of speculative reason in theology is limited to understanding the revelation, to inferring by starting from principles, to organizing and finally to criticizing, contradictory formulas. Speculative reason cannot offer a positive criterion to religious truth.

2. PRACTICAL REASON

The foundation of religion, we are now told, must be sought in moral obligation, the *form* of duty with which practical reason bids us clothe our acts. The criterion of the *matter* with which the same reason enjoins us to fill this form is the possible universalization of the act. Emmanuel Kant and Charles Secrétan, in their splendid discussions on the philosophy of liberty, have proved, even by their very work, that in this principle reside the elements of a philosophy of religion conceived from the religious point of view. The contentions of this school may be summarized in Secrétan's words: "Duty, of which conscience is a part, gives us God and our liberty of choice which are both equally essential dogmas."[1]

Three shades of opinion may be discerned in this group. First, those for whom duty is an object of science, for whom faith begins only by starting from certain religious postulates: God, liberty, immortality (Kant); next, those for whom duty is itself an object of faith (Renouvier, the neo-Kantians); and, finally, those for whom the obligation begins only with the arbitrary decision of the ego to place itself under obligation. One is not bound except by being bound freely, "because one desires it strongly" (Gourd).[2]

---

[1] Secrétan, *La philosophie de la liberté,* preface to 3rd ed., p. xxvi.

[2] Bavinck justly remarks that Kant seems sometimes to make the postulates themselves to be the necessary consequences of duty laid down by practical reason (*Kritik der prakt. Vern.,* ed. Kirchmann, Heidelberg, 1882, p. 172, note). It might be asked why the postulates should not be objects of

Scripture itself knows but one legislator capable of causing life and death in a spiritual sense (Luke 12: 4–7): "It is God alone who has consciences subject to His laws by night". [1] His law is worthy of respect of itself, because it flows from the internal and infinite justice of God, and because justice, or rather the Just One, is worthy of respect in Himself.

We are too great to take orders from any will other than that of God, or of one who commands with a divine delegation; we are too little to be a law unto ourselves. Thus, to the autonomy of reason, Calvinism opposes the theonomy of the total ego (Boehl). It will be readily understood that Calvinism cannot, and would not wish to, make any use of Kantian postulates. It may have recourse to what is incorrectly termed the judicial proof, which is nothing else but consciousness that we have of our dependence in regard to God in the moral order, of our responsibility in regard to Him. We can never accept the idea that the human mind can ascend from the sovereign autonomy of practical reason, or of the human will, a blind faculty giving itself its own laws, to a God whose rôle is merely to play the property man on the stage of moral activity.

As against the efficacy of this ethicalist principle to serve as a support to religion, let us observe that it leads easily, as Boehl shows, [2] and inevitably, as Bavinck reminds us, to atheistic conclusions.

Little by little, the good is substituted for God, culture for cultus. The thing may be grasped so much more readily than the reality, which will not accommodate itself in the slightest degree before the imperatives of our moral autonomy.

Thence, by way of Manicheeism, we approach the degradation of the idea of God. We do not suggest that this process is the inevitable conclusion of ethicalism, but it is certainly one of its probable issues and its proximate temptation. Is it not more disinterested, and more in conformity with the spirit of duty, for duty to renounce the hope of any compensation or recompense other than the satisfaction of duty accomplished, and any sanction other than that of remorse? If so, future life and God are without value from the moral point of view, and consequently, from this same point of view, without reality. In fact,

science, like duty. On the other hand, it seems more in harmony with the spirit of the system to attribute the affirmation of the postulates to the moral disposition of the subject (*ibid.*, p. 172, s. 175). For the three views that we have indicated, *vide* Kant, *Kritik der prakt. Vern.*, p. 159 f; Secrétan *op. cit.*, lecture ii, *ad fin*, p. 42; J. J. Gourd, *Les trois dialectiques*, Geneva, 1897, p. 67.
[1] Calvin, *Com. on James*, iv, 11, 12.
[2] E. Boehl, *Dogmatik*, Amsterdam, 1887, p. 21; H. Bavinck, *Geref. Dog.*, I, p. 269.

although Kant has clearly shown that a distinction must be made between value and reality, many of his epigones, confounding the one with the other, deny the reality when the value has disappeared. The primary inspiration of ethicalism is as little religious as possible. Religion signifies the sovereignty of God, ethicalism the autonomy of man.

In its primary or Kantian phase, this autonomy is still restricted by the fact that the affirmation of the categorical imperative is a scientific necessity. In the second phase, with the most favourable intentions towards religion, the passion for autonomy, for the liberty of independence, exalts itself to the point where God, conceived as pure liberty, as absolute caprice, exists, as in the system of Duns Scotus, only for the purpose of communicating this liberty to man. Nevertheless, a certain restriction is maintained: one remains obliged by obligation to oneself. With Gourd, this last inconvenience is impartially rejected: let him oblige himself who wishes to do so. In this way he who obliges himself will depend henceforth only on his own will. The process has arrived at its term: God becomes "the least real of beings", a personification constructed or chosen arbitrarily in order to favour the dynamism of the personality endeavouring to affirm itself in the contact "with inco-ordinables". We are driven to the conclusion that practical reason is as impotent as theoretical reason of furnishing us with a criterion for judging the truth of a religious proposition.

Immorality demonstrated is as certain a sign of error for practical reason as is contradiction for theoretical reason. The law of justice: to each his due, is immutable, universal; because it is the law of the divine mind itself, which is indeed autonomous. But the concrete applications of law are subject to the sociological conditions of each historical milieu, while on the other hand we have only an absent and analogical conception of the absolute justice of the infinite being. It is impossible for us to decide *a priori* what God, who owes nothing to anyone, since He has received nothing from anyone, owes to Himself, in respect of future sinners. Our concrete maxims, which imply the immutable principles and universals of justice, are valid for the conditions of life made for humanity. They would be otherwise if, for example, we were bees endowed with intelligence. We cannot then erect them into universal laws, which must govern all minds, least of all the absolute mind. The impossibility of demonstrating logically, in every case, that the ways of God are just, does not in any way prove that they are unjust. It proves only that our mind is limited and that there again it finds, in the sphere of voluntary action, mystery, a sign of the presence of God, which it had previously encountered in the sphere of theoretical speculation.

3. SENTIMENT

This philosophy of religion—it is contestable that there is one —presupposes four moments of religious knowledge. First, there is an obscure phase, when things happen in the subliminal consciousness; secondly, certain perceptible modifications appear in the light of the psychic consciousness; thirdly, should the occasion arise, there is an arbitrary and autonomous decision to translate subjective emotions into ideas; and, finally, the ego proceeds to a translation beyond all possibility of verification.

We have said that the decision to proceed to a translation proceeds from a pure voluntarism, and that it tends to an illusive construction. We find the proof of our assertion in the following passage which gives us Bois' conception of inspiration: "God inspires: man translates this inspiration into ideas, into words, and there is revelation. But, in this translation which is man's work, man employs the opinions current in his epoch, the scientific and philosophical ideas of the moment";[1] this is the philosophy of "the emotions of the heart, of the modifications of the moral consciousness and of the will."[2] It is expressly understood that each one will make whatever he wishes of these emotions and modifications. The religious man will introduce into them the direct action of a divinity distinct from himself; the non-religious thinker will regard it as useless to go beyond himself as a subject.[3]

It is scarcely necessary to demonstrate that such a conception of revelation is in radical opposition to that of the Reformers, Calvin in particular. It is not a question of divergence in detail, but of a principle which decides the whole question; an *articulus stantis vel cadentis ecclesiae*, a doctrine on which depends the decline or the vigour of the Church. It is important to realize clearly that, on this point at least, neo-Protestantism is not a continuation of the Reformation, but something entirely and radically different from that movement. Historical Protestantism was intended as a reform of the Church. Neo-Protestantism, whether it wishes it or not, represents another religion altogether. The man who would remain faithful to the Reformation believes without doubting that the Holy Spirit exercises His mysterious action on the human soul at the outset in pouring

[1] Henri Bois, *Philosophie de Calvin*, Paris, 1919, p. 4.
[2] *Ibid.*   [3] *Ibid.*

the treasures of His power into the dark depths of the "subliminal consciousness". This action has as a result the manifestation of the object to the subject as real, causing the latter to bow before the revealed majesty of God. He does not believe in the Holy Spirit only but also in the Word who speaks intelligently to the thought. He believes in the revealed Word. His faith adheres to certain truths, which are not just "inarticulate sighs", but the communications of thought, the thought of God, to the thought of man.

And there is, in the revelation which God communicates to us, in its content as well as in its purpose, a "splendour of truth" which lifts the soul to the regions of divine faith. In the religion of sentiment, of emotion, on the contrary, there is but one certain thing: the subjective emotion. "The riches of the subliminal consciousness" and the agent who produces them, are alike unknown. The decision to translate is unpredictable, and the translation, if perchance one decides to make it, will be of doubtful value. The text, similar to phosphorescent inscriptions traced on a wall in the night, is too unstable for anything certain to be drawn from it. Nothing of this sort can account for the fact of the certainty of the faith.

Again, if it were desired that the emotions and modifications of the subject should serve as premises to a line of argument, then we should be brought back to the rationalistic position. Those who claim that we know more than the ego and its modifications, and who desire that our judgments on existence, relative to God and our fellows, should rest on reasoning, unconsciously fall back on the ontological proof. They are commonly reproached, indeed, with inferring ontological existence from logical necessity. In both cases, the abyss which separates the ideal order from the real is cleared at a bound. [1] But the supreme objection to this method of sentiment, of religion considered purely as an affair of the heart, is that it cannot furnish a criterion clear enough to enable us to distinguish that which is divine from that which is purely human, or even perhaps satanic, in the form given to the interior impulsion, whether by unconscious automatism or by formal liberty. We know, of course, that every positive reality, every force, physical or spiritual, every intellection, every act, as to its *matter*, comes from God, the cause of causes. The criminal, at the moment of perpetrating a crime, exists only by His power. All vital impulses, all the

[1] T. Ziehm, *Psychophysiologische Erkenntnistheorie*, Jena, 1897, p. 6. The author extends his remarks concerning rationalist philosophy to the historic proof of the existence of God based on universal consent, a proof invoked also to demonstrate the existence of the external world.

intelligence which translates itself in actions of every kind proceed from God. But, finally, there is sin, there is the personality of the free agent who imprints on all this a criminal or insane *form*. This form exists first of all in the subliminal ego. How are we to distinguish this unwholesome operation from that which the Divine Spirit accomplishes, tending to reform that which, in us, is deformed and empty? The theology of the heart by itself is powerless to tell us. It can only appeal to the instinctive reactions of sentiment, to what it calls the Christian consciousness. This consciousness is indeed an experimental reality, but it has no value apart from the environment in which it has been formed. The satisfaction which a Roman Catholic experiences in his devotion to the Sacred Heart, or on a pilgrimage to Lourdes, has the same right to be called an experience of the Christian consciousness as the severe and sober enthusiasm of a Huguenot peasant in the Cevennes. By what criterion are we to distinguish between these two types of Christian piety? We must not confound the experience connected with the origins of religion, the sensible intuition of God, and of our absolute dependence on him, with the reactions which this experience provokes in our sensibility. These reactions result largely from the influence of the environment which has helped to mould us; they cannot therefore enable us to judge the environment. Predestination, which, for Calvin, is a sweet and comfortable doctrine, excites a strong aversion in Arminius or Bois. Where are we to look for the authentic Christian consciousness in a case like this?

We must seek another way which will lead us to a philosophy of religion, or, in other words, to a science of faith. According to Scripture (John 7: 18; 8: 50), the sole intrinsic criterion, or, to use the language of Calvin, the sole touchstone capable of being "a mark of divinity", is faith itself in its vital tendency. It is also called "the principle of the analogy of faith". The intuition which conditions faith is, as we have observed, that of our dependence on God. This intuition is not complete until the natural religion of man has been restored and the tendency and inclination of virtual faith has been awakened. This tendency arouses the intuition by its jealousy for the glory of God. For it, a dogmatic proposition is religious according to the measure in which it sets in a clear light the unique character of the sovereignty and independence of God, on the one hand, and the absoluteness of our subjection to Him, on the other. Note, in passing, that faith, in so far as it is the instinct of piety, never confounds the infinity of God with indeterminacy. The more

35

jealous it is of the rights of God, the more it feels that he is a *nature*. To be sovereign, it is necessary to be not only something but someone, a personality determined by itself. "Absolute indetermination", the deity proposed by Scotus and Secrétan, is the slave of his own blind will. God is sovereign only on condition that the primacy of the intellect is maintained.

Thus, the sign of the presence of a divine revelation and the key which permits us to open its seals and understand its sense, is the presence of a doctrine which agrees with what we call the analogy of faith. It is clear that subjective religion is a spiritual fact, and, that being so, it must be judged spiritually. Religious truth can have no intrinsic criterion other than a religious one, and this criterion is conformity with the faith. Faith is the internal principle of dogmatics, as Scripture is its external principle. Calvin has very clearly formulated this principle in his *Epistle to Francis I* and in his commentary on the texts cited above.

CHAPTER 4

THE ORGAN OF RELIGIOUS KNOWLEDGE

We have said that the method of rational demonstration, applied to natural religion, has been approved not only by Protestants, but by Calvinistic Protestants like Guélincx,[1] Heydan, and Charnocke, whose *Discourses upon the Existence and Attributes of God* are still popular in England and enjoy the consideration of distinguished divines.[2] But the method in question is contrary to the spirit of Calvinism. It is irreconcilable with some of its essential doctrines. Moreover, it conflicts with the general consideration that the faculties of man have been gravely injured by the Fall.

According to primitive Calvinism, the knowledge which we have of God as Creator has for its organ sense of the divinity (*sensus divinitatis*), which is nothing less than faith in exercise. This faith forms an integral part of human nature as originally conceived by the Creator. Man before the Fall had, in some sense, the vision of God, because his heart was pure. After the Fall, his nature was totally corrupted, extensively, of course, and not in an equally intensive manner. There remains in man "the seed of religion", which is this primitive sense of *numen*, of the divinity. Through a consideration of the creation, preservation and government of the world, the light of nature by itself is sufficient to lead man, even in his fallen state, to the certainty that God exists and has a right to his trust and worship. But, by the aid of this light alone, he cannot attain in the slightest degree knowledge of the true God. A god, indeed, he may envisage but not God. The Confession of La Rochelle excludes expressly intelligence and reason, as means of approaching God: "We believe that man, having been created

---

[1] [Arnold Guélincx (1624–69), Belgian philosopher, author of *Metaphysica vera* (1691) and Γνῶθι σεαυτόν sive *Ethica* (1675), the first definitely to systematize the theory called Occasionalism, previously propounded by Gérauld de Cordemoy and Louis de la Forge.]

[2] E.g., R. B. Girdlestone, *Old Testament Theology and Modern Ideas*, London, 1909, p. 62. We ourselves recognize the great value of Charnocke's work, but the date at which it was written (1682) furnishes a clue to the fact that he feels the contrary influences of Descartes and Gassendi in philosophy. At this period, Reformed theology entered upon an era of decadence: its leading theologians were men like Amyraut and Cocceius to whom Charnocke often refers with respect.

37

pure and perfect, and in conformity with the image of God, by his own fault fell from the grace which he had received . . . so that his nature became totally corrupt. Being blinded in his mind and depraved in heart, he lost all integrity, so that even the light which he possesses transforms itself into darkness when he seeks for God, and this in such fashion that man can in no wise approach God by his reason and his intelligence."[1]

It is strange that the philosophers and theologians who claim to be able to establish religious certainty and to give its criterion by the aid of the natural faculties alone, never dream of asking themselves whether the state of these faculties is such that by their exercise one can establish anything other than more or less solid opinions. They take it for granted that, from the moment when a revelation appears in nature, it is necessary that this latter should be proportioned to our powers. Otherwise, they think, it would scarcely be able to serve any other purpose than to occasion new errors.

But Calvin and Reformed theologians in general affirm that such is precisely the case. Our Reformer holds that the religious sentiment, delivered over to its native ignorance, is one of the most fruitful sources of error.[2] This is one of the consequences of sin which carries with it its own punishment.

The presuppositions of the philosophers in question would be convincing enough if it could be proved that our cognitive faculties are in their primitive state of integrity. But this is precisely what we deny. That natural revelation originally sufficed to reveal God has scarcely been contested. But, on the other hand, it is a capital article of our faith, which experience confirms in the most striking manner, that actually humanity is not in its original state; and that, since its "imbecility" relative to the knowledge of divine things does not exclude a perverse disposition of the will, God chastises the carelessness and ill-will in "giving efficacy to the spirit of error". This note is by no means exclusive to Calvinism: it is taken for granted by Aquinas and Pascal. Strictly speaking, there is nothing contrary to dogma in admitting that one can prove a god but not God. Positive faith is not the product of an act of man. It is indeed an act of man, but this act is determined by an efficacious movement of grace. Faith is a gift of God.

The external principle of this faith is not the natural light, but the sacred Scriptures which serve as "spectacles" to us, in

---

[1] *Confession of La Rochelle*, art. ix: *Westminster Confession*, cap. XXI, arts. i and ii.
[2] *Inst.* I, vii. 3.

order that, by their means, we may decipher the book of nature and read therein the name of the true God. Without doubt, God has written His name in the sky with the stars. "The heavens declare the glory of the God" of power: but, even so, it is necessary to have eyes to see and ears to hear. To "declare" moreover, is not to prove by syllogisms: it is to give a testimony which the hearer remains free to accept or reject. It is easy to see, then, that it is impossible to remain a Calvinist from the formal point of view and to admit the apodictic method of proof.

In order to see how untenable is the position of Calvinistic theologians, like Charnocke, who have admitted this method, one has only to compare the explanation which this theologian gives to Hebrews 11:3 with that of Calvin. The difference between the points of view is striking.[1]

It should be observed that the insufficiency of the subject receiving the revelation is not the only result of a perversion of the will. This is connected also with an original weakness of the understanding. "Having such a spectacle quite evident before our eyes, we are not in blindness because the revelation is obscure, but because we are alienated from sense and because, in this respect, not only the will but also the ability is defective."[2]

The true starting-point for a philosophy of religion is to recognize faith as religious capacity restored by grace, as an organ of knowledge: faith which sees in Scripture the source and rule of its knowledge. If it is thought strange that the Reformed theologian should proceed thus, and if he is charged with shutting himself up in a circle, we reply that there is no logical fault at all in the fact of raising oneself to a reflexive certitude by abandoning spontaneous certitude. A philosophy termed independent cannot indeed do otherwise.

To arrive at an epistemology and an ontology, it is necessary to employ the organ of certitude that one possesses: there is always an intuition at the base of all reasoning. The most critical mind is obliged to start from a point which it considers certain. We cannot believe in the value of a line of argument except by virtue of an intuition which shows us either the identity or the harmony in which it connects the terms.

Faith is a certitude based on a testimony: faith conceived as an organ of knowledge. Independent philosophy knows no other testimony than that of rational or sensorial evidence. But it must not be imagined that such a faith is beyond the reach of

---

[1] *Vide* App. II, p. 388.   [2] Calvin, *Com. on* 1 *Cor.*, i. 21.

all attack. Experience proves that adhesion to the testimony of a witness may be defective. Even there, scepticism remains a fact. The doubt which raises its head cannot be overcome except by an act of supra-rational faith: an act of faith in the religious sense of the term. This act will be unconvincing to the sceptic in so far as it rests on a rationalistic foundation and maintains the principle that we should hold as true only that which has been proved. In fact, on the one hand, he does not see any reason which constrains him to give credence to fallible witnesses, with human faculties: while, on the other, God who guarantees to him the value of reason, cannot be demonstrated.

We have remarked that Reformed theology considers religious faith to be an integral, essential element in human nature, even in its state of integrity before the Fall. It is not, as for Catholic theology, a simple *donum superadditum*, a supernatural element superimposed on human nature. Obviously, the faith of man not yet fallen could not have for its object that which is specific in Christian doctrine. In particular, the promises of the covenant of grace were unknown to him. The primitive faith could only have been that which Calvin calls faith in the Creator God: the intuition of the reality of God, of His presence, of the divinity of His word: man's recognition of the state of absolute dependence in which he found himself as a creature in regard to his Creator.

Our Reformer's doctrine, more than any other, emphasizes the fact that when it is a question of God and divine things, that which is natural and normal, and which must be the starting-point, is faith: while doubt on these great subjects proceeds from the moral and intellectual decadence of man as a sinner. As we shall show later in detail, faith in God and in His existence is in fact so bound to all the fibres of our nature that we should have to cease to be human to lose all trace of it. No one can by his own powers rediscover the true God, the normal knowledge of God. But there is no man who, in the depths of the profaned sanctuary of his own soul, does not perceive the presence of this God by the aid of an intuition whose certitude equals that which he has concerning the existence of all other things: this God, whom he knows as someone or something sacred and inviolable, as a *numen*, as an abstract phantom which wears the mask of the absolute and which always floats on the horizon of his thoughts.

While Calvin and his spiritual sons postulate as a fact that God, His existence, His presence, His love, and His promises, are the objects of certain faith; they are much more logical in their view of the religious consciousness than the scholasticism of the Council of Trent. The latter, it will be remembered, claims to find God by the reason. Now what is it a question of knowing and making known? Not the indefinite, still less the infinite totality of beings, but the God of religion, the "Spirit infinite, eternal and unchangeable in His being, wisdom, power, holiness, justice, goodness and truth",[1] in fact God Himself.

But there is an axiom which our older theologians never tired of repeating because everybody accepts it and so few take it seriously: *Finitum non est capax infiniti*—the finite cannot comprehend the infinite: finite reason cannot prove it, still less comprehend it. Sense cannot attain the invisible spirit nor reason circumscribe the infinite essence. In order to reach God, it is necessary then to come out from oneself and be raised above oneself, by superhuman infinite means, a means operative in us, since it is we ourselves who must know, but which is in its principle, in its total act and achievement, a creation of God[2] adapted expressly to its object, a sense of God at the same time as it is a movement towards God.[3]

In other words, it is necessary that God should have subjects capable of knowing Him, and with that purpose in view He must create or restore faith. If we say that God cannot be known in His essence, but only in His qualities, this is not for the reason suggested by Hamilton. To think, he said, is to condition; and God is absolute. Yes, no doubt; and for us also God is indeed Absolute.[4] But, on the other hand, the Absolute does not exclude all relationships but only such as impinge on His independence: the thought which grasps its relationship of dependence in regard to the Absolute, does not act on Him and does not establish this relationship: it submits to it and merely recognizes its reality.

If we do not admit as possible, as a fact capable of rational demonstration, anything other than the existence of a more or less indeterminate god, and not that of God, it is by no means for the reason suggested by Jacobi.[5] This thinker objected that to demonstrate God would be to make him depend on our own reason. But the ideal order is not the real order. Moreover, the result of a demonstration would do no more than place the

---

[1] *Shorter Catechism*, iv. [2] *Vide* App. III, p. 389.
[3] *Vide* Peter Brunner, *Vom Glauben bei Calvin*, Tübingen, 1925, p. 132 ff. The author of this excellent work gives numerous references on the subject taken from Calvin.
[4] *Westminster Confession*, II, i.
[5] Jacobi, *Von den Göttl. Dingen*, Werke IIIb, 368, 567.

reason under the necessity of recognizing the existence of God. Consequently, even in the ideal order, it is the reason which would be dependent on the constraint exercised over it by the object, that is to say, by God. We believe that a demonstration of the existence of God should not be attempted because God being "sensible to the heart"[1] the demonstration is useless, and being credible in Himself ($\alpha\vartheta\tau o\pi\iota\sigma\tau os$) having in Himself the right to be believed, the demand for the demonstration is illegitimate. For, in order that His existence should be believed, it is sufficient that God should show Himself: we ask nothing more in order that we may believe in the existence of finite beings. In the last resort, then, God is knowable only by the intuition of faith.

In this way, faith, as a means of certitude, comes to the aid of epistemology and criteriology. Our study then will have to admit of three principal parts; the first treating of knowledge in general and of the principles in the sciences; the second, of the nature of religion and of religious knowledge, that is to say, of the reality which is proper to it; the third, of the objective value of this knowledge.

---

[1] The term "heart" is understood in the Pascalian sense of "sensible consciousness" and not exclusively of sentimentality, vide *Pensées*, ed. Brunschvicg, sec. IV, 277, 278, 282.

CHAPTER 5

INNATISM

Bacon and Descartes are specially regarded as the creators of
"modern" philosophy, but, in reality, its origins can be traced
back to the medieval period, and the two great currents which
divide it are already discernible among the scholastics. These
two currents are *innatism*[1] and *empiricism*. Descartes was an
innatist; Bacon an empiricist. At one moment, the powerful
genius of Kant seemed to cause the two currents in the rigid
forms of his system to meet and mix. Time, which is an objective
reality, whatever Kant may have said about it, time which
allows that which is hidden to manifest itself, did its work: the
two currents separated again, until the sociological school of
Durkheim attempted another factitious fusion. The innatist river
lost itself finally in the ocean of the illusion of collective representations. It is decidedly in the other regions of thought that
philosophy will have to trace out a route leading to the objective
knowledge of the ego, of the world and of God. Innatism, under
all its forms, at least until Fichte inclusively, makes the mind of
the subject of knowledge no longer the organ but the source of
this knowledge. It is thus profoundly egocentric. It tends to
enclose the ego in itself and to remove from knowledge its
character of transitive act. Its tendency may be summarized in
this paradox: we do not know the object, precisely because we are
in a relation of knowledge to it. In the idealist form of this view,
it will follow that we know only the ego and its states. The logical
goal of this system is solipsism. For idealist philosophy, it is only
through a form of reasoning, which establishes itself with ever-
increasing difficulty, that we can hope to attain the external
world, our fellow men and God.

With Descartes (innatism of ideas) we find this school still
hesitating to formulate its principle. Sometimes it seems that
the ideas must be like images, imprinted in the mind, sometimes like reproductions of the real, due to a spontaneous
activity of the intelligence, more or less in contact with this real.
But even in this case "the constitutive principles of the innate

[1] [Innatism (Latin *in* + *natus*, inborn), a theory of philosophy in which
ideas or principles are considered to be present in the mind at birth, either fully
formed or requiring some additional experience for their complete formulation.]

ideas, form and content, are resident in the intelligence . . . the virtual precapacity of these ideas in the intelligence is more than simple power, more than the simple capacity to receive them or to form them on a strange model offered by the sensibility. For this would be Aristotelianism. Now, Descartes argues against the peripatetic adage that there is nothing in the understanding which has not been originally in the senses:[1] an adage destined to become, rightly or wrongly, the rallying cry of empiricism".[2]

Briefly, the innatism of Descartes is still "only virtual", and for this reason it can easily be confounded with the innatism of the faculties of the intelligence alone. The danger of the tendency is not even fully appreciated. Although pointed out by the Calvinistic theologian Voetius, it was misunderstood by some theologians who shared his faith, such as Wittich, Van Till in Holland, Glauberg in Germany. The success of Cartesianism among theologians as authentically Roman as Bossuet and Malebranche, is well known. Yet there can be no doubt that the system involves in latent form, one of the fundamental errors of rationalism, namely, that reason is not merely the organ but the source of knowledge. Other germs are at work in this system: egocentrism makes itself felt in the fact that the ego is presented as known immediately, considered as a spiritual substance of which the whole essence is capacity to think. This logically illegitimate identification of the intuition of thought with the intuition of mind is the false starting-point of the affirmation that it is impossible to reach external reality except by a line of argument concerning experienced sensations.

Hence the menace of solipsism, which will take shape in other systems. We shall soon find ourselves driven to a denial of the possibility of the influence of soul over body. Mind and matter are juxtaposed one with the other in the organism and made entirely heterogeneous. We are tending by way of occasional causes (Guélincx) and of the vision in God (Malebranche), towards the Leibnitzian denial of the possibility of transitive action, towards the monads which "have no windows by which anything can enter or depart".[3] At this moment, modern innatism receives its formula: "Our ideas, even those of sensible things, proceed from our own depths."[4]

It is a fact fraught with consequences affecting all modern thought that nominalism commanded the formal adherence of

[1] *Discours*, Part IV, ed. Adam and Tanney, tome VI, p. 37.
[2] J. Maréchal, *Le point de départ de la métaphysique,* Part II, p. 45.
[3] Leibnitz, *Princip. Philos.*, n. 7.
[4] Leibnitz, *Nouveaux essais sur l'entendement humain*, I, i.

the greatest philosophical genius of the period. There is nothing real except singular substances. Beyond these nothing exists but "pure names". Universals have no reality at all. [1]

Far from bringing nearer the living reality, the scientific process of abstraction and generalization is an attempt to co-ordinate reality by artificial means; the more abstract the idea, the farther we find ourselves from the real. The real in its entirety being unintelligible, the sensible elements of space and time which remain refractory to intelligibility, proceed to rejoin Descartes' secondary qualities and are relegated to the sphere of subjectivity. Time and space remain no more, except in relation to succession and coexistence, until Kant makes of them simple forms of sensibility.

But, in spite of these seeds of scepticism, with the first successors of Descartes we find ourselves still in the full floodtide of rationalist dogmatism. Minds are dominated increasingly by the Cartesian maxim: "Hold as true only that which has been proved." Already, with Wolf, the point is making its impact on orthodoxy. He marks the transition between *Le discours de la conformité de la foi avec la raison* of the author of the *Théodicée*, and unbelieving and dogmatic rationalism.

The latter was the victim of an accident: Hume appeared and aroused Kant from his dogmatic slumbers. Henceforth, rationalism must efface itself in the presence of criticism. It has to reconcile itself to the inevitable: reason is losing its empire over objective external reality. Its proud certainties have collapsed. The Scottish David has vanquished the Goliath of dogmatism. In order to preserve its values for theoretical reason, to save science, and, if possible, to lay fresh foundations for natural religion, a new dominion must be established for the understanding.

Kant will relegate to the unknowable the world in itself, the *noumena*. But the *noumena* evoke in the subject a world of representations, the phenomena. It is these phenomena which the understanding encloses in its innate and subjective forms: time, space, the categories. The intelligence will impose its *a priori* synthetic principles of causality, harmony and permanence of substance. It is by the aid of the categories that the intelligence arrives at its judgments in the matter of representations.

Practical reason, in giving its imperative law to action, will lead the understanding to postulate the three dogmas of natural religion: God, liberty, and immortality. Thus, on the one hand,

---

[1] Leibnitz, *De stylo philos. Nizolii*, n. 28.

science will be saved; and, on the other hand, religion will be established within the limits of reason.

There is indeed this disadvantage that the world of science has become a sort of purely subjective phantasmagoria without any resemblance to reality; that the world of religion is no more than an end in itself and exists only as a sort of hypothetical construction raised on the real enough foundation of the autonomy of reason.

After Kant, the effort of his successors, Fichte, Schelling, Hegel, is directed towards the attempt to explain the passage of the subject to the object. Fichte shows that the matter of the representation is inseparable from its form, and that thus the elements of knowledge are laid down by the ego, *a priori*, in an act of absolute liberty.

The difficulty born of Kantianism disappears with the reduction of the non-ego to the ego. Hence, a metaphysics of the evolution of the ego. The ego is at first not that which is, but that which ought to be; the Ideal, the Absolute, Necessity, the creator of the world. In the first stage of its evolution, the pure ego is unconscious. Then it produces the non-ego, the external world, realization of the Ideal. This is the second stage of the evolution. At the third stage, by reflection, the ego becomes conscious of its identity with the non-ego. The latter is, in fact, no more than the realization, by means of evolution, of the former. Thus, the object is derived from the subject and subjectivist innatism attains its apogee. The spirit of Kantianism is respected: faith in Necessity is the principle of all knowledge.

Schelling endeavours, on the contrary, to make the subject proceed from the object, which he styles the Absolute. The Absolute, principle of the ego and the non-ego, "is neither the one nor the other, although it is the cause of both: a neutral principle, indifference or identity of contraries."[1] An evolution analogous to that of Fichte will give us both the real and the ideal, nature and history. Arriving, with art, at the end of its evolution, the absolute finds an intimate union between the conscious and the unconscious, above the real and the ideal, and knows itself as the Identity in philosophy.

Hegel, correcting his two predecessors, finds a bond between the subject and the object more subtle than either, something even less definite: the Idea, and the most empty and at the same time the most general of all ideas, the abstract Idea of Being. From the necessity of existence inherent in the Idea, he infers the reality of that which is rational. From the dialectical

[1] *Werke*, X, p. 92.

necessity of anything real, he infers the rationality of all that is real. Thus, the order of reality and the order of thought are identical. Modern idealist pantheism is thus seen to be the product of an attempt to solve an epistemological problem: that of explaining the passage from the subjective to the objective. More faithful to the spirit of Kantianism is the phenomenalist criticism of Renouvier[1] and perhaps also that of Gourd, although the latter is mixed with numerous Hegelian elements. We know only the phenomena, and it is futile to imagine that we know things in themselves. (Note in passing that in this manner a bridge is built which will enable us to arrive at rationalist empiricism.) But among these phenomena which are our states of consciousness, there are those which can serve as organizing principles. These are the categories of thought. They could be denied, but we prefer to apply them, since they are the conditions of reasoning, and since it pleases us to organize our thought in a coherent manner.

Thus, in arbitrary fashion we bind ourselves to the principles of identity and contradiction. Thus, all knowledge becomes in its final analysis a convenient adaptation to practical conditions, derived from the autonomy of the ego. It is the subject which gives a law unto itself in a sovereign manner, not only in the sphere of practical activity, as Kant wished, but in the sphere of thought contemplating and organizing the phenomenal reality, the only one which exists for us. We must needs affirm the *coup d'état* of liberty. We find it at the very root of our reflective thought. We must needs deny the infinite, because it places this thought in the presence of contradictions and impossibilities. The god postulated by neo-Kantianism is finite and limited. We are still in the meshes of innatism: the possibility of an ideogeny of representations conditioning experience and thought is rejected.

Modern innatism, the historic course of which we have tried to sketch, had an ideal, but it has had finally to confess itself impotent to realize it. Descartes, whom Gerdil rightly called the father of the new philosophy, thought he could give metaphysics a series of proofs *more geometrico*. Spinoza believed himself to have realized this dream. The voluntarism of Kant, Fichte, and Renouvier definitely abandons such a project. Modern innatism has condemned itself already by repudiating the ideal which was,

---

[1] [Charles Renouvier (1818–1903), strongly influenced by Leibnitz and Kant; his philosophy has been called "phenomenological neo-criticism", its peculiar feature being that it denies the existence of all transcendental entities such as thing-in-itself, the absolute and the *noumenon*.]

historically, the reason why it set itself up in opposition to medieval philosophy.

When innatism makes the ego the source of the ideas that we have of things, it produces a confusion analogous to that which would exist if one were to identify the eye, the organ of vision, with the objects which reflect their image in it. In reality we have no innate ideas; the psychological consciousness gives evidence against innatism. We have no virtual innate ideas, that is to say, we have in our reason neither the form nor the intellectual elements, of the ideas of the ego, of spirit, of God. It is one thing to have a consciousness of oneself as affected by an external object which reveals itself in the representation, and quite another to have the intellectual concept of the ego or of a different mind. So far from having adequate ideas of these realities, we can only form very incomplete negative and analogical ideas of them.

That which is innate in the mind, that which is virtual in it, is not an idea: it is the capacity for noticing a necessary relation of identity or of harmony which binds the subject to the attribute of a judgment. Thus, the proposition $a=a$ is properly, despite the tautological form of the formula, a synthetic judgment. For, in this proposition, there is, in the attribute, something more than in the subject, viz., the intuition, of the necessity of the identity. But the fact that it is synthetic does not prevent this judgment from being a judgment of material necessity, as the scholastics say: this is the law imposing itself objectively on the intelligence—and causing it to be intelligence—which is thus innate in the latter. The existence of the understanding itself is very evidently innate. That goes without saying. Innate ideas cannot appear necessary except in the erroneous presuppositions of the philosophers whom we are combating.

If, instead of admitting the organic unity of the living substance of a material organism informed by a mind, one decides, with Descartes, on a simple juxtaposition of soul and body, of a substance unextended and of a substance extended, most certainly he will have to proceed from it, whether he likes it or not, either to the "vision in God" of Malebranche, or to the innateness of the idea of being, with ontologism (Gioberti). [1]

But we are not obliged to create the pseudo-problem: how can two heterogeneous substances act on one another? If, with the

[1] [Vincenzo Gioberti (1801–52). His fundamental problem was the relation between sensibility and intelligibility. Being creates existence. The universal spirit becomes individual by its own creation. Thus, the source of individuality is not subjective but divine, vide B. Spaventa, *La filosofia di G.*, 1863.]

author of the *Monadology*, we deny the possibility of the transitive action of one finite substance on another, we shall be compelled to derive everything, even sensible representations, from our own mind. But if we consider that the action of the finite Monad is not all of one piece for the agent and the patient, but that it is in the patient, and that if expenditure of energy takes place, this fact is explained not by the action of the agent, but solely by the reaction of the patient, then all Leibnitz' objections against transitive action disappear. Where is now the necessity of the total representation of the universe in the Monad? There is no longer any reason to imagine innate ideas. It is the object which furnishes its matter to our knowledge. Nor are there innate patterns of the sensibility, as maintained by Kant. It is well known that this philosopher made time and space the subjective conditions of sensible perception. These two representations were for him the pure forms of all representation, forms necessary and universal because they are produced by the constitution of our sensibility.

But this necessity is susceptible of quite another explanation. It is sufficient to admit that duration and extent, and hence real time and space, considered in abstract, are not subjective forms of our sensibility, but properly the real and objective forms of our being itself. We are essentially beings of time and space because we are finite beings. Our mind itself is subject to the law of succession and it is determined by space. Subject to changes, involved in incessant movement, in a continual passage from potentiality to act, itself a power of an ulterior act, placed incessantly between two abysses, the past which is no more and the future which is not yet, having only a fleeting shadow of the reality which God alone possesses, we have no other experience of being than that of an act, power of another act, of a virtuality which tends to action. We cannot then imagine anything other than successive duration, subsisting even when we have annihilated by thought all finite beings. But in reality this successive duration, of which time is only an abstraction, is not a subjective form: it is all that we possess of reality.

On the other hand, finite beings, because they are such, occupy a definite or circumscribed space, because they have extension or merely because they exist. Consequently, if we were to suppose other finite beings to be annihilated, we should still not be able to annihilate, in our imagination, the remainder of the objective experience of our own nature. For the imagination would remain a container empty, hypothetically, of all content. It would be infinite, because we cannot imagine limits which might not be comprised in it. In fact, we cannot escape from the experience of our own objective reality. Now, our extension is finite. Hence the impossibility for us to imagine anything which cannot be overflowed by the infinite. And this infinite we cannot imagine except as a finite which repeats itself indefinitely. Here we have that imaginary space (and time) which Kant confounded with real space and time, themselves abstractions of concrete duration and extension. It is against imaginary time and space that Kant brings his objections to bear. But real time and space are always finite, with a commencement and a conclusion which coincide with the beginning and the end of being, its duration and extent.

There are no longer any innate forms of the understanding. Nominalist premises, which modern philosophy has borrowed from Occam and thus from the Middle Ages, must be rejected. Leibnitz is mistaken when he claims that only particulars are intelligible, and that beyond this we have nothing but mere names. Undoubtedly universals do not exist apart from things [1] but it is equally evident that we have no reason to believe that they exist only in the mind, and that they are subjective elements, devices of which one makes use in order to establish science (Gourd).

It is not, in fact, our mind which governs the representations furnished by sensible representation. It is not this which models them in the mould of its forms, which connects them by the relations which it imposes on them. On the contrary, it is the mind which is governed by the constraint placed upon it by objective reality. It is the experience of reality which imposes categories on it. If there is something intelligible in the sensible, and the constitution of science proves that there is, the mind can abstract from it the universals which are really in it.

That we do not govern the object is proved by the fact that we have no consciousness of this claimed discretionary power. We do not impose our intellectual forms on the representation. Otherwise, it would be understood, strictly speaking, that we classify beings in different categories, but no reason can be given for the fact that our mind may hesitate to form a judgment regarding the same object, which is at first little known, then better known, and it may revise its judgment in proportion as it becomes better acquainted with the object: it is therefore the object, our consciousness attesting it, which governs the subject.

The universals are in the things and the real relations which

[1] It should be remembered that universals are the genus, the species, the difference, the characteristic, and the accident.

connect them are objective. In fact, independently of any act of the mind, things are what they are and their relations are what they are. It seems difficult to dispute that it is not our mind which creates the relation of unequal size that we observe between the cedar of Lebanon and the hyssop. The mind is compelled to accept this relation which exists quite apart from all its operations. There is an objective relationship between two finite beings, when a determination of the one is a function of a determination of the other.

Now, the determinations of beings, the bonds which unite them and the facts which differentiate them, are anterior to the intuition which the mind can have of them. To claim that a relation does not exist for us, unless a subjective operation of the understanding intervenes, is merely equivalent to saying that we do not know it before it has imposed itself on us. This does not signify that it has not real existence, even for us. We can, in fact, suffer through it cruelly without knowing it. Moreover, the fact that we do not feel ourselves justified in deciding what relations may exist between certain objects, shows that if the mind puts its power into action when it recognizes the relations between things, it feels controlled by them when it affirms a certain determined relation between certain things.

A real relation, perceived intuitively and of which we cannot doubt, is that of our dependence in regard to certain of our representations, that is to say, more precisely, of the constraint of the object. But, it may be asked, are we not entirely subjective in relation to our representations? Are not the latter merely modifications of the ego? Does not sensation, a fact of agreeable or painful consciousness, seem more capable of helping in our adaptation to reality than in teaching us about it? Is it not incommunicable and for that reason eminently subjective? Must we not admit that reasoning concerning sensible data leads to insurmountable contradictions? Here, we are told, lies the proof that sensation is purely phenomenal and corresponds to nothing objective. To sum up, we know only the ego and its states. We cannot escape from it, and there is no decisive reason for supposing an unknowable "x" beyond the phenomenon which would be the thing in itself.

In the first place, we notice that this reasoning starts from a sort of unformulated rationalist postulate, which leaves itself clear of the argument. Briefly, it amounts to this: all reality is intelligible and there is no reality but the intelligible. Now, here is an assumption which the facts contradict. The psychological consciousness, in fact, puts us into contact with the supra-rational, for the consciousness of the relative implies that of the absolute. It also puts us into contact with the sub-rational perceived by the senses. The material world certainly contains the rational. This is what renders possible science, which is knowledge of the universal and of the necessary. But there is always in the sensible reality a residue objective enough, which is not knowable for us except through the senses and the imagination. Here we have the reason why one cannot convey any vivid conception of any sensation whatever to anyone who lacks, from birth, the sense to which it corresponds. But the sensations are objective, since one can communicate to him an analogical idea of them. It is sufficient for this purpose to appeal to his knowledge of the other senses which he possesses in common with the rest of humanity.

Sensation is so little subjective essentially that it is one of the principal bonds of communion between men. It is altogether wrong to give the chief place in sensation to the effective element of pleasure or pain to which actually most of the sensations are indifferent. But there is not one of them which may not be representative, or rather presentative of the object. With them it is the object which becomes immanent in the subject. Every sensation tells us something about the physical, chemical or radio-active nature of bodies. The sensations are not pure modes of the mind. If they contain a hyperphysical element, they are nevertheless essentially organic.

In fine, three sorts of object are immediately present to our consciousness: the supra-rational, the rational and the sub-rational. When we desire to know the sub-rational by our reason alone, we find ourselves in the presence of formidable difficulties; for the latter can only have an abstract notion of the former. There is a residue to which it cannot attain, namely, that which is, properly speaking, sensible. From this proceed the contradictions which reason thinks it discovers in imaginary time and space, then in the real time and space which it confounds with the former. The same fate overtakes ratiocination when it claims to comprehend God. He is the incomprehensible: one cannot then speculate on his essence. It is evident that one cannot give a real definition of a being who is *ex hypothesi* above all genera and all specific differences. The definition, in fact, depends precisely on the genus and the difference. Thus, one can only give a descriptive definition of God. It follows that one cannot comprehend Him, since definition, in itself, is the result of comprehension. This does not prevent us from having a certain intellection of Him: from knowing Him in fact, as being totally diverse and not as simply different from all others. (*Quis ut Deus?*) Nominalism implies the negation of the reality of every idea which is not altogether individual. This negation leads again to the denial of the reality of space and time. But the nominalist principle is not an axiom. It will be seen later that if the genus and the species have no existence outside individuals, the individuals are only intelligible because they contain these realities formally in themselves.

We have said that the password of idealism consists in claiming that we have no consciousness except of the ego and its states. Now this formula expresses only very partially and imperfectly the result of introspection. What is true is that we have no consciousness of the ego except on condition that we have consciousness of a non-ego. The consciousness of the ego, in a finite being, is always a consciousness of an opposition to that which is not the ego. The starting-point of certitude is not "I am." In order to remain reality, the formula must be modified and completed. It is necessary to say: "I am conscious of the ego as affected by the non-ego in the representation made present to me." The modifications of the ego are indeed the result of the actions by which objects internalize, and manifest themselves to us, or else reactions of the ego consequent on the intuitive knowledge which we have of objects in relation to and acting in us. It is in this sense that Martensen, a Lutheran theologian far removed from pantheism, can maintain that we have a consciousness of God.[1] Such an expression would be improper if consciousness were defined as the internal knowledge of the states of the ego, but we hope to show that this definition is too narrow. The object is not known except on condition that we come out of ourselves and that the object enters into us. The consciousness is also consciousness of this communion with the object, of this double movement which we call the knowledge of the object.

By sensation we can have immediate knowledge, intuition of the object. This is possible because the ego, both spiritual and organic at the same time, is not a phantom which haunts the organism. It is the organism itself, informed by the spirit, a unique substance, but composed of the body, which is the matter, and of the soul which is the form. Sensation, being a fact which is both mental and physical, places us directly in the presence of bodies. There is no need for argument or reasoning in order to know them. Sensorial knowledge is an immediate intuition in all reasoning. The infant and the brute, while

---

[1] Martensen, *Christian Dogmatics*, trs. Urwick, Edinburgh, 1866, p. 5.

incapable of reasoning, perceive the external world. As for the vibrations which accompany the sensations and which have their repercussions in the nervous system, these are by no means the causes of sensation. The proof lies in the fact that we have no consciousness of them whatever. They constitute the environment which conditions sensation and renders it possible. But this environment is real. Thanks to it, the ego can know that anterior to itself and to every created thinking ego, the world has had a long history of which geology, palaeontology and prehistory attempt to yield the secret. If there are only subjective phenomena, what can be the meaning of geological facts? Are these phenomena? But then one would like to enquire what is a phenomenon which does not appear in itself, since a geological fact is not a fact of consciousness, and one which does not appear to any consciousness at all, since *ex hypothesi*, it is anterior to all consciousness. Geology compels us to turn our eyes towards a past from which all consciousness is absent.

It seems that Gourd would have us imagine the contrary: "Facts", he tells us, "exist only in and through consciousness." This is a well-worn idealist cliché, but it conceals a difficulty. The solution suggested may be stated thus: "Facts produce themselves only in the measure in which the consciousness produces itself: they originate only at the moment when they are grasped." We used to think that the examination of a plutonian rock gave us information concerning what happened long ago, but now it would seem that we were in error. The rock tells us nothing about what has happened. In reality there is no past at all. We are the victims of a sort of inverted illusion. We may be mistaken but this seems to be the conclusion at which the philosopher of the *Trois dialectiques* arrives. Notice how he continues: "Consequently, there can never be regression but only progression, in the quest for causes." It might be thought "that we move back from a time less ancient to one more ancient." Yes, that is true, everybody thinks so, but it seems that this is not the case. What actually happened then according to idealism? "In reality, we only advance from the present moment to one that is to come." If a new Nicodemus, a reader unaccustomed to the paradox of phenomenalism, were to ask: "How can these things be?" this is the reply which he would receive: "The series of facts of consciousness, even when it is a question of tracing back towards the past, does not unfold itself except in the direction of the present to the future."[1]

---

[1] J. J. Gourd, *Un vieil argument en faveur de la métaphysique*, p. 380: quoted by L. Trial, *J. J. Gourd*, p. 359.

"Yes," we reply: "the series of facts of consciousness, in the theory which the author constructs, as an explanation."

But actually, this explanation obliges him, in the present instance to recognize a state of objective reality greatly anterior to these states of consciousness, and the difficulty remains: what are these unperceived and imperceptible phenomena? Where do they reside? Certainly not in the ego, which did not then exist, not in God, since we are forbidden to find him at the climax of the series of phenomena; not in themselves, for it would be rather drastic to deduce from the consciousness the phenomena of eruption or erosion or any other similar fact.

We conclude that the sensations which give us information concerning the past, equally with those which give us information concerning the nature of present objects, testify in favour of the objective existence of the external world and contain the refutation of phenomenalist idealism. Innatism, in the final term of its evolution, innatism become phenomenalist, breaks itself against the rock of sensible experience, against the resistance of objective and experimental reality. It is for empiricism to tell us if it is in a better position to give us a theory of knowledge.

CHAPTER 6

EMPIRICISM

Innatist rationalism has attempted to bring reality into the Procrustean bed of the ideas and forms of the human mind. Empiricism, on the contrary, endeavours to mould reason on experience, or rather to make the former emerge from the latter. Consistent innatism intended us to draw all our knowledge, even that of sensible things, from our own depths. Empiricism desires that sensorial experience may be, in some sense, not only the source of the content of our knowledge, but even the creator of the understanding, the organ of knowledge.

From this point of view we do not think that the empirical school has the right to annex Lord Bacon. Although it is not always realized, the position of this philosopher is a philosophical transposition of his theology. In the first place, the formula *mens est tabula rasa* is no sort of sure criterion, enabling empiricism to reveal itself. This formula was that of medieval orthodox scholasticism, and of systematic Calvinistic theologians like Peter Martyr. Far from presenting us with an ideogeny derived from sensation or from association of ideas, it denies all psychological systematization based on introspection, and it is to revealed theology that it sends back those who wish to construct a psychological science.

The importance assigned by the author of *Novum organon* to experimentation, and to the establishment of a system of inductive logic, has in itself nothing specifically empiricist. It is here, perhaps, that one can speak of the philosophical transposition of theology. Bacon extends to knowledge of cosmic reality what Calvin predicated of knowledge and of the faith.[1] In the English philosopher may be found what one seeks in vain in Descartes: a theory of the limits of natural and revealed knowledge.

What he says concerning the inability of natural theology to give us the knowledge of the true God, the rôle to which he confines it, which consists solely in repelling atheism, all this is certainly very far from the high aims of scholasticism. It is well known that the latter claimed and still claims to give a rationalistic foundation to revealed theology. It would have us find God

---

[1] *Inst.* I, x. 3.

at the conclusion of its syllogisms and establish a speculative science of the divine essence.

Bacon himself thought that one could, by the light of nature, arrive at the knowledge that there is a God who ought to be adored, but that only revelation could enable us to know the true God and the nature of the service which we owe to Him. Now this is not empiricism: it is simply Calvinism, or, if one prefers it, Paulinism. What he says concerning the loss of free will and the darkening of the light of human intelligence falls within the same category.[1]

At the most one notes that he seems more pessimistic than Calvin concerning the competence of reason after the Fall. We believe that, if he was indeed the precursor of empiricism, he was so unknown to and in spite of himself. What must be acknowledged, we think, is that being English, Bacon's empiricism is in the condition of a latent tendency, like rationalism among the French and metaphysical speculation among the Germans. It is this ethnic tendency which is responsible for the fact that his theological premises are accentuated in a direction which may be felt to foreshadow empiricism and positivism.

But Bacon was under the influence of Calvin. It has been remarked how little the latter describes the faith psychologically.[2] Our Reformer was too occupied with God and the promises of God, objects of faith, to confound dogmatics with the description of the states of soul of the subject who believes. Moreover, his notion of total corruption causes him to mistrust extremely the results obtained by introspection when the interests of the subject are at stake.[3] It may indeed be said that the abuses of introspection in the religious life are a deviation from and even a debasement of Calvinism. Now this distrust of interior observation that we notice in Calvin becomes with Bacon a doctrine of scientific methodology. He precedes Comte in his refusal to consider psychology as a science, employing for this purpose terms which remind us of a contemporary empiricist.[4]

Once more this is simply an exaggeration of Calvinistic antipsychology. Nevertheless, the exaggeration is not as complete as one might think. Actually, Calvin assigned only a subordinate

[1] De augm. scientiarum, V, i. 1: Etenim illuminationis puritas et arbitrii libertas simul inceperunt, simul corruerunt.
[2] P. Brunner, Vom Glauben bei Calvin, pp. 2, 112, notes 1 and 2; vide also App. IV, p. 390, for B. B. Warfield's view.
[3] Calvin, Inst. III, ii. 10: "So much vanity has the human mind, so filled is it with divers refuges of lies, with such hypocrisy is it enveloped, that it frequently deceives itself."
[4] Vide App. V, p. 390.

rôle to psychological facts which he examined in the light of history or of what we now call ethnography. And it is remarkable that the philosopher, McCosh, who introduced into the New World physio-psychological experimentation at a time when a too exclusively subjective method prevailed in psychology, was both a realist philosopher and an eminent Calvinistic divine.

Many examples of Calvin's influence on Bacon could be given. Here is one, among others: Calvin's revulsion from the subtle and artificial dialectic of his Occamist opponents to whom he commonly refers under the name of sophists, is well known. This repugnance was, in general, shared by the Reformed doctors of the first period, and even increased as a result of the fear which they felt lest their hearers should be led astray by the captious reasonings in which certain of their adversaries excelled. In order to meet them, they had to appeal to the specialists of their party, like Peter Martyr.[1]

On this point, again, Bacon furnishes us with an example of the extension of the fundamental tendencies of the faith which he professed to the sphere of general knowledge. Discussing the perversity of the human mind, he declares that dialectic is weaker than the evil that it sets out to cure, and that logic seems to be little better than a snare filled with thorny subtleties. "An abyss separates it from the subtlety of Nature, and if one thinks of what it cannot comprehend at all, it is in fact more apt to establish and confirm error than to open the way to the truth." Bergson will say later, of the intelligence in its entirety, what Bacon says of one of its processes, the syllogism.

But mistrust of the syllogism in the sciences of observation, which extends itself to other sciences also, is still not empiricism. It is rather the symptom of a tendency towards empiricism.

Locke himself is no more than a semi-empiricist. One may ask whether his virtual latent ideas might not have been a possible ground of conciliation between Leibnitz and himself. He is fundamentally a nominalist; this is above all what characterizes him. Condillac is a true empiricist but his system is puerile. In our view, David Hume is the true father of uncompromising empiricism: that of a John Stuart Mill, and, with one ruinous concession, that of a Herbert Spencer.

True empiricism is associationism. Intuitional and neo-rationalist empiricism are scarcely more than unsuccessful attempts at escape made by the human mind, for which the

---

[1] *Vide* App. VI, p. 390, for an interesting letter on this subject by Beza, then at the Colloquy of Poissy, apropos of Peter Martyr.

atmosphere of a too radical empiricism ends by becoming unbearable.

The leader of the modern form of empiricism, namely associationism, is John Stuart Mill, who continues the phenomenalism of Hume. For him, all psychological facts bring us back to the sensations: the relations of association (contiguity and resemblance) are the laws of their different groupings and combinations. The necessity of the alleged ideas of reason arise, they tell us, from the indissoluble character of certain associations of sensations. It is itself the result of habit become all-powerful.

Inductive reasoning is only a consecution from the particular to the particular, of the type: this flame has burnt me; this will burn me. Two ideas habitually associated in the mind constitute a couple. The appearance of the one is followed by the expectation of the other; thus, for example, "the law of causality, which is the pillar of inductive science, is only the familiar law which arises from the circumstance that one observes the invariable succession of a natural fact by relation to a fact which precedes it."[1] Alexander Bain perfected Mill's system in conceding to the association an active nature: "attraction of sameness".

There are numerous objections from the intellectualist side which render this system unacceptable. Ideas cannot bring themselves back to sensations. Actually, they are coexistent with them but there is no transformation. Moreover, in practice it is impossible to confound the perceived sensation of a long object, where image can be reconstituted, with the idea of a line of the same length, but with one dimension only: length. This idea, which, in the present case is a concrete one, can be clearly conceived by the mind, but it is absolutely impossible for the mind to imagine it.

The general idea is still farther removed from sensation. An attempt has been made to explain its formation by superposition of images (composite images). But we would say, with Cardinal Mercier, that the destinies of the general idea and that of the composite image are totally different. The more the composite image is overburdened and applies itself to a greater number of objects, the more it becomes blurred, obscure, indefinite; while, on the contrary, the more the general idea gains in extension, the more it becomes distinct, clear, precise. We are here, then, in the presence of two contrary evolutions; which shows us that we have to do with two distinct objects. The necessity which connects two ideas in our mind by association, and in virtue of

[1] J. S. Mill, *Logic*, III, v. 2.

which the one evokes the other, is a fact. But it is a fact of such an accidental character that we instinctively seek the *raison d'être* for it when it confronts us.

In evoking the habit as a general reason for the fact, either the empiricists make a simple description, in which case they explain nothing; or else they think they indicate to us the true, sufficient and universal cause of the apparent necessity of the ideas of reason. In this case, they disown their own system at the very moment when they are claiming to prove its superiority. This system in effect excludes all rational explanation by its very essence.

The error is altogether too obvious. We accept then the first alternative. The empiricists are describing simply what has taken place. The real not being basically rational, a description of the mental process has to serve instead of explanation. But it so happens that this description is inaccurate. It must be admitted that the human mind is often guilty of the sophistry *post hoc, ergo propter hoc*. Sometimes, however, the mind notices its error. We would ask what operation it performs when it corrects itself in this manner. It often happens also that notwithstanding the presence of invariable successions, the mind declines, sometimes rightly, sometimes wrongly, to recognize a chain of causality.

Rapid variations of temperature are generally followed by illness which, in the absence of proper treatment, may result in death. If invariable successions always tend to establish a relation of causality, how does it come about that such a large number of uncivilized people refuse energetically to recognize the real and natural cause of death, and try to seek the explanation of it in certain spells or mystical influences? The successions established between these practices and the actual death are very variable indeed. Thus there must be something other than invariable succession which makes us think we know and can verify a relation of causality.

On the other hand, there is the famous succession of day and night that always reappears in this discussion. It remains no less a stumbling-block for empiricism. No one thinks he can establish a relation of cause and effect between these two phenomena. Bertrand Russell was probably the first philosopher to express his readiness to admit the existence of such a relationship on a systematic basis.[1]

It was obviously necessary to arrive at some such conclusion:

[1] *Mysticism and Logic*, Longmans, 1918, p. 193: "We shall not refuse to say that night is the cause of day."

Mill's solution is clearly inadequate. According to this thinker, the reason why the invariable succession of day and night can yield no more than a separable association is that it is not immediate.

It is evident that there are some successions which are not immediate, and which the mind unites inseparably by the chain of causality, such as the breaking of a dam caused by the slow accumulation of water, comparable for that matter to the rapid succession of night and day in the tropics. On the other hand, the parallelism between psychic states and those of the organism is constant and invariable. Yet still the human mind, not only the mind of the philosopher, but that of uncivilized people, separates the soul from the body to the point of failing to recognize that there is any chain of causality between the states of these entities.

We must be content, then, with Bertrand Russell's admission, though it shocks common sense and even scientific reason. Empiricism claims that, in its origin, induction amounts to no more than an instinctive movement analogous to that of the child who hastily withdraws his hand when a flame recalls to him his first burn, by association, as it does to an animal. In such a case, we should have to admit that the certainty of the sciences of observation would have a poor intellectual foundation.

In reality, however, the succession that is offered us as an example has nothing in common with an induction, even if it is spontaneous. Induction which derives the general from one or more particular cases, rests on a rational principle which is its logical foundation. This principle is the principle of sufficient reason. It has for an instrument experimentation which would be impossible, on its part, without the principle of negligibility.

Balfour asks "whether principles without which no inference from experience is possible, can be themselves inferred from experiences?" No doubt, as in the suggested case of the flame, "experiences may produce habit, and habit may produce expectation, and this process may masquerade as induction. But expectations thus engendered belong to the casual series, not the cognitive." [1]

Thus the presence of rational principles is the condition of induction and experimentation. If it were otherwise, it would be impossible to explain how the higher animals, which have sensations similiar to ours, are incapable of assimilating our scientific

[2] *Theism and Humanism*, p. 206.

knowledge. Even Herbert Spencer, himself an empiricist, has nevertheless urged this objection with a severity of language that we should not have dared to bring into our criticism. But he thinks he can parry it with the aid of his theory of evolution, which, like Aristotelianism, allows him to admit.the presence of innate aptitudes. This theory purports to explain these aptitudes empirically by heredity.

"If there exists nothing at birth, beyond a passive receptivity for impressions, why should not a horse be educable as well as a man? Or, if it is claimed that language makes the difference, why do not the dog and the cat, which have the same domestic experiences, arrive by this means at the same kind of intelligence? Accepted in its current form, the hypothesis, which grants everything to individual experience, implies the uselessness of the presence of a definite nervous system, as if it had no account to give of a fact of this sort! It is nevertheless the fact which matters essentially, that which the critiques of Leibnitz and others indicate in a sense. . . . Supporters of this hypothesis, ignorant as they are of the mental evolution due to the autogenous development of the nervous system, deceive themselves as grossly as if they were to connect all growth of the body with exercise, without borrowing anything from the innate tendency to assume the adult form."[1]

Thus the admission is made, and it comes to us from one of the leaders of the empirical school: intelligence is innate of itself; the human mind is furnished at birth with tendencies and rational aptitudes which the animals do not possess. In order to explain this fact, Spencer has recourse to the hypothesis of evolution; thus, he substitutes for individual habit, the hereditary habit of the generations of species from which man has descended.

We accept the admission and reject the hypothesis, for reasons which we shall give later, and because, if it were true, it would explain nothing. Neither time nor any number of intermediaries could make a physical movement become a sensation, nor a sensation become an idea; nor a habit, even if hereditary, become the principle of contradiction. These states may succeed one another, but they cannot transform themselves the one into the other. Each is separated from the other by an abyss; there is no continuity but a sudden leap, a new commencement and complete heterogeneity.

Meanwhile, there is still the mystical evolutionist who presents

[1] Herbert Spencer, *Principles of Psychology*, quoted by Renouvier, *Logique*, I, 311.

us with a rejuvenated form of the transformist theory of knowledge, namely Bergsonism. Some progress has been made, however, for here mechanism gives place to teleological dynamism. According to this system, intelligence is a result of instinctive defence rather than of passive adaptation,[1] that is, the faculty of creating one's own tools.

The hand is the material organ of which "creative evolution", the *élan vital*, makes use in giving an account of development from brute matter. It represents nothing less than a transformation of the mind in the act of dying. Intelligence, the organ of defence, the faculty of invention, can give us no information concerning the basis of reality. This latter is, in fact, all movement, spontaneous and unpredictable. The representation that the mind makes to itself of reality is, on the contrary, necessarily static. The only reality that it can grasp is that of matter, that is to say, petrified spirituality.

Geometry is a successful enough science of this reality. But only intuition can attain reality in its moving and fluid transformation, and by this we understand, not the intuition which provides the data with which the understanding is concerned, for that focuses our attention on those aspects of reality which have no vital importance except for practical matters; but rather primitive intuition, that of the child: it is this kind of intuition which must be re-established in order that reason may be required to abdicate its function. It is thus we rediscover "the immediate date of the consciousness".

Knowledge would be identical, from this point of view, with the action even of creative evolution, in which each one of us is at each instant a totally new moment. Moreover, there are only new moments irreducible to each other in the homogeneity of the flow of the real. The illusion of intelligence is precisely to believe in the possible repetition of the same fact. Nothing can repeat itself, reproduce itself. All is perpetual creation of new forms (nominalism).

Have we been able in these few rapid lines to give an exact idea of the "new philosophy"? Is our exposition itself a creation of our own intuition? We hope we have been able to reproduce

---

[1] Spencer defines life as "the continuous adjustment of internal relation to external relation" (*Principles of Psychology*, 120). This would be true of intellectual life. Knowledge may be no more than adaptation. Thus Le Dantec teaches that "experimental notions result from the contact of our ancestors"— these ancestors are, according to his ideas, snails—"with solid bodies": they have enabled us to arrive at arithmetic and geometry. Fundamentally, Bergsonism is not far from this manner of understanding the origins of intelligence. But the *élan vital* is creative rather than receptive.

a fact already stated, viz., the exposition of Bergsonism. When we say that this philosophy deserves praise for having returned to a certain realism by its resolute affirmation of the reality of time, and for being thus a partial reaction against Kant's forms of the sensibility, we have done it justice, we hope, with the consciousness of having wished to be as objective as possible in our exposition. There is considerable difficulty in fixing the sense of certain words as used by Bergson. It has been remarked that intuition, in particular, under the pen of this philosopher, appears to have a signification almost as vacillating and incapable of fixation as the "discoveries of creative evolution" itself.

We ought perhaps to explain what has been said already concerning the superiority of intuition over intelligence, as being the affirmation of the primacy of instinct over discursive reason. It seems that there may be a double confusion here. It has been said that instinct in man does not oppose itself in its higher functions to intelligence. Human sensibility is intelligent. It is discernment, choice between (*intel-lectio*) the true and the false, the just and the unjust, the natural and the artificial.

Discursive reason must not be confounded with intelligence or wisdom (Abraham Kuyper). Reason, instead of being contemplative, as it is in the case of intelligent sensibility, is constructive, synthesizing: it prolongs and extends the limits of intellectual intuition by the aid of a formal reasoning automatism. When it is guided by intelligent intuition, it is *ratiocinata*, reason dominated and guided by the reality apprehended to the sensible intelligence. [1] It is thus a sure guide within the limits of its competence.

When it substitutes itself for intelligence, and claims to derive reality from its own depths: when, from the faculty of synthesis and control, it claims to become a creative faculty: then all the reproaches that Bergsonism and pragmatism address to the intelligence must fall again on this ratiocination.

This fundamental distinction between reason and intelligence is made, perhaps unconsciously, by the empiricists of the school of Bertrand Russell. "Reason", says the latter, "is a harmonizing, controlling force rather than a creative one." Up to the sphere of pure logic, it is intuition, which in the first place, apprehends the new. [2] We should prefer to say, however, that the terms of a line of argument cannot be connected except by intelligent intuition.

In the second place, we cannot approve the idea according to

---

[1] [*Ratio ratiocinata, raison raisonnée*; lit., reasoned reason. *Ratio ratiocinans, raison ratiocinante*; lit., reasoning reason, independent reason.]

[2] *Op. cit.*, p. 13.

which the real is a continuum in which for simple practical reasons one carves out, arbitrarily, certain generic and specific parts. This effacement of frontiers, this negation of all qualitative limit, is an irresistible propensity due to the presence of pantheism, as Kuyper has very clearly indicated.[1] The multiple is the stumbling-block of pantheism. It is not surprising then that it tries to convert it into a shapeless conglomerate and to reduce its diversity to certain unstable and fugitive manifestations of a reality always identical with itself, even when it evolves. This is what Spinoza would call "substance"; Hegel, "idea"; and Bergson, *élan vital*. But if there is anything which is repugnant to this confusion, it is principally the intuition of the difference, which is still one of these universals perceived intuitively as essential to things.

We observe, it is true, that reason has a tendency to restore all things to unity. But when it is reason rationally systematized, the unity that it seeks is the identity of the universal intelligible (genus and species) abstracted from the particular.

Now, this intelligible cannot be abstracted from it unless it is formally contained in it. A lion which seeks its prey in the desert is neither a moment of its prey, nor of the reed boat which glides down the Nile. The lion, the prey, the boat, are distinct and real entities, essentially irreducible the one to the other: they are separate substances, which the intelligence and systematic reason alike forbid us to confound.

It is objected, and with justice, we think, that if the intelligence has been and is a faculty of effectual defence, it can only be so because it perceives the true and not the false. It has been further observed that, from the point of view of evolution, instinct is a utilitarian function and that whatever may be said about instinct in opposition to intelligence, it is certainly not infallible. With reason it shares the doubtful privilege of being subject to error. There is yet another grave criticism to make against the new philosophy, namely, that it has linked up its lot with the doctrine of transformism. Now, genetic evolution, which has never been more than an hypothesis, is a very uncertain foundation on which to rear a structure of this sort. Under the blows of scientific men, the foundation is beginning to move and the movement seriously threatens the stability of the new building, which is already showing cracks and looking old before the time.[2]

[1] Abraham Kuyper, sen., *De Verflauwing der Grenzen*, G. A. Wormser, Amsterdam, 1892.
[2] *Vide* App. VII, p. 391.

It seems evident that the new philosophy gives those who are not dominated by the illusions of transformism [1] the impression of something rather old-fashioned. It is strange to be told, for example, that man is intelligent and reasonable because he has a hand at the end of each arm. One asks oneself, involuntarily, why the ape, a quadrumane, has not achieved an evolution parallel to, or even more perfect than, that of man. We appreciate that the monkey's hand has not evolved as fast as man's, or, rather, that its evolution has been different, but quantity should surely have made up for quality, the latter being approximately equal on both sides. It is certainly not the primacy of instinct over intelligence which will give us an acceptable theory of knowledge.

It seemed that, after Kant's unsuccessful attempt at con- ciliation, there was nothing more to be done but to record that the conflict 'between innatism and empiricism was insoluble.

Innatism shows that to attempt an explanation of reason by means of accidental associations is to destroy it. Empiricism has also its moment of truth, when it insists on the dependence of the human mind in regard to nature, on the fact that experience alone provides it with the matter of its knowledge, and that it is the instrument and not the source of this knowledge.

This is, indeed, the fundamental error of innatism: to believe that the mind embraces and bends experience in the pincers of its innate forms. But to us it appears abundantly demonstrated that empiricism is incapable of explaining even the possibility of experience. Habitually, it seeks for reasons; the necessities of the system oblige it to show us only causes or, rather, facts which by hypothesis have no connexion between them.

*　　*　　*　　*　　*　　*

The *sociological school* in France, with Durkheim, proposes an ingenious solution of the conflict. First of all, it offers a very pertinent criticism of the two tendencies under discussion, from the exclusively individualist point of view. The individual, it recognizes, is certainly real. Society is composed of concrete individuals. But, and it is this that they have neglected to notice, society is more than a mere collection of individuals. Just as a chemical compound is a new body, so society is a new reality qualitatively different from the individuals which compose it. There are individual representations, accidental results of contingent experience; and there are collective representations, necessary as a social bond; and it is these collective representa- tions which appear to the consciousness as *a priori*. These are

[1] Cf. Louis Vialleton, *L'origine des êtres vivants: L'illusion transformiste*, Plon, Paris, 1929, pp. 363, 378.

judgments invested with such authority that they must be believed without proofs, under pain, for the individual, of cutting himself off from the social body.

The principle of identity, the categories of space and time, moral obligation, etc., are collective representations which have their origin in social representation *par excellence*. This representation is religion. The sign of a social representation is the *a priori* obligatory character with which it is invested. Religion itself, before becoming belief, is collective emotion; ceremonial performed in common, distinction of the sacred (collective) from the profane (individual). Belief in God is, in no sense, a necessary element of religion: the social origin of religion, morality and logic, renders it possible that these phenomena may be illusions.

Society is a fact, natural and real: religion, logic and morality, are the products of a cause, rooted in reality. These products, then, are true—true, let us say, in our turn, like hallucination, which also has real physical causes, while it remains a deformed and deforming interpretation of them.

After all, this analogy between religion and hallucination should not be too uncongenial to the founder of the sociological school. It is known that he had already established his system, destructive of religious objectivity, well before he studied the religion of the Australian aborigines, basing it on *a priori* arguments.

Ethnography and hierography, interpreted more or less arbitrarily, do not intervene here except as means of polemic. They are required by the exigencies of the case merely to give these interpretations the reassuring appearance of an impartial and scientific presentation of facts. [1]

For the moment, we are concerned only with what Durkheim has told us of the origin and legitimacy of our logic: later, we shall consider the necessity of the principle of reason. His ideology and ideogeny we reject, but we are disposed to accept his ideography, on condition that it is purged from its exclusiveness and that a due account should be taken of the contribution that it makes as well as of the reactions which it has provoked.

The ideological character of the system is positivist rationalism. The $\pi\rho\hat{\omega}\tau o\nu$ $\psi\epsilon\hat{\upsilon}\delta o\varsigma$ does not consist in the attribution of a distinct reality to social facts. We recognize that these facts are things, for the same reason that we recognize the objects of the other sciences. It consists in the positivist postulate itself. This

---

[1] The documentary proof of our statement is given by G. Richard, professor of social sciences at Bordeaux, in *L'athéisme dogmatique en sociologie religieuse*, Strasbourg, 1923.

is how we understand this postulate: we know only sensible facts; the true object of sovereign and impartial reason is simply the study of these facts and their relations.

It follows that the method of social science must be the kind of experimentation which will endeavour to put on one side individual opinions and sentiments and explain quality by quantity. It will give up explanation by means of the psychology of the individual, in order to consider only the external signs accompanying the initial states and transformations of societies. Effects will thus be traced to causes in reliance on the supposed axiom, which is no better than a sophism: "The same effects result from the same causes."[1]

Thus, on the one hand, we have facts purely sensible and observable: on the other, a reason which is claimed to be impartial in the judgment of the scientist, because it is that which is social in him. All social facts, and even religion, will be amenable to this sovereign tribunal. We shall thus obtain, it is said, not a type of science relevant to a particular philosophy, but science itself, positive and independent.

Our first objection is that this ideology is false. At the very moment when it proclaims itself impartial, it opposes the question preliminary to all the claims of religion. It employs against theology the method of exclusion by "legitimate presumptions" so dear to the Catholic and Jansenist controversialists of the 17th century. Then, when it has thus driven its adversary from the arena, it commits suicide.

When we accuse positivism, and, in general, independent science, of partiality, we wish it to be understood that we do not suggest that those who maintain these points of view are in the slightest degree lacking in intellectual integrity. We say only that the very idea of an independent science, of a science without preconceived principle, is irrealizable. This results precisely from the great amount of truth in Durkheim's affirmation, according to which the individual is, in large measure, the product of his social environment.

Long before Durkheim, theology, and more particularly Calvinism, insisted on this dependence of the individual on the community.

Now, every social environment is either given, or in process of transformation. It is, therefore, impossible that the scientist, who, let us remember, forms part of it, should approach the object of his study without bringing to it the preconceived ideas that he derives from the social influences which have moulded

<hr />

[1] Durkheim, *De la division du travail social*, pp. 35–50.

him. The principles from which he starts are necessarily collective and social, even when he tries to react against his environment. Reaction is always, in some sense, conditioned by action. All that can be asked of him is that he shall apply honestly the principles which he imposes on himself. We do not suggest that Durkheim has done otherwise.

But it is obvious that he is mistaken when he considers himself to be in a perfect methodological state of indifference to the religious idea. He is not indifferent. He cannot be so, because the thing is psychologically impossible.

He considers himself to be without preconceived ideas, but listen to this: "The theoretical importance which has been sometimes attributed to primitive religions has been able to pass for the sign of a systematic irreligiosity which in *prejudging the results of the research vitiates them in advance* [italics, ours] . . . in any case, one would not expect this to be the point of view of a sociologist: it is in fact the point of view of sociology that a human institution should not rest on error and untruth, and that otherwise it could not endure."[1]

Thus, Durkheim says expressly, and believes, that the sociologist does not prejudge the result of his researches. But how can he fail to recognize that this is not the case? Durkheim has certainly prejudged the result of his own researches, at any rate, in a negative sense: and he still does so when he excludes, on principle, the supernatural action of grace in explaining the birth of faith.

It is for science, we are told, to search out the cause of religious facts; and these causes are not necessarily those which the believer imagines them to be. It so happens, however, that, according to his principle, these causes are necessarily other than those which the believer imagines, when he is not a Pelagian. For Durkheim, they are, and can only be, social, and, therefore, natural causes. He knows it in advance because he is a positivist, and thus prejudges that it cannot be otherwise.

He has no wish to deny the reality of the power of religious experience. He recognizes that it is the experience of a power on which the believer depends, and which enables him to get beyond himself. But in order to explain this fact, if one admits "that there really exist beings more or less analogous to those which the mythologies represent to us, it must be recognized that the only fire at which we can warm ourselves, morally, is that formed by the society of our fellows: the only moral forces by which we can sustain and increase our own are those which

[1] Durkheim, *Les formes élémentaires de la vie religieuse*, p. 2 f.

other people lend us."[1] The reason being that these divinities cannot act on us, unless we believe in them. Faith, however, can only come into existence through the action of the social body.

We, on the other hand, acknowledge another principle. We say that, in order that the social environment should act, and faith should come into existence, it is necessary for God to act in the first place both in the individual and in the social environment. We believe further that the only moral forces by which we can sustain and increase our own, and those which come to us from the social environment, are those which proceed from God.

Our objection to Durkheim is, not that he realizes that the individual draws from the forces in the social environment, but that he regards these as the only ones, thus excluding the immediate action of God on the individual independently of the social environment. His point of view and our own are in opposition, but both are capable of being defended. It cannot be maintained, however, that the man who makes either his starting-point is independent of all preconceptions of religion.

Moreover, it is as impossible for Durkheim not to act in accordance with his positivist ideas as it is for us not to take into account our religious preconceptions.

We recognize that there are not two formal logics. But there are at least two material logics. There is the logic of those who, like Durkheim himself, deny the Fall and its consequences— again, an anti-Augustinian preconception—and who explain sin as antagonism between social constraint and the need for individual independence; and there is the logic of those who, with Calvin, believe in the Fall and total corruption. According to them, as according to Paul, the φρόνημα τῆς σαρκός the natural mind, is "enmity against God".

From this point of view, as Abraham Kuyper has shown, there are necessarily not two verities: the truth is one, not two, scientific methods; the method is universal; but two views of facts, two principles of interpretation of the method; and, although this will scandalize modern theologians, two sciences. This would appear to be an original and fundamental concept of Calvinism restored and reaffirmed, on the ground of modern science.

We do not acknowledge an independent science, on the one hand, and a science enslaved to prejudices, on the other. Nevertheless, there are two sciences, both necessarily dependent: the one, of the natural mind; the other of the mind regenerated by

---

[1] Durkheim, *Les formes élémentaires de la vie religieuse*, p. 336.

the action of grace. Neither the one nor the other of these scientific schools is, by nature, exempt from faults against formal logic. No one is infallible.

Here, for example, is an error which has slipped into Durkheim's ideology. When he claims that the same effects spring from the same causes, he imagines himself to be enunciating the inverse of this other principle in virtue of which, all things being equal, the same causes produce the same effects. A little attention would have enabled him to avoid this error. Everyday experience shows that identical effects may be the result of very different causes. Suicide may be caused by despair, by the collapse of religious convictions; or, on the other hand, by fanaticism or by the exaltation of chimerical hopes.

We note that the enfeeblement of social authority, as well as the extension of this authority—causes absolutely contrary the one to the other—may produce effects externally identical. Thenceforth, the explanation of quality by quantity, commended by Durkheim, may be a constant source of error.

Moreover, if sociological ideogeny were true, the first suicide whose causes would call for investigation would be that of the theory itself. Indeed, if our categories arise from accidental habits, and by irrational hypothesis, from some primitive clan, which has long disappeared in the mists of pre-history but which survives in our logic, nothing remains true. Consequently, the sociological system which claims to explain the birth of these ideas is itself not true. We cannot, in fact, affirm anything except by making use of our categories. Now, we are informed that these categories have no other relations with reality than those which may exist between a dream and the psychological cause of which it is the illusory interpretation. Here, again, when we ask for reasons, we are presented with causes. It is surprising that, at this stage, anyone can confound the causal order with the cognitive order.

But Durkheim's ideogeny, in so far as it is original, is unacceptable. And when he tries to make it acceptable it ceases to be original. It comes back again to that of our own theologians.

Our categories of time and space have their origin, sociology tells us, in the necessity of fixing the regular rendezvous for the celebration of feasts, sacrifices and other ceremonies, perpetuated in the hierarchical divisions of the encampments organized by the clans, then in the very form of the camps themselves.

"It seems evident, on the contrary," says Parodi[1] "that the mere existence of ceremonies or of regular tasks, that the mere

---

[1] *La philosophie contemporaine en France*, p. 155, n. 1.

distinction of the clans and the tribes and of their respective places in the camp, presuppose the logical categories and are not possible except by reason of a preliminary intervention of the ideas of time, space, causality, on the principle of contradiction, etc."

This seems all the more evident when we consider that, in human societies, these rendezvous and these divisions are not uniform, like those of animals belonging to the same species. These, then, are purely instinctive facts, corresponding to more or less accidental representations which betray the intervention of the factor of liberty. Now, liberty is no more than a *lubentia rationalis*, a rational spontaneity. Reason, or rather intelligence, the source of liberty. It is presupposed by the manifestations of free activity.

When Durkheim has an idea of the kind of objection that is about to be raised, and which he tries to forestall, he hastens to return to the truth, and, in doing so, departs from his system. He does nothing but repeat, in terms scarcely different, that which others have said before him.

After having said that social representations are irreducible to individual representations, he makes a ruinous concession in a footnote: "Besides, this irreducibility must not be understood in an absolute sense . . . *all* that we wish to establish here"— it is, then, the essential totality of his system that Durkheim wishes to confide to us—"all that we wish to establish here is that, between the indistinct germs of reason" (in the individual) "and reason properly so called" (in the collective conscience) "there is a distance comparable to that which separates the properties of mineral elements of which the living thing is formed and the characteristic attributes of life once it is established."[1]

Do not cavil at the author's comparison. It seems as if, here, the opponent of evolution has become a transformist himself. He believes that the properties of the mineral elements which constitute the living thing are "the indistinct germs" of life. There remains, between the germs of reason and reason itself, the difference which separates a germ from the perfect organism.

But this is not new. It is the doctrine which has been traditional with us since the time of Calvin, who took it over from the scholastics.[2] When our Reformer would determine the extent to which common grace has enabled reason to function after the Fall, preventing human intelligence from sinking lower than

---

[1] *Les formes élémentaires de la vie religieuse*, p. 22, n. 2.
[2] *Vide* App. VIII, p. 392.

that of the brutes, he begins by distinguishing two spheres: that of "terrestrial" things and that of things "celestial". "Under the former category"—that which concerns us now—"are comprised political doctrine, the manner of ordering one's house aright, the mechanical arts, philosophy, and all those disciplines which are termed liberal."

The order followed by Calvin is significant. The social order takes first place: after which come, successively, domestic economy, industry, philosophy, and the sciences which branch off from it. It is not surprising that he gives pride of place to what he calls the police, to the civic order, for "to wish to reject it is human barbarism, since it is not less necessary among men than bread, water, sun and air: while its dignity is much greater: for it is not concerned only with what men eat, drink, and are sustained with in their life . . . but with what humanity consists in among men." [1] But whence comes the possibility of the social order and what does it prove?

On the question of origin, Durkheim tells us: "if the psychic nature of the individual were absolutely refractory to social life, society would be impossible." [2] Elsewhere, he appeals to the gregarious instinct. Calvin says, more clearly: "In so far as man is by nature companionable (literally, a social animal) he is inclined by a natural affection (literally, instinct) to maintain and preserve society." [3]

Up to this point, agreement between the two writers is complete. What they say is very useful, but there was nothing new about it, even in the 16th century. For Calvin, as for Durkheim, society is the environment necessary for the development of the "germ" of reason among men. It is this idea which has preserved for Calvinism the rights of the state. Thus, on this question, a theologian as affected by Cartesianism as Samuel Endemann is in agreement with a theologian as formally correct as H. E. Gravemeijer. Basing himself on an experience which he believes to be experimentally verified, he denies that the individual deprived of external instruction can attain to the verities of natural religion solely by the powers of reason. [4]

What conclusion can be drawn from the fact, recognized on all sides, that man is a social animal? Durkheim has told us

---

[1] *Inst.* IV, xx. 3.   [2] *Loc. cit.*

[3] *Inst.* II, ii, 13: *Quoniam homo animal est natura sociale, naturali quoque instinctu, ad fovendam conservandamque eam societatem propendit.*

[4] *Theol. Dogmat.*, Frankfurt on Main, 1782, f. 9. *Si vero quaeris an homo omni institutione externa, imprimis revelatione divina, destitutus sola rationis vi theologiam naturalem condere potuerit nego; exempla sunt qui inter feras adoluerunt.* Cf. Gravemeijer, *Gereformeerde Geloofsleer,* I, p. 33 ff.

that there are "rudimentary germs of reason in the individual". Calvin has said the same thing, but he draws from it the obvious conclusion. After the Fall, the individual, with his germs of reason, is logically anterior to society: "Hence it is that the minds of men have general impressions of civil order and honesty . . . in every man there remains some seed of political order." [1]

Here, what Durkheim styles "collective representation", Calvin calls "general impressions"; and Zanchius, later,"common notions". Durkheim speaks of "rudimentary germs of reason". Calvin employs the technical expression, borrowed from Augustine, of *semen*, seed (a certain seed); moreover, he employs this term in the sense of aptitude, which is Durkheim's sense. Calvin knows as well as Augustine all the difference that separates the seed from the perfect organism. On this point, also, the agreement is striking. Only Calvin draws the necessary conclusion: "Here, we have ample proof that, in regard to the constitution of the present life, no one is devoid of the light of reason." [2]

Actually, society by itself has no power to create reason. Durkheim hesitates to recognize this, but is finally obliged to do so. The existence of animal societies is a fact. Durkheim tells us that the isolated individual is an animal; but, here, he contradicts himself, since he is forced to attribute to him a germ of reason, however "rudimentary" it may be. The child or man who has grown up among wild beasts is not an animal but a potential man. No doubt, the seed can only germinate in appropriate soil: in this case, social life. It is this which secures that "humanity shall exist among the humans", as Calvin says. But reason, in the state of virtuality, of aptitude to co-operate in the social order, is the *conditio sine qua non* of the origin of all human social order.

It must be added that the social environment does not act alone in provoking the germination of the seeds of reason, morality and religion. Individual intelligence, the physical environment, the influences and scenes of nature, temperament, native qualities, each play a part which Durkheim has certainly underestimated. Actually, there are in his theory two systems. There is a system of primary importance: his own, properly speaking, and he cannot sustain it; also a secondary system constituting, shall we way, the second line of

---

[1] *Inst.* II, ii. 13 : *Ideoque civilis cujusdam et honestatis et ordinis universales impressiones inesse omnium hominum animis conspicimus . . . manet tamen illud inspersum esse universis semen aliquod ordinis politici.*
[2] *Ibid.*

defence. But, on this line, the sociological view shows no superiority over theories as secular as those of Marion or Tarde, or over theories as theological as those of Calvin, Kuyper or Bavinck, which represent society as the necessary condition for the formation of religious and intellectual thought.

Having completed our survey of the great theories of knowledge, we note that empiricism and innatism remain opposed in sterile conflict, and that the two attempts at reconciliation by Kant and Durkheim respectively have failed. The innateness of the forms, the presence of categories of the understanding, the obligatory character of rational imperatives, is, for the first named, a mystery. The second thinks he can give a satisfactory explanation of it: but confronted with the rational, in germ, in the individual understanding, and the rationality of the real, he stops short. He is quite prepared to accept Herbert Spencer's relative innatism: but we have seen that this, again, ends in a *cul-de-sac*. It is in a form of moderate realism that we shall seek the true solution of the problem.

CHAPTER 7

KNOWLEDGE AS AFFECTED BY CONSCIOUSNESS

Jean Jacques Rousseau, by his theory of the social contract, made collectivity a conventional creation, due to the agreement of the individual wills concerned in it. For the men of the 18th century, the *Encyclopédistes*,[1] and the *Aufklärung*,[2] individual reason is an autonomous faculty, everywhere the same in itself, and they continue to believe the Cartesian dogma that good sense is, of all things on earth, the most evenly distributed. Good sense is reason.

Durkheim on the contrary, tends to make the individual reason a creation of the collective consciousness: and man, in isolation, an animal. Durkheim, and in a general manner, the progress of ethnological science, seem to us to have scientifically discredited the ideology of the 18th century, which exercised, and still exercises, such a mischievous influence over certain groups in Protestantism.

We have endeavoured to show what is exaggerated in Durkheim's theory, and to restore it to proportions more in conformity with the results of a sober review of the facts. It remains for us, now, to specify as far as possible, the part played by natural factors in the acquisition and development of knowledge, the existence of which we have already noted, namely, the individual, environment and society.

We have already said that the human individual is indeed an animal, but one capable of thinking by concepts, and of raising itself by abstraction to generalization. We have recognized that an orthodox theological tradition, long anterior to Durkheim, does not hesitate to admit that the individual, accidentally isolated from his fellows, would differ very slightly from the

---

[1] [*Encyclopédistes*, the contributors to the *Encyclopédie ou Dictionnaire raisonné des Sciences, des Arts et des Métiers* (1751–72), edited by Diderot and D'Alembert, among whom were Voltaire, Rousseau, Grimm, Quesnay, Turgot, Marmontel, Holbach, Duclos and Jancourt.]

[2] [*Aufklärung* (German), Enlightenment, in its historical perspective the cultural atmosphere of the 18th century in Germany, France and Britain which also affected American thought in B. Franklin, T. Paine, and the leaders of the revolution. It crystallized tendencies created by the Renaissance and stimulated by scepticism and empiricism. The term is more particularly applied to tendencies represented by Lessing, Reimarus, Wolff, Eberhard, Kant, and Goethe.]

higher animals. But, as Durkheim admits, "there is something social in him", innate in him. Virtually he would still be a man.

In fact, normally, man, even if uncivilized, receives by education, by the language he is taught to speak, which expresses the soul of his people and of his race, that which becomes the form of the majority of his intellectual representations, modes of feeling, reasoning processes and prejudices.

The social influence is enormous, and it is so much the more irresistible in that it is least perceived by the individual. The individual, in fact, who is never merely an individual, but who is a person formally free, is often impelled by his personal character to develop in reaction against social conformity. But one only reacts against what is felt as a constraint, as incapable of assimilation by the personality. On the other hand, that which is appropriated unconsciously, that which integrates itself in us, governs the progress of our thought, even in the freest of its investigations.

In this sense, the seeker always depends on his social environment. This latter may be in process of formation, of dissolution, or simply in a relatively stable condition. From which it follows that there is no such thing as independent science. Everybody starts, invariably, from undemonstrables, which are the syntheses of common notions, ἔννοαι κοιναί with his personal intellectual tendencies.

Further, science resides properly in the collective consciousness of a society, of a given culture. The individual never possesses more than a part of it. Now, it is incontestable that human societies are not all at the same level of rationality. Reason, the faculty of generalizing attains to generalization only by abstraction. To abstract the intelligible from the sensible, in order to generalize, is its proper function. But this function is not at the same stage in all human societies. Even if one wishes to regard reason as a collective faculty, it must be conceded that its function is accomplished only in and through individuals.

There is no reason to think, however, that abstraction must everywhere attain perfection the very first time. On the contrary, the task of abstraction which rests on observation, is slow and difficult. *Primum vivere, deinde philosophari.* The cares of daily existence, and the struggle for life, take priority over the exigencies of thought. Consequently, a tribe which lives from day to day amid the hazards of the chase, or by fishing, will transmit to the individuals by its language only a limited number of abstract ideas. The primary source of the conceptual representations of an individual, even if very gifted, will be much poorer in a tribe of Hottentots than in a Greek deme or in the most backward of our European villages.

Collectivity, then, does not act on the individual by merely furnishing him with the material of his ideas: the individual still depends on the degree of rational generalization to which the society of which he forms part has attained, and he depends on it for the number of ideas which he possesses originally.

But there is another factor which Durkheim appears to have left in the shade, namely, the physical environment. It is from our sensations that we derive our general ideas. No doubt, "the rôle of words is precisely to permit us to form general ideas."[1] But these general ideas are not arbitrary. They are common to the men of a certain period being in a certain environment, and are imposed by the nature of the sensations experienced and by the associations which these provoke. Divisions of time, e.g., associate themselves naturally with the movements of the celestial bodies. It is only when we come to certain magical ideas, the efficacy of words, action from a distance, etc., that we cannot show that they have their origin in the psychological experiences of the child, provoked by physical causes.

If the individual were not in correspondence with the physical environment which he receives in the nature of things, it would be impossible to explain the generality of the ideas which one finds everywhere, even in the most advanced societies, without any question of propagation by tradition. They have only become collective, and almost universal, because they have been suggested to the human mind, everywhere the same, by individual physical experiences common to all men.

Disregard for, or underestimation of, the influence of the physical environment on the formation of ideas, and the exclusive rôle assigned to the collective consciousness, appears to us to be due to this error: namely, the tendency, by no means confined to the sociological school, to consider reason, collective fact, as the objective element; and sensation as the subjective and individual element.

Now, as we have already remarked in passing, sensation is certainly an individual fact, in the sense that it is incommunicable to those who are not placed in the same physical conditions as the one who experiences it. But it is objective, not merely

---

[1] Sechehaye in R. Allier, *Les non-civilisés et nous*, p. 212. In pp. 201–215, Allier gives a conclusive demonstration of the influence of the physical environment on the formation of quasi-universal magical ideas.

because it reveals the object to us but still more because we know that all those who are placed in the same conditions as ourselves will experience the same sensations as we do. We know it because the object appears to the subject as connected with reality by a necessary relationship, and because it is axiomatic: a belief on evidence that, *ceteris paribus*, the same causes will produce the same effects. This is because we credit other men with the same senses and the same sensations as ourselves. The sensation that we experience is thus, for us, the means of escaping from our subjectivity, and of realizing the viewpoint of other people. The representative element is the same for them as for us.

As for the affective element of pleasure or pain, we freely admit that it may differ in certain instances, because, in our own case, experience shows that habit may modify our manner of appreciating a sensation which remains identical with itself, under the representative relationship. The affective element is thus the only part played by subjectivity in the sensation; but, as we have remarked, it is far from existing in all the sensations. The greater part of them are indifferent in this respect.

It is precisely on this undeniable fact, that there is something subjective in sensation, on its affective side, that Durkheim builds in order to explain why the authority of the collective consciousness of reason, prescribing rules of conduct, is so often defied by the individual. He cannot visualize more than two possibilities of seriously explaining this phenomenon: his own, which we have just outlined, and the doctrine of the Fall. Nevertheless, there are others. There is that of Pelagius, for example, which appeals to the individual free will and to imitation. There is the view that explains sin by the precedence, in time, of the physical instincts of animal life, developed long before the dawn of moral consciousness in each individual. But sociology does not concern itself with such explanations: they are too individualistic for its liking. It would be out of place for us to discuss them here, since they raise the question of hamartiology, which is a section of dogmatics proper.

At this stage in the discussion, Calvinism again finds itself face to face with the sociological theory: and, under honourable conditions since its adversary recognizes that, even though its explanation may not be accepted, there is no other serious alternative than that which Calvinism offers, namely, the doctrine of the original Fall.

Now, it seems to us impossible that, on reflection, anyone could be content with the sociological theory, however ingenious it may appear. Actually, it reduces the spiritual conflict to a conflict between the reason, considered as a collective faculty, and the individual sensuality: or, if one prefers it, the subjective sensibility. In these circumstances, reason is law, always in the right, formally at least; sensuality is individual caprice and, when it opposes reason, disorder or sin. It may be at work in the collective judgment, but, in order to triumph, it must begin by being a crime against the social order.

We regard this as an unwarrantable restriction of the sphere of sin. Corruption is total, extensively, if not intensively. It extends to all the human faculties. Sin has its seat, not merely in the world of the sensible passions, which it perverts and lets loose, but also in the will, which it enslaves: and in the understanding, which it liberates from dependence on its real object and on the creator of the object. There is sin of the intelligence. Sin overflows to the aesthetic sphere also. It extends further and higher than the sensibility and the will. It has its seat in the very centre of the intellectual consciousness of man. If reason were normal, it would consent to remain *ratio ratiocinata*. We should not see it aspire to become *ratio ratiocinans*.[1] The disharmony in us is not produced solely by the revolt of the senses against reason. It proceeds from the fact that every faculty of the soul tends to become normally an end in itself, autonomous, egocentric.

There is not merely the concupiscence of sensuality. The concupiscence of the flesh, in the Pauline sense, embraces also the concupiscence of practical reason; the pride of life and the concupiscence of theoretical reason; the covetousness of the eyes, to use the Jansenist expression. The practical reason, which proclaims itself autonomous, sins: for there is only one lawgiver, namely God: and this lawgiver it ignores, in order to instal itself in his place.

The theoretical reason, even if collective, sins also when it claims to derive reality from its own depths, to impose after a sovereign fashion its forms and relations on experimental reality: for it ignores its subordinate rôle of organ or instrument conditioned by the true objective, in order to constitute itself the supreme norm and source of knowledge. It also replaces the supreme authority of the fact laid down by God, by His own proper authority, and enthrones itself in the temple of science, on the altar before which the truth is adored. It sins also when it claims to usurp the rôle of the other faculties, in the act of knowing, comprehending the infinite and arraigning God before the bar of its own tribunal.

[1] *Vide* p. 64 note.

It goes without saying that the sin of the reason is rather in intention than in fact. When it claims the right to establish relations among things it changes nothing in the reality as it is or as it appears. The cosmos, the universe, still remains conditioned by laws higher than itself on which it depends absolutely. These laws are so evidently decreed by an intelligence that, rather than deny it, human reason is obliged to claim that it is itself which creates them, equally with the world of representation (Kant).

Reason can change nothing in reality, but the intention is not lacking. Kantianism and the systems connected with it are revelations of the state of sin to which the understanding has been subjected, because, being unable to make the human mind the creator of reality, they make it the creator of a world of phantoms. Thus, the absolute dependence of the human mind on reality and the divine laws which govern it is transformed into an imaginary sovereignty of its own laws over itself. As Baader observes: in the order of knowledge as well as in the order of the moral law, God is everywhere displaced by man.[1] In Kantianism, it is the individual that is concerned in this displacement; in sociology, it is society. For Durkheim, in effect, the collective consciousness corresponds to the representation that believers have of God.

It follows from this that sin is not only a conflict between reason and sensibility but a conflict between the supreme reason, on which all depends, and the subordinate reason, which would rid itself of its dependence. Durkheim's explanation, then, cannot survive an analysis of the facts. Since, according to him, there is no alternative but the Calvinistic explanation of original sin, on his own showing, this demands consideration.

Now, Calvinism distinguishes between the normal state of human reason before the Fall and the abnormal state of this reason afterwards, a distinction which enables it to take a clear position of principle in the conflicts between faith and reason, dogma and science. The intelligent consciousness, in its primitive state, is a pure reflex of divine intelligence. It awakens and functions under the action of the physical and social environment on which the individual depends. The imperfections of reason which are evident in the individual do not proceed

---

[1] Quoted by Abraham Kuyper, *Pantheism's Destruction of Boundaries*: "The fundamental error of his (Kant's) philosophy is that man is autonomous and spontaneous, as if he possessed reason of himself; for it transforms man into a god and so becomes pantheistic."

merely from the fact that, like the clan or people among whom he is called to live, it does not at first attain the highest degree of culture and generalization of which it is capable: these imperfections result from a social and hereditary fact, from a much more general type of solidarity. Each individual has, in himself, something social; or rather, human. He is a personal, concrete realization of humanity itself—and humanity is in a fallen, sinful state.

Sin, before being a fact of the voluntary order in the individual, an individual transgression of deliberate purpose, is an innate tendency out of harmony with the law of the divine intelligence. This orientation is the result of a free act which has vitiated at its source all human development, the development of this collective consciousness, of this organism, which is a system of individual consciousness all united in the same stock. For God "hath made of one blood all nations of men for to dwell on all the face of the earth." (Acts 17: 26.)

Sin is, in itself, a negation: but a negation in regard to something positive, a defect introduced into the relative perfection of the finite being. It is an effort towards total disorganization, towards death. Thus, for Reformed theology, the persistence in humanity of reason, even if vitiated, is a fact apparently abnormal in this abnormal state caused by sin.

For Calvin, the existence of imbecility and idiocy shows us what all men would have to expect if an intervention of divine power had not produced a limitation of the natural effects of the initial fault. God has not willed that humanity should altogether sink into bestiality. His common (general, collective) grace has in view, in the first place, the preservation of a minimum of humanity among the sons of Adam. It proceeds according to the method of election, like particular (special) grace which has in view the reconstitution of a new humanity according to the Spirit.

The action of the former is more extensive than that of the latter. The human race is the social environment in which common grace is exercised, while the sphere of activity of particular grace is the Church. The action of common grace maintains the social instinct among men, a natural inclination to respect social authority, and for the right of superiors to take command. Calvin observes that this instinct persists, even among brigands. It maintains among the intellectually mature a developed aptitude to generalize by abstraction, and to exercise the formal activity of reasoning in a sufficiently correct manner.

In a later section, we shall show that common grace preserves a religious aptitude in fallen man. It is sufficient to say here that, from the Calvinistic point of view, the arts and sciences, philosophy, and religious and social institutions, are the ordinary effects of common grace. The faculty of invention and what is called genius constitute its extraordinary effects.

On the other hand, if common grace canalizes sin, and limits its disastrous effects for the individual and the community, it cannot regenerate the sinner. It follows that the latter, in whom formal reason may exist in an efficient state of operation, should be able to excel in those branches of knowledge the object of which has only a remote relation with his normal religious purpose. When it is otherwise, his subjective tendency fundamentally opposed to God will manifest itself.

This is particularly the case with the disciplines of the mind, such as ethics, law, sociology, literary and historical criticism, metaphysics and theology. On the other hand, in the purely formal sciences like mathematics, and those into which ontological principles do not enter, the subjectivity of the sinner, considered as such, is practically non-existent.

Obviously, these theses which, for us, are articles of faith, can be only unproved and unprovable hypotheses for those strangers to the action under which our faith is born. It must not be forgotten, however, that, as Durkheim admits, they remain the only serious explanations of the facts, if his thesis is set aside. And we have seen that it must be set aside.

Moreover, it is useful that these theses should be known, in order that our attitude to reason and the senses in the conflict with religious truth may be understood, and in order to show how it is that sometimes we invoke the testimony of reason and the senses, and at other times refuse it. This is not the result of arbitrary dispositions, suggested by the accidental exigencies of a discussion, but the reflected application of systematic principles. We believe that, apart from physical or mental malady, the reason can function formally in a correct manner. A formal contradiction is thus, for us, a mark of error. We believe that, in a subject in good health, the senses function normally and render present to us the qualities of the object and the object itself. In consequence, their testimony may be trusted.

In this, we are being consistent with ourselves, because reason and the senses, according to our faith, are instruments of knowledge willed by God, efficacious while they exercise themselves in the sphere for which they were intended. Common grace maintains their integrity among those whom it exempts from infirmities and sickness.

Our theologians are thus justified in invoking the testimony of the senses and the authority of reason against the theory of transubstantiation. For they see in the latter not only palpable contradictions but an implicit denial of the value of sensible knowledge. Moreover, a contradiction is not a mystery. An illusion cannot constitute the central "miracle" of religion.

They are justified, also, in denying that the senses grasp the whole of reality: and in refusing to reason the right to consider itself the source and norm of reality. There can be, and are, objects each of whose elements is intelligible to reason, even when it is unable to form a synthesis of them. Partial intellection may be possible where comprehension is impossible.

Insoluble opposition gives us no right to affirm that there is contradiction. The Calvinist knows that men possess integrity relative to their senses and their reason only by a precarious title. If he believes in such formal integrity, it is because faith teaches him that it is God's purpose to preserve mankind in general, in order to serve as a sphere of action for special grace.

Under the influence of their social environment and of the spirit of the age (the power of which completely dominates the majority of minds), philosophers and thinkers sometimes declare certain principles that confront religious certitude to be axiomatic and demanded by reason. In such cases the believer is not guilty of any inconsistency if he replies with a plea of exception. Indeed, he must do so, because he knows that natural reason, like the other faculties, is set in opposition to God and divine truth; but, above all, because he knows that such authority as reason has retained after the Fall is dependent on the action of common grace.

*   *   *   *   *   *

We are now in a position to see the relations that exist between the three factors of knowledge: nature, society, and individual reason. The source and norm of our scientific knowledge consists in the objects of the natural environment: in the objective relations which connect them and which are perceived by the intelligent sensibility. In matters of secular science, the fact proved is the supreme authority. The fact can be grasped only by the individual, by the particular reasonable and sensible being. Experience is a revelation of truth to the individual. But the individual owes to the collective consciousness, to the social environment, the preliminary communication of the treasures of experience communicated by the generations which preceded him, expressed in the prevailing language, traditions and ideas.

The individual does not reach nature by study without having received a certain intellectual bias imprinted by society.

Society is his indispensable instructor: the individual owes it everything except his innate aptitude to think by concepts. He cannot be too grateful for this. But the authority which he should ascribe to it is purely pedagogical: or, to employ the technical term of theologians, ministerial. This authority is subordinate to the higher authority of God, who reveals Himself both to the community and to the individual. At a given moment, it may appear evident to the latter that the social representations of a certain period are opposed to well-known natural or supernatural facts. In this case, the individual is not bound by the authority of the body social. He commits no crime in ranging himself against it. What binds him is the supreme authority of the known fact; for every fact is, in the natural order, the revelation of a divine decree.

CHAPTER 8

MODERATE CRITICAL REALISM

Knowledge is a relation between the subject knowing and the reality which, in so far as it is known, constitutes the object. Now, we have seen that *innatism* tends to idealism. And idealism tends to a denial of the possibility of knowing the object, and even, in phenomenalism, to the annihilation of the object It recognizes no other knowledge than that of the ego and its states. We have remarked that the paradox of this theory of knowledge consists in the fact that, since there is a relation of knowledge between the subject and the object, the object is unknowable.

The subject, shut up to himself, cannot escape from himself except by a *salto mortale*, a *coup d'état* of the will to believe. The way of reasoning is too difficult. Science is merely the organization of interior representations introduced by the mind into its own states of consciousness. *Empiricism* appears to preserve the object but leads to a sort of dissolution of the subject. Intelligence is simply the result of accidental coincidences, a fact which vitiates it at its source. It is only distinguished from other things by a greater complexity of relations which seem to be interior to itself. Knowledge is merely adaptation to an irrational state of things.

The relations between things are what they are, but there is no guarantee that they will not be something quite different in the next moment. Experience tells us what is: it cannot teach us what must be. Logical necessity itself is reduced to the experience that certain phenomena exclude others in our consciousness. Thus we never perceive at the same time light and darkness, noise and silence (Stuart Mill).

Now, these theories satisfy neither religion nor theology, the science of religion. They might do so if religion were exclusively an affair of the heart, and if theology were purely and simply the psychological description of states and modifications of the religious sentiment. But, as we have pointed out, it is nothing of the kind.

The religious question is, above all, an alternative between two terms: truth or error, the vision of reality or illusion. This is true even of those doctrines in the appreciation of which sentiment plays its part, in the first place, namely, those which relate to the eternal destiny of the individual.

To the sinner who lives as if reality was synonymous with the material world, religion declares that beyond the tomb it is not annihilation but justice which awaits him. To those who fear death, or who mourn loved ones, religion affirms that the last word does not belong to death, but to life eternal. To those who are perplexed by the spectacle of injustice and evil reigning in the world, religion promises "new heavens and a new earth, wherein dwelleth righteousness." (2 Peter 3: 13.)

In regard to these affirmations which speak to the heart, the question which demands an answer is always: are they true? If one replies affirmatively, but adding that truth is merely the agreement of thought with itself, or that it is identical with the useful, with that which enables us to enrich our personalities; if one goes on to say that truth is no more than an adaptation to the reality of the moment, the enquirer may feel that such answers are beside the point. When he asks if these affirmations are true, what he wants to be told is whether their content will manifest itself to his consciousness at a given time, as really as the rising and setting of the sun: as the alternation of the labour of daytime and the repose of night; as the moment when he must leave the land of the living to enter the mysterious regions of the dead. On these questions one does not demand a speculative demonstration: what one wants is a practical knowledge of the same sort as that which we have concerning the most ordinary events of daily life. If it could be proved that such a knowledge was impossible, no one would concern himself about these doctrines. This is the reason why the religious man and the theologian cannot, in the long run, be content with the noetic theories of which we have just spoken. Even for knowledge in general, we must start with doctrines which are more respectful of the fact of knowledge.

The spontaneous knowledge of sensible objects, in the several orders to which they belong, is not a question but a fact. Science is not bound to demonstrate its possibility nor even its reality, since that is granted. It has simply to specify the concept, to indicate the conditions, and to show the ontological presupposition which this fact implies.

For the believer, religious knowledge is also a fact. The reality of divine things, and the source of the knowledge of these things, are the same for the simple individual as for the theologian. There is no such thing as a privileged position here.

This is naturally true of the theology which accepts the

special theory of religious knowledge. But, since religious knowledge is a particular case of knowledge pure and simple, theology cannot be disinterested in theories which imply negation of the most certain of all facts: denial of the objectivity of what the believer knows. Most assuredly, philosophy, epistemology, and physiopsychology are autonomous sciences, even as theology is an autonomous science.

But if every discipline is autonomous in its own sphere, none is independent of its particular principle. If the revelation of God is a fact, no thinker conscious of this fact has a right to ignore it. Conversely, no one who is deprived of this intuition can honestly act as if he had experienced it. Thus, there are two philosophies of belief: that of believers and that of unbelievers.

The illusion of the supernaturalist school of apologetics consists in thinking that it is possible to pass legitimately, by a process of philosophical and historical demonstration, from religious doubt to religious faith. Doubt and faith are states of mind which reveal radically opposed orientations of what is most profound in the personality. They are principles, drawn from personal experiences, which dominate all reasoning, and cannot, therefore, be derived from the latter.

A faith created by scientific demonstration would not be the faith but a science, probably a pseudo-science. Faith is a gift of God. On the other hand, a faith which can be dissolved by reasoning is not the faith but a rational counterfeit of it: true faith is inamissible.

The philosophy of belief which, among the philosophies of believers, appears to us best to take account of the facts, is moderate and transcendental realism. According to this realism, the object exists apart from and independently of the subject, except when the subject itself forms the object. This is, therefore, true realism. On the other hand, the certainty of the existence and externality of the object is granted by a factor which goes beyond sensation: this realism is, therefore, transcendental.

The philosophical reaction now in progress is particularly favourable to the reconstruction of a realist theory of knowledge. The revival of Thomism in France, Italy and Germany, and the reaction of American and British neo-realists, are facts which work in our favour.[1] It is no longer singular to reaffirm that

---

[1] Concerning this reaction, consult René Kremer, C.SS.R., *Le néo-réalisme americain*, Louvain, 1920; and *La théorie de la connaissance chez les néo-réalistes anglais*, Louvain, 1928. We would remark that the father of modern American neo-realism was the Calvinistic theologian and philosopher, James McCosh, author of *Realistic Philosophy defended in a Philosophic Series*, 2 vols., London, 1887.

secondary qualities are as real and give us as faithful an image of the object as primary qualities. In fact, the distinction between the two orders of qualities has scarcely any defender to-day.

However this may be, from the realist point of view, we say that knowledge by concepts is a state of consciousness of the subject which seems in itself to be determined by the constraint of the subject and derived from it. Knowledge thus presupposes a conscious subject, that is to say, one which, in itself, appears as opposed to one or several objects: as an ego opposed to one or several non-egos, distinct from it and yet united to it. The object, in so far as it is an object, a known reality, is in a certain sense one with the subject. For, if the separation were total, the object would be to the subject as not being. Still worse, it would be possible to enquire whether the subject itself was susceptible of having a distinct self-consciousness; since, otherwise, it could not distinguish itself from anything else.

In the act of knowing, determined by the subject, the subject cannot appear to itself as accomplishing this act, unless it is conscious of being modified by the object, at the same time external to it, distinct from it, and, in a certain sense, immanent in it. Thus, in knowledge, the consciousness that the subject takes of itself is jointly responsible to the consciousness that it has of the objective externality of the object. We are, here, in the presence of an immediate datum, from which proceeds the irrefutable certainty that we have of the existence of an objective reality, telling of an external world.

We see at once the fallacy which underlies the idealist postulate that we can know only the ego and the states of the ego. We could not know anything at all, not even the states of the ego itself, if we did not know it as modified; and, because modified by the object, considered as reality, opposed to the ego, distinct from it, and yet in communion with it and united to it. It is this communion, this intimate union, which constitutes the very act of knowledge.

It is equally evident, in opposition to empiricism, that there is a kind of certain knowledge which reveals itself to the inspection of the intelligence as legitimate, but which is extra-rational and even transcendent and anterior to all reasoning. This kind is knowledge which is such that, if it were denied, the subject would have to deny itself as capable of knowledge, for the simple reason that the content of this knowledge is the condition of conscious thought.

Thence it comes to pass that, even when it is incapable of refuting the arguments of idealism, common sense maintains an unshakeable faith in the existence and independent persistence of its act of knowing things, men and God, as they appear to it. We know with certainty that the house in which we dwell does not return to nothingness, nor to the bosom of God, when we have quitted it.

Knowledge, we have said, is a state of consciousness. This state of consciousness may be defined as a certain immanence of the object in the subject. There is certainly immanence, since it is in the consciousness that the object appears to the subject. It is the nature of this immanence which remains to be determined. As regards material objects, it cannot consist in the invasion by these objects, matter and form, of the ego subject. The latter is not a vessel that can be filled in the material sense of the term. Moreover the representation reveals these objects as external to us. Nor would it suffice if the form of the object, in opposition to its matter, became internal to us: for the form, becoming that of the conscious ego, could not realize the degree of union of identity between the subject and the object, which knowledge presupposes. [1]

Matter and form, in fact, are always opposed in the mind; and remain in this opposition, even when their synthetic unity is realized in a concrete being. Now, in the act of knowing, the subject and the object maintain clearly the distinction which places them in opposition one to the other; nevertheless, there is realized in this act, not simply a synthesis, comparable to that of form and matter in the being, but a compenetration of immanence which can only be expressed by the term "identity". This is not of course, a total identity, resulting from confusion of the subject with the object. On the contrary, it is an identity resulting from an ideal immanence of the object in the subject; that is to say, by the specifying action of the object, the subject is ascertained to transfigure its manner of existence as an intelligible or sensible image of the object. This image, being a scodification of the conscious ego, is itself conscious. We are conmious of acting only in so far as we are acted upon by the object: *acti agimus*, says Zanchius.

The object, present in the subject, since it acts upon it— presence can have no other meaning—is thus represented or better presented in the subject, by a mode of this subject which, let us not forget, is fundamentally of the same nature as the object. Only like can know like at all adequately. [2]

---

[1] *Vide* G. Maréchal, *Le point de départ de la métaphysique*, Part V, p. 68.
[2] Zanchius, *De op. Dei*, lib. II, cap. iii, f. 750; Aquinas, *S. Theol.*, I, 124 c. *Cognitum est in cognoscente secundum modum cognoscentis.*

We are conscious of not knowing objectively except in the measure in which by this action of the object on us, we ourselves determine to distinguish the object and to specify it, thanks to the effort of the attention and of the observations. If, instead, we were to impress on the object the forms of our sensibility and of our understanding, as Kantianism would suggest, the system of representation would be not knowledge but misunderstanding; and, what is worse, a systematic misunderstanding of the object.

But things happen quite differently. In the full light of the consciousness in its transparent setting is revealed the constraining and sovereign action of the object, which modifies us and causes to spring forth in us this luminous state of union with it that we name knowledge. Observation does not reveal in us any *a priori* form of sensibility or of understanding. Empiricism is right when it denies that the admission of such forms is a necessary condition of knowledge.

Experience reveals, and, in spite of the denials of empiricism, reflexion confirms the fact, of which we are immediately conscious, that we possess a faculty, an aptitude, a spontaneity, potential even in the new-born babe, which develops in conjunction with the organism, tending to realize the immanence of the object in the subject; the sensible, both temporal and spatial in sensible images; the intelligible in concepts: the supra-rational in ectypical analogies.

Always and everywhere, it is the conscious ego, endowed with intelligence, which perceives the object, more or less completely, more or less exactly, but always immediately. This fact alone explains the invincible certitude which imposes itself on us concerning the reality of a sensible and spatial external world, despite errors of detail into which we fall sometimes and which we have to rectify.

In the opposing camp, this is admitted freely in the case of knowledge of sensible objects, provided that one takes the viewpoint of the subject in regard to the object: "but if we, as it were, turn round and, beginning at the other end, consider the relation of the perceived to the perceiver, no similar statement can be made."[1] And, for this reason: "Science requires us to admit that experience, from this point of view, is equivalent to perception; and that perception is a remote psychological effect of a long train of causes, physical and physiological, originally set in motion by the external thing, but in no way resembling it"[2] (e.g., nervous modifications, vibrations of the ether,

---

[1] A. J. Balfour, *Theism and Humanism*, p. 155 ff.   [2] *Op. cit.*, p. 166.

accelerated electrons which constitute such a material object). "But why should the long train of unperceivable intermediaries that connect the perceived with the perceiver be trusted to speak the truth?"[1]

The cause of this suspicion, in our judgment illegitimate, seems to reside in the following fact. The organism and the physical surroundings—conditions of perception—are considered as secondary intermediate causes which interpose themselves between the ego perceiving and the object. The intelligence or the subject knowing, is, on the one hand, considered somewhat as in a situation parallel to that of a blind and deaf bird, perched on a definite spot in a cage, which corresponds to the organism. In this condition, it is able to perceive only the vibrations of its perch, produced by the contact of external objects and will interpret them as best it can.

Nervous excitement, vibrations, etc., are, from this point of view, causes of sensation, which sensation incidentally bears no resemblance at all to the object. At most, it is a sort of signal, noticed by the subject. We consider that this manner of representing the relationship between the soul and the body, between the perception of sensible images and nervous excitement, is influenced by a contradictory metaphysic.

In the subject, there is presumed to be a juxtaposition, a coexistence of two realities, external the one to the other, in such a way that they may be compared to the coexistence of a prisoner and his prison, of a pilot and his craft. On the other hand, these realities are so homogeneous the one to the other that the mechanical movements in the body can produce purely psychical effects such as sensible images in the mind. Now, the union between soul and body, whatever ontological realities are implied in this expression, is much closer than that which unites a pilot and his craft. If it were otherwise, "when the body was wounded, the mind would experience no sorrow on that account; it would merely perceive this wound, as a pilot who notices that something has been damaged in his vessel."[2]

A spiritual philosophy that takes facts into account can only conceive the union of spirit and body as of the closest possible kind, as a synthesis of two substances, constituting a new substance, combining two elements, a new being, neither a phantom

[1] A. J. Balfour, *Theism and Humanism*, p. 166 ff. In this book the author summarized the arguments which he had developed in *The Foundations of Belief*.
[2] Benedict Pictet, *La théologie chrétienne*. Geneva, 1721, livre 5, ch. vi, p. 377, col. 1.

nor a corpse, nor an angel in an animal; but an animal verte-
brate, vertical, bimanous, endowed with reason and the power
of speech, a living creature informed by a spirit. The presence of
the spirit in that which is sensible in the organism can only be
conceived under the mode of a spiritual presence. The spiritual
presence is distinguished from the corporal in that it is total in
all parts of the being in which it realizes itself.

On the other hand, it is impossible to consider the modifications of the nervous system, the vibrations, etc., as *causes* of
perception: they can be no more than its conditions.[1] It will be
conceded, and, indeed, cannot be well gainsaid, that we have no
conscious representation at all of these nervous vibrations. The
brain and the nerves which converge in it may well become the
objects of our representation, but only in the physiological and
anatomical study of the human body. Clearly, we do not form
the sensible image by taking knowledge of the nervous vibrations. These vibrations cannot act on our spirit, considered in
isolation from the body, without our consciousness taking
notice of it. Between a mechanical movement of purely material
bodies, however rapid and complicated, and a psychical phenomenon, however simple, there is an abyss that cannot be bridged.

There remains only this alternative: the perception of the
sensible image is the act of a creature like man, living a life at
once sensitive and intelligent; the act of a synthetic being, both
physical and hyperphysical, who is not merely intellectual and
spiritual, neither body nor spirit, but a living soul.

This act is that of a spiritual being endowed with material
organs, which put it in immediate communication with material
objects. It is clear that a pure finite spirit cannot know bodies
except by the aid of innate forms. A simple material organism
could have only physical sensations, more or less associated and
bound together.

It is the same spirit bearing form of the body, and thus of the
senses, which perceives the external object directly, that is to
say, transfigures itself subjectively to its image, identifies itself
with it. It perceives sensible objects because and inasmuch as
the senses serve as windows opening to outside space. By means
of these senses, the mind perceives material objects in the vibratory environment of the ether, and the sensation is not a purely
psychical phenomenon. It is the complex state of this synthetic
being which is man.[2]

---

[1] Cf. H. Bavinck, *Geref. Dog.*, I, p. 231 ff.
[2] Aquinas, *S. Theol.*, Id. q. 77, d. 5: *Sentire non est proprium animae, neque
corporis, sed conjuncti: potentia ergo sensitiva est in conjuncto sicut in subjecto.*

It follows from this that we have no *a priori* right to doubt the testimony of our consciousness when with full conviction it affirms itself to be in intimate communion with the object.

No doubt, there is a physical environment which conditions sensation. In order that the perception may be faithful, the sensation must take place in the normal environment, that is to say, in the one in which the subject is called, normally, to pass its existence. Further, the subject must be physically sound: in a normal state of alertness. But all this gives no sufficient reason for suspicion.[1] Still less does the very real difference which exists between the sensible image and the vibratory environment conditioning the reception constitute a reason of this kind, permitting us to entertain *a priori* doubts concerning the resemblance between the image and the object. There is no resemblance at all between the chant which rises beneath the vaulted roof of Westminster Abbey and the waves, long or short, which place this chant within reach of my ear in my study in Paris. Nevertheless, even from the idealist or phenomenalist point of view, which is that of Balfour, the identity of its emission at Westminster and of its reception in Paris is certain. The environment, in spite of numerous intermediaries, does not necessarily deform the transmission. What reason, then, have we to suppose that it is otherwise with regard to the sensible perception of that which the object is in reality? Such a supposition is altogether gratuitous and contradicts our intuition.

There is nothing astonishing in the fact that alteration of the organs or an unforeseen change in the environment can bring confusion into the perception. Everything human is fallible: even an intuition can be distorted, since the subject which experiences it is not absolutely simple, and can, itself, be distorted in one of its elements or in the relations which ought to exist between them. It is so, also, in the cases in which the intuition is too feeble to be distinctly perceived.

What are we to conclude from this? Simply that it is sometimes necessary to check the data of one sense by those of the others: to check our whole system of sensations by that of our fellows; and sometimes also to modify the physical conditions of our sensations. But we have no right to deny, categorically, the testimony of our consciousness, served by sound senses, normally disposed, exercising their action in an environment appropriate to the exercise for which they were made. Faith in the testimony of the senses lies at the foundation of all our scientific knowledge. And it is inconsistent to invoke the

[1] Cf. Zanchius, *De op. Dei*, lib. II, cviii, f. 104 ff.

existence of the nervous system, which is only known by the senses, in order to discredit their authority.

Since knowledge is essentially the identification of the object with the subject, revealing itself as nevertheless distinct from it; since it implies the transfiguration of the subject into the object, it is very necessary, as we have said, that there should previously be homogeneity of nature between the subject and the object. No collective consciousness can put any individual whatever into relationship with an object radically different from himself.

Now, our knowledge is not only particular, contingent, sensible, but it is also susceptible of generalization. It permits of the discovery of necessary relations. It can raise itself to intelligibility by the aid of a generalizing abstraction. But we are conscious of finding in things this intelligibility, these rational relations, which we have not put there.

Our categories, our universals, are certainly not independent entities anterior to the things themselves. This would be the thesis of extreme realism. Nor are they reduced to non-existence apart from the human mind, as the conceptualism of Abelard would have it. That attenuated form of nominalism, clumsily expressed by the Parisian doctor, then learnedly elaborated by Kant, will not suffice. These rational relations are the terms given by the things themselves. They are in them (universalia in rebus). All that we have to do is to abstract and systematize them by reason, after having perceived them.

Take, for example, any concrete object whatever: by abstraction, I see no more in it than a solid. I am assured, however, of certain relationships subsisting in it, under the form of geometrical propositions. At first, I doubt. But, in proportion as the demonstration unfolds itself, my doubts are shaken and, finally, I pass from doubt to certainty. What has happened? I have been convinced by the weight of logical evidence, by the relationships of identity or of agreement, resulting from the very nature of the object. If it were I who had imposed on the subject the laws of mind, I should deny or affirm it without hesitation. If I doubt, it is because, before allowing myself to be convinced, I am expecting the object itself, that is to say what is intelligible in it, to impose the objective majesty of rational necessity on my mind, which will then have no alternative but to perceive it.

What effects rationality in man is that he is able, not only to see that things are, but that things are necessarily that which they are; that between the denial and the affirmation of a thing there is no intermediate position; a thing is either *per se* or it is dependent on other things; it has its necessity, in itself, or its necessity is derived, hypothetical. But, from the moment that it exists, it is under a certain necessity. Being what it is, it cannot be the same thing and something else.

The principle of identity, the principle of the excluded middle; the principle of causality; these are things which impose themselves on the mind. Its innate prerogative is its capability of being sensitive to this logical constraint of rational and objective reality.

It is not, as Stuart Mill suggests, because we verify it through our objective experience that certain things exclude themselves in actual fact—that the sensation of noise banishes from our consciousness the sensation of silence, for example—it is not, we say, in consequence of experiences of this kind that we arrive at the principle of contradiction or the principle of identity. It is because we perceive noise to be the negation of silence that we should be astonished if, *per impossibile*, we were to realize in experience the contradiction that our mind sees as absolutely incapable of realization (Renouvier). I realize that it is only conditionally necessary that a noise should be produced; and, on the other hand, I realize that, if it is produced, I am compelled to recognize that silence, the negation of noise, does not and cannot ever co-exist with it.

If things did not disclose themselves under the rational form of their identity or of their harmony: and if we did not already perceive this necessity, we should not even be able to recognize that the fact advanced by Mill was true, or to suppose that it might be so; which supposition we are, otherwise, not in the least disposed to admit.

Suppose that we could know it, and that the persistence could arouse expectation in us, the expectation would remain a doubtful anticipation: it might exist in fact, but we should never see that it was founded on right. Now, rational principles present themselves with authority: they claim unconditional adhesion. Durkheim, dealing with this matter, considers that he can explain it by saying that principles are the commands of the collective consciousness. If this were indeed so, we suggest that the acceptance of the authority of reason would appear to be contrary to reason.

Empiricism remains, therefore, in the presence of this mystery which its principle forbids it to explain and which its impotence leaves inexplicable: the mystery of the absolute authority of the principles of reason and their agreement with the reality which reveals itself as intelligible. If, by chance, it were to accept a rational explanation, it would destroy itself. For empiricism, indeed, the rational has no reason, nor even cause, in the proper sense of the term: it can have only antecedents. This system would plunge the rational, by its roots, into the irrational.

On the contrary, human reason cannot find the basis of its authority in itself. The very existence of scepticism furnishes proof of this: the theory fails to justify rational constraint in the presence of intelligence, "which contemplates with fixed and quiet regard whatever reason discursively considers."[1] Now, we cannot trust in our own reason to the point of believing that the more we advance towards abstraction, the more we embrace reality; we cannot comprehend the harmony which exists between the reason which thinks and the world which is the object of thought, except on the condition of realizing that both reason and the world have their common principle in an original and creative intelligence.

It follows that reason must flow from and reflect the supreme intelligence.[2] It follows that the world must be the realization of thought *ad extra* and the voluntary realization of this supreme intelligence. Thus, we see that objective truth is not merely an adaptation of thought to things. It is the agreement of the created thought which sees the intelligible in the things, together with the creative thought which has placed the intelligibility in them. Thought, our thought, can only agree with thought. Consequently, reality must be the expression of a thought, seeing that thought is capable of agreeing with it.

The only objective truth which thought can conceive is that which constitutes the thought of the absolute being in his sovereign independence. Indeed, we must say, with the old divine: "If God were not, there would be neither true nor false."[3] He appears as the crown of the theory of knowledge, since He is the supreme guarantee of the dignity of the human mind.

The philosophy of science, in a powerful current, is drawing us towards religion.[4] Balfour observes: "The highest conceptions of God seem to approximate to one of two types which, without

---

[1] *Inst.* I, xv. 6.
[2] Calvin, *Com. on John*, i, 1–5; F. Gomar, *op.* 220 f.; G. Woltjer, *Idée en réel*, 1896, p. 28 f. in H. R. Woltjer, *Over de Beteekenis der natuurwetten*, Amsterdam, 1925, p. 58.
[3] *Campegii Vitringa, aphorismes*, III, in A. Schweitzer, *Die Glaubenslehre der evang. reformirt. Kirche.*
[4] *Vide* App. IX, p. 393.

prejudice, and merely for the sake of convenience, I may respectively call the religious and the metaphysical. The metaphysical conception emphasizes His all-inclusive unity. The religious type emphasizes His ethical personality. The metaphysical type tends to regard Him as the logical glue which holds multiplicity together and makes it intelligible."[1] To meet this objection, it is necessary for us to determine the nature of religion and of religious knowledge.

[1] *Theism and Humanism*, p. 19.

CHAPTER 9

THE MEANING OF RELIGION

The theory of knowledge leads to the affirmation of a God who is at once transcendent to reality, since He establishes it by His originating intelligence and His will: and at the same time, immanent to this reality, since He constitutes its "logical cement". In this way, as we have said, it arrives at the threshold of religion.

This last affirmation can be justified only if theism is understood to be the normal condition of the true religion. In this case, we must endeavour to determine what is the essence of religion and to realize that it is essentially theist and specifically distinct from science.

Since Schleiermacher, religion in modern Protestantism has been, as to its origin, simply an affair of the heart. Its sphere being that of sentiment, it can add nothing to our knowledge. It translates into symbols and metaphors the experiences and aspirations of sensibility, which congeal into abstract dogmas. Religious affirmations are thus not judgments of fact but judgments of value. The founders of religions, the prophets and reformers, are those who, in the crucible of their individual consciousness, have elaborated the original emotions which they experienced, and which they propagated forthwith by a sort of contagion.

Thus, religion is, above all, personal and subjective. By addition, it becomes a social bond and evolves dogmas, rites, and religious organizations.

If it is asked what constitutes religion in the strict sense of the term, the answers vary extremely. Religion consists, says one, in a sentiment of absolute dependence in regard to infinite totality (Schleiermacher); in the issue glimpsed in the conflict between the aspirations of the ego and the constraint of nature (Lipsius, Sabatier); in the distinction between the sacred and the profane (Soederbloom): in the realization of the personality (Gourd, Eucken); in the affirmation of the fundamental axiom of the conservation of value (Höffding); in the sentiment of mystery, at once repellent and fascinating (Otto).

In the conflict of definitions, it would appear that they are all in agreement on one point: God is in no sense essential to religion. The principal end which it pursues, in one form or another, is salvation or deliverance, conceived as individual or social, or as both at the same time.

The point of view adopted by Schleiermacher has, no doubt, the great merit of bringing an important truth to light: namely, that there can be no true religion apart from piety. Actually, this truth had already been proclaimed by Calvin, who declared that God is not truly known when piety is absent, and that the knowledge of God consists in living experiences rather than in cold theoretical speculations. [1] Certainly, one cannot insist too strongly on the fact that a religion which is no more than intellectual belief, a system of mummified traditions, is nothing; or, at any rate, is a very small thing. Nevertheless, the point of view of Schleiermacher, and the moderns in general, confounds the organ of religious belief—mystical sensibility and emotivity, aptitude to perceive and recognize the presence of God, or of the Word of God—with the material content of religion.

In assuming the starting-point to be the subject, neglecting to rely upon the object, and determining specifically the nature of religion as religious consciousness, Protestant Modernism, and, with it, a certain type of Catholic Modernism, is following a method abandoned for good reasons in the most recent classifications of scientific and intellectual disciplines.

What is still more serious is the fact that one is thus definitively shut up to the subject and cannot emerge from it except by an arbitrary act of the will (voluntarism). The seeker remains free to regard the facts and experiences of the religious order as purely subjective. We have remarked that this is expressly recognized by a theologian of the weight and authority of Henri Bois. But we have already objected that, in religion, what matters practically is to know that one is not the plaything of auto-suggestion: in the presence of the tomb, we want to know whether eternal life is a reality or not.

Finally, if Protestant Modernism is right when it sets in evidence against the sociologists the rôle of great personalities in the development of the religious life, one has to admit that it also misunderstands historical reality at one point. It is wrong when it claims that these personalities are limited to interpreting the states and emotions of their religious experience; they are always presented as tied to a tradition and as messengers reproducing a revealed word which constitutes the originality of their message. No doubt it was necessary that this word should

[1] *Inst.* I, x. 3.

be grasped in the depths of their consciousness. In this sense it had to become interior in them. But it was perceived as transmitted to their ego from outside and as declaring itself to be of divine origin.

In the final analysis, history knows no founders of religion. Actually, there are only reformers, who may be at the same time initiators. The individual, however great he may be, is always attached to the past by the bonds of a tradition. All we know of human nature and its history forbids us to admit that religion may be born one day in the consciousness of a religious genius. Man is a religious animal, as truly as he is a social animal. Religion dates from the awakening of his intelligent consciousness. It is the product of a divine revelation, that is to say, of a manifestation of God in the spirit of man and in nature.

The irreducible disagreement which exists concerning the very notion of religion proves that the various definitions put forward do not place us on the solid ground of positive science but merely on that of arbitrary subjectivism.

Sociologism imagines itself to have discovered the promised land of objective, or, rather, positive certainty, by defining religion as the product of social authority and as expressing itself by collective emotion and ceremonial. Here, also, we have part of the truth: the individual, isolated from all social tradition, far from formulating a dogma, could not even speak. Indeed, he could not even think clearly.

Very willingly, then, do we concede to Durkheim that a religion despoiled of its social elements, rites, dogmas and social authority, would no longer be a religion. At most, it would be the ruins of a religion. But the fact that there are rites, dogmas and religious groups, and that all this forms an integral part of religion, does not authorize us to conclude that all sorts of rites, dogmas and collectivities are of a religious nature, or that religion may be reduced to these elements.

There have been scientific dogmas: transformism and the simian origin of man; the indestructibility of matter; the indivisibility of the atom. Shall we say that these more or less outmoded dogmas are religious? There are, in China, rites of politeness practised by persons of good education. [1]

In order to show that the existence of religion is entirely dependent on rites and ceremonies, one must define, first of all, what constitutes religion. It is true that the rites and dogmas of

[1] R. P. Huc, *Souvenirs d'un voyage dans la Tartarie, le Thibet et la Chine*, IV, pp. 73–103.

which we have just spoken always rest on the authority of a social tradition, or on social bodies like the academies, the universities, or the court. But even when the religious and social authorities are not differentiated in a human group, we have no proof that the group, so far as it is such, originates the religious fact. This is not even the case when the chief or the ancestor of the group is more or less identified with a divinity.

The true explanation consists in acknowledging that the social authority has felt an instinctive need to found itself on a higher authority, in appealing to the subjective religious inclinations of its subjects.

Ordeals and juridical oaths mark the precise point at which social authority is compelled to admit its impotence and to appeal to divine authority; a fact which proves that society has as much need of God as the individual. We must admit, then, that social beliefs and rites are not of necessity wholly religious facts; and that, when these beliefs and rites are religious, they are not the whole of religion. If these beliefs are to be efficacious and these rites practised when there is no one to witness them, it is necessary that, in his heart, the individual should believe subjectively and that he should fear the effects of ritual negligence. Rights and taboos fall into desuetude when the flame of interior piety, of subjective religion, is extinguished.

In the final analysis, Durkheim holds that the "germ" of social consciousness, which is the creator of religion, resides in the individual. Each individual, he admits, has in himself both an individual and a social element. The range of the sociological thesis is singularly reduced by this avowal. To us, it seems to amount to this: in a favourable atmosphere, like that of the clan assembled for a festival, a solemn dance or banquet, that which is specifically social in the individual, its religious instinct, finds occasion for development and expansion. The cult of the totem, taboos and rites, will flourish on the hardy stock of traditional religious beliefs, born in contact with other minds and in communion with them.

Thus presented and understood, this thesis appears to us to be simply the truth. It is in conformity with the strictest Calvinistic orthodoxy: we find it in a passage, already quoted, from a Calvinistic treatise on dogmatic theology published in Holland in 1876 by H. E. Gravermeijer: "Excluded from all social life, without language, deprived of education, the natural aptitude for spiritual realities is arrested in its development, like reason itself. In proof of which may be cited the case of those who, as a result of peculiar circumstances, grow up in a desert solitude, without having received any instruction."[1] If this is what sociologism maintains, if it does not refuse all attention to subjective religious phenomena, we do not see what there is to object to in it.

The two schools that we have just tried to characterize—subjectivism (Schleiermacher) and sociologism (Durkheim)—concentrate their researches on the same object, the reality of which is recognized as being above all doubt, namely, the fact of religion, in so far as it is a psychological and social reality.

The agreement, or, as one might say, the unanimity, in the authentication of the fact, is a serious presumption in favour of the supposition that we ourselves seek to establish in the presence, not of a certain view of the mind, but of a positive datum of reality. On the other hand, the persistence of disagreement between minds experienced in scientific methods, and starting from the same principle of the exclusion of the transcendent[2] and of the independence of science, seems to us to indicate that they are both dominated by some *a priori* system, by certain powerful tendencies which prevent them from grasping reality in its complexity. The disagreement bears on the fundamental constituent of religion. Some see in it a state or activity of the individual, while, for others, religion is "essentially social".

Let us then construct a synthesis and say: Religion in the objective sense (cultus, dogma, institution, rites) has its source in personal piety and beliefs: but this piety and these beliefs cannot originate, express or perpetuate themselves except in a social human environment. With the old divines, we distinguish *religio-subjectiva*, piety, from *religio-objectiva*, cultus.

The *sensus divinitatis*, the sense of the divinity, in contact with the *numen*, with God "in whom we live and move and have our being", is indeed according to the teaching of Calvin, a germ of religion. The intuition of God is an objective fact of which the individual is the subject.

It is because God is perceived immediately as the power immanent in us, as the mystery which fills us with fear, as the source of all that has a value for us, that piety or subjective religion which is made up of these sentiments, becomes possible.[3]

[1] H. E. Gravermeijer, *Leesboek over de Gereformeerde Gelofsleer*, I, p. 33 ff., Groningen, 1876.

[2] The expression comes from Flournoy, *Les principes de la psychologie religieuse*, Geneva, 1903, p. 8, according to H. Bois, *La valeur de l'expérience religieuse*, Nourry, Paris, 1908, p. 28.

[3] The reader may perhaps have the impression that we have borrowed this analysis of subjective religion from Otto and the neo-Frisians. But Peter Brunner has shown that Calvin preceded them in this direction, *vide* p. 41 of the present work.

AN INTRODUCTION TO REFORMED DOGMATICS

And it is piety which is the condition of collective religion, of the social religious fact.

Piety is a state of individual sensibility, provoked by the intuition of the presence of God in the subject. It is thus essentially personal. But, since it is the intuition of the object, it can only be called subjective improperly in order to indicate that it is a state of the subject.

Religion, the system of beliefs and ritual prescriptions, is itself a social institution, in the sense that it presents itself always as a pact of peace concluded between the divinity and his adorers. This pact or alliance may be concluded with a natural group: a family, a clan, a nation; or with a spiritual group which superimposes itself on the natural groupings and ends by overflowing them (the Church).

Now, even if it be supposed that, in all these cases, the collective religious institutions or religions are due to the deceitful initiative of seducers, or to the illusions of fanatics, one fact remains which preserves a real value for them: namely, that indirectly, at least, they have their origin in the intuition of God in the individual consciousness and in the existence of the religious consciousness, which is a natural phenomenon.

Having elucidated a fact specifically different from all others, the religious fact, we are in a position to ask if the concept of God, conceived as "logical cement", connecting together the multiplicity of phenomena, rendering them intelligible, is religious or not. This is important for the determination of the relations which must exist between religious and scientific thought.

If piety were a purely egocentric affair, if Höffding was right when he reduced subjective religion to faith in the conservation of value, the word "value" being taken in its utilitarian sense,[1] one would have good ground for asking in what respect the God of acquired knowledge, the metaphysical type of the idea of deity, could serve to nourish piety. But it is not so. Piety feels an instinctive sentiment of repulsion before the cynical statement of William James: "Not God but life, more life . . . is the end of religion. God is not known, He is used."[2]

To claim with Achelis[3] that there would be no religion in the subjective sense if sorrow and need were absent from our universe, is to set at defiance all psychology. For that state of affairs to exist, it would be necessary that one of the most

[1] *Philosophie de la Religion*, p. 11.
[2] Cited by H. Bavinck, *Geref. Dog.*, Vol. III, p. 678.
[3] T. Achelis, *Abriss der vergleich. Religionswissensch.*, Leipzig, 1908, p. 36.

abundant sources of misery should be dried up, namely, sin. Now if sin had no existence at all, there are two sentiments which would still not be atrophied. The sentiment of reverence for infinite wisdom and holiness and the sentiment of gratitude for infinite bounty: these would suffice, by themselves, to engender some sort of worship. Consequently, even in a world exempt by hypothesis from all suffering, prayer would continue to flourish under the form of adoration, praise and thanksgiving. The absence of suffering does not imply the abolition of the creature's sense of absolute dependence on God, the Creator, and pre-server of his being. The fact that they have not seen or felt this suggests that the religious instinct of certain hierologues must be terribly atrophied and reduced.

What is true, and can be verified by introspection as well as by observing the religious manifestations of other people, is that the instinct of piety tends to produce the exclusive veneration and the disinterested worship of God, known and loved. In its profoundest manifestation, this instinct is monotheistic and theistic. It is only in a subsidiary sense that the religious man seeks in God the protector and the tutelary genius. It may even be said that to seek for aid, succour and protection, is only religious in so far as it finds expression in prayer. Now prayer is, indeed, a manner of glorifying the one to whom it is addressed, since it implies that he who prays is in a position of dependence and postulates the omnipotence of the God invoked. It implies the first article of the Apostles' Creed: "I believe in God the Father almighty . . .".

He who has recourse to magic practices or to scientific means may, indeed, postulate the conservation of values, but he does not perform an act of religion on this account. This act appears only in prayer, a fact which refutes Höffding's theory that it is sufficient for the conservation of values to be postulated in order that religion may result. It must be admitted that, with many people, demonism and personal preoccupations often take precedence of zeal for the honour of God. But this does not authorize us to posit an irreducible opposition between the idea of God as a moral being and the idea of God as the original and constitutive mind of the cosmic order.

This last idea is not less indispensable than the first to give satisfaction to the fundamental tendency of piety, which is theocentric and not egocentric, religious and not eudemonist. To believe that God, the supreme reason, is the "logical cement" of reality, the guarantee of the subordinate reason of man, this is, first of all, to place Him above the necessity of proof, since

He is acknowledged as the principle and guarantee of all demonstration. Having left behind the sphere of rationalistic dialectic, we find ourselves at once in that of intuition and religious faith. In the second place, this gives a sacred and religious character to rational and experimental truth. The relations which exist between facts are thus conceived as pre-existent in the divine intelligence; they are established by God. The facts themselves are his thoughts, realized and manifested in time. From this point of view, the evidence of reason and of the senses must be considered as a revelation of God. "In his light", cried the psalmist, "we shall see light."

Thence it follows that to pervert the facts, to falsify an argument consciously is not only to sin against honour: it is to place a sacrilegious hand on something divine. Truth is separated from lying, as the sacred is from the profane. This is one of the characteristics of religion, essential in the eyes of certain hierologues. To maintain this idea of God, called metaphysical, but in reality ontological, is again to place in evidence the absolute independence of God and the absolute dependence of the beings who are not God. Without the intuition of this double fact, there can be no religion.

From this point of view, it must be realized that the infinite intelligence sees all the possibilities of the ideal order: that it chooses sovereignly by its decree those whom it calls into existence, bestowing on all these contingent beings the hypothetical necessity of becoming and the forms of this becoming. That in this way the acts of moral creatures, having received the form of free acts will remain free in their nature, while being at the same time hypothetically necessary in their futurition. Thus satisfaction is given both to the exigencies of religion, which require that all should depend on God, and to the needs of morality, which require formal liberty, in order to safeguard responsibility. These two orders of exigencies are carefully safeguarded by Calvinistic doctrine.[1]

Reformed theology presents us with a magnificent synthesis of what may be called the ethical or religious idea of God, and the idea called metaphysical. From the religious point of view, it is important to notice that to deny the metaphysical God and preserve only the ethical God, is to jeopardize precisely that egotistic security which is our chief concern. We believe that the great law laid down by Christ finds its application here: he who seeks to save his life shall lose it, and he who loses his life shall find it. Balfour is surely right when he says: "The religious

[1] *Westminster Confession*, iii, arts. 1–2; v, arts. 1–4.

type [of the idea of God] emphasizes His ethical personality. The metaphysical type tends to regard Him as the logical glue which holds the multiplicity together and makes it intelligible."[1]

A grave defect of a section of neo-Protestantism, namely, Ritschlianism, is to imagine itself able to dispense with the synthesis and vote for the religious type of God. It is not realized that the revelations and promises of a moral deity who is not, at the same time, the sovereign or reality, the source and guarantee of the value of reason, cannot be the object of an absolute, a religious, faith. At the outset, this god, from whom the ontological attribute of absolute simplicity is missing, cannot guarantee to us his veracity. The latter is no longer his essence itself: it is like our own, a quality superadded to his essence. We admit that it is there, since, *ex hypothesi*, the divinity that is presented to us is an ethical god. But there is no absolute guarantee that what the synthesis has produced will not be discredited by analysis, dissolution and even decrepitude. Even supposing that, for all practical purposes, we can count on his veracity, this god cannot guarantee to us his own infallibility. On the admission of his theologians and prophets, his knowledge, passive like our own, increases according to the measure in which the indeterminate future of the acts of the free will of creatures unfolds itself. But is it not obvious that this divine knowledge may be subject to error like our own? Reality is external to him, as to us. The future is almost as mysterious to him as to us. Who or what, then, can guarantee to him the agreement of his intelligence with reality?

Buddha Sakyamuni, disputing with Brahma, warned the latter of a fall, more or less distant at the time, and revealed to him that even he had to submit to the law of Karma. He was destined to be swept away in the infinite torrent of transmigrations. Here we have a human sage speaking to a god.

The "moral person" type of deity, lacking metaphysical attributes, would have good reason to fear the same fate, and his adorers would be equally able to share this fear. Luther rightly says that "a God is someone in whom man can place his confidence." He is speaking, of course, from the religious point of view. That is why a deity reduced to a mere ethical entity, a limited god, cannot be the God of religion.

To be religious is, above all, to have a thirst for God, in the language of the Psalmist. But this is not simply to feel a kind of sympathy with Him and to resign oneself, if necessary, to the

[1] *Op. cit.*, p. 20.

invention of a phantom in order to assuage one's thirst. It is to thirst for "the living and true God", the dispenser and guarantee of truth; for one who can apply to himself the words of Him whom Christians worship: "I am the Truth."

Can this longing be satisfied by that knowledge of God which is inherent in our minds? The sense of our dependence, our limitation, our nothingness, in the presence of a superior being, is indeed a condition of religion, of piety; but it is not piety itself. It does not constitute its essence:[1] it is merely its germ. This sensible intuition is not, in itself, a clear idea of God: it is the impression produced in us by His ceaseless activity in governing and preserving His creatures. This dependence may be supported with impatience and anger; but, on the other hand, it is always the case that, apart from the help of revelation, any abstract conception which one may form of God is either inferior or erroneous. We need no proof of this than the full flowering of natural religions. Spontaneous knowledge of God, by itself, cannot lead us to true religion.

This spontaneous knowledge of God, inherent (*insita*) at the dawn of the psychological consciousness, is indeed a knowledge of one of the aspects under which God appears to us. He appears to us as the mighty being who rules us entirely, inclines and attracts us to Himself, and sometimes, indeed, repels us. To know God by this intuition is thus to have a consciousness of being inclined, bent, drawn, under His domination. This knowledge is essentially inclination, aptitude, religious instinct. It is because we know Him in this manner that we can recognize the truth of the idea of God which revelation presents to us and can be religious. But it is still necessary that the idea itself should be suggested to us by the social environment and religious tradition. Knowledge of God acquired by the spectacle of the universe, by the effect of reflection, if it is deprived of the help of a positive revelation, is equally incapable of leading us to a correct theology.

Scarcely does the human mind arrive at the conclusion that the cause of the world can only be conceived as a cause analogous to our thought before it denies this analogy, whose necessity it nevertheless recognizes, by reducing it to a form empty of all content, as, e.g., did Romanes.[2] Or, perhaps, confounding the order of thought with the order of reality, it will make its god of a purely abstract word, without any influence at all on

---

[1] It will be observed that here we part company with Schleiermacher. With the Reformed theologians before his date, we consider the intuition of dependence solely as a germ or anticipation of religion.

[2] *Thoughts on Religion*, p. 87 ff.

the physical world or on our personal life, and ruling only the world of our representations. This is the conclusion which Brunschvicg, the spokesman of contemporary rationalistic idealism, has reached.[1] Others, more sensitive to the fact that, in the vast field which we seek to comprise in the meshes of our reasoning, there are certain elements refractory to all co-ordination, will make the "inco-ordinable" the acknowledged divinity, and will charge the mind with creating for itself a sort of phantom whose right to exist is due to the *fiat* of the human will. This is the counsel given by Gourd and approved by his disciple and admirer, Trial.[2]

Here we see the tendency towards a god who is an ethical, simple personality, with no incommunicable attributes, a limited personality: and behold the human mind is spinning theories once more.

There is the courageous group of Catholic neo-scholastics who believe that they can establish a veritable science of God, the elements of which have been furnished by the proofs and reasonings acknowledged by Thomas Aquinas. We admit that the philosophers of this group arrive, in actual fact, at conclusions which conform, generally speaking, to the doctrine of God resulting from the data given by the Biblical revelation; but we consider that, despite the rigour of their dialectic, they have been guided and directed unconsciously by the data of this very revelation and by the teaching which they have received from the Church.

Here is the reason why we consider this to be the case. In their view, the perfect being is the one who, in his absolute simplicity, is the sublime equivalent of a being who has all the positive qualities of which being is susceptible. Formally, this idea, which for our part we accept, is quite clear. The human mind can rise to it without any great effort. The difficulties commence when it becomes a question of attaching the idea to a living content, matter on which the mind can act. It is then seen that frequently the determination of the positive qualities again raises judgments of value, which depend for the most part on subjective principles: they are matters of personal appreciation. Thus, Aristotle assumes as a principle that there are some things that it is better to ignore than to know, and concludes from this that God, pure act, does not know the world, and does not act upon it except by the mystical attraction which He exercises over all creatures.

[1] *Nature et Liberté*, p. 149.
[2] Louis Trial, *Jean-Jacques Gourd*, Nîmes, 1920, pp. 339-345.

If the Catholic neo-scholastics judge invariably that the positive qualities susceptible of being raised to this eminent degree are precisely those recognised by orthodox Christian theology, this implies that they are.unconsciously determined, in their judgments of value, by the happy preoccupations of their piety and religious faith. In fact, the admirable analogical concept of the God whom they present to us is never encountered except where the teaching of Scripture is known. We see, in this authentication, an experimental confirmation of our own psychological presumptions.

The psychological, historical and rational methods have failed in their attempt to determine the nature of religion and to explain its origins. They have sought this explanation in factors which were not, in themselves, religious, and they conclude by destroying the object of their research.

At this stage, it will be convenient to 'notice a different principle and method. Instead of confining our attention to psychology or the social environment, in order to ascertain whether, by some happy chance, human facts will justify faith in the objective existence of God, considered as an hypothesis, and in the divine origin of religion, let us follow a contrary route: namely, that trodden by Calvin in the 16th century, and by the Calvinistic dogmatic theologian, Bavinck, at the beginning of the present century. [1]

For the principle of doubt, let us substitute the fact of religious knowledge and of the certainty which is proper to it. To the principle of the exclusion of transcendence, we bring a correction. We postulate the necessity of taking into account, in religious researches, God, His reality and the fact that He reveals Himself. Believers know by experience that there is a spontaneous knowledge "Naturally rooted in the minds of men" (*cognitio Dei insita*: Calvin). [2] This is the side of the truth more or less clearly seen by subjectivism. There is also an acquired knowledge of God (the *cognitio Dei acquisita* of the older theologians) by means of the study of nature. [3]

We consider the act by which God reveals himself, whether in nature or in the human mind, as in itself a revelation. For the moment, let us even abstract from what is called positive revelation. Natural revelation could only manifest God to us as creator and ruler of the world, even if sin had not rendered it

---

[1] *Inst.* I, iii. 1; H. Bavinck, *Geref. Dog.*, vol. I, p. 286 ff.

[2] *Ibid.*, I, iv. 1: *Omnibus inditum esse divinitus religionis semen, experientia testatur.*

[3] *Ibid.*, I, iii and v; H. E. Gravermeijer, *Gereform. Gelofsl.*, I, i, pp. 11, 26 ff.; H. Bavinck, *Geref. Dog.*, II, xxiv and xxv.

obscure. If we confine ourselves, provisionally, to this revelation we shall find that it is sufficient, by itself, to explain the existence of the fact of religion, individual as well as collective. In the case of the spontaneous knowledge of God, His presence is felt by a sensible intuition of the religious man (*sensus divinitatis*), with a certainty analogous to that which accompanies the perception of the external world by the senses, or the perception of logical agreements and identities by the reason.

It must be observed, however, that religious intuition, in order to be as real as sensorial intuition and natural intuition, is of a different order from these last two. It is the witness of a mind to other minds, and the value attached to this witness depends on the moral and ontological quality which manifests itself in it. Religious intuition is the result of a testimony which God renders to Himself in the presence of created spirits, endowed with intelligence, by the action of His presence immanent in them. The certitude which this testimony can create is the highest that it is possible to conceive. It is faith, in the religious sense of the term. The intuition is designated by the term faith, because by this word is generally understood adhesion to a testimony.

When the witnesses are beings like ourselves, faith is naturally less certain for us than the testimony of our own senses or that of rational evidence. This is because, in the ordinary language of everyday life, to believe is opposed to certitude, to knowledge. It is not so in the religious life, for here the witness reveals himself as God, as the Being who is the source and guarantee of all truth. In religion, belief is a faith based on divine authority and it excludes "all doubt" (Calvin). It may be objected that it is also a matter of experience—Calvin recognizes this himself—that the firmest faith may have to struggle against the most obstinate doubts of temptation.

We reply that it is equally a matter of experience that the certainty which excludes all doubt and the uncertainty which excludes faith can co-exist in the same mind. This is connected with the fact that the internal testimony of God to the mind of man is grasped chiefly by a contemplative faculty, the sensible intelligence. God is spirit—not demonstrable by reasoning, for He is Himself the principle of all demonstration. From this there follows the possibility of a conflict between the certitude of the intuition of the faith, which has for its organ the intelligent sensibility, and the data of the senses or the results of our reasonings.

The lack of harmony between our faculties, in consequence of total corruption, renders psychologically possible this paradox of a profound certitude of religious intuition co-existing in the same individual with speculative doubts arising from temptation. This fact has also an analogy in the natural order, in which there may be, for example, a conflict between the work of the imagination and mathematical certainty.

Our starting-point is thus made in the certain data of religious intuition which serves as a spiritual cement to the Reformed Church. We shall place ourselves at the very heart of religion to determine its nature, origin and value.

It will be observed that, in speaking of religion, we do not use this term in an abstract or general sense. Religion exists only in concrete religions, in societies and individuals in which the fact of religion is realized. This is the reason why we consider it to be impossible to place oneself in the living centre of this abstraction called religion. By religion we understand that special sphere in the bosom of which we encounter God, the real source from which the faith of real believers draws sustenance; the religion according to which it becomes evident to us that we must live the life of faith; that which provides us with the means of realizing the principal end that gives life its direction; that in which we wish to die. It is our faith that this religion is the Reformed Christian religion.

If it is objected that we should approach the subject with complete scientific detachment, we reply: when it is a question of disciplines, whose object is in the spiritual sphere, impartiality is impossible. This is because spiritual facts are so intimately united with the personality of the seeker that the only thing one has a right to demand is objectivity, absolute intellectual sincerity.

Indifference is not conceivable, is not possible, in this sphere. [1] Let each one start with the principle which he holds to be true. It is his right and his duty to do so. We have the same right and duty to start with ours. The results, the facts recognized and explained, will justify our method.

It will not do to say that this procedure is anti-scientific. To suppose a problem to be solved, for the purpose of interpreting and explaining facts, is a recognized procedure in natural disciplines. We do not see why we should be forbidden to use it in religious science. That which is a provisional hypothesis for those to whom the explanation is proposed, may very well be a proved certainty for him who proposes it.

---

[1] J. Severijn, *Spinoza en de gereformeerde Theologie zijner dagen*, p. 1 ff.; H. Bavinck, *op. laud.*, vol. I, p. 286; J. R. Illingworth, *Reason and Revelation*, London, 1902, p. 96; Boegner, *Dieu, l'éternel tourment des hommes*, 1929, p. 55.

Does the theological explanation of the Reformed Faith render a better account of the facts than other explanations? That is the whole question.

For pantheism, God is infinite in the sense that he constitutes the totality of the real. He is thus confounded with the reality of which our world, and conscious personalities in particular, form part. This is the case even with those personalities which he raises to the consciousness of himself and possesses.

For deism, on the contrary, God is indeed the supreme being, but He is not, properly speaking, infinite. By the mere fact that He has created, that He has placed other beings in His presence, He has limited Himself. These beings are not His dependents, except in the sense that He is the source of their existence. Actually, they are quite independent of him, since He cannot touch their liberty without destroying it. Thus, for deism, God has commanded and acted once, in order to give existence and laws to creation. But it subsists by itself and the beings which compose it act one upon another, and God must obey the laws which He has made. (*Semel imperat, semper paret*). Free beings are absolutely independent in their acts, not only of God, but of all natural laws, internal or external.

Pantheism does not, and can not, know more than one first cause, unique, identical with the infinite. There are no true secondary causes in this system. What it calls secondary causes are but sporadic variations, more or less ephemeral, more or less stable, of the one totality. Fundamentally, the multiple is no more than an idea in the mind, and liberty no more than an illusion. When the illusion is dispelled and the idea in the mind gives place to the consciousness of universal identity, man knows himself to be one with God. He is God, or at least a necessary moment in the history of God. At that point, he becomes religious. For the religious pantheist, what is evident is God: and what is doubtful is the world. What is misunderstood is the human personality, created liberty, distinction from God.

Even deism can scarcely be said to recognize secondary causes. In the material world, these causes, after having received their first fillip, act by themselves: transmit their action to other objects, which will proceed in the same manner. God is wholly exterior to the interaction of secondary causes. In the spiritual and moral world, this limitation and this externality of God are more evident still. Indeed, liberty consists in absolute independence.

This point of view has the actual effect of rendering the

sensible and intelligent consciousness practically impermeable to the intuition of the real presence of God and of His activity immanent in our souls. It is very difficult for a deist to be in the slightest degree religious. The fact that deism is possible shows to what point some systematic preoccupations, such as the desire to safeguard a certain conception of moral responsibility, can distract attention from a fact as clear as the consciousness of our absolute dependence on God, present and acting in us, in such a manner that we live and act through Him.

But pantheism and deism are not the only possibilities: *tertium quid datur*, there is a third thesis. Following Augustine and Aquinas, Calvin and Reformed theology have refused to admit the presupposition common to the two schools that we have just placed in opposition one to the other. This presupposition can be formulated, we think, in the following manner: all that is conceded to divine causality is withdrawn from created causality, and conversely.

Calvinism, on the contrary, maintains that God is so powerful that the more really He acts, the more reality the creature has in his being, his action, and his liberty: *Providentia Dei causas secundas non tollit sed ponit.*[1] If Calvinism can thus affirm that the activity of the first cause, far from nullifying secondary causes, gives them their substance, their force, their reality— indeed, establishes them—this belongs to the idea of God by which it lives, which it confesses and defends. It denies itself the right to establish this idea in an arbitrary fashion. It believes that the idea can be found in elements furnished by the sacred Scriptures, the source of its dogma. What it finds there is the affirmation of a morally perfect being,[2] of that being whom Balfour represents as the God of religion, but whom he wrongly, as we see it, places in opposition to the God of ontology. The perfect God, in awakening in the believer sense of his own moral wretchedness by comparison with him, produces "the horror and astonishment with which, as the Scripture recounts, the saints have been afflicted and cast down whenever they beheld the presence of God."[3]

But this morally perfect God is at the same time the being whose essence is infinite and spiritual.

---

[1] Wolleb, cited by H. Bavinck, *op. laud.*, II, p. 663.

[2] *Inst.* I, i. 2: "If we once begin to raise our thoughts to God and reflect what sort of being He is and how absolute the perfection of that justice and wisdom and virtue to which, as a standard, we are expected to be conformed, what formerly delighted us by its false show of righteousness will appear polluted with the greatest iniquity."

[3] *Loc. cit.*, 3.

It is precisely in proposing to faith these ontological attributes that Scripture erects a barrier against the pantheistic speculation which conceives the infinite under the aspect of the spatial continuum: "His infinity should surely deter us from measuring Him by our sense, while His spiritual nature forbids us to indulge in carnal or earthly speculation concerning Him." [1]

The ontological aspect of God, in itself, arouses a sentiment of fear. But, as is reasonable, this fear is of an intellectual order. It corresponds to the *mysterium tremendum* of Otto. It is the sentiment of the nothingness of the *ratio ratiocinans* in the presence of the abyss of the immensity of God who is a Spirit. It is important to remember that this God is absolutely one: not only is He unique, but He is perfectly simple in His essence. On the other hand, He is not the "solitary of the heavens" predicated by deism. In Him, the highest and most perfect social relationship is realized. One and simple in His essence, God is triple in His hypostases. The God of Calvinism is essentially the Triune God. For Calvin, and for us, if the Trinity of Persons is abstracted, "there remains only the bare and empty name of God, without virtue or effect, fluttering in our minds." [2]

"In one sole divine essence, we have to consider the Father as the commencement and origin, that is to say, as the first cause of all things: then the Son who is His eternal wisdom: and finally the Holy Spirit who is His power everywhere diffused yet residing always in Him." [3]

It is in so far as He is triple in His hypostases, that God is creator in the full sense of the term. The Father is the first cause of being, and it is by His wisdom and spiritual power that He creates. Wisdom is this "logical cement of things" which Balfour represents to us as the God of science. The spirit is the originating power of all movements and of all life. This God is, in the absolute sense, creative causality, organizing not only in respect of representations, as Kantianism would have it, but of objective reality. For, being infinite power, it is on being that He acts, as much as on thought.

Contrary to the deist view, "the power of God cannot be inactive," says Calvin: "He does not possess omnipotence without using it." [4] No doubt He is the *causa causarum* because He gives being to things; but He is so supremely and, in a sense which is far more important in the eyes of our Reformer, [5]

[1] *Inst.* I, xiii. 1.   [2] *Ibid.*, 2.
[3] *Inst.* I, xiii; *Geneva Catechism*, iii.   [4] *Geneva Catechism*, iii.
[5] *Ibid.*, iv.

because He causes them to continue in being by the same act of creation, which is continuous. He infuses into them the power which makes them real secondary causes at every moment of their existence. It is in Him and by Him that, according to the word of the Apostle, they "live and move and have their being"; vitality, movement and existence, all that they have and do which is positive, they owe to Him. The acts of subsisting, moving and living, are, formally, the proper acts of creatures; they are the subjects of them. But, materially, these same acts are God's actions, for it is He who predisposes, moves and applies the secondary causes to the actions which they perform, conformably to their nature, sometimes in a necessary manner sometimes contingently, sometimes in harmony with their liberty.[1]

Thus, for a secondary cause to be conscious of itself, to know that it exists and moves and lives, means simply that it perceives the actions of which it is the subject as at the same time, although in another respect, altogether the actions of God: it is therefore to perceive itself as created, quickened and moved by Him and to perceive Him as present in us by His immanent action.

From this point of view, the only one that can be called properly religious, self-consciousness is identical with the "Kreaturgefühl" of the neo-Frisian school. This consciousness of the presence of God is, properly speaking, the act of the religious man. No doubt the irreligious man possesses it, as though by a lightning flash in the night, but he does not recognize God in His continuous activity. He is there all the same, present and acting, as in every conscious creature. Thus, Calvin concludes, logically, that God is immediately perceived by intuition as present in the very act of subsisting which we accomplish. "We see now that all who do not know God do not know themselves: for He is present not only in the excellent gifts of their understanding but in their very essence; for their essence or existence is due to none but God, and all other things have their subsistence in Him." Thus, our Reformer finds it strange[2] that it should be possible for us "to say that in perceiving Him, we do not perceive Him."[3]

In so far as He is the creator and preserver of being, activity and life, God is perceived as "the fountain of all good". So Calvin tells us, and experience confirms his statement. Thus, love

---

[1] *Westminster Confession*, v, art. ii; H. Bavinck, *Geref. Dog.*, II, p. 666 ff.; cf. pp. 352 ff. and 410 ff.
[2] *Com. on Acts*, xvii, 28.   [3] *Ibid.*, v. 27.

is joined to fear, and these two sentiments, when they proceed from a sense of dependence and are ideally orientated towards the absolute, constitute the essence of piety or *religio subjectiva*.

For the Christian, in any case for the Calvinist, the sense of dependence is no vague intuition towards a determined infinite: he knows that he depends on the infinite being. The absolute towards whom his fear and love are directed has a name: He is called God, the Father and the Lord. The Calvinist knows it, because it is this God Himself who declares it in Holy Scripture, and because to this Scripture He sets the double seal of the testimony of His Spirit and of the inward persuasion which results from it.

But what happens to those who do not know, or who misunderstand, religion? What can religion mean to them? We have said that in perceiving the acts of which they are formally the causes, they are perceiving the acts of which God Himself, by His creative and regulative action, is materially the efficient first cause, in all that these acts have which is positive, real and good; and the deficient first cause in all that they have themselves which is morally or physically deficient.

They have God then present at the root of their being and of their activity, in exactly the same way as believers. They cannot even be conscious of themselves except for an act of God's continuous creation. Where it concerns finite objects, what puts the perceiving subject into contact with them is causality. The presence is nothing else but the causality by which the object acts on the subject, in order to become, in a certain sense, immanent to him, in such a way that it is by his action that an external being becomes an object. What we perceive is the being himself, in so far as he is the object or acts upon us: the intelligence, on its part, tends spontaneously to abstract its essential characteristics from the object perceived, in order to develop from them the concepts which constitute its intelligible representation.

It is this same process which unites the human mind to God in the act of knowing. The intuition can be, is, in fact, confused, in the mind of the "natural man". He is in contact with God, ontologically; but separated from Him by an abyss, morally and sentimentally. Moreover, religious ideas, or even merely ontological notions, developed by the natural reason, must be, in the first place more or less vague and inexact. Nevertheless, the essential thing, deformed, disfigured, diminished, may be recognized in it. In all religions we find the notion of a being on which the subject depends for his happiness or woe. This notion is formed spontaneously by the human mind, thanks to the elements furnished by the intuition of the presence of God.

In the natural religions, such as those of uncivilized tribes, and in artificial religions, like theophilanthropism, e.g., the Spirit proceeds in a manner analogous to that which is postulated by the ethicalism of neo-protestantism. There is, in the first place, the intuition of God inherent in the human mind. Then a notion, more or less abstract, is elaborated: the mind tends spontaneously to translate intellectually the sensible intuitions of a specifically religious experience.

It must be observed that if this experience of the sentiment of total dependence in regard to God were properly interpreted, it would not in the least involve the pantheistic view according to which formal liberty is an illusion. Consequently, the reaction of deism in the name of morality would have no *raison d'être*.

According to the Calvinistic interpretation, the sentiment of dependence, precisely because it is the intuition of being the object of continuous creation by one who is omnipotent, becomes also an intuition that we are limited in our essence and activities: but, far from being a source of depression, this sentiment has a stimulating and dynamic effect. In fact, it is perceived as the gift of a real measure of true subsistence, distinct from God: as a continuous influx of power and of life: as the inexhaustible causation of that rational spontaneity which assures us at least an interior independence in regard to other creatures, and which is, properly speaking, liberty. By it we are liberated from the yoke of the impulses of blind hereditary instinct. By the deliberation of the practical reason and intelligent choice among mediate values, we escape from the restraint of logical necessity.

With Wittich, we say that when God predisposes us to action, it is then that we act most freely: that the more efficacious and all powerful is His action in us, the more are we the masters of our acts and the less do we feel that they are determined by an external force. For, when God predetermines an action, it is a free action that He predetermines: He does not annihilate that which He creates.[1]

The conviction that, in each particular case, the futurition of

[1] Quoted by Leibnitz, *Les Essais sur la bonté de Dieu et la liberté de l'homme*, no. 298: *Quia enim Deus operatur ipsum velle, quo efficacius operatur, eo magis volumus: quod autem, cum volumus, facimus, id maxime habemus in nostra potestate.* Leibnitz misunderstands the Reformed theologian. He is mistaken in thinking that the latter reduced liberty to an illusion. If the free agent perceives neither logical necessity nor constraining impulsion, the reason for it is that neither the one nor the other is present. If it were otherwise, the fact would be apparent to the consciousness.

our choice has been inserted in the chain of the divine decrees, does not destroy our consciousness of not being constrained in this choice. God does not bend the will except in conformity with the laws of liberty. The reasons which determine us depend on our own judgments of value in a contingent manner. The act is formally free, since the formal power of execution is given to us in the deliberation.

God does not create evil, which has no essence and which is nothing but a negation, a defect in the good that He creates. He does not cause it, but, finding it, he moderates or directs it in such a manner that, in spite of himself, the wicked man works in the direction of the final triumph of that which is good.

To realize that all our actions are directed by God in such a manner that by their means, willy-nilly, we always fulfil His decree, is to realize that our acts will be all the more free in that they are decreed, together with ourselves, by a being who is so powerful that the more He acts, the more liberty He confers on those beings which He creates and directs according to the laws of their nature. Experience shows that the more this is so, the more the act is felt to be free: for, we repeat, the consciousness perceives in it neither logical constraint nor natural necessity: and if it fails to perceive them, it is because these factors are effectively absent. It is the sovereign action of God which gives liberty its true reality, at the same time that it limits the possible deviations.

We acknowledge that the liberty of independence in regard to God is incompatible with the truths of the Faith and with religious intuition, even as it is incompatible with the requirements of a sound philosophy. [1] We consider, therefore, that there is good reason for believing that, between the determinism of the pantheist, whether dialectical or mechanistic and philosophical, and the vague indetermination of the deist, there lies a third possibility.

We are not thinking of the God of Spinoza or the God of Duns Scotus. We have in mind the God of Augustine, Aquinas, Calvin and Pascal, the infinite riches of whose power is so real, so great, that He establishes true secondary causes, communicating to them an *esse*, a *posse* and a *velle*: an essence, a power and a will, which constitute them intelligent and spontaneous causes, that is to say, formally free and responsible, subject to one sole necessity, that which results from their absolute dependence in regard to God.

It follows from this that "no man can contemplate himself

[1] B. Pictet, *Theol. chr.*, vol. I, p. 502 f.

without immediately turning his thoughts towards the God in whom he lives and moves: for it is perfectly obvious that the endowments which we possess cannot possibly be from ourselves: nay, that our very being is nothing else than subsistence in God alone." [1]

The second consequence which flows from our conception of the immanent causality of God is that, naturally inherent in the human mind, there is an idea of God as real and present (*cognitio Dei insita*). This conclusion is laid down by Calvin as an incontestable starting point: "We regard it as beyond question that a sense of divinity is indelibly engraven on the human heart. . . . This is not a doctrine which is first learned at school, but one concerning which every man is his own master and teacher from the womb." [2]

Belief in the existence of God is one of those common notions which the human mind forms, by its own natural inclination through contact with experimental reality. Because man is sustained and directed by God, there exists in him an aptitude to seek his foundation in God and an inclination to make a place in his life for religious thought and action. This may be termed an innate idea, provided that the epithet "innate" is not understood in the sense of latent, and still less of actual; the idea of God is not innate, except in the sense that it is inherent in our nature; that we are naturally inclined to form for ourselves a notion of the ego and of the external world. [3] The aptitude for religion is innate in the same sense as aptitude for language.

We must never lose sight of the fact that the natural and subjective are not placed in opposition to the social but only to the acquired. The natural man that we have in view, the subject of religion, of subjective religion, is the social man born and reared in a human environment endowed by it with language, the minimum condition for the origination and expression of elementary notions.

The individual ordinarily receives from his clan, his people, his Church, a traditional conception of religion, which he appropriates by reflexion, aided by the contemplation of the spectacle presented to him by creation. He thus forms for himself the notion of a deity. This notion is partly the result of the spontaneous working of his mind and partly the result of an external contribution (*religio objectiva : cognitio Dei acquisita*).

Even when God reveals Himself to a community, the internal sanctuary of the personal consciousness of each individual

---

[1] *Inst.* I, i. 1. [2] *Ibid.*, I, iii. 3.
[3] C. Hodge, *Systematic Theology*, I, pp. 340, 360.

constitutes the source from which the divine flame draws its strength. There cannot be a tribal, national, universal, or ecclesiastical God who has not previously been perceived in the consciousness of a believer. If the latter had no sense of divinity, at least in a rudimentary stage, all acquired and collective religion would have no more than an artificial and ephemeral existence, even supposing that it could exist at all. Subjective religion is the necessary condition, the soul of all objective religion. Let us see if observed facts are in agreement with our conclusions.

CHAPTER 10

THE UNIVERSALITY AND PERSISTENCE OF RELIGION

To experience the power of existing and acting, as we have observed, is to experience the presence and immanent action of God. The God who appears thus is invested with a character considered by Reformed theology as specifically divine. He has sovereign independence and underived existence (aseity). He is the being *a se* (by Himself), that is to say, the principle of His being is not in anything external to Himself: He is the being who alone is, in an adequate sense of the term. [1]

It follows that man cannot be defined merely as an erect bimanous being endowed with reason, with the faculty of speech. This definition omits a specific characteristic of the idea of man. Man is a religious animal; indeed, the only one. This explains the reason why he alone can have a clear consciousness of the immanent activity of God in himself. Being a specific characteristic of human nature, religion is a universal and indestructible fact. This is why, in spite of everything, the existence of God is experienced even by the unregenerate, at least occasionally.

To throw light on this first fact, we will appeal to two pieces of evidence which give it irrefutable confirmation. In the first place, the intellect infers immediately, everywhere and always that by the fact alone that something exists, something exists of itself. Every man, even a deist the least disposed to admit our conception of divine causality, knows that something exists of itself and that he depends on it. Slightly modifying Herbert Spencer's thesis, we can say that the absolute, that is to say, the independent, is implied in the consciousness that we have of being relative and dependent.

In the state of blindness to which we have been reduced by the Fall, this something often appears under a vague enough outline. The concept that is formed may identify it with the totality of beings, the unique substance, etc. In any case, the human mind cannot escape from some sort of representation of

[1] *Inst.* I, x. 3; *Com. on Acts*, xvii, 28: "Properly speaking, He alone is, and as to ourselves, we exist in Him in so far as He gives us strength and sustains us by His Spirit."

something which subsists and in which all finite beings move: an infinite space endowed with an eternity without succession, which Clarke considered as the *sensorium* of God, the abyss from which whole worlds emerge and which the Gnostics worshipped. Even when the human mind has emptied God of all life, the image of divinity is still perceived and felt to be indestructible.

The second piece of evidence is a fact connected with one of the grossest misrepresentations and exaggerations to which the divine reality can be subjected. But, as in physiology, this kind of extreme exaggeration affords an opportunity for studying normal reality. The fact is the persistent attraction which pantheism exercises for many minds. The pantheist maintains that God is perceived to such an extent that one may doubt everything except Him.

It must not be imagined that this view is exclusively the product of philosophical reflexion which has arrived at a high degree of refinement and maturity such as we find already in the Vedas, in Hegel or Schopenhauer. On the contrary, we find it extremely active among peoples of little culture, and, even there, elaborated into a sort of coherent system. This is the case with the Zunis of Mexico and the Bataks of the north of Sumatra.[1] The *Hâi* of the former, the *Tondi* of the latter, is the universal and identical soul, which diversifies itself in concrete beings and animates all. In the background of the uncivilized pantheists is found the widespread concept of what is designated in hierography by the name of *Mana*. This name was discovered for the first time by Bishop Codrington among the Melanesians. The equivalent is to be found in the *Manitou* of the Algonquoins, the *Wakonda* of the Sioux, the *Orenda* of the Iriquois, the *Mulungu* of the Ysos on the east side of Lake Nyasa.[2]

It is some superhuman power or influence, supra-sensible, more or less impersonal, but capable of dwelling in persons as well as things. This power may be conceived as a divine matter, or rather substance, at the same time formidable and desirable. The beings which are impregnated with or enveloped in it partake of the sacred character which attaches to it: contact with them defiles. This notion of a divine principle diffused everywhere is associated also with what is called the prelogical, or better (according to Allier), paralogical, mentality. This type of thought approaches very closely to pantheism, as we shall see. It is, perhaps, one of its intellectual principles. According to

---

[1] J. Carpenter, *Comparative Religion*, p. 83 ff.
[2] *Ibid.*, p. 80 ff.

this view of the mental functions, the most diverse beings, such as a parrot, a plant, and a man, or a group of men, may be regarded as identical. [1]

These sorts of identifications, so strange to the Occidental mind, do not imply indifference in regard to the principles of identity and contradiction on the part of uncivilized peoples, as Lévy-Brühl incorrectly imagines. They suppose, rather, that confusion, that effacement of the lines of demarcation, that nebulous intuition of the fundamental identity of contraries, which is one of the surest symptoms of the presence of the pantheistic virus.

The paralogical turn of mind we believe to be nothing else but the spontaneous and unpolished form of the learned nominalism and pantheism, the majestic systems of which, as constructed by the philosophers of the most ·modern and cultured peoples, excite our admiration. Now, pantheism, especially in its mystical form is merely an illusory intuition of the identity of the ego with the infinite being, with God, the universal soul of things. Things themselves are merely transient expressions or modifications of this universal soul.

The examples which we have cited, taken from among uncivilized peoples, show that this identification of God with the creature is natural, perhaps inevitable, at a certain stage of culture. So general and persistent an illusion, often declaring itself to be at the summit of human thought, must have some foundation in reality.

There are mystics, whose reason is perfectly sound, who can, and frequently do, arrive at a state in which they believe themselves to be so united to God that they end by crying, in moments of religious exaltation: "I am God!"

In attempting an explanation of such extreme theories in metaphysics and such strange affirmations in religion, we shall begin by admitting that God must indeed be very near to man, that He must dwell within him and be perceived as so doing in order that these things may be possible. What sane religious experience calls "union", and, therefore, distinction, pantheism calls "identity". Both are in agreement regarding the reality of the fact of the intuition of God. The disagreement exists in the intellectual order. It is explained by Blondel as a difference of mental disposition. At the root of pantheism lies an error of

_____
[1] C. Blondel, *La mentalité primitive*, p. 66: "A Huichol, e.g., sees without doubt almost like ourselves, in the wheat, the deer, Hikuli . . . classes in which are grouped objects. But . . . in proportion to the identity of their mystic properties . . . the Huichol compares the wheat, the deer and Hikuli to the point of identifying them."

ontology and of logic that we will designate by one word, "nominalism".

But the agreement is there. And we consider that this harmony, in the same religious experience, between such a large number of men of all races, at all imaginable degrees of intellectual culture, implies, as the only satisfying explanation, the reality of the fact of divine immanence.

But, it will be said, what of the deists? We know that they conceive God not only as distinct but as separated from the world. They do not believe in the possibility of attaining to Him, otherwise than by way of discursive reasoning and postulate. Do they not also experience the same fact of the immanence of God in the same immediate manner? Doubtless, we reply, but this proves only that, in our fallen state, presumptions of all sorts, some of a very exalted character, may contribute to obscure and dim the clear vision of the interior judgment. Someone has said that a deist is a man who has not yet had time to become an atheist. Actually, moralism and endemonism are both unconsciously orientated towards atheism. They lead there inevitably unless the subject has a confused intuition, a dim perception of this interior presence of God, in virtue of which His existence is still affirmed when, logically, it ought to be denied.

In the constraining form posited by the "proofs" of the existence of God, in the logical necessity recognized as a postulate, we see, as it were, the dialectical interpretation of the immanence of God, of which the deist is still the object.

This seems to us evident in the case of the ontological and cosmological proofs. The appeal to the sensible perception of the immanence of God by the human mind is scarcely disguised in the former. All that it affirms, fundamentally, is that it is impossible not to see that the affirmation of the existence of God is necessary. The second would not even be conceivable unless it was based on our sense of being contingent creatures, surrounded by contingent creatures like ourselves (*Kreaturgefühl*) whose principle of existence and duration is transcendent.

As much can be said of the proof from movement and the necessity of a prime mover himself unmoved. In our judgment, this proof is nothing but a particular application of the cosmological proof. On the other hand, to postulate God and the future life, in order to give morality its absolute sanction, is merely to obey a confused intuition that, at least in the restricted sphere of practical activity, "all our powers and forces consist in subsisting and being supported by God", according to the saying of Calvin already quoted. It is to admit that we regard

God as the efficacious stimulus, the psychological mover indispensable to perseverance in good works.

There is, however, one case which seems to present more difficulties than the theoretical denial of the immanence of God professed by deism. There are those who have had bitter experience, all too real this, of the absence of God from their soul. They would like to believe, they tell us: they stretch out the hand to grasp God and they have the impression of finding, instead, only a void. What they would like is a miracle in which God should reveal Himself visibly. In themselves they find only aspirations unsatisfied and without hope of satisfaction.[1] We acknowledge that this experience also corresponds to a reality.

With Bonaventure,[2] we would say to those who wish to see, physically, in order to believe, that it is not true that all certain knowledge must necessarily be acquired by the bodily senses. The soul knows itself and it knows God by means of other organs. To demand that one should perceive God by the senses, to declare that one will not believe in Him except on this condition, is to repudiate the use of that *sensus divinitatis*, that sense of God which is in us, and in consequence to deaden even more a sense which is already weak through desuetude. Every organ condemned to inaction tends to lose its aptness for its function.

And it is because those of whom we speak have fallen into this error that they no longer perceive the presence of God. Bonaventure recognises this clearly when he says: "Although God is present, we know Him as absent because of the blindness and darkness into which our understanding is plunged."[3] Once more, the organ which is not exercised tends to become atrophied. This is also true of the religious sense. It must be admitted, too, that in addition to this acquired atrophy, there may be, among certain individuals, a congenital atrophy analogous to that with which the bodily senses may be affected. These particular cases of congenital religious inaptitude do not in the least diminish the

---

[1] *Vide* M. Boegner, *Dieu, l'éternel tourment des hommes*, p. 33 ff., for characteristic examples of this state of mind drawn from Marcel Arland's *Étape*.

[2] [Bonaventure (1221–74) O.F.M., born at Bagnorea, near Viterbo, studied at Paris under Alexander of Hales, and in 1257 was made Superior-General of the Franciscan order. His chief works are *Commentaria in IV L. Sententiarum*, *Itinerarium mentis in Deum*, *Questiones Disputatae* (*Opera Omnia*, ed. crit., 10 vols., Quarachi, (1882–1902). His philosophy is Augustinian with Aristotelian modifications in his theory of intellection and matter and form. But his Divine Exemplarism, Illumination theory, and tendency to stress the psychological importance of the will, derive from Augustine. (E. Gilson, *La philosophie de S. Bonaventure*, Paris, 1924.)]

[3] Quoted by H. Bavinck, *op. laud.*, II, p. 40.

value and objectivity of the religious sense which is proper to humanity, or rather, which is a specific characteristic of it. With good reason, Herring asks: "Are the results of natural science less objective because they cannot always be checked by blind and deaf people? Why then, should not aesthetics, ethics or theology, be free to ignore the judgment of those who do not possess the faculties with which to perceive the values or realities of the aesthetic, moral or religious order?"[1]

On the other hand, those who suffer and are distressed because they do not feel the presence of God, if they do not perceive Him as the One by whom they were made, know Him, nevertheless, as the One for whom they were made. They have already verified experimentally one of the first affirmations of the catechism, namely, that without Him life is more miserable than that of the brutes: that it has no meaning that satisfies their reason.[2] When God moves us, if He turns us towards Himself and thus raises us above ourselves, He attests so imperiously the reality of His being and of His action that, while it may please us to misunderstand it or to wish to take our stand on our external senses in order to admit it, our instinct warns us, by the misery of our state, that we are in an abnormal and fundamentally false position. It is thus that the religious sense, outraged in its testimony, takes vengeance every time an erroneous epistemology leads us to pretend that we do not know God, while all the time we feel His action in us.

One thing is certain for every man who takes the trouble to reflect on the enigma of his presence in the world, at this moment of time which is assigned to him, with his specific qualities, distinguishing him from the brutes: the intelligence of which he is so proud; the liberty, which emancipates him from physical constraint; the vital powers which sustain him above the abyss of non-being from which he has emerged. If there is one certain fact for such a man, it is the existence of a source of dependence on a mysterious power, which he fears as one fears that which is immense and impenetrable; in which also he confides instinctively, since he struggles and works in order to live, thus affirming implicitly his faith in the author of life; which his instinct moves him to implore in distress; whose wrath he fears, when he feels, more or less obscurely, that he has provoked His displeasure by violating his unwritten law. The objective existence of the deity, therefore, is not and cannot be in question

[1] J. Herring, *Sub specie aeterni, réponse à une critique de la philosophie de Husserl*, Part II, *ad fin.*
[2] *Geneva Catechism.*

for any man conscious of his being and his activity in himself. In this sense, there are no atheists. That power which is of itself and independent of anything other than itself, and the fact that we are dependent on it—these are objects of immediate intuition. "I know that there is something—one does not, necessarily, say 'someone'—above me." This is a common affirmation, by which those who cannot repeat the Christian creed express what remains to them of the "religious sense".

There may be no atheists, but in practice there are impious people, sybarites and dilettantes. In the theoretical sphere, too, there are those who form a narrow and anthropomorphic conception of God and who can easily be led to treat Him as they treat anyone else who does not obey all their behests. There are also those who empty the concept of God of all living or spiritual content, who regard Him as blind fate and thus atrophy in themselves the instinct of prayer and worship. One does not invoke a deaf deity and so, in the long run, the mind finding itself unable, without degradation, to bow before anything but a higher mind, ceases to worship. In this way, an intellectual error may dry up the sources of the religious sensibility. The belief that one is dependent on an abstract principle or impersonal power, so far from normally engendering religion, in the sense of piety, produces a despairing rebellion in some, and in others a discouraged indifference.

If this instinctive belief in the mysterious source of our being is to blossom into absolute adoration, into victorious faith, into prayer which comprises both ardent desire and unconditional submission, there is one condition necessary, although it is insufficient of itself to produce such effects. This is that the mind, relying on its own sense of piety, should reject all that reduces and limits the God thus intuitively perceived and that it should at the same time raise to an infinite degree all the positive qualities of this Being, especially His bounty and power. This is the *via negationis* and the *via eminentiae* of philosophy; but, as we have observed, these ways are not sufficient in themselves to bring us to God. In order to come to the Father, we must tread the *via crucis*, the sorrowful way of renunciation: the road which leads to the living God must pass by Calvary.

The considerations which we have just developed help us to understand in what sense it can be said that man is, by nature, a religious animal and that religion is universal. It is clear that this cannot be understood in the sense that religion can never be accidentally atrophied by the absence of a favourable environment nor systematically undermined by consciously hostile influences. No doubt such accidents do happen to a considerable number of people some of whom declare themselves strangers to all religious unrest. Nor have we any *a priori* right to question their sincerity.

The proof of the universality of the religious instinct is furnished by the universality of the beliefs and practices having for their object that which is held to be sacred. Proof still more striking, if possible, may be found in the unexpected recurrence, among those who profess that they have no religion, of these beliefs and practices, which reappear in a distorted form. We would even say that the special form of these recurrences is specially instructive.

Socinians, and many Arminians, have disputed the fact of the universality of natural religion to which we appeal as a proof. They have done so, and still do so, in a systematic manner. They will not let it be said of man that before the Fall he was endowed with a knowledge of God which formed an integral part of his nature. In virtue of dogmatic premises, the divine image in which man was originally created must be reduced to his dominion over the other creatures. [1]

In the 19th century some who shared these views tried, in the name of science, though with a zeal scarcely consistent with scientific objectivity, to discover tribes without religion among the most degenerate specimens of humanity. The existence of such tribes became, for many, almost axiomatic. Thus Broca wrote in 1886: "It is beyond question that there exist among the lower races peoples without cultus, dogmas, metaphysical ideas, collective beliefs, and, consequently, without religion." In the previous year, Lubbock compiled "a long list of peoples entirely without religion." [2] Little by little this catalogue has been reduced by the researches of scientists, whether unbelievers or not, until nothing now remains of it. To-day no one takes seriously the arguments used by Socinus against Calvin, or by Broca against Quatrefages, and it may safely be said that never has there been found among all the tribes of man one so degenerate as to be devoid of any vestige of religious belief. [3]

[1] *Racovian Catechism*, xcii, 46–49; Fock, *Der socin*, p. 307.
[2] V. A. Reville, *Les Religions des peuples non-civilisés*, I, p. 13; J. Lubbock, *Les origines de la civilisation*, tr. Barbier, Paris, 1877.
[3] [Cf. Plutarch, *Adv. Colsten Epicureum*: "Go round the world and you may find cities without walls, literature, kings, houses, riches, money, gymnasia or theatres. But no one ever saw a city without temples and gods, one which does not have recourse to prayers, oaths or oracles, which does not offer sacrifice to obtain blessings or celebrate rites to avert evil." Cicero, *de Leg.*, i, 8: "There is no people so fierce and savage as not to know that they must have a god, although they may not know what sort of a god it should be." Clement of Alexandria,

Even if the contrary were the case and such a tribe were to be discovered, we should still have to define man as a religious animal. The definition should be based on the essential elements, ignoring the accidents. Man is a religious animal in the sense in which we call him a reasonable animal and say that rational ideas are universal, although there are individual fools and idiots and tribes of morons.

The facts of the recurrence of the religious instinct put this universality in its true light and prove to us the persistence of religion. They surprise by their frequent strangeness and by the apparent inconsequence of the manifestations which they assume, thus proving that man is incurably religious. The case of Auguste Comte reappearing with the attributes of the high priest of the religion of Humanity is evidently not an isolated example, since the positivist philosopher was able to establish a Church with relatively numerous adherents.

The truly astonishing progress of that particular form of superstition which causes those who engage in hazardous pursuits to resort to "chance" and seek protection through possession of a mascot or fetish deserves attention, for it enables us to observe the spontaneous activity of the religious instinct at work creating mental representations which are proper to it, when the traditional forms appear to be outmoded or are regarded as inefficacious. The study of these facts presents difficulties analogous to those encountered by the explorer who interrogates uncivilized people regarding their beliefs. Like them, the superstitious modern man has not always sufficient courage to confess his intimate beliefs. Moreover, they are often men of action little disposed to observe with attention the phenomena of their inner life. Nevertheless, there are those who avow boldly their faith, even if they do not always analyse it. "Many aviators practise fetishism", writes Matisse. "Paulhan never flies in his aeroplane without carrying with him some mascot. Other aviators have different fads and some none at all." [1]

It is true, of course, that not all aviators, not all motorists, have these "fads": but, when they do have them and the fact is generalized as a sort of mental epidemic, they show how the idea of God as hidden in their minds (or simply the idea of a

---

Strom., lib. v, n. 260: "All nations, whether they dwell in the East or the remotest shores of the West, in the North or in the South, have one and the same rudimentary apprehension of Him by whom the government of the world has been established."]

[1] G. Matisse, *Les ruines de l'idée de Dieu*; collection: *Les hommes et les idées*, Paris, n.d., p. 11.

special divine providence) replaces the dead or inadequate notion by a representation which is often confused, but which corresponds to the intuition of a real power on which they feel that their happiness or their misery depends.

This intuition, as we have said, is still not piety, subjective religion, but it is the foundation of it. The St. Christopher of the Catholic chauffeur, the mascot doll of the atheist or deist chauffeur, is, for practical purposes, his personal God. "A God", said Luther, "is he in whom one trusts." The intellectual value of these representations appears as nothing to the convinced Protestant Christian or to the positivist philosopher. Those who would not consent for anything in the world to embark without their mascot are generally conscious of their belief. The fact that they do not attempt to justify it does not matter, for the intuition on which they build as a foundation is so strong that it resists all rational arguments. Man feels God within, and when he no longer believes in Him, he tends to fashion a mental image of Him which is gross or ridiculous, according to the measure of his theological aptitude.

This tendency is specially noticeable among those whose occupations expose them continually to danger. But it is notorious that it exists among men who are otherwise very cultured and disciplined intellectually by the powerful and liberating influence of scientific methods. Matisse finds himself obliged to admit that "many men of a very positive mind are the slaves of certain superstitions. It so happens that these superstitions are of exactly the same order as those of the sailors and chauffeurs which we have just called to mind, and that they must find their explanation in the same cause."

This aptitude, this general inclination among uncivilized peoples, which we encounter again in the full positive culture of the 20th century, shows that the divinity who is recognized and honoured in practice, if not specifically the object of an act of faith, is the God of personal representation. The other divinity, that of the official religions or of the state, even if recognized as real, has no religious importance at all for the individual. It can only have this importance for him in the measure in which this divinity can be believed in and acknowledged by him as his God. This happens when the personal God who reveals himself to the chief of the clan is recognized as exercising his benevolence towards each one of the members of the clan in particular. By an analogous process this tribal deity becomes national and even universal. This, at any rate, is what emerges from the researches of Boscawen on the origin of theocracies in the *Semitic* race. [1]

Man begins, not by the adoration of a crowd of divinities peopling a pantheon, but by the worship of a god who reveals himself to him personally. If he becomes a polytheist, it is because a subsequent experience leads him to think that his personal divinity does not always resemble that of his neighbour, who is in conflict with him and protected like himself, by his god. But, in this case, it would be more appropriate to speak of polydemonism than of polytheism. [2]

These gods are only, so to speak, particular centres in which an identical divine substance concentrates itself, which itself dwells in a supreme spirit too exalted to occupy himself with men. They are rather tutelary genii than gods. Their multiplicity in no sense excludes the general concept of a supreme divinity, who is the source of their power.

Man feels himself dependent on the absolute, of which it has been said that particular divinities are only its small change; delegates, as it were, like the guardian angels and patron saints of medieval Christianity. In practice, the supreme God may shade off in the horizon of thought and the foreground may be filled with an innumerable crowd of genii, spirits of the dead, secondary divinities. But these are scarcely more than derivatives and particular incarnations.

Moreover, with Max Müller, we believe that henotheism [3] preceded polytheism, but we cannot accept his definition of the former as a sort of inadvertence on the part of the polytheist whose object of worship is the one in whom, at the moment, he recognizes all the divine virtues, the reason being that, in the act of worship, he has lost sight of other gods.

Actually, for primitive peoples, a god is only worshipped because he is the bearer, or rather the form, of this divine force, everywhere identical with itself, of that *mana*, this *manitou*, etc., which is properly divinity, ultimately God. Hence it is a matter of indifference whether one personified natural force or another is invoked: each and all of them are merely the small change of the God whom man bears in his heart. By these roots, henotheism plunges into monotheism, an unstable monotheism which

---

[1] W. St. Chad Boscawen, *The First of the Empires*, London, New York, 1903' Pref., p. xiv.

[2] C. P. Tiele, *Manuel de l'histoire des religions*, Paris 1885, p. 18: "The religions dominated by animism are remarkable in the first place for a mixed, confused, uncertain doctrine: a polydemonism without order, which nevertheless does not exclude belief in a supreme spirit."

[3] [Henotheism (ἑνός, one + θεός, god), belief in one god as the deity of the individual, family or tribe without asserting that he is the sole God.]

the tendency to unity, a law of the human mind, easily diverts towards pantheism in the lowest social stages, as we have seen.

One knows how indifferent is the paralogical mentality to the stability of forms and also with what facility it identifies the beings that appear to us as endowed with an irreducible and uncommunicable essence. Von Hartmann arrived at a conception of henotheism analogous to that which we have just outlined. [1] We believe it covers all the facts.

What appears to us to militate in favour of the view that monotheism antedates polytheism is that, not only is it becoming more and more evident that the majority of polytheistic cults recognize a chief among the gods, a veritable supreme being in the divine domain, but that, wherever practical polytheism holds sway, this higher deity remains at the back of the polytheist's mind. He appears to have lost his religious importance through the myths and legends of which he is the hero and the nature of the cultus practised. This god is generally considered to be too great, too remote, or too good to be usefully invoked. There are some cases in which this religious decadence can be historically verified: for example, in popular Catholicism or among the Chinese. [2]

The well-authenticated existence of a spontaneous religious tendency, of a prodigious theogenic fecundity, and this even among tribes with lower civilizations, allows us to infer, as against Frazer, if not that religion is anterior to magic, at least the simultaneity of these two manifestations of the psychic activity of man. Frazer has well observed that the essential distinction between religion and magic lies in the fact that, in the former, man assumes a suppliant attitude in regard to the powers which he invokes: while, in the latter, he imagines that he can command them as a master, e.g., the slave of the lamp in the *Thousand and One Nights*, by means of procedures whose secret he holds.

But we cannot accept his view that primitive man had recourse to prayer, having previously proved the futility of issuing commands to sacrifice, because the rite had shown itself to be inefficacious. The reverse could be equally well maintained and, indeed, is maintained to support their case by contemporary

[1] *Das religiöse Bewusstsein der Menschheit im Stufengang seiner Entwicklung*, Berlin, 1882, p. 57.

[2] Science and theology are beginning to visualize independently the possibility of proving the primitive character of monotheism: *vide* a bibliography in Bavinck, *Geref. Dog.*, I, pp. 310–329; R. Allier, *Psychol. de la conversion chez les peuples non-civilisés*, I, p. 279 ff. and 284, n. 6, indicates the most recent work on this subject, which has been investigated in detail by Frs. Schmidt and Maréchal.

atheists. When Matisse remarks that processions and fasts have been replaced by prophylactic processes in the struggle against epidemics, he is saying the same thing. [1]

But these two suppositions are discredited by observation. Among uncivilized peoples, magic is as active as religion, which it opposes and implies at the same time. On the other hand, hygienic services among the civilized, even when directed by unbelievers, if they are run on intelligent lines, in combating disease, must take into account that imponderable thing which is called "mass morale". Nor can they afford to despise the aid of religious institutions. In communities not blinded by the spirit of systematic negation, one sees the same authorities which prescribe prophylactic measures appealing for the help of religion.

In the second place, not only is the co-existence of religion with magic and science an observable fact, but this fact does not necessarily suppose any inconsistency in those in whom it is found. The sorcerer, the doctor and the scientist, control, or think they control, certain particular facts: but it is still on the express condition that they submit strictly to the process which conditions their success. Thus, they are intuitively conscious of dependence on a certain order of things, and that this dependence is absolute. If, for example, the magician believes that the knowledge of the processes which he employs is due to a revelation of a divine being: if the doctor and the scientist believe that the natural order was introduced by God in creation, and that their own scientific aptitude and knowledge are His gifts, they are perfectly consistent in maintaining a religious attitude. The priest who believes that he transubstantiates a host into the body of Christ by virtue of the sacramental formula which he pronounces, performs, technically speaking, an act of magic. But, as he believes at the same time that he holds his personal power from God, mediately by the intermediary of the sacerdotal succession, and that the sacramental formula is of divine institution and revelation, he professes to perform a religious act at the same time and is perfectly consistent. We have no right to affirm *a priori* that belief in an order of things supposed by magic and science is necessarily anterior to belief in a being who is the revealer and organizer of this order.

Finally, we have seen how, in the least favourable circumstances, produced by the dominance of a positivist "scientific" mentality, with its hostility to historical and traditional institutions, the religious instinct is represented in forms analogous to those of uncivilized peoples. We believe that, if this does not

[1] *Op. cit.*, p. 71 ff.

always happen, the reason must be sought in the general tendencies of our civilization which strongly oppose the natural aptitude for religion. This being the case, it is unthinkable that, in an environment as favourable as that of the paralogical mentality, and among the dangers which attend the life of savages, these inferior representations of henotheism should have to await the repudiation of magic as inefficacious in order to manifest themselves, and that, at the same time we should know that this repudiation never happens in such an environment.

We are now in a position to say what religion is in the proper sense of the term. In the first place, it presupposes an idea, inadequate perhaps, but at least correct, of God known as all-powerful and all-good, the source and dispenser of all good things. This constitutes the necessary intellectual element. One can only love and adore what one knows. Afterwards comes the affective element, the particular sense of the dependence on this God of all that exists: the sentiments of fear, veneration, love and, finally, confidence: in a word, faith. These sentiments receive their specifically religious note from the fact that they are known in relation to the absolute.[1]

Ideas and sentiments presuppose a revelation of God to the mind of man by the creation, preservation and government of dependent beings, and hence God entering into relationship with man. Moreover, if it is true that we cannot think of him without becoming aware of the need for consecrating ourselves to his service, it is impossible to know *a priori* by what acts and what abstentions he wishes to be served, or even if things of this character exist: revelation is still necessary here. If nothing abnormal had happened, this would suffice: but conscience and revelation warn us that something abnormal, namely, sin, has happened and that it has resulted in a rupture between God and ourselves.

It is not sufficient, then, that God should reveal Himself in nature and the human mind as all-powerful and good. He must restore the broken bond of union by a covenant and attest it to us by a definite revelation that He offers the assurance of His paternal benevolence to all to whom the message comes and who comply with the conditions laid down for the realization of this covenant. We find in Scripture, the inspired document of revelation, the supreme source and norm of religion. God is thus the efficient cause of religion: the religious consciousness is not the efficient cause, but merely the material cause, of religion: the receptive organ. Revelation in agreement with the instinct

---

[1] Hoornbeek, *Theol. practica*, II, 205 ff. *Absoluta dignitas et potestas Dei . . . absoluta subjectio*; H. Bavinck, *Geref. Dog.*, I, p. 245.

of piety and reasoned reason (*ratio ratiocinata*) regards God as the efficient cause of religion, His glory as its principal final cause and our salvation as its subordinate end.

Reason left to its own resources (*ratio ratiocinans*) with the aid of the light of general and natural revelation can construct for itself the idea of a god or of a plurality of gods, a sort of intellectual idol: it can invent means for attracting to itself his benevolence: it can prescribe a cultus and a rule of conduct. The name of religion may be applied by analogy and extension to this arbitrary cult, but wherever we find the notion of a higher power on which we depend, the sentiment of this dependence and the idea that one can enter into relationship with him in order to attract to ourselves his benevolence, will tell us that, in the abstract and general sense of the term, we are in the presence of religion in embryo. Developed religion presupposes a cultus and leads to a social organization. This is indeed the definition of it proposed by Jastrow.[1]

But we would add this observation, in our judgment essential: that a distinction must be made between religions of spontaneous growth, which all claim for themselves a positive revelation, and religions of artificial formation, like the cult of theophilanthropy, the religion of Auguste Comte, etc., which content themselves with intuitions of reason or of sentiment. These religions are, to the spontaneous type, what Esperanto is to languages of natural growth.

In the final analysis, God is the efficient cause (*principium essendi*), of all religions. But the natural cause, the subjective state, impresses on non-revealed religions the deformations which constitute them in reality pseudo-religions. Modern substitutes for religion, the cult of abstractions, like truth, universal order (Haeckel's *universum*), the moral order, etc., attest the indestructible religious consciousness in man, the reality of the intuition of dependence. But it is quite improperly, by abuse and metaphor, that we invest these tentative positions with the name of religion.

The general concept of religion that we put forward does not claim to express all the riches and complexity of the religious fact. We believe that to be impossible. But, at any rate, it conforms to popular usage and it is not contrary to any conclusion generally accepted by the science of comparative religion. Moreover, it has the advantage of tracing a clear line of demarcation between religion, on the one hand; and magic, science and metaphysics, on the other.

[1] M. Jastrow, *The Study of Religion*, New York, 1904, p. 170.

CHAPTER II

RELIGION, MAGIC AND SCIENCE

Magic and science present themselves as knowledge of the order of the universe. Magic rests on adherence to certain principles which our sociologists have explained and formulated, and which they designate the laws of the identity of the object with the sign: of like recalling like; of the transmission of qualities by contact; of the efficacy of words and formulas. The practice of magic is based on an adherence, implicit at least, to these or similar principles. These relations are supposed to govern reality. Fundamentally, magic is understood to be a mass of information which enables its possessor to dominate things and events in a more or less complete fashion. These principles are, we believe, the product of the spontaneous activity of the human mind, proceeding by hasty generalizations and fortuitous or habitual associations. In brief, magic is a badly constructed science. It is a nominalism and a pantheism for which real distinctions and the law of natural causation have no gnosiological[1] significance. This is a state of mind that we describe, with Allier, by the epithet "paralogical"[2] rather than by the term "prelogical", invented by Lévy-Brühl. Actually, "uncivilized" man is as logical as anyone else: he is blatantly so, like a child. But his knowledge is based on other principles than that of experimental logic. He has, nevertheless, a basic bond of logical coherence: belief in the unity of the principle which integrates reality and in an order of reality governed by magical laws. We have seen that this principle finds clear enough expression among certain savage tribes.

Science consciously obeys the laws of logic laid down by Aristotle and Bacon. No doubt the scientist may be influenced by regressive tendencies, like empiricism and pantheism, but, in practice at any rate, he methodically applies the laws and directive principles of reason. The natural causative sequence, even though reduced to certain sequences practically indissoluble and constant, remains the principle of natural laws. The discovery

---

[1] [Gnosiology (γνῶσις (knowledge) + λόγος (discourse)), the theory of knowledge in so far as it relates to the origin, nature, limits and validity of knowledge; as distinguished from methodology, the study of the basic concepts, postulates and presuppositions of the special sciences.]

[2] [A paralogism is a fallacious syllogism, an error in reasoning.]

by experiment of constant relations between phenomena is itself the proximate goal before the scientist: his remote goal being the acquisition of power over things and events.

Strictly speaking, his goal is the same as that of the magician, except that the means and objectives are differently concerned. The technical processes of "uncivilized" tribes, often very ingenious, and presupposing remarkable qualities of observation, patience and sagacity, are condemned to stagnation because they are associated with magical practices and inviolable traditions. Among the civilized, these same processes are susceptible of constant improvement, because they are subjected to the incessant revision by a science which knows no other law than that of the relations between generally recognized facts.[1]

But magic and science, while differing in principles and methods are alike in their general presupposition of an order of reality and in the goal which both pursue, namely, obedience to laws in order to control things. The most abstract and theoretical sciences originate from and produce a utilitarian technique. They are born of practical necessity and in this necessity find one of their most efficacious stimulants. Magic also undertakes to satisfy the same needs. Even the most disinterested of religions are not necessarily indifferent to these needs: some there are, indeed, that adopt this attitude, which advocate renunciation in the ascetic sense and which have, as it were, an appetite for death. This proves that religion, in itself, is not a technical process in competition with those of science. Even those religions which interest themselves in the temporal needs of man, like Christianity, for example, make no claim to teach him the technical means necessary to ensure the satisfaction of these needs. They aim rather at putting the worshipper into such relationship with the deity that the judicious employment of the means suggested by the science of his age and environment may be favoured by the benevolent aid of this deity.

They claim to act chiefly on the agent, by imparting to him a precious substance like the *mana* or a superhuman grace: but, so far as religion is concerned, it is a matter of indifference whether phenomena are governed by the law of resemblances or by any other law. If they were governed by the law of resemblances, it would be necessary to conform to it in order to obtain the desired result: to depict a hind transfixed by an arrow in order to secure success for the chase. But religion remains, in its essence, substantially the same for those who do not entertain such conceptions.

[1] *Vide* R. Allier, *Les non-civilisés et nous*, p. 53 ff.

It is conceivable, however, that the predominance of magical ideas may tend to alter the interpretation of the rites and sacraments in revealed religion and to introduce magical concepts and practices into the others. A religion can adapt itself to the introduction or the preservation of these elements and still retain a character of high spirituality which places it almost at the summit of the hierarchy of religions. In proof of this may be cited classical Lutheranism, with its sacramental theories.

Magic, in itself, is neither morally good nor bad, religious nor anti-religious. It can be placed at the service of all causes, the better as well as the worse. It is a *Weltanschauung*[1] which we believe to be out of date in regard to physical facts.

We exclude it carefully from our theological interpretation of the sacramental rites of our religion, because we believe it to have no foundation in the sacred documents. But if the authority that we recognize in Holy Scripture were to reveal to us that some of its laws, like that of contact, for example, had their application in the hyperphysical sphere, we should be willing to accept the position as do the Lutherans. On the other hand, we cannot admit a purely symbolical conception of the sacraments, in the name of rationalist mentality and natural causation.

The natural sciences and the rationalist mentality are quite incompetent to judge the question of knowing whether or not God presents, offers and guarantees, with the visible symbol, the invisible grace which it represents. The mental functions do not assume the livery of empiricism or rationalism: they may be fulfilled in the sphere of realism.

Sometimes, it is true, the religious revelation touches on the subjects which the natural sciences study on their own account, following their own methods, which they base solely on reasoning and observation of the facts. Examples of such cases are the dogmas of creation, of the unity of the human species, and of moral liberty. There is, indeed, a theological cosmology and a theological anthropology, too: but the world and man are studied in them only from the angle of their dependence on divine sovereignty and the conditions of salvation, and not with a view to satisfying scientific curiosity. Were there such things as a revealed astronomy, geometry or geology, which is not the case of course, these sciences would not, *ipso facto*, be religious.

On the other hand, if the scientist by the aid of the methods

---

[1] [*Weltanschauung* (German): world-view, perspective of life, conception of things.]

with which he deals and the facts which he knows, discovers that his conclusions are not at the moment in harmony with the interpretation of theologians, he need not trouble himself nor be disturbed for this reason. If he is a believer, or merely well informed in regard to modern conceptions, he knows that scientific theories are not immutable dogmas, or "unquestionable" certainties, but merely provisional working hypotheses: and that theological interpretations are also susceptible of revision. Let each pursue his own task and God's time will correct men's errors. The theologian need not be in a hurry to accommodate the interpretation of the sacred texts to the scientific theories of the day. The latter are too soon outmoded; but "the word of the Lord endureth for ever."

CHAPTER 12

THEOLOGY AND METAPHYSICS

Metaphysics, or, more exactly, ontology, endeavours to satisfy the natural curiosity of the human mind which seeks a knowledge of the quiddity[1] of things. The offspring of θαῦμα or wonder, it is essentially a speculative discipline and in this respect differs necessarily from religion and theology, which is a practical discipline. The latter can, indeed, furnish solutions which satisfy curiosity to a certain extent, but this is by accident. Its nature and essence, the ends which it proposes to itself, are otherwise. Religion reveals to us what we must know in order that God may have the honour which is His due: in order that we may acknowledge Him as God, as *ens independens* and sovereign. In the second place, it proposes to teach us how we shall find in Him our supreme and eternal happiness. It is essentially an applied discipline. Revelation imparts to us, with authority, the ontological notions necessary in order that we may realize these ends: it appeals to faith. Speculation leads to these, or to contrary notions, by its own means. It appeals only to the authority of the light of nature.

Should these certainties of faith, founded on a divine testimony, conflict with the hazardous and uncertain speculations of metaphysics, the religious man does not hesitate to sacrifice the second to the first. To be sure, he must feel intensely grateful to Kant for having definitely destroyed the arrogant boast of philosophical dogmatism which proclaimed its intention of supplanting the revealed faith, henceforth useless, by a theology demonstrable by reason alone.

Experience shows that, by making a happy use of the ntuitions of common grace, the metaphysician who is ignorant of, or misunderstands, the particular and positive revelation, can achieve an abstract and formal concept of the divine quiddity and define it as pure act, the perfection of being, the infinite and spiritual essence. He can even clothe these intuitions of grace with a dialectical form which will give him the illusion of a rigorously scientific demonstration. But the moment he wishes to give a content to this abstract concept, he will find himself

---

[1] [Quiddity (Lat. *quidditas*, whatness), essence; that which is described in a definition.]

obliged to appeal to judgments of value, in order to determine certain positive qualities of being. Can the knowledge of an imperfect object, like the world, in other words, can omniscience, be regarded as a positive value: and is it of more value to be an ideal than a living and acting reality?

The reply to these questions depends not on speculation but on intuitions determined by the moral and spiritual dispositions of the seeker. The person who is not guided by a revelation which prescribes these judgments of value for him, and which disposes him inwardly to accept them, will put into the formal concept of pure act, of perfect being, not the divine reality but the image projected by his own eyes. He may approach the sanctuary, he may enter in and worship, but he will not have taken a single step towards God. The being whom he acknowledges and worships is an idol, the creation of his mind, a deformation resulting from a corrupt heart. [1]

The religion whose mental representative element formulates, organizes and synthesizes itself in dogmatic theology is not, therefore, an ignorant metaphysics in a rudimentary state which should give place to a scientific metaphysics. It differs from this by the ends it pursues, by its concrete content, method, and principles. Both functions may co-exist in the same mind: they must never be confounded.

The presupposition of the physical sciences is that nature is a cosmos, an intelligible universe, in the sense that it is bound together by relationships susceptible to investigation and understood by the mind[2]; and this to such a point that the idealists are able to persuade themselves that it is they and their intelligence which create the cosmos. This suggests irresistibly to front-rank scientists (even if, like Romanes, they are not theists),[3] explanation by means of an intelligent cause of a spiritual order. Reality is bound together and conditioned by intelligible relations. This leads idealists, like Brunschvicg, to describe the universal mind as the organizer of the representations to which he reduces reality.

These conclusions, even when they remain at this stage and

---

[1] *Inst.* I, iv. 1–4; *Com. on John*, xiv, 1, *sub titulo*: *Dei somnia sua adorant.*

[2] On the other hand, the cosmos is not a theorem which unfolds itself in accordance with the law of a logical or mechanical determinism. It is the result of an act of the divine liberty. In this sense, Meyerson rightly says that science everywhere encounters "irrationals", *vide* M. Boegner, *op. cit.*, p. 103.

[3] It is well known that G. Romanes, who had lost his faith in consequence of his eudemonist and rationalist premises, through contact with the theory of evolution, recovered it through a series of reflexions and intuitions of which he has left us traces in some posthumous notes edited by Bishop Gore under the title *Thoughts on Religion*, London, 1902.

continue to be hostile to religious theism, prepare the mind to accept the notion of an infinite being, whose intelligent mind is originative and creative in his knowledge and will: they prepare the way, in fact, for the acceptance of the specifically theological notion of the eternal decree of divine providence and predestination which lies at the heart of Calvinistic theology.

We have said that by this means science leads the mind towards religion, because the latter essentially has God for its principle, its object and its end: that religion is inconceivable without God, and that God is not to be found by speculation; that the infinite does not manifest Himself by means of metaphysics but through the intuition which contemplates the revelation in nature and in the Word of God, at first oral, then written.[1] There may be conflicts in detail, but, taking it as a whole, the general direction is orientated towards religion.

The "moral person" god of the religious man, according to Balfour, being none other than the ontologically perfect God, is identified spontaneously in his faith with the deity who is the "logical cement" of metaphysicians and philosophers.

A god who was merely a "moral person", neither creator nor preserver, nor supreme ruler, *logos* and infinite dynamic of the mind, could be the object of only a very restricted and conditional faith. His knowledge, if it were not the origin of all reality by an almighty and free choice, would be fallible. Like ours, it would depend on things. The future being contingent, free acts, in themselves imprevisable, would increase his knowledge in the measure in which they developed in time: and, like Brahma, he would run the risk of one day meeting a sage, like Sakyamuni, who would disclose to him his own future dethronement. The god of Renouvier, for example, who knows that he has begun in or with time—who knows it, at any rate, because his theologians teach it to him for he himself is incapable of conceiving infinite duration otherwise than as contradictory—such a divinity must fear he may come to an end one day. He depends on another god, real but unsubstantial: the principle, mysterious for him as for us, of the laws of being.

Unless piety is seriously weakened by ethicist preoccupation, by a desire to maintain a certain concept of moral liberty, or by a radical eudaemonism, it can never accommodate itself to such a god. The soul of true piety is faith, absolute confidence of

[1] *Conf. gallic.*, art. II: "God manifests himself to His creatures in the first place by His works, as much by their creation as by their conservation and conduct: secondly and more clearly by His Word, which at first was revealed by oracle and has since been committed to writing in the books that we call Holy Scripture."

the heart, certainty that the highest value will be victorious. How can the god who is merely a "moral person" be the guarantor of this victory of good over evil, of life over death?

The God glimpsed by science, if the idea of him is quickened and developed by the elements and corrections furnished by the law and the prophets, by Christ and the apostles, is precisely the one for whom the religious soul knows itself to be made and in whom it believes.

It is claimed, however, that between science and religion there exists a radical conflict of principles. This opposition consists in the fact that the mainspring of science is the principle of phenomenal causation, while religion supposes a direct intervention in the order of things by God, the supra-phenomenal cause, acting as Judge, Saviour, Instructor and King in concrete cases. Science presupposes that each phenomenon finds its explanation in an anterior phenomenon, and is itself the cause of an ulterior phenomenon. The series of natural causes knows no commencement and no lacunae. Religion, on the other hand, implies a free intervention of God, the first cause, whether in response to prayer or not. Here, we are told, is an irreducible opposition. Höffding appears to us to have formulated the argument with the greatest vigour. He starts with a concrete case, in which the opposition between the religious explanation and that of science seems to him to burst forth in its keenest form. A shipwreck takes place. The religious explanation attributes it to a moral cause, seeing in it a punishment, a trial, a deliverance willed by God. Science, on the other hand, assigns to each phenomenon certain proximate natural causes: a shipwreck, for example, is caused by a variety of natural circumstances: a faulty navigation, a storm. These proximate causes are themselves scientifically connected with a natural causal series which, it is suggested, excludes all divine intervention. Where, indeed, can a place be found for God? Not at the origin of the causal series, for the causal series of phenomena knows no origin. There is no point at which the human mind can pause in order to allow the supreme cause to intervene. Each causal series is infinite and only the spirit of the system can rule the possibility of an infinite plurality.[1] This cannot be the case with any link in the chain, for science knows only natural phenomena, united without the slightest fissure by the bond of causation. There is therefore a conflict of principles between the scientific causal

[1] We say plurality, not number. Number is by definition numerable and thus evidently finite. But it is not evident that all plurality is a number (Mihaud, *Cardinal Mercier*).

explanation and the religious casual explanation. "If the meteorologist is right, the pastor is wrong."[1]

We shall not ask Höffding how he knows that God, whom he considers to be unknowable, cannot manifest His intervention by an extraordinary phenomenon, modifying the order of things; nor why what is termed a miracle must be regarded as out of the question. What makes the religious explanation so interesting is precisely that it claims to be applicable to the humblest events of the natural and ordinary course of existence. The religious man sees God in them as clearly as in the most dazzling miracle. If it were otherwise the religious explanation would be applicable on very few occasions.

In the first place, the application of the principle of causation to being does not in the least imply that, in virtue of this principle, one must never pause in tracing the series of causes. The principle, as it is usually formulated: "Each effect has a cause", is nothing but a piece of tautology. The Kantian formula "Each fact which appears has a cause", says all that is required. It is not by any means a principle of reason. It is possible to think without this principle. The advocates of free will—absolute commencement—the nominalists, like Bertrand Russell, are proofs of this. The principle of causation is an anticipation of the reason which persuaded us of the universal and at any rate relative intelligibility of things. Let us formulate it in this way: all that is contingent has a cause which renders its existence intelligible. But this principle does not specify whether things have their *raison d'être* in themselves or elsewhere. It is the idea which we formulate either of the intrinsic necessity, or of the contingence of a thing or of a fact, which warns us that we must pause or continue. A deist who believes only in first causes, at least when it is a question of free agents, stops short with his formulated notion of himself as a free agent and feels no need to proceed further, for he thinks himself to be in the presence of a first cause. His conception of the nature of liberty is sufficient to remove from him all temptation to proceed further. The idea is false: but it is sufficient that it should be able to stop him, in actual fact, thus invalidating the thesis of the infinity of causes in the past. In the same way, if God is conceived as the *ens sui sufficiens a se*, the Being who is self-sufficient, the Being by Himself, no one who thus conceives Him will feel the need to imagine anything anterior to him: the

---

[1] [*Si le bureau des longitudes a raison, le pasteur a tort.* The *Annuaire du Bureau des Longitudes* corresponds to the Nautical Almanac in Britain and to the similar publication of the Cambridge Observatory in U.S.A.]

reason is satisfied by this line of thought. God does not cease to be a mystery to it, but it is incorrect to say that divine causation merely replaces one mystery by another: for God, while remaining mysterious and incomprehensible in His essence, appears clearly to the mind as the necessary principle, partially intelligible, of the universal intelligibility of things.

It is clear that God, the Being who, by definition, possesses in Himself all the positive qualities of being, possesses *ex hypothesi*, the quality of existing necessarily. His place in a natural causal series can only be, first of all, "in the beginning". Where must we stop when tracing the series of beings as distinct from phenomena? We must do so at the point where science, or ontology, put us in the presence of a principle which is the condition of the scientific explanation of things, and which does not possess in itself its *raison d'être*, matter, movement, force. It cannot be affirmed of these principles that they are necessary, in the full sense of the term, except in virtue of a gratuitous presumption: and the principle of causation compels us to ascend still higher. For it is obvious that there is nothing in their essence which authorizes us to think that the latter implies existence. Since, on the other hand, it is sufficient, by hypothesis, to explain reality, there is no reason to assign to them an anterior natural principle. If we accept the principle of causation as applying to reality, we are compelled, therefore, to decide for an infinite, eternal, supernatural cause, namely, God. The religious man thus places God at the beginning of the causal series, which have caused the shipwreck of which Höffding speaks. But he does not content himself with this: if he did so, he would be no more than a deist or a Pelagian.

Let us suppose that, at this point, the human understanding was so corrupted by the Fall that it had to accept the Kantian principle of an infinite series of causes extending back into the past. The religious explanation would still hold good. It may be asked where we should place the divine intervention in a natural causal series, conceded provisionally to be infinite. It would not be "in the beginning", since, in our provisional hypothesis, there is no beginning. Nor would it be in a space between the links, since, in our provisional hypothesis, there is no interruption of any sort. Where then would it be? The reply must be: Everywhere! In each link of the chain; in the substance, even, of each cause; in its duration and efficacy; in the order and direction in which it appears: to sum up, in the reality, power and disposition, of each cause. For the believer in the living God, almighty and infinite spirit and mind, this insertion of each cause in the causal series is nothing else but the result of the free divine pre-ordination, in eternity. He is in all causes, including the free causes. He co-ordinates them with the blind causes: with the motives which determine without compelling. [1]

Continuous creation implies continuous government. Causes, whatever they may be, have no efficacy apart from that which is communicated to them. [2] The principal power granted to created causes is obediential power. The constant relations which we call natural laws are simply "divine habits": or, better, the habitual order which God imposes on nature. It is these habits, or this habitual process, which constitute the object of the natural and physical sciences. [3]

The miracle, in its form, is nothing but a deviation from the habitual course of natural phenomena, provoked by the intervention of a new factor: an extraordinary volition of God. There is, thus, no violation of law, as scientifically defined, since every scientific law supposes this restriction, explicit or implicit: all things being equal in all respects.

The extraordinary thing can be recognized by anybody in its quality of fact, but it cannot be grasped as divine except by the religious consciousness. That, alone, is competent to pronounce on its character, as such, for it is the sense of divinity. Moreover, a miracle cannot be accepted as a proof, except by the religious consciousness. Science, in the physical sense of the term, cannot decree the impossibility of miracle *a priori*. Its means are too limited to enable it to do that.

If, by hypothesis, God confers extraordinarily on any cause, in virtue of the obediential power inherent in every cause, a quality which it does not possess habitually, or if He withdraws one from it, things are no longer equal in all respects. But science has no means of knowing whether this takes place or not. Philosophy cannot place any limit at all on the divine liberty. On the other hand, science is not concerned with the eventuality of the miracle. Its object is to enable man to foresee, in order that he may have power. In order that the prevision may be practically possible, it is sufficient that the natural order should be practically invariable. Now, this is presupposed by the very concept of miracle. What renders it astonishing is its extreme rarity. For the natural order itself, in a broad sense, may be described as a perpetual "miracle", and should always excite the astonishment which lies at the foundation of all ontological

---

[1] Bavinck, *op. laud.*, II, 189 ff.; 389 ff.; 502; 655 ff.; 661, 664 ff.
[2] *Inst.* I, xvi. 2.
[3] A. Kuyper, *E voto dordraceno*, I, 239 ff.

science, and at the same time, the admiration and fear which are among the elements of religion. [1]

Höffding's objection seems to us to militate against deism, because the latter system rejects the activity of the first cause in its universal immanence, and he would appear to admit various independent first causes. It seems obvious that this conception of divine causation and of created free causality cannot be classified as religious. The objection also militates against those who, while admitting a certain divine concurrence, understand it as sharing its activity with that of secondary causes. But the deists can no longer imagine that their view represents the condition of agreement between belief in God and science. Contemporary science, in fact, does not demand the presuppositions which Kant thought to be indispensable.

Without going as far as to claim with Bertrand Russell that the very idea of cause is useless to mature science, the latter being occupied only with invariable functions, we maintain that the scientist has no right to presume anything beyond the practical stability of natural laws. These latter are not promulgated by *natura naturans* [2] in the same manner as a public decree or order. They are the habitual relations which the Creator has imposed on *natura naturata*. [3] The scientist is limited to ascertaining and verifying this natural order, which he calls law. He does not derive these laws *a priori* from his mind, as Descartes would have it. He learns them by experience and by experimentation. Now, experience only tells us that which is, namely, the habitual stability of the order of nature. This stability is sufficient for a relatively certain prevision to be possible, that thus we may be able to find our way in the apparently inextricable chaos of phenomena.

There is, therefore, no conflict of principles between the presuppositions of science and those of religion. The determinism taken for granted by the former is not absolute. There is no absolute guarantee that it is universal, that it does not admit of gaps and exceptions. But, if the contrary were true, that this determinism of contingent laws, connecting contingent beings among which some are free and cannot be determined except by final causes, it can and must be considered, from the religious point of view, as governed by the providential action of God,

---

[1] *Inst.* I, xvi. 1: "And it is necessary that in this respect principally we should differ from the pagans and all secular peoples in maintaining that the power of God shines upon us in the existing state of the world as well as in its first origin."

[2] [*Natura naturans*: nature naturing, a scholastic term for causal principle.]

[3] [*Natura naturata*: nature natured, the complexus of all created things.]

who realizes in time, by physical premotion and efficacious grace the sovereign decree enacted by Him in eternity.

The God who gives to nature its order and its laws is He who inspires the prayer of the believer. Thus, harmony is pre-established between the prayer of the heart and the course of events: between the petition and its response.

CHAPTER 13

THE REAL CONTENT OF RELIGIOUS KNOWLEDGE

In describing piety or subjective religion as a sentiment of dependence, fear, love, and confidence, we have not indicated any sentiment which, taken by itself, can be called specifically religious. These sentiments enter into the warp and woof of all our relationships, personal and social. They are only religious in consequence of two characteristics: the nature of the object to which they relate and their qualificative degree of intensity.

In order that a sentiment may be religious, its object must be divine, and this sentiment must itself assume a specific quality. Now, a being is divine, he is a god, when, in his sphere of activity, if not in his essence, he is the possessor of a power independent of the conditions which govern other beings in this same sphere of activity. He is still a god, in fact God himself, when he is identified with the cause of these conditions or with these conditions personified: necessity, fate, an almighty will, etc. He is properly God when he is considered as the being absolutely independent of all that is not himself and as the sovereign master of the conditions which he has himself imposed on created beings.

Sentiments are, on the other hand, specifically religious when they are affected by the note of the infinite and when they have for an object God or divine beings. The idea may be more or less clear or more or less confused: but, after all, the idea precedes the sentiment. Knowledge, a certain rudimentary theology, normally precedes the movements of piety.

If the divine power were not known at least as an enigmatical power and, for that reason alone, to be feared, it could not be the object of religious reverence. Now, the only being worthy of exciting in us the sentiments that we have enumerated is the being who is absolutely independent, all-powerful and all-good: the being infinite and perfect: God. Perfect piety, that is to say, piety extending fear and love to the infinite and confidence to the absolute, is not rationally possible nor morally legitimate except in regard to the absolute, perfect and infinite being.

The acceptance by the mind of the fact of our absolute dependence can be logically conceived only when it acknowledges itself to be in the presence of God, and of the infinite God.[1] The question arises: is the analogical knowledge which Reformed theology proposes to us[2] sufficient, supposing the reality of God to be admitted, to allow us to claim possession of such a knowledge of Him as is required in order to engender piety. The question is important. It is clear that minds like our own, immersed in a finite and material organism, cannot possess an adequate knowledge of an infinite pure spirit. The only knowledge that we can have of God and of the facts of the infinite or purely spiritual order must be analogical. Thus, if analogical knowledge were devoid of all real content, we should be condemned to religious agnosticism. But such is not the case. Analogy, it is true, explains only a similarity of relationships. The only identity that it can claim is an identity between them. It is in this respect that it differs from adequate knowledge which takes cognizance of the identity between the elements of the nature of the beings compared. But, on the other hand, the identity of the relations, understood by analogy, is implied in the nature of the things. It is essential identity. There is a similarity which belongs to the essence of the relations between two or more beings. It is thus that, in creating, God has willed that nature should be a revelation of what He is in relation to us and for us.

To know these analogical relations is, therefore, to have a knowledge which, while partial, reflected and anagogical (the way of eminence) is not on this account less surely founded on the essential relations belonging to the nature of things. It is by the essential quality of the relations of similarity envisaged that analogy differs from equivocation and simple metaphor, both of which can yield only a symbolical knowledge. The symbol, the metaphor, the equivocation, also suppose a certain similarity of relationships, but one that is purely accidental, poetical: it can even be established in an arbitrary fashion by a simple convention.

It is by accident that the constellation *Canis Major* recalls vaguely the shape of an actual dog. It is poetical imagination which sees in the snow a shroud enveloping the earth. It is by convention that the ceremonial gesture of a priest lifting his hand above the congregation tells us that the latter has been sanctified or set apart. These similarities among accidental relations, by themselves, teach us very little concerning the intimate

[1] Hoornbeek, *Theol. practica*, II, 205.
[2] Calvin expressly indicates analogy as a process of the knowledge of God, *vide*, e.g., *Com. on Jer.*, xxiii, 5; Zanchi, *De nat. Dei*, formulates the theory of this analogical knowledge, following Aquinas; as does H. Bavinck.

nature of the objects compared. Without a verbal commentary, indeed, they would teach us nothing.

The astronomical and physical knowledge furnished by the two metaphors given above as examples is obviously very slight, although not absolutely nil, since it informs us of real accidents. But the accident is not exactly an object of science. Moreover, this purely metaphorical knowledge cannot be compared, strictly speaking, and as to its content, with analogical knowledge, which is the ordinary mode of religious knowledge. The latter enables us to know, by the aid of essential and therefore permanent relations, the ontological properties of the objects which it presents to us. The metaphor and the symbol address themselves to the imagination; the analogy speaks to the understanding.

The symbolo-fideist theology of Auguste Sabatier and Eugene Ménégoz is sharply divided from Thomist and Calvinist theology by its theory of knowledge. Analogy gives religious knowledge a substantial content, and dogma an element of stability, permanence, and absoluteness, which the modern Paris school is powerless to impart. The latter merely throws dogma into the whirlwind of the evolution of intellectual culture.

CHAPTER 14

CERTAIN DOCTRINES CONSIDERED IN RELATION TO EPISTEMOLOGY

One of the features which gives Reformed theology its peculiar character and religious value is that it proclaims, like no other, the sublime paradox that the God of religion who desires to be for each of us a Father and a Saviour,[1] is precisely the One whose infinite essence and incommunicable perfections are the object of the vain speculations of metaphysics. By this affirmation it echoes the religion of the prophets. "Thus saith the high and lofty One that inhabiteth eternity, whose name is holy: I dwell in the high and holy place, with him that is of a contrite and humble spirit, to revive the spirit of the humble and to revive the heart of the contrite ones" (Isaiah 57: 15). It is this paradox which gives religion its mystery: which gives piety its ecstasy of sacred wonder which custom cannot stale: which gives Calvinism its pre-eminence above all other theologies.

Pantheism claims that the two concepts of God united in religion are irreconcilable. Deism, on the other hand, declares this synthesis to be dangerous for religion and morality. Both agree in denouncing it as leaving us in an agnostic position. There is no way of escape except by choosing between the metaphysical and the ethical concept. Pantheism attacks the dogmatic concepts of God as Father, Lord and King, which correspond to those assigned by Calvin to the religious idea of God as "Master and Lord, Father and Saviour."[2]

Perhaps the most complete critique of this has been made by Höffding, who objects to the ascription of personality to God and declares that monotheism leads to a religious paradox, reducing the idea of the deity to antimony: "God is immutable", says scholasticism; and "God is the most mutable of beings" says Kierkegaard. In his preliminary remarks, he observes that the "figurative ideas" in question express and suppose relations: from which he infers that they can never lead to an absolute conclusion.[3] If by this he means that there is incompatibility between the ideas of the absolute and of the relative, we simply

---

[1] *Geneva Catechism*, xxi.   [2] *Ibid.*, xxxi.
[3] *Op. cit.*, p. 76.

deny his premise. The absolute, as we understand it—as all the world understands it, pantheists apart—does not exclude every relation: it excludes only relations of dependence. If Höffding merely means that we cannot, by speculation, grasp God in Himself, that we cannot have an absolute knowledge of Him apart from relation and comparison with ourselves, we are ready to subscribe to his view. In so doing, we are merely affirming our agreement with classical Calvinism.

Speaking of God, Calvin says: "His essence is incomprehensible in such wise that His majesty (*numen*) is indeed hidden far from our senses. . . . His virtues are recounted by which He is demonstrated to us, not as He is in himself but as He is towards us."[1] So that this knowledge consists rather in living experience than in "vain speculation."[2]

The quiddity of God, God considered in Himself, is totally inaccessible to us: we can only know His qualities in relation to ourselves.[3] This is implied in the notion of analogical knowledge in which there is nothing that need trouble us. The idea of God, the absolute cause, as we have seen does not exclude all relation. If it did so, religion would be impossible, for religion is relation to God. Religion excludes only those relations which are not susceptible of demonstration, whether in virtue of His nature, His essential relationships with created nature, or His free decree.

The identity supposed to exist between the terms absolute and non-related would make a pseudo-idea of the absolute. It would deny the relation of the absolute to our minds in the very act of stating such a relation. This relation is established by our concept of it, whether, that is, we consider it as in relation to or distinct from us. This would, indeed, be a contradiction: for either this relation is acknowledged, in which case the absolute is not absolutely absolute; or it is denied, in which case the very thesis that the absolute is identical with non-relations is denied.

From this it will be evident that the foundation of the general criticism made by Höffding and Romanes (in the agnostic phase of his thought) of the "figurative ideas" of religion is faulty. These figurative ideas are, it will be remembered, the ideas of king and lord: of father and person. Applied to God, they express the fundamental dogmas of religion. The method of Höffding and others consists in showing that if these ideas are sublimated (the way of eminence) it will lead us to recognize in the being thus sublimized a nature entirely different from that

[1] *Inst.* I, v. 1. [2] *Ibid.*, I, x. 3.
[3] *Ibid.*, I, ii. 2.

CERTAIN DOCTRINES CONSIDERED

of the kings, lords, etc., to which the analogy relates. Thus, for example, an infinite person would have nothing in common with what we know as a person in ordinary experience. Thence, it is concluded that these ideas applied to God are concepts totally devoid of all thinkable content.

We acknowledge that it is with good reason that we say that God, in His essence, in His qualities, transcends all beings. We subscribe to this with all our heart, for it agrees with the word of the prophet already cited: "God is most high, whose dwelling is eternity and whose name is Holy." Holy, that is to say, separated, ontologically and logically, separated absolutely, from all that is not Himself. As Calvin says: "His essence is the object of adoration rather than of scientific exploration."[1] Having said this, however, we maintain that Höffding only arrives at his conclusion by begging the question.

The point under discussion is whether by analogy we can have a qualitative knowledge of being whose quiddity is inaccessible to us, precisely because we know that this quiddity and these virtues are what they are in an eminent degree. To know this is, surely, to know Him already as perfect, as realizing in a supreme degree the equivalent of all the positive qualities of finite beings. But to know Him thus is to be totally ignorant of Him no longer: it is to know Him by means of an idea which declares that He is the ocean of being and that He differs totally from the abstract conception of being in general (*ens generalissimum*). The concept of perfect being is the richest of all concepts: the concept of being in general, the poorest. The latter has no separate existence; an abstraction from the totality of finite beings, it is nothing but the phantom without distinct reality imagined by pantheism.

But, since the "totally different" who reveals Himself to us is such only in so far as He realizes, in an eminent degree, what is known by experience, it is clear that this "known" is merely the ectype, the analogical reproduction of this "totally different", who is its archetype. The known, being the realization of a thought of the Creator, reflects in an infinitesimal degree, indeed, but, after all, reflects something of the glory and of the "virtues" of Him who is its archetype. In all that is positive, the "known" accessible to our thought bears the impress of creative thought. The relations which unite finite beings among themselves and then finite beings and their qualities possess certain analogies with the divine being and the intra-divine relations.

These analogies, not only yield a sufficiently vital material

[1] *Inst.* I, v. 9.

knowledge of God but they are also capable of offering a precise, though limited, knowledge of the essential element or elements of identity of relations which we must hold. For, by the method of negation, from the proved analogies, we can eliminate all that is limitation: matter, inferiority, dependence on outside things: the term of comparison chosen in order to construct an analogical idea is thus taken in its essential acceptation and stripped of its accidental modalities.[1]

This abstract concept is obviously not capable of being imagined. So far as the imagination is concerned, it is a concept to which no sensible image can be applied: but, since it is composed of intelligible elements contained in sensible beings, it is not empty of meaning for the understanding. On the contrary, it is strictly scientific, for it is general, universal, and we know that there is no science but that of the general and that all things, general and universal, are objects of science.

The reason why nominalists claim that concepts thus formed are empty of all thinkable content is because they themselves think of images, and naturally they want clear images. The moderate realist, on the other hand, asks only for intelligible concepts. For him the concept of a myriagon, which he cannot naturally translate into a sensible and clear image, is a concept as strictly intelligible as that of a pentagon, so easy to construct by the imagination.

It is one thing indeed to conceive an idea ; quite another, to imagine it. Pantheism, true to its confusionism, tends continually to lose sight of this distinction. When it abandons itself to nominalism it confounds, with equal consistency, the empirical conditions of the realization of an idea taken for granted in our world, with the essence of this idea. Knowing for example, that the opposition between the ego and the non-ego constitutes personality, that the rhythm of finite life is formed by a succession of actions and passions, it immediately takes these accidental modalities for the essence of personality.[2]

These modalities belong, of course, to the personality only. Strictly speaking, they are merely accidents in the logical sense of the term. What causes a being to be a person is essentially this: that he is a rational and intelligent substance. To say that the nature of God is personal is to say that intelligence is one of His essential attributes. It will be noticed that we say that the divine nature is personal and not that God is personal.

---

[1] [Modality (Kant: German, *Modalität*), concerning the mode—actuality, possibility or necessity in which anything exists.]
[2] Höffding, *op. cit.*, p. 80 ff.

This is because the latter formula is not exact from the trinitarian point of view. God is not a person: His is a personal nature which has its real triple centre and support in three hypostases.

But, reduced to the affirmation that God knows Himself and knows things in an intelligent manner, the idea of personality applied to Him and thus carried to infinity, preserves a sufficiently intellectual residuum, since it is not permissible to speak of unthinkable notions. The man who prays, who believes that his prayer is prompted by an infinite Spirit and received by an infinite Intelligence, cannot accept the view that it would be all the same if he were to replace this affirmation of his faith by another, namely, that prayer has its origin in the unknowable and that it is in the unknowable that it loses itself.

The same must be said of the analogies of Lord, King and Father. Höffding reproaches the analogy of Lord-King with implying an eternal relation between "different" beings. He finds this relation ridiculous, no doubt because he is unable to conceive of God as otherwise than identical with ourselves. But what is absurd for the believing reason, at any rate, is to reduce the infinite being to this degrading confusion.

No doubt, there is nothing more interior to us than God: *Quid interius deo?* But at the same time, there is nothing which is qualitatively more external and more transcendent. At the moment, however, this is not the point under discussion. What is in question is whether that which is essential and formal in the notions of Lord and King can be predicated legitimately of God.

Now, the essential point in these ideas is the notion of a will normative for us, served by a power capable of annihilating all opposition and of protecting efficaciously. To affirm these things in an eminent degree is evidently not to lose all contact with reality. The same remark agrees with the analogy borrowed from human paternity. In spite of Höffding's suggestions, the essential idea of paternity does not in the least imply "the maternal relation", nor the pedagogic preparation of children for independence in regard to the father. These are characteristics proper to human paternity only and are therefore the accidents.

The essential idea is this: a being is the principle of projection into existence of other beings, or of another being of the same substance as itself. Properly speaking, then, God is essentially and absolutely Father. He is so, without having need of creatures, by the eternal generation of His Word. [1] In an

---

[1] Athanasius, *Orat. cont. Arian*, ii, 2; *ad Serap.*, ii, 2; *de decr. Nic. syn.*, xii.

improper sense (*aequivoce*), symbolically, He is the Father of all creatures. In an analogical sense, by adoption—the very term is clearly analogical—He is the Father of the elect: to all who believe, says the Gospel, He has given the power to be made the sons of God.

This term, adoption, stripped of its juridical accidents, preserves the very intelligible residuum that God treats believers as an adoptive Father, full of tenderness, would treat the son whom he had admitted into his family. When we say that God is a Father to believers, inasmuch as He adopts them as His children, the essential idea of adoption that we have just defined remains the intelligible residuum of the affirmation. The belief that God is our Father by right of creation and by an act of free grace is by no means a vague notion. On the contrary, it has in view a very precise idea.

In becoming immeasurably profound, this idea plunges into the mysterious and incomprehensible, losing nothing of its strict precision in the process. Astonishing, unmerited, exalted above all known psychological conditions as is the fact, the essential notion of adoption remains unchanged. It is only after the pedagogic preparation which is necessary to bring the son to his majority that it corresponds to a positive reality in the religious life.

It is not astonishing, perhaps, that Höffding, who appears to be a stranger to these most gracious and profound modalities, has not been able to see this fact. But the fact is there. God is the Father of the predestinated, not only because He treats them with a truly paternal love but because He is an educator in this precise sense that he arranges events in such a manner that we can pass from the spiritual minority (observance of literal prescriptions) to the spiritual majority, to the spontaneous distinction between good and evil (Hebrews 5: 14). Naturally, it is not a question of us becoming independent of God. But does not a king's son remain always, even when he has attained his majority, the subject of his father? And, as believers, are we not sons of the King?

Finally, Höffding claims that the images of Lord and Father are inconsistent when God is represented as demanding a bloody sacrifice to appease His wrath. That would imply the relationship of "a cruel Oriental lord", and not that of a father with his children. Hence, the impossibility of constructing a coherent system from images, according to his view. The point to be noticed is that dogmatics, which has for its object our relations with the infinite being, must not undertake the task assigned to it by modern theology and seek to simulate the internal unity to which every system of pantheistic metaphysics aspires in vain. It is understood that the notions and analogies of which it treats are unfathomable mysteries at the points at which they touch the infinite.

But it can make, or at least it can aspire to make, syntheses of mysteries. The doctrines of divine sovereignty and divine paternity express realities as objects of faith which the intelligence can formulate and specify, and the harmony of which can be perceived by the reasoned reason (*ratio ratiocinata*). But independent reason (*ratio ratiocinans*) can have no adequate notion of it, and is thus incompetent to declare that the notions which it cannot explore are contradictory. And the faith which receives them in virtue of a *Deus dixit*, of a divine authority, can and must anticipate their internal accord. Otherwise, theological science would be incapable of making a synthesis between two certain data of the faith, such as the divine sovereignty and the divine paternity, and it would not be able to arrive at any other conclusion than that of its own infirmity.

As to the association of ideas insulting to the faith of orthodox Christians, which Höffding's mind entertains, such as the associations of the divine demand for a bloody sacrifice and the caprice of a cruel oriental lord, it is nothing more than a psychological phenomenon which can only be explained by ignorance, misunderstanding, or forgetfulness of the basis of dogma. It is not a reason which is invoked here but a case of irrational physical repulsion.

In this fashion, we find ourselves transported into the uneasy and obscure realm of passion, situated below the spheres in which discussion can be profitable. But it will suffice to take knowledge of the actual dogma that is supposed to be false, in order to see that the accusation of cruelty is calumnious. Whether the necessity of the bloody immolation of the Redeemer results from an arbitrary decree (Scotus, Occam, Gabriel Biel, Luther, Zwingli); from the exigencies of justice (Irenaeus, Basil, Anselm, Beza, Piscator, Voetius); or from reasons of convenience; or whether the demands of the human conscience are taken into consideration (Athanasius, Gregory Nazianzen, John Damascene, Augustine, Peter Lombard, Thomas Aquinas, Calvin, Zanchius, Peter Martyr, Twisse), there is no question of a cruel lord. Under any hypothesis, he who immolates himself is not a person taken from among humanity as a scapegoat: that would be the Nestorian heresy. On the contrary, it is the offended One Himself, God, one of whose hypostases assumes a human nature

in order to become possible and to be able to suffer for and instead of, the offenders. The subject who sacrifices himself is not
the person of a man but the second person of the Trinity, God,
who has taken on Himself a human nature. The formula of the
dogma is: one person and two natures. The bond between the
natures is hypostatic and the person providing the bond is
divine. If, with Scotus, we professed the primacy of the will over
the intelligence in God, we might, indeed speak of caprice: but
even then it would be the sublime caprice of the love which immolates itself, and the King would be cruel only towards Himself. If it be said that the ecclesiastical dogma is defective from
the point of view of exegesis or of metaphysics, we can discuss
the matter; but we are confident that, for every unbiassed mind,
a correct exposition will suffice to refute the accusation that it
has anything to do with the cruelty of an oriental tyrant.

It is inevitable that deism, even when it calls itself Christian,
should charge orthodoxy with agnosticism. Bois directs his
criticisms specifically against Calvinism, indicating as the source
of Calvinistic agnosticism what he calls its infinitism,[1] invoking
as proof of this the Calvinian notions of the incomprehensibility
of the essence of God, of the image of God in man, of the subjectivism of certain dogmatic formulae, of the cause of the
decree of predestination. We shall not stay to consider these
notions except from the epistemological point of view, the only
one which concerns us here.

It is well known that Renouvier was a determined opponent
of the idea of the infinite. Bois shared the hostility of the leader
of the French neo-critical school, like him conceiving the infinite only under the numerical aspect of totality of beings.[2]
He attributed the notion to a Philonic and neo-Platonic
origin. "It is because of its infinitism, latent or avowed, that
Calvinism is so profoundly agnostic."[3]

It is true that Calvin, like the schoolmen, believed the divine
essence to be infinite.[4] But for him, as for them, the infinity of
God is of the qualitative, and not quantitative, order; and
Bois is mistaken when he identifies Calvin's conception of the
infinity of the divine essence with this "notion contradictory in
itself"; the infinity of actually realized quantity. For the
Reformer confesses no less firmly that the divine essence is
spiritual.

The essential and replenishing presence of God in the universe

---

[1] Bois, *La Philosophie de Calvin*, Paris, 1919, p. 14 ff.
[2] *Ibid.*, p. vi, n. 1.   [3] *Ibid.*, p. 6 and *passim*.
[4] Vide *Praelect. in Jer.*, xi, 18.

must not be conceived otherwise than under the spiritual mode. Aquinas had already said: "The infinite is encountered, properly speaking, in the order of quantity . . . but infinity cannot be attributed to God except in relation to spiritual greatness." [1]

In other words, the term "infinite" is applicable in the positive sense to the imaginary space which we represent to ourselves under the mode of the material, concrete space, in which we cannot register limits that are not contained therein. By analogy, we employ this term as an epithet of the spiritual essence of God in order to express the truth that this is perfect in a supreme degree: and that nothing can be added to it in respect of reality because it is by itself and in itself, being; and because, properly speaking, God alone is, eternally, immutably. It is important to notice that thus, for Calvin, the infinity of the divine essence is formally and immediately the eternity of being, in the proper and unique sense: that is to say, aseity. This is taught everywhere in Scripture, for the sacred name recurs in it continually. It is only as a legitimate deduction that the omnipresence of the divine essence can be affirmed. But, while we acknowledge that it has a religious importance of the first order, since it serves to distinguish God from false gods, the moment it becomes a subject for scientific subtlety, it develops into one of those idle and sterile speculations which Scripture does not formulate explicitly because its purpose is not to give us empty knowledge. What it does teach explicitly is the infinity of the providence and the knowledge of God. [2]

It will thus be seen how contrary to the truth is the view that Calvin put in the foreground the metaphysical attribute of the infinity of the divine essence which he confounded with the infinity of the essence of God. To say that this essential omnipresence is not taught explicitly in Scripture is merely to repeat what Calvin has already said. He declares, in effect, that the passages which are habitually adduced to establish it either ought not to be explained in this sense or cannot be so explained without violence. [3]

---

[1] *Contra gentiles*, i, 43.

[2] *Inst.* Latin text of 1554, I, x. 2: *Jehovah, Jehovah . . . animadvertamus eius aeternitatem magnifice illo nomine bis repetito praedicari.* What corresponds to this paragraph in the French edition of 1560 will be found in paragraph 3, thus: *Son éternité et son essence résidant en lui-même sont annoncées par ce nom Jehovah . . . qui vaut autant à dire comme celui qui est seul.* His eternity and His essence residing in Himself are announced by this name (Jehovah) . . . which is equivalent to saying that He alone is. Cf. *Com. on Acts*, xvii, 28: "God distinguishes Himself from all (every) creature(s) in naming Himself Jehovah . . . in order that we may know that, properly speaking, He alone is."

[3] *Vide* App. X, p. 394.

While holding this to be the case, he does not dwell on it. Moreover, he cannot conceive this omnipresence as other than spiritual, according to the formula *totus in toto*. Thus, we are very far from the infinitude of extended greatness. Indeed, Calvin joins to the epithet "infinite" that of "spiritual", precisely in order to combat the idea of an infinite diffusion of substance which Bois imputes to him. He declares, moreover, that it is in order to avoid this interpretation that he does so: and he says this in a passage which the dean of Montpellier invokes in order to show that Calvin's notion of the incomprehensibility of the infinite "proceeds from pantheism and returns to it."[1]

Here is the passage which, strange to say, Bois quotes: "The infinity of His essence must affright us if we are not careful to measure it in this sense, and His spiritual nature must prevent us from vainly speculating concerning Him in an earthly or carnal manner."[2] If this severe critic of Calvin had taken the trouble to read the development of a dozen lines of which his quotation forms the conclusion, he would have seen that Calvin declares that spirituality joined to infinity, as he understands it, in the divine essence, will suffice to refute the speculations of the philosophers; and, in particular, of those who interpret the essential infinity as an extended (and thus quantitative) diffusion: "What is shown to us in Scripture concerning the infinite and spiritual essence of God is said not only in order to overthrow the foolish dreams of the vulgar but will serve equally to discredit all the subtleties of the profane philosophers." What subtleties are these? There is the quantitative infinite, the affirmation of which is imputed to Calvin at the very moment when he condemns it. "One among them thinks he has found a fine aphorism saying that God is what we see and what we do not see."[3] Here is the equation: infinity=everything. "Now, in speaking thus, he imagined the deity to be apportioned (*in singulares mundi partes divinitatem transfusam esse*) throughout the world." How does Calvin now estimate this notion of the infinite which Bois attributes to Him? This is what he says: "It is true that God, in order to keep us in sobriety, does not give us a long account of His essence, yet by the two titles that we have quoted [namely, infinite and spiritual] He destroys the vain dreams of men and thus holds in check "the audacity of the human mind." Calvin concludes with the quotation given by Bois, in which the Reformer says the very opposite to what is attributed to him. In the first part of this quotation, he rebukes

[1] *Op. cit.*, p. 11.   [2] *Ibid.*, p. 13.
[3] The idea is derived from Seneca, *Praef.* lib. I, *quest. nat.*

the extravagant speculations of the schoolmen, and, in the second, those of the pantheists[1] who understand the omnipresence of God as a material diffusion of substance.

It is all the more astonishing that this pantheistic notion should be attributed to Calvin, seeing that it was this very point which provoked the most tragic of all his conflicts, namely, his controversy with Servetus. The *Institutes* by itself makes this sufficiently plain.[2]

The pantheistic notion of numerical infinity leads to the idea of God as unknowable. It would not be surprising to find that the qualitative and spiritual infinity of Calvin and Aquinas led to the incomprehensibility of God, which is by no means the same thing. Two different ideas naturally produce two different results. Bois is mistaken in assimilating the infinite of orthodox theology, which he attacks in the person of Calvin, to the All and the Number: but he is no happier when he assigns to it a Philonic and neo-Platonic origin. It is beyond the scope of this work to study the Philonic and neo-Platonic notion of the infinite,[3] nor is it our intention to dispute the abstract possibility of quasi-direct borrowing by Calvin from this philosophy, via the pseudo-Dionysius. Calvin knew and criticized the latter, while recognizing that there were good things in it.[4] He would have no reason to turn to current ideas, floating in the intellectual atmosphere of the times, as Bois seems to think.[5]

As a direct proof of borrowing by Calvin from a "non-Christian philosophy", Bois points to the fact that the Reformer has these curious lines on the subject of the angels: "God finds that there is folly and vanity among the angels, He finds fault with the angels . . . although they are His servants . . . Behold he finds no steadfastness in His saints (i.e., angels) and the heavens are not clean in His sight."[6] As an indirect proof, Bois offers the absence of the idea of the infinite from Scripture. "The idea of the infinite", he claims, "is not Biblical; it is to be found neither in the Old Testament nor in the New."[7] In his

---

[1] The word is relatively recent, dating from John Tolland in the 18th century; the idea is as ancient as the human mind fallen through sin.

[2] *Inst.* I, xiii, 22.

[3] This idea in neo-Platonism seems to us to signify the indefinite, the indeterminate; cf. Zeller, *Philos. der Gr.*, V, 485 f.; 497.

[4] *Com. on Acts*, xvii, 34: "As for the book of the divine names, while it contains things which one need not altogether reject, it is nevertheless more subtle than religious."

[5] *Op. cit.*, p. 4 f.

[6] *Opera*, xxxiii, 724, quoted by H. Bois, *op. cit.*, p. 63.

[7] *Op. cit.*, p. 66.

proofs of fact, the neo-critical theologian is particularly un-happy. He sees in the words of Calvin, which we have just quoted, and in others preceding and following them, and which form a commentary on them, the proof that Calvin believed in an infinite justice in God, in comparison with which the (finite) justice of men and angels paled: "like the stars which seem clear and shining during the night but which lose all their light when the sun appears on the scene"; and the learned professor is certainly justified in this conclusion. Where he is mistaken is in thinking that these words and their commentary are of Philonic inspiration. They are merely translated, for the most part, strictly literally from the Book of Job (4: 18–19) on which Calvin comments faithfully. Thus, whatever may be said, it is in the Bible and not in Philo that Calvin finds this con-trast between the infinite justice of God and the finite justice of the creature. This is sufficient, after having demolished the posi-tive proof, to invalidate the proof built upon the pretended absence of the idea of the infinite from the Bible. We would add that in the New Testament this opposition between the infinite goodness of God and the finite goodness of the creature is so marked that Jesus, in a saying universally acknowledged to be genuine, rejects the epithet "good" which the rich young man attributes to Him and declares that it belongs only to God (Mark 10: 18). He would thus have approved the words of Job, adopted by Calvin, on the imperfection of the angels. And he was an infinitist in the manner of the author of the Book of Job and of his gifted commentator. Besides, as the latter observes: "the Scripture so frequently and so plainly declares that there is one only God, of an infinite, eternal and spiritual essence, that there is no reason to make a long proof of it", [1] provided that one does not confound the infinite of Calvin, the synonym of perfection, with that of Spinoza, the synonym of the diffuse extension of the unique substance, equivalent to the totality of being. The first notion places us in the presence of the mystery of being and thus

---

[1] Nevertheless, certain texts may be indicated whose exactness leaves nothing to be desired. Infinity, in relation to being, is the plenitude, the im-mutability, of being: Exod. 3: 15, 16; John 5: 26; Mal. 3: 6; Jas. 1: 17. Absoluteness in relation to time is eternity without succession: Ps. 90: 2; John 8: 58. In relation to space it is immensity overflowing: 1 Kings 8: 27. In relation to power, omnipotence: Luke 1: 37; Mark 14: 36. In relation to thought, fathomlessness: Rom. 11: 33, etc. We merely mention these texts at random. We are absolutely unable to understand how anyone can say that the idea of infinity is absent from the Bible. Not to entertain such an idea would imply that one was not persuaded psychologically as to the co-ordination of space and imaginary time. The infinite is taken for granted by the simple fact that it is impossible to imagine a limit which is not contained in it. Consciousness of the infinite is implied in that of the finite.

protects us against the illusion of the possibility of attaining to an adequate knowledge of God. But it also preserves us from agnosticism, for it is because of what we know of God that we know that it is impossible for us to comprehend His essence and that we adore this essence instead of making it the subject of a philosophical enquiry.

We need not dwell long on the proof of our Reformer's agnosticism drawn from the modifications that he made in his notion of the image of God in man. In the *Psychopannychia* published in 1542, Calvin maintained that Adam's body was not an element of the image of God, who is spirit and can have only a spiritual image; by 1560 he had come to believe that the image of God resides not only in the soul but in the body also. He would thus seem to have become an agnostic or to have ceased to be so: "in the measure in which one insists on placing the image of God in the body as in the spirit, in this same measure one weakens . . . one tends to regard the spirit and the body as inadequate symbols of a God who is as much above the one as the other, who is in the final analysis an unknowable x."

If it is a question of measure, let us reassure ourselves: Calvin is nowhere near agnosticism. For, forced to concede to his adversary, Osiander, that, after all, the soul is not the whole man and that our bodily form, distinguishing us from the beasts, brings us closer to God in the same measure. Calvin writes in the edition of 1560: "How greatly the glory of God shines forth even in the outward man: nevertheless there can be no doubt that its seat is in the soul." Then, leaving as it were, regretfully, the concession with which he is reproached, he continues: "I will not contradict it at all, provided that this point remains always granted, that the image of God which shines clearly in these evident marks or even shows some little glimmer is spiritual: for some who, like Osiander, are too speculative, place it as much in the body as in the soul, mixing as it were, the earth with the sky." Thus Calvin concludes that the body "shows some little glimmer" of the image of God. His agnosticism is an insignificant matter after all.

Orthodox theologians admit freely that divine realities cannot be expressed adequately in human language. Professor Ridderbos, a contemporary Calvinist theologian, remarks that Scripture "is written in human languages, under the sentence of the curse of the confusion of tongues, and which are, for yet other reasons, imperfect vehicles for the transmission of human thoughts, and, *a fortiori*, of divine thoughts."[1]

[1] J. Ridderbos, *Gereformeerde schriftbeschouwing*, p. 26.

This is Calvin's view also. Apropos of the mystery of redemption, he writes: "In Scripture the Holy Spirit ordinarily uses this manner of speaking: that God was the enemy of men until they were reunited to Him in grace by the death of Christ . . . now, such a manner of speaking is accommodated to our sense, in order that we may understand better the misery of man's condition without Christ. For, if it were not clearly expressed that the wrath and vengeance of God, and eternal death, were upon us, we should not understand sufficiently, and as we ought, how poor and miserable we are without the mercy of God and we should not value at its true worth the benefit which He has shown in delivering us."[1]

From this it follows, one may say, that such a manner of speaking has only a subjective value and is designed solely to express or to provoke these sentiments in man . . . and, if so, are we not complete agnostics in regard to God? Certainly such a manner of speaking has only a subjective value but it is not designed solely to provoke subjective sentiments. One has only to read the paragraph which follows to see that, behind these subjective forms, Calvin recognizes and formulates objective realities which teach us, not indeed the mysteries of the divine essence, but what God is objectively for us. Let us hear Calvin and we shall realize how much he has been misunderstood not only by his heterodox enemies but even by his friends. "Now, it is indeed true that God, in using such a style, accommodates Himself to our ignorance. For He who is sovereign justice cannot love iniquity, which He sees in us all. We have thus matter enough in us to cause us to be hated by Him. Moreover, in regard to our corrupt nature, as also to our evil life, we are always worthy of the hatred of God, born in condemnation, and guilty under His judgment."

Here we have the objective fact, which this manner of speaking expresses in such a way as to provoke in us subjective sentiments adequate to the objective reality.

But why then does Calvin consider the formula of redemption as a manner of speaking? For the reason that it is a question of surmounting a logical difficulty. The love of God is the cause of the sending of His Son into the world. It is true anterior to the reconciliation procured by His death but nevertheless this death was necessary.[2] This difficulty will be surmounted if one takes into account the first objective fact that we have just noticed: God hates us in so far as we are sinners; also the second objec-

----

[1] *Inst.* II, xvi. 2, quoted by H. Bois: *op. cit.*, p. 15.
[2] *Supra* just before the quotation by H. Bois.

tive fact, which is this: "Because God does not wish to lose in us that which is His, His benignity still finds in us something to love: for, already, while we were sinners by our own fault, nevertheless we remained always His creatures."

And Calvin proceeds to show that God, who loves us in so far as we are His creatures, conceived the plan of redemption in order that sin might be expiated and that thus the reconciliation provoked by His love might be sealed at the foot of the Cross. We have not to enquire here whether, as we believe, his reasoning is valid. The question is simply whether our Reformer had in view merely the subjective facts and was thus the precursor of symbolo-fideism. We think we have furnished proof to the contrary. The richness of the divine realities always overflows in infinite measure the most beautiful and the most profound dogmatic formulae. It does not in the least follow from this that the latter are designed solely to provoke sentiments. While they are designed for this purpose they also invariably shed some intellectual light on the reality. They have always a residuum of "truth" intellectually intelligible and objective.

As to predestination, it might be said to favour or express agnosticism in the following manner. Calvin says that "it is nothing else but the order and dispensation of divine justice, which cannot be held worthy of blame, however secret it may be."[1]

Now here, it must be acknowledged, and Calvin is never tired of repeating it, we are in the presence of the most profound and formidable of the mysteries which Scripture proposes to our faith.

Formally, predestination must be understood to signify "the eternal counsel of God, by which He has determined that which He wills to do to every man. For He does not create all in the same condition but ordains some to eternal life and others to eternal damnation. Thus, according to the end for which man is created, we say that he is predestined to death or to life."[2] What renders the mystery insoluble is that, on the one hand, God being just, the destiny reserved for the reprobate could not be what it is if they were not unworthy; while, on the other hand, God being the independent Being on whom all things depend, the determinations of His will could not be caused by creatures. Thus, the object of the decree is not man considered as already fallen and rebellious, but man considered as creatable,[3]

---

[1] *Inst.* III, xxiii. 8.   [2] *Ibid.*, xxi. 5.
[3] *Ibid.*, xxiii. 8: "As if God had not determined what He desired the condition of the chief of His creatures to be."

and due to fall[1] certainly, yet nevertheless freely. In this sense Calvin is a supralapsarian. "The foundation of predestination does not rest on works at all. If, therefore, we cannot find another reason why it is that God accepts His children except that it so please Him, we shall also be unable to find any other reason why He rejects others, except His will."[2]

The question can be put in these terms: things being so, in what sense, intelligible to us, can God be said to be just? Is not the expression: "justice of God" devoid of meaning, and are we not thrown back into agnosticism?

If Calvin had been a nominalist, like Occam, or merely an advocate of the *dominium absolutum* of Duns Scotus, we should have to reply in the affirmative. But the dean of Montpellier, confronted with the evidence adduced by Calvinists, is obliged to admit, with a certain bad grace, indeed, but to admit all the same, that such is not the case. The will of God is, for us, the reason beyond which there is nothing to seek. But this will is not caprice: it possesses in itself its reasons, and its reasons are just.[3]

It will be agreed by some that the God of Calvin is not that of Scotus or Descartes. He does not say: "it is just because I will it", but: "I will it because it is just." On the other hand, it has been contended that "his doctrine is that of Spinoza, who sees no more resemblance between divine and human justice than exists between the constellation of *Canis major* and a barking dog: it is the Kantian doctrine of Sabatier concerning the god Noumenon, the unknowable God, the God x in itself."[4]

Two arguments are adduced to support this identification of Calvinian predestination with Kantian agnosticism.[5] In the first place, a dilemma: if the justice of God is incomprehensible because it is infinite, of two things one follows: either this infinity is quantitative or it is qualitative. In the first case, there is no more difference between the good and the bad than between plus or minus. In the second case, the good, the justice, the holiness of God, have nothing in common with the things which bear the same name in man.

We reply that spiritual things cannot be weighed, measured or counted: the infinite in God is not one attribute added to

---

[1] *Inst.* III, xxiii. 5: "I say with Augustine (Ep. cvi) that the Lord created those who, as He certainly foreknew, would go to eternal perdition, and He did so because He so willed."

[2] *Ibid.*, xii. 11.

[3] *Inst.* III, xxiii. 2 and *passim.*   [4] H. Bois, *op. cit.*, p. 24.

[5] It is curious to note, in passing, that Fouilles in his *Idées Forces* connects Kantianism with Calvin, approaching the question from an entirely different angle.

others. The divine virtues are synonymous with unlimited perfection, and between them and ours is a difference of quality, such as must exist between a thing perfect, essential, original and archetypical, on the one hand; and a thing imperfect, accidental, derived and ectypical on the other. But, since the justice of God is the original of which justice in angels and men is the reflexion, the shadow or the schematic copy, it cannot be said that this qualitative difference destroys all relationship between the two terms. There exists an analogical relationship. There is an identity of abstract concept: Do no wrong to anyone, render to each what is his due.

Thus, we emerge from the mists of Kantianism. When Jesus says that God alone is good, He does not evacuate the phrase "goodness of God" of all meaning, but He enriches the idea to such an extent that it surpasses all conception.

Here is the argument: It is essentially unjust to force an innocent person to become guilty in order that he may merit damnation. To claim that we shall realize the justice of the matter when we are more enlightened is equivalent to saying that what is obviously evil to-day will be good later, and to laying down a principle of moral agnosticism which recalls that of Duns Scotus.

We agree; but our opponent has missed the whole point of the mystery. It is no question of believing that God is just in forcing an innocent person to sin and in consigning him to the chastisement which is its consequence. On the contrary, in its supralapsarian interpretation, the dogma teaches precisely that the objects of the decree of reprobation "were not unworthy of being predestined to such an end."[1] The mystery is involved in the relations which must exist between a Being perfectly holy and just, on the one hand, and creatures that He is about to create holy and free, but who, He sees, will certainly sin if He does not restrain their liberty from the moment when they are placed in the presence of the moral trial to which He agrees that they should be subjected. To reply, with Calvin, that we must leave this problem with God does not make one an agnostic. It is simply to be profoundly religious, and reasonable also; for it is clear that we lack the elements for forming an opinion on the subject.

To say, with Bois, that free acts are by definition incapable of being foreseen is not to convict Calvinism of moral agnosticism: it is simply to beg the question. In fact, Calvin's thesis is precisely that an act of which the futurition is certain can be perfectly free in its mode of realization.[2] In order that the

[1] *Inst.* III, xxiii. 8.   [2] *Ibid.*, I, xv. 8.

futurition of any act whatever may be certain, it is sufficient that the reasons which determine it should in fact be known or foreseen. In order that this act should be free, it is necessary and sufficient that the said determining reasons should not annihilate, in the agent, the formal and physical power of the contrary act: that he should have the psychological power not to will that which he does will.

The world of realities issues from the order of possibles conceived in the infinite intelligence by a voluntary decree: all reality thus depends as to its futurition on God. On the other hand, the means employed by God are such that they do not destroy the formal liberty of the creature; but, on the contrary, establish it in all its spontaneity and rational lucidity.

The world of reality, ordained and directed by God is a universe in which the realm of values has its place. Now this realm, through the contingent judgments of which it is the object, is a sphere of liberty. The divine decree of which creatures are ignorant is not the determining reason which dictates their conduct. The determining reasons are those of which they have consciousness and which express the profound aspirations of their spontaneous personality, the orientation being actually taken by this conscious spontaneity, deliberately, and, therefore, freely.

In this case, it would seem that all that exists must owe its origin to the first causality. This is so, for God is sovereign: but since sin, or free disobedience, has made its appearance in the world, the divine causality is deficient, not efficient. This deficiency corresponds to a directive permission, as distinct from the naked permission of Pelagius.

Since sin is in the world, God is doubtless the material cause of every positive act; but it is equally true that, formally, we are the causes of our own actions. By means of that which is defective and negative in them, we impart to them spontaneously their bad qualities. Being the subjects of our acts, we are thus responsible for them. God does not create the evil in us: He does not impel us to it; but He finds it in us and directs it in such a manner that He limits its more disastrous effects.

We conclude from what has been said that the attempt to reduce to agnosticism the most religious form of the Christian concept of causality represented by Augustinianism, Thomism and Calvinism, has proved a failure. The analogical knowledge of the dogmas criticized remains a knowledge substantially real and formally scientific, although partial, inadequate and consisting in reflected images.

CHAPTER 15

CALVINISTIC REALISM AND SOME TYPES OF RELIGIOUS EPISTEMOLOGY

Before examining the bearing and value of religious knowledge, it seems opportune to specify formally the type of religious knowledge that we mean to establish; and, for that purpose to compare it with the principal present-day theories, which we shall classify in conformity with the division of general knowledge as innatism, empiricism and realism.

Innatism (*vide* note p. 43) is the theory maintained by Auguste Sabatier, disciple of Kant, and Henri Bois, disciple of Renouvier. The former may be considered the most important representative among us of the philosophy of noumena and phenomena. The latter is the dogmatic exponent of the philosophy of phenomena.

Empiricism in religion leads to a utilitarian theory of knowledge (pragmatism) the most influential French representative of which is Le Roy, disciple of Bergson and metaphysician of the philosophy of becoming. To these theories are opposed the neo-scholasticism and the intellectualist neo-realism which profess the philosophy of being. It is with these various currents of thought that we propose to compare our view, which, for the sake of brevity, we shall designate, Calvinistic realism.

Sabatier was responsible for introducing orthodox Kantianism into French-speaking Protestant theology,[1] and for this reason we refer to him rather than to Lobstein's *Introduction à la théologie protestante*, or to Neeser's *Religion hors des limites de la Raison* or his *Problème de Dieu*. Generally speaking, we believe our criticisms of Sabatier to be valid against the two theologians whose names we have just mentioned, because, like him, they are orthodox Kantians, at least in regard to the general theory of knowledge.

By his piety and his religious affinities, Sabatier remains a Huguenot, a Calvinist modernized by Schleiermacher. By his philosophical formation, he reminds us, above all, of Kant. In his system there are at least two minds in conflict, like Jacob and Esau in Rebecca's womb. There is the Huguenot nourished

---

[1] Auguste Sabatier, *Esquisse d'une philosophie de la religion*, Fischbacher, Paris, 1897.

by the Scriptures who meets God in the consciousness which he feels of his utter dependence on the universal being. It is this God who has decreed his destiny, outside of and apart from himself. It is to this Being that he turns in prayer. For this Parisian theologian, the prayer of the heart is religion in action. Religion is thus essentially the consciousness of an immediate relationship with God, which realizes itself pre-eminently in prayer. It implies God entering into vital relationship with the subject of religious knowledge. By the contagious contact of the experience of Christ, this knowledge of God, the master of destiny, becomes the knowledge of God, the heavenly Father of believers. So much for the sensible knowledge of God.

But, for the intellectual knowledge of God, the Kantian critique, which also has a place in Sabatier's thought, conceives things quite differently. Religion does not originate in the prompting of the mind of man by an intelligible word of God. The cry of distress which is the prayer of the heart, religion in action, springs from the conflict between the constraint imposed by phenomenal reality and our aspirations to independence: between the constraint of scientific determinism and faith in liberty, as a condition of moral life. Hence religion is a hunger containing in itself the principle of its appeasement; a question which implies its own reply; a desire for liberation because it is a hope seizing an object experimentally. The subjectivity of the religious man invests this object spontaneously with intellectual colours suggested to him by the forms of his judgment and of his sensibility.

He creates poetic metaphors, naïve and spontaneous symbols, which translate objective reality as well as they can, and later become the matter for a process of intellectual elaboration, the result of which is dogma: a purely symbolical juridical and consequently provisional expression of the spontaneous experience of the religious soul in contact with an indestructible and permanent reality.

Thus, dogmas, petrified and mummified symbols of that which is spirit and life, are all subject to the law of evolution, with its fatal cycle of birth, growth, decay and death. There remains only the experience of piety which attains its culminating point and assumes its normative value in the consciousness of Jesus, in the centre of which is revealed the fatherhood of God.

Now the contradiction between the experience of Sabatier the Huguenot and the theory of Sabatier the Kantian consists in this: in the experience, one has the vision of God such as He is, such as He is towards us, no doubt, but after all such as He is objectively and independently of us. The experience is properly the experience of a relation with an object which interiorizes itself in us.

In the theory, on the contrary, what we see is the concept destitute of an unknowable noumenal being, of a cause x of this "enrichment of life" which is religion, x concerning which we can say nothing to the point; concerning which we cannot even be sure that it is not merely what the English call "our better self", our ego in its better aspect; concerning which we cannot even know whether it will survive a possible disappearance of our globe. It is not difficult to see that the origin of this contradiction must be sought in Sabatier's acceptance of the philosophy of the noumenon.

Since we do not know, it is said, anything about the noumenon but its existence and causal action; since the phenomenon alone is accessible to us, it is very clear that our phenomenal experience does not give us any knowledge other than that of the modifications of our own states of consciousness. We are enclosed in our subjectivity, as within the walls of a prison, and on these walls we trace certain symbols, consoling indeed, but without any special objective significance.

It cannot be said that either Scripture or the immediate data of religious experience—experience which Sabatier described so well because he has proved it—brings the confirmation of its authority to this philosophy.

With Renouvier, we see the opposition of the noumenon and the phenomenon taking place in the phenomenon, sufficing by itself and constituting the entire reality. But what about the noumena which serve as causes to phenomena? Why should the law of causality operate outside the phenomenal series? Besides, these series are finite in number, while they themselves are necessarily finite. In fact, an infinite number is a contradiction in terms.

At this point, one has to admit absolute beginnings. Thus if we "reconcile phenomena with God" (that is to say, in the language of the critical school, if we reconcile existence with Him) we must indeed admit that God Himself has a beginning. Renouvier does not shrink from this terrible conclusion and refuses to God, in whom he believes, immensity in space and eternity in relation to time. French Protestant theology has had, in the person of Bois, an eminent representative of this tendency. With his master, he has a pronounced aversion to what he terms infinitism.

The philosophy of the phenomenon, as Renouvier and Bois

understand it, is intended as a reaction against Kantian agnosticism, that of his *Critique of Pure Reason* and that of Sabatier's *Esquisse*. In our opinion, the reaction was inevitable. On this point, we concur entirely with the verdict of Ménégoz: "Kant, despite his strong Christian heredity, paved the way, without knowing it, for the great movement of ideas which to-day corrodes religious thought and life as acid eats away metal."[1]

Agnostic positivism, with its atheistic degeneration, is in the Kantian succession. In actual fact, an absolutely unknowable God cannot be logically postulated as real by the practical reason, as long as the critique of pure reason exists. The latter invalidates the conclusions of the former.

But the question is whether the neo-Kantian attempt to restore the reality of the object of religious faith has succeeded. We doubt it. The god which Bois gives us in his theory is, indeed, this time, an unknown divinity, a god constructed according to the mean measurements of an anthropomorphic psychology.

Nevertheless, in the same way as Sabatier, Bois had truly found God in his sensible experience, such as He is towards us, but independently of us. Listen to him: "By a spontaneous intuition I know in the most indisputable manner that my being mingles with one which overflows and envelops it: with a consciousness of which mine is the reflexion, with a life of which mine is but the continuation and the radiation. You may regard me as the victim of hallucination and I shall not take offence, because you cannot possibly experience what I experience."

If the Christian has encountered God, the philosopher has had to keep the infinite out of the way. He could not do otherwise, since he accepted the Kantian premises, at least in regard to the idea of space. Moreover, he starts from Kantian postulates: the God that he finds immediately in his experience as a Christian, he postulates as a philosopher in order to rescue Duty. Here we have a conflict between religious experience and the exigencies of the theory.

The critical theory in its native form such as appears in Renouvier can scarcely be integrated into a Christian system of dogmatics without previously having to undergo profound modifications. Moreover, the religious consciousness the most completely independent of tradition feels an instinctive repugnance, in the measure in which it is religious, to the idea of a god who must have had a beginning; a repugnance equal to the protestations of reason confronted with the idea of a being who must

[1] Fernand Ménégoz, *Le problème de la prière*, p. 28.

have been the cause of himself, in the sense that he must have caused his own existence before existing.

Bois is not troubled by this logical contradiction, but he realizes the uneasiness which is provoked in the religious consciousness by the doctrine of a temporal god. Hence, he introduces into the system of Renouvier an amendment intended to deceive the thirst for eternity which characterizes the religious consciousness. Before time, which commenced with creation, and which implies, from what it is, a successive existence in God, he had a simultaneous existence.[1] But it must be understood, of course, that he is a stranger to all beginning.

Unfortunately, Bois can only introduce this happy correction into Renouvier's theory at the price of a disastrous concession and, it would seem, of insoluble contradictions. In fact, to acknowledge in God an existence simultaneous and without commencement or termination, is precisely to acknowledge Him to be immutable and infinite in the order of duration. The "infinitists" could scarcely ask for more. All that they might require would be a statement as to what precisely we are to understand by simultaneity.

But then what becomes of the fundamental principle of Renouvier's phenomenalism according to which it is a contradiction in terms to speak of the infinite as realized? This principle is, nevertheless, accepted by Bois. But how, then, can he speak of a simultaneous duration? Surely, to do so is to make another disastrous concession.

And here lies the contradiction: if the mode of the existence of God is simultaneity, that is to say, if the mode is that of an immutable duration excluding all change in the Being who persists, it follows that the appearance of successive duration, which is ascribed to Him with the introduction of time, can only occur in this simultaneous duration: that it is simultaneous to Him; in other words, that He has successive duration in an immutable manner. Which amounts to saying that God, simultaneously and in the same respect, has an immutable simultaneous existence and that this existence is successive. The principle of contradiction could scarcely be more openly ignored.

Moreover, it is maintained that while God is not infinite, He is, at any rate, perfect. But if He is perfect, how can we admit that He may be mutable in His essence? If He changes, it can only be in order to acquire positive qualities which He does not

[1] H. Bois, *Revue Théol. Quest. Relig.* Montauban, Dec. 1, 1898. In the issue for May 1, 1899, the author maintains his point of view against Eugène Ménégoz, who defends the same notion of eternity as the Arminians.

possess: to lose them or to barter them in exchange for equivalent qualities.

In the first case, this would show that eminent perfection was not His at all, and that He was not yet God: in which event it would be evident that God had not begun.

In the second case, it would not be eminent perfection that He possessed. From that moment, He would be no longer God, and we should indeed have a God without commencement, but it would be a God who comes to an end.

On the third hypothesis, it must be admitted that He is not yet God before changing, since He has not the qualities with which He is going to replace the preceding ones: while, after the exchange, He will still not be God, since He will lack the qualities which He has renounced in order to acquire new ones.[1]

In this case, there is perhaps a god, but there never has been and is not yet God. This is the real significance of the theodicy of Bois. The god whom it presents is no more than a *primus inter pares*, forming part of the series of beings similar to himself, of which he is merely the primary term. He is a good genius endowed with a relative perfection of the same order as can be realized, theoretically, at least, by any creature whatsoever.

God being mutable, the generic and relative perfection recognized in Him is always threatened with degradation. Who cannot see that His moral and psychic stability is endangered by this instability, this ontological corruptibility?

Kant founded faith in God on duty, and thus, in our judgment committed a grave error. But, even so, what he postulated was God, all the same. Neo-Kantianism, as modified by Bois, merely postulates one being greater than the others, and is not certain even that he will be always capable of sustaining the cause of the categorical imperative, which it is his function to defend.

On the other hand, one cannot help being surprised that after the striking parallel which he has established between sensorial experience and the intuition of God, with the "coefficient of reality" which he recognizes in this experience[2], the critical theologian should feel the need for founding faith in the existence of God on a moral postulate, like that of duty which has been so seriously questioned by the sociological school.

The law of our practical independent reason does not demand respect for its own sake. It does not permit us to postulate "phenomenon" (that is to say, existence) for God. On the contrary, this law deserves respect only because it is the impression

---

[1] B. Pictet, *Théol. Chrét.*, 1731, I. p. 238.
[2] H. Bois, *La valeur de l'expérience religieuse*, Paris, 1908, p. 53 f.

produced on us and in us by the majesty of the normative divine will; i.e. for the same reason as the religious intuition of our total dependence in regard to God: as the impression produced on us and in us by His living, essential, real presence, and by His creative action which is continuous and therefore ruling and sovereign.

In the order of action, the only law which can claim absolute obedience is that which expresses the will of the absolute being. He alone deserves absolute confidence in the order of thought and this confidence in the order of thought is obviously the condition of obedience in the order of action.[1]

Actually no one but God can be infallible, because He alone is the originator and ruler of reality. He is the only one whose veracity demands our faith, for He is unique perfection. Apart from faith in God, we can conceive only a moral and speculative scepticism, or rather a confidence, at the same time credulous and vainglorious, in certain imperatives which, nevertheless, are of no more value than the person who formulates them.

In the final analysis, faith in our practical reason, far from forming the basis for our faith in God, builds solely upon Him and His authority. He alone renders the authority of reason intelligible to reason.

Thus, innatism, Kantian and neo-Kantian, in other words moral rationalism, is seen to be incapable of reconciling its idealist theories with real religious experience.

Is Bergsonian empiricism any better? We think not. Despite what he wrote in a letter to Fr. de Tonquedec[2] he gives neither a theistic theodicy, nor a refutation of pantheism of his *Evolution Créatrice*. If certain lines in his work are studied, however, it may well serve as a starting-point for a certain philosophy of religion.

We are indebted to Le Roy for a systematic explanation of these consequences.[3] With regard to the knowledge of God, we note the same agreement between his view and that of Calvinistic realism as exists between the latter and the piety of an Auguste Sabatier or an Henri Bois. Le Roy admirably defines the idea of God the Creator when he says that: "between the world and God there exists a relation of total dependence reaching to the depths of the being." For this Roman Catholic thinker, as for us, "it is by His immanence in us that we attain to God as

---

[1] *Voluntas signi*: the will expressing itself in a law as distinct from the *voluntas decreti* which decrees what shall be.
[2] June 12, 1911; *Les Etudes*, Feb. 20, 1912.
[3] E. Le Roy, *Le Problème de Dieu*, Paris, 1929.

our inward source, deeper in us than our very person. . . . In attaining to Him we perceive Him . . . as an impulsion reaching beyond our actual nature, our finite nature, always and infinitely."[1] Let us say, in passing, that in this agreement on the subject of religious experience, between men whose theological premises are very different, there is something which pleads powerfully, irresistibly, in favour of the objective reality of the fact experienced. On the other hand, the nature of the disagreement on the intellectual formula makes us presume, with no less force, that these are philosophical and theological doctrines which are incompatible with the certainties of religious experience.

Now, it is our conviction that Bergsonism is one of these philosophical doctrines. His theory of knowledge and his metaphysics are opposed by the immediate data or religious intuition. The doctrine of knowledge presented in his *Nouvelle Philosophie* appears to be nothing more than intuitive realism superadded to intellectual empiricism. According to this philosophy, it is sensibility which brings us into contact with God, as the source of our being. And it does this because it is sensibility which extends to reality in its original and living form. The mind can only deform reality by introducing it into the framework of space. Intelligence being the product of phylogenic evolution is essentially a defensive adaption in a given environment.

The natural consequence to be deduced from this is that the intellectual formulae of theology represent, at best, pragmatic truth. Thus, to say that God is personal, for example, signifies merely that we ought to conduct ourselves in relation to Him as if He were a person, in order that our spiritual life may prove successful.

Le Roy was originally attracted to this agnostic and pragmatic conclusion,[2] but turning again to the traditional teaching of his Church, this disciple of Bergson attempted another step in the direction of a doctrine of knowledge which should be really analogous to reality.[3] Henceforth, dogmas must be no longer simple rules of conduct: they must possess also a character of "direction" for thought. Thus our knowledge of God is not pragmatic but regulative as well. In saying, for example, that He is personal, one is following the objective law of the mind, regulating its own movement when it tends towards Him.

[1] *Op. cit.*, p. 284 ff.
[2] *Dogme et critique*, Bloud, 1907, pp. 11, 32.
[3] *Op. cit.*, pp. 274 ff. and 281.

This change of view shows notable progress in the direction of an analogical knowledge of God. Nevertheless, we have not arrived there yet, for, on the hypothesis of regulative knowledge, what we know is not that God is for us, independently of ourselves: it is not a quality of God grasped analogically; what we know is a tendency of the mind: it is not God but ourselves thinking of Him.

Thus God, while close to us in sensible intuition, remains perfectly inaccessible to religious thought. Our thoughts concerning Him may have no value whatever, and so the conflict is renewed between the God of philosophy and the God of religious faith. What is threatened now is not only the authority of the mind but also that of God. According to revelation, worship is not due to me nor to the direction of my mind, but to God. But we cannot adore that which we do not know in some sense. What we need to know, in order to worship, is not our subjectivity thinking of God but the qualities actively present in Him.

Shall we be told that we know Him in fact in sensible intuition as the source of our being, as a perpetual spring, as a supernaturalizing impulsion? We insist then that God cannot be so distinguished, as the principle is from the result, if the intuition which receives the impression of the action of God is not that of an intelligent sensibility.

If the metaphors suggested to us have no intellectual content, they mean nothing. If they have an intellectual content, and if this intellectual content is purely regulative, they teach us nothing. If this content expresses what God is for us, independently of us, well and good. Only then the theory of knowledge which is presented to us is false. It breaks down in contact with the immediate data of religious experience.

Certainly they have an intellectual content in Le Roy's system, but this content is such that it cannot be embraced by Christian theism. It is a pantheistic monism, not a monism of substance nor of idea, but a monism of becoming, of the process of duration, to which all reality is reduced.

Here we see the incompatibility of the new metaphysics with theism. Like Bergson, Le Roy denies expressly, and in good faith, that he is a pantheist, but his pantheism is not less evident than Bergson's. It is the dogma of the creation and conservation of new substances which forms the impassable barrier which prevents us from reducing the world to nothing more than a modality of God. Between the God who is eternally and the creature who commences to become, there must be total diversity from the ontological point of view, absolute irreducibility. There must, therefore, be numerically distinct substances.

Now, Bergson and Le Roy agree in making the total reality into a unique and continuous process of becoming in which God and the world are both swept away. Of the mysterious, nothing remains.[1] Any infinite hiatus or gap in the origin of the series of beings must be denied as unintelligible.[2] If there is no hiatus between God and the origin of the series of beings, it is because there is continuity uniting the evolution of creatures with that of God: thus, together, God plus the world constitute a unity. This is pantheism indeed.

No doubt the reason why the creators of the *Philosophie nouvelle* can believe, and believe sincerely, that they are not monists, is that they teach heterogeneity, the absolute novelty of the moments of the true duration which rests, interpenetrates, and organizes itself in a unique whole. The reality is becoming in the sense that it is the continuity of irreducible moments of being. If two similar impressions are never identical, with all the more reason is God not identical with me. Here, again, we see a reason why our philosophers speak of *creative* evolution.

It is strange, however, that they fail to see that if reality is essentially continuity of becoming, the heterogeneous moments which appear in it are no longer new aspects of a unique reality. From this point of view, it is very true that reality is not a homogeneous thing which passes into heterogeneity, as materialistic monism would have it. This is understood. But it is none the less a "perpetual springing forth". God, the world and the individual form a unity: mixed in one stream, their perpetual fusion constitutes total reality.

Again, we find ourselves immersed in a complete system of pantheism. If I depend on God, He in His turn depends on me in His becoming, and therefore in His intimate reality, since my free acts, being entirely new, are incapable of being foreseen. Henceforth, He will have to adjust Himself, by new and unforeseen discoveries of Himself, to the disastrous modifications which it may please me to introduce into the process of becoming. But we have shown in connexion with neo-Kantianism that if God could change, and change under the influence of the creature, he would be no longer God: at most he would be a god. Bergsonism, which began as a reaction in the direction of realism

[1] Bergson, *L'Évolution Créatrice*, Paris, 1907, p. 270.
[2] Le Roy, *op. cit.*, p. 34.

and the objectivity of knowledge, abandons us to a desolating religious agnosticism.

If, however, we have found God in the witness which He gives to Himself in us, we must at all costs abandon Kantian conceptualism, neo-Kantian rationalism and Bergsonian empiricism, in favour of a realist philosophy which can be harmonized with the certainty that forms the basis of our theocentric theology.

Thomist neo-scholasticism, on the one hand, and the realist intuitionism of certain Protestants on the other, approximate in different respects to Calvinistic realism. They, too, are concerned with establishing the objective reality of God and show a definite tendency towards the recognition of His absolute sovereignty.

The neo-scholastic presents us with a solid theory of general knowledge, thanks to which we can escape from conceptualism and innatism, through the rôle ascribed to experience, without on that account falling into empiricism. This theory gives complete satisfaction to those who, like ourselves, have no desire to discredit knowledge in the act of explaining it. The same thing may be said of the way in which Thomism conceives the nature of the intellectual knowledge of God and of spiritual things, analogical and ectypical.

Unfortunately, through reaction against the ontology of Gioberti in our day, as formerly through reaction against a certain ultra-Augustinian mysticism, Thomism would have it that the acquisition of this knowledge of God must be made exclusively by discursive reasoning. Now the impression produced immediately by God in the religious soul is a fact of experience, so far as we are concerned. In the order of religious thought, He is a first principle which can, and in fact does, impose itself on the intellectual sensibility with irresistible force. At this point, we find ourselves unable to accept the conclusion of Thomist epistemology.

The case of Thomism goes to show that believers, even when endowed with a high degree of spirituality, may have so slight a sensible intuition of God that it passes unperceived or, at any rate, is indistinct enough to be confounded with the constraint of a logical argument.

In the presence of this fact, we can only bow our heads: the Spirit, according to our Lord's words, breathes where and as He will. But it follows from this that the Thomist system presents a grave lacuna, because it does not sufficiently take into account a fact too general and too constant to be relegated to the order of exceptional cases such as the experiences of the great mystics.

On the Protestant side, Fernand Ménégoz in his *Le problème de la prière* makes a determined effort to supply a theocentric solution to the problem. His solution is one of the most original of those which approximate to Calvinism without actually identifying themselves with it. In any case, it is the most important of its kind which has appeared recently in France, for which reason we have chosen it as a standard of comparison with our own point of view.

For this Strasbourg professor, prayer, considered from the angle of the subjectivity of the believers, is the most general, and at the same time the most essential, act which expresses and actualizes religion. It implies, between God and man, a relation of person to person, and even a relation of co-operation of man with God. This being so, we are told, in substance, the problem of prayer is the religious problem *par excellence*. To acknowledge the objective value of prayer is by this very fact to recognize religion in that which is essential to it.

Rightly condemning the illusory method of the postulates, the author asks us to place ourselves at the heart of religious experience. This experience has, according to him, two principal stages, at the first of which man is conscious of his total dependence on a transcendent decision, in ascertaining that the world is what it is, conditioned as it is when it could have been otherwise, and that his ego forms part of this conditioned whole. This is the stage of the "religion of destiny".

To this elementary stage there succeeds that of the "experience of God", at the moment when the pressure of destiny, realized by all the world, is replaced by an internal testimony of the Spirit of God. This testimony is perceptible only by "a special subjectivity, a good will apart from which it remains inoperative." It reveals to me not only a destiny but a glorious destination. It is thus an entreaty addressed to our free and faithful co-operation. "It is only by the religious relationship active in himself by praying, that man can attain to a complete knowledge of himself and of his real destination."

Let us admit at once that there is something in this term destiny, so full of transcendent will, which recalls the terminology and the predilections of our great Calvin.[1] In the insistence with which the objective reality and sovereignty of the divine initiative are placed in relief, there is something more Calvinistic still. The fact of experience of the coefficient of objective

---

[1] Calvin, in his *Com. on Psalm CV*, speaking of "that which God has decreed for each one of us" makes this remark: "And it pleases me well that the French call this in their language *Destinée*."

reality which accompanies the intuition of God is properly stressed.

But the sympathy and admiration which the work of Fernand Ménégoz inspires in us must not prevent us from stating quite frankly the criticisms which it evokes from a Calvinistic point of view. In the first place, we cannot subscribe to the view, in our opinion, savouring of pietism, according to which power by itself expresses the religious relationship between God and man. It is certainly "the principle exercise of faith in God . . . by means of which we call upon Him, in order that He may reveal Himself as present to us."[1]

But the relation which exists between the Being invoked and the person who invokes Him is by no means the only living and personal religious relationship, realized through an inward attitude, which can exist between God and man. There is also the receptive attitude of the disciple receiving the instruction of the Master within, and of the Word without. Basing his statement on a celebrated passage in Paul's Epistle to the Romans (10: 14) Calvin lays down "that there cannot be any true invocation of the name of God which has not been preceded by a right knowledge of him."[2] Thus, it is faith, or more properly knowledge of the faith, which conditions prayer, before the latter can, in its turn, condition faith. "Now", observes Calvin, "according to Paul, faith proceeds from the Word of God." From which it follows that the living religious relationship preceding that which involves prayer is the relationship of Master to disciple, or, more concretely, of God who reveals Himself and who promises, to the believer who adheres to and confides in Him.

The attitude of Mary sitting at Jesus' feet and hearing His teaching constitutes a religious relationship. The Huguenots who risked the galleys through hearing the preaching of the Word in the "desert" knew that by this act they were entering into living relationship with God.

It is the Spirit of God who creates faith, in all its degrees, in the soul, and it is He who afterwards raises up prayer. All this He does with complete sovereignty as to the choice of means, but the ordinary method which it pleases Him to follow is the social means of the preaching of the Word of God confided to the Church. As a rule, it is this instruction which precedes and awakens the consciousness, at first latent and virtual, of the presence and action of God, who is perceived as the power on whom we depend entirely.

---

[1] *Inst.* III, xx. 1.   [2] *Com. in loc.*

And now, what is the intelligible content of this theocentric intuition, whether illuminated or not by the light of a positive revelation? What type of prayer must result from it? What philosophical premises does this intelligible content suppose? This remains for us to examine. In so doing we shall notice in what respect our conception differs from that of the author of *Le problème de la prière*. According to him, as we have seen, the pre-religious intuition, anterior to positive revelation, leads to the "spontaneous and violent religion of destiny." The vision of destiny makes itself known in the mind of man by direct intuition. This is evidence, but of another order than scientific. It consists in the fact that a man feels himself to be placed in the presence of a previous decision on which his destiny depends. He sees himself as the plaything, inwardly free, of a will more intelligent than his, which leads him, despite himself, towards its own ends. He is, or rather thinks himself to be, a free element in a determined whole.

That this static conception of dependence does actually exist in some minds we should not dream of contesting. It leads as the author wishes to the drama of Greek tragedy.

But Calvin had seen that the elementary intuition of dependence at the stage preceding revelation could also assume a dynamic character. In this case, destiny can be conceived as the first total and universal cause of life, of which the impulsions of our own will are merely moments. Stoic fatalism is the philosophic form of this manner of interpreting religious intuition.

However this may be, for Ménégoz, the appearance of religion, properly so called, results from the revelation that we are called to collaborate with God in order to attain our true destiny. The pressure of destiny thus resolves itself into a solicitation of free co-operation witnessed by the testimony of the Spirit of God to the spirit of man.

In our view, true religion makes its appearance when the intuition of total dependence in regard to God is purified from the elements of deism (religion of destiny) and pantheism (determinatism, naturism). What is revealed to us, then, is the opposition between the destination which the normative will of God the Creator assigns to us, namely, to glorify Him and find in Him our supreme good, on the one hand; and the lower ends towards the pursuit of which our will tends with deliberate and constant purpose, on the other hand; also the misery which this opposition implies for us; also the vision of the absolute necessity of changing this tendency and our utter impotence to do so.

We are conscious that, even in our wilful opposition to the end imperatively assigned to us by God, we do not cease to depend entirely on Him, since our evil spontaneity is always directed in such a way that we cannot accomplish the ill that we would, except in so far as God slackens the reins; we know that we should not exist for a moment if He allowed us to relapse into nothingness; we are conscious moreover that our moral inability to escape from the slavery of our own will renders us liable, by a just judgment of God, to condemnation and death.

Henceforth, solicitations of collaboration can afford us no relief. If God were a synergist, like Melanchthon and Ménégoz, no one could be saved. Succour can only come by an efficacious divine initiative making us realize the tragedy of opposition between our will and that of the lawgiver: so disposing our sensibility that we feel this opposition to be insupportable and that we cry earnestly for deliverance.

Further, if God himself testifies in His Word, sealed by the witness of His Spirit, that He offers us the fruit of the redemptive act and that He is determined to answer a cry for help by the gift of His grace, it is psychologically impossible that a sense of our helplessness, coupled with the knowledge of the divine promise grasped by faith, should not cast us on our knees and provoke the prayer which is always heard.

The sense of misery and the faith in deliverance which determines and conditions such a prayer imply that the law of the Lord is our supreme end, because it is the cause of our being; that the realization of our end is our supreme good; that God offers Himself as our Father and Redeemer: that He inspires, understands and hears the prayers of the faithful: that He is thus personal, in the highest sense of the term, which implies the trinity of hypostases.

But, far from supposing, at the initial stage, a co-operation between God and man, prayer, like the religion from which it proceeds, implies the strictest monergism: we act, indeed, in the act of faith, in the prayer which springs from this mystical knowledge, but only because and in so far as we are acted upon, even in regard to formal causes.

Prayer produced by the confidence of the heart in God whose "transcendental decision" (Heim) has ordained our destiny; prayer, shall we say, like that of Christ in Gethsemane (Mark 14: 36) is a supplication which will always subordinate man's desire to the realization of the immutable decree of the wisdom of God. It can never be an attempt to act magically upon God in order to induce Him to modify His decree. In saying to Him:

"Thy will be done", we finally renounce our own will. "We renounce it", says Calvin magnificently: "that God may frustrate all the projects that we have formed contrary to His will, and that He may create in us a new heart and mind, in such wise that we will nothing of ourselves but that His Spirit wills in us so as to render our will conformable to His."[1]

Prayer is not designed for the purpose of revealing our needs to God or instructing Jesus Christ (Matthew 6:8), for if it is addressed to a Person, it is to One whose knowledge, like His power, is infinite. Prayer is an honour due to God; but it is a necessity for us in order that we may be determined to will and to act, not with God, but under His impulsion, who delivers us from ourselves and from the power of evil. It is in this that our true liberty consists.

Thus understood, prayer is not logically intelligible unless it forms part of a theology that is not merely theocentric but truly theistic; a theology which does not confound God with the world, but which does not conceive the world except as pre-ordained, created, preserved, directed, in a sovereign manner by God. This theology will be the expression of the intuition and the knowledge that we are not moments of God, nor beings independent of Him, but that, distinct from Him, we do not exist except of Him, by Him and for Him. In order to depend on something, one must be distinct from it; otherwise, it is inter-dependence of which we are speaking and the instinct of piety as well as revelation forbids this.

Such a theology demands a certain ontology. No doubt, methodologically, philosophy and ontology are free disciplines, but it is none the less true that if we wish our thought to be coherent we must resolve to have the ontology of our theology.

This intellectual necessity supposes the restoration of the notions of substance, time and space, the religious value of which consists in the fact that they permit us to form analogically the concepts of being by itself (*a se*), of eternity and immensity.

We are finite substances, limited in our being and in our action. To the question in what consists such and such a thing, we reply, according to the case, that it consists in another thing or that it consists in itself. The growth of a plant which grows is in the plant. It is a modification, an accidental determination of this plant, but the plant consists in itself. It is not the mode of another being; it is its own material cause. It is in this sense that

---

[1] *Geneva Catechism*, xxxix.

we say that it consists by itself. To have in itself its own *raison d'être* is to be a substance.

In this sense, we are conscious of being substances. Moreover, the notion of substance does not exclude dependence on an efficient cause distinct from itself. It is the defect of Spinoza's definition that it neglects this fact. Finite substances are indeed by themselves (*per se*) they are not of themselves (*a se*).

These substances are limited in their being. They are the seat of accidental modifications which determine and constitute their evolution. They have a starting-point which marks the commencement, the first limit of their being. On the other hand, certain modes are realized in them which sometimes coincide (simultaneity) and at other times are mutually exclusive. The mode which we perceive as excluded by the other constitutes what we call the anterior. That which excludes is the posterior (temporal succession). The mode appearing in the consciousness at the point at which it suppresses the other constitutes the essentially mobile limit of the present. These accidental determinations can be enumerated under the category of anteriority and posteriority. This enumeration is extrinsic time. The metaphysical movement, constituted by the continual change of the mutually incompatible determinations, is duration or intrinsic time.

We are substances limited in our action. Man, a composite substance, a body informed by a spirit, has an immediate dynamical and mechanical action. The immediate dynamic action is that exercised by the mind. The immediate sphere of immediate physical action is a spirit circumscribed, informing a body; this is the organism itself. The measure of this organism constitutes what we call intrinsic space. The negative interval extending itself between the limits of many bodies is the real extrinsic space.

The limited character of the presence and of the mechanical action of bodies among themselves appears from the fact that they cannot act immediately on one another except by their parts; the action and the presence of bodies are always essentially partial.

We are indebted to Bergson for having reaffirmed the objective reality of time. His philosophy stresses the notion of the relativity of time which is triumphing with Einstein in modern physics, but which is still unrecognized among neo-critical theologians.

But the affirmation of the objectivity of time is not enough for the religious instinct, which requires to express in terms of objective reality the limited and fragmentary character of the presence and action of the creature in contrast with the infinite character and presence of the Creator. It is this which renders indispensable the restoration of the objectivity of space. Extension is, moreover, an immediate datum of sensation. At first the eye sees certain spots which, prior to the education that it is about to receive, it perceives on one plane only; it never sees geometrical points which, in any case, have no real existence. Once one admits the objectivity of space, critics of the philosophy of Bergson, attacking intelligence, whose sphere would be spatial unreality, fall at a single blow.

The epistemology of our theism is thus that of the primacy of intellectual intuition; this is a realist epistemology according to which, to adopt the language of Bois, contradicting his own idealism, the other beings are "within" the data of experience, "within" the modifications which occur in us, "as much as we are ourselves."[1]

A knowledge of God and of other beings which was not the intuition of their anteriority to our mind, which was not a transitive act, would merely be ignorance of the existence of God and the world. If we admit that our judgments of present existence can be no more than the conclusions of reasoning, we shall be very quickly driven to solipsism.

The act by which we know God in elementary religious experience and that by which we know sensible beings are analogous. Neither in one case nor in the other can truth be confounded with usefulness for action. For a theist, truth on all planes of knowledge is and can only be a harmonizing of our thoughts with the thought of God, which is reflected in our mind when the objects which we perceive recall to it the intelligible light by which the creative light causes them to appear in the dark abyss of our immense ignorance.

In the next Part, we shall examine the objections which may be raised against the bearing and value of religious knowledge in so far as it is defined and specified confessionally.

[1] H. Bois, *La valeur de l'expérience religieuse*, p. 53.

PART TWO

THE FOUNDATION AND SPECIFICATION OF RELIGIOUS
KNOWLEDGE

CHAPTER I

PRELIMINARY AND METHODOLOGICAL QUESTIONS

In our first Part we have endeavoured to show that there is such a thing as religious knowledge and to define its nature. The present Part treats of the prolegomena to Reformed dogmatics. Its object is to determine in a scientific manner the course which dogmatics must take and to elucidate the value of its degrees of specification from the viewpoint of that section of scientific criticism which forms the epistemology proper to dogmatic theology.

We shall bear in mind that dogmatics, properly so called, as distinct from its prolegomena, is that canonical science which aims at determining, formulating, and connecting systematically and genetically, in such a manner as to construct a synthesis the mysteries of religious faith: that is to say, the divinely revealed verities which must constitute its content.

It must be understood that, for us, knowledge is not religious unless it has as its object verities concerning the glory of God and the salvation of man. If, in accordance with the ideas of the author of the Book of Enoch, it had pleased God to give us a revealed cosmography, the data of this cosmography would be of the greatest interest: but, even so, they would not come within the scope of dogmatic thinking.

We have referred to degrees of specification of religious knowledge. What we mean is this: the mind in its attempt to proceed logically towards a theological position having a fundamental meaning finds itself nonplussed the moment the idea which it is pursuing loses itself in extension and enriches itself in comprehension. Every definition must be made according to the genus and the specific difference.

To arrive at Calvinism, for example, we must start with theism and persevere along the lines of theistic thinking. But that is not enough by itself. It is possible to conceive a purely speculative theism, concerned exclusively with solving theoretical problems, such as the origin of contingent beings or the passage from power to act.

Calvinism tends spontaneously towards a practical and religious theism. It seeks to know God only that it may render

Him the honour which is His due; by confidence in His promises, by obedience to His commands, by the prayer of petition, and by thanksgiving for all the benefits of which it acknowledges Him to be the supreme source. [1]

But, if Calvinism were to halt there, it would not differ in principle from Mohammedanism. It would be merely a purer form of religious theism than Islam, since it vigorously repudiates the primacy of a capricious and tyrannical will in God and confesses that the divine will, sovereign and free as it is, without doubt, contains in itself reasons, unknowable indeed to us, but none the less holy and just. [2]

Here, again, the ways diverge. Calvinism desires to be, and is, Christian. The Gospel of Jesus, the Christ, is God's message to humanity, and Calvinism knows no other. It is a theism both religious and Christian.

Now, by the "Gospel" may be understood two messages differing one from the other in extent. The term may be restricted to the "essence" of the teaching of Jesus of Nazareth, as it is given in the Synoptic Gospels (*evangelium Christi*).

On the other hand, this *evangelium Christi* may be regarded (with Mark 1: 1) as only "the beginning of the gospel of Jesus Christ"; and it may be held that the Fourth Gospel in affirming that God "gave His only-begotten Son" for the salvation of sinners who shall believe in Him (John 3: 16), has thus sublimely epitomized it. In that case, it is the gift of the person of Christ and his saving work which constitute the Gospel properly so called (*evangelium de Christo*).

Discussing this very point, Troeltsch has shown that the most exalted theism can be found in association with the first manner of understanding the Gospel. Thus one can be at the same time an excellent theist and a mere Socinian. Calvinism is committed to another view, and, by the agency of the greatest of its synods, it has defined that the *evangelium de Christo* is the substance of the Gospel. [3] By this definition, it places itself in the tradition of the great councils and of the Fathers who guided their decisions, [4] and declares itself part of oecumenical Christianity.

The acceptance of the supreme *magisterium* of the Holy Spirit, speaking in and through the Scriptures which He has

---

[1] Calvin, *Geneva Catechism*, i; *Inst.* I, ii. 1 ff.

[2] The contrary opinion is qualified by Calvin as abominable and sacrilegious (*quod non modo falsum esse concedimus, sed tanquam foedum sacrilegium detestamur*), *De Aeter. Dei praedest.*, op., vol. VIII, p. 342.

[3] *Can. Dordrac.*, c. i, art. 2, 3, 4; c. ii, art. 5.

[4] *Confession of La Rochelle*, art. vi.

inspired, sets Calvinism in the way of orthodox Protestantism. Its principles of discrimination and spiritual interpretation of divine revelation, the *soli Deo gloria* preferred to the *sola fide* of Luther, gives Calvinism its own physionomy in relation to the other types of evangelical Protestantism.

It is natural to think that, if a dogmatic theologian has decided to make Reformed principles, rather than any others, the basis of his studies, it is because he believes these principles to be well founded. But the personal conviction of this theologian is an accident. It is useful, therefore, to preface the exposition of a dogma with an introduction giving scientific reasons for proceeding in the proposed direction and making plain the epistemological legitimacy of the principles adopted.

It is not here a question of proving the reality of what the believer hopes, and holds firmly as seeing the invisible, of proving it with the aid of independent reason. This is impossible for a Reformed theologian, since the Scripture teaches him that it is precisely faith which is "the substance (hypostasis) of things hoped for, the evidence of things not seen" (Hebrews 11 : 1).

What has to be made plain is the epistemological legitimacy of the method of dogmatics, the internal principle of which is the faith (*fides qua creditur*) which the Spirit of God witnesses as being His work (*testimonium Spiritus sancti*).

We must be on our guard, therefore, against confounding the *introduction to dogmatics* with the religious initiation and instruction by means of *catechetics* and *homiletics*. The introduction to dogmatics can, accidentally, provoke the birth of faith in a soul, or partially modify it in the direction indicated by the dogmatician.

But this is not its proper rôle, any more than it is the rôle of dogmatics to provide an ecclesiastical community with its rule of faith. Dogmatics cannot and must not serve as a substitute for *symbology*.

Let us explain: Faith comes through the preaching of the Word of God, which is the normal and habitual instrument of efficacious grace and the determining factor of belief. This preaching can be catechetical or homiletical. The catechetical form is designed for religious initiation. The catechism and the catechetical explanation are conditioned by practical considerations. Their object is to communicate to the catechumen that which he must know in order that he may render to God the honour which is His due, find the way of salvation, and become a spiritually responsible member of the Church.

The plan of the exposition must be determined by pedagogical considerations. The content must limit itself to that which is strictly relevant to the object in view. Theological questions which have only a remote connexion with practice must be avoided. For example, the catechism teaches the Incarnation of the eternal Son of God for the salvation of sinners who repent and believe, because it is the content of the *evangelium de Christo*; but it does not enter into the question whether the Reformed are right as against the Romans and the Lutherans when they teach that the subject of the Incarnation is not the divine nature but the person of the Word. This question is of a high scientific interest. It has a considerable importance for replying to certain objections which unbelief and heresy raise against the Incarnation. But it cannot figure in the programme of religious initiation, because one may be an excellent Christian without being aware that such a question exists, or, knowing that it exists, one may yet be ignorant of what reply should be made to it.

Homiletics also aims at expounding Christian truth, by explaining the Scriptures, in order to provoke the birth of faith, and at developing and confirming it when it is born. But here it is no longer a question of expounding the Christian verities in systematic order by means of a sort of "higher course" of religion. It is rather a matter of making the Scriptures known and relating them to the actual needs of souls. Preaching, in this sense, must be essentially prophetic. The matter of his teaching is furnished to the preacher either by the contents of the book of Scripture which he is explaining or by his knowledge of the needs and difficulties of his flock. The needs experienced by the members of his congregation, and the dangers which they incur, may lead the preacher to treat of scientific questions which would be out of place in an elementary catechism.

There is scope here for pastoral prudence. The essential thing is that the preacher should never forget that his function is to act as an "ambassador from God and that what must form the basis of his teaching is the Word of God" addressed to sinners, who tend naturally to misunderstand God's sovereign rights and who need to be taught the way of salvation and sanctification.

Those who have heard the Word of God, who have acknowledged it to be divine, and who, as a result of this acknowledgment, have placed their trust in it, those are they who have the gift of faith and who bear within themselves the testimony of the Holy Spirit. They have no need to study dogmatics in order to arrive at the highest degree of certainty to which man can attain. The way lies elsewhere. It is in the practice of the divine will, in the experience of natural impotence and of the presence of grace, in personal communion with Christ and, for that reason, in a faithful use of the Sacrament of the Eucharist and in persevering prayer.

Thus, contrary to what has been sometimes maintained, the normal object of theology is not to test and verify the value of the faith, starting from a principle external to itself or to divine authority.

What profit then can be expected from the study of systematic theology (including the prolegomena)? And on what condition can the maximum profit be derived from it?

To those who have not faith but whom the action of grace predisposes to receive it, the study of dogmatics and of its introduction may bring accidentally that which the catechetical instruction of the Church would have given: like the catechism, like preaching and, we may add, like ecclesiastical symbology, it endeavours to place the spirit of man in the presence of revealed truth. It differs from those other disciplines in being occupied solely with formulating and systematizing that which is given to it as revealed, in taking into account only the scientific demands of the believing mind, without concerning itself with the spiritual needs or aptitudes for which catechetics and homiletics are designed.

It differs from *symbology* in not being limited to the mere statement of the agreement realized *hic et nunc* by a particular Church in the understanding and confession of revealed truth, agreement which it claims from its members as a bond of unity and from its ministers as rule of instruction. Dogmatics being a canonical science determines scientifically and *in abstracto* what must be believed, even if the state of the minds within the Church does not permit one to anticipate that the ideal will be attained immediately. But, as it always presents the divine revelation, it may so happen that souls disposed to faith by grace will find in this contact with religious truth systematically presented, with the didactic severity demanded by science, the best apology for the Christian faith.

To those who have faith, but whose initiation and spiritual education have been badly directed from a given point, the introduction to dogmatics and dogmatics proper may bring the occasion and be the instruments of the necessary rectification.

They may indeed bring unexpected solutions to intellectual difficulties which press heavily on the certitude of faith.

Moreover these difficulties present themselves—it can only be through the work of the enemy—to the mind of more than one believer whose faith is sound and whose confession is pure. Founded as he is upon the rock, his certainty remains victorious, but he suffers through not being able to give an account of the hope that is in him.

He would like to close the mouth of the enemy of his faith, or at least to induce in him an intellectual respect for it. In such a case, spiritual means are no longer sufficient. He can only arrive at this result by scientific and precise knowledge of the problems which present themselves to the mind in relation to Christian dogma.

Finally, the scientific knowledge of dogma, by imposing on the mind a discipline of strict precision, helps to dissipate the misunderstandings which arise among believers through disputes over words and, on the other hand, to unmask heresy sheltering under the vagueness of a formula imperfectly drawn up. In this connexion, one has only to recall the part played by the ὁμοούσιος in the Arian controversy and by the *non praevisa fide* in the controversy with the Arminians.

In the spontaneous faith of the Christian who is a stranger to dogmatic studies, often in preaching also, especially in popular preaching, mind and sentiment are undifferentiated. After all, in the nature of things it is the intelligent sensibility which believes, but it often happens that, as a result of imperfect differentiation, discussion becomes impassioned and divisions are embittered on points the importance of which is relatively secondary. In such circumstances a purely didactic and systematic study of religions may render inestimable service.

Both dogmatics and its prolegomena are frequently charged with "dryness". Now this dryness is precisely their quality. The preacher and the apologist may aim at exciting and persuading, for that is their rôle. The dogmatician, on the contrary, must seek to convince. No doubt, he must speak only of the things which he knows and if he speaks of personal experiences, he must himself have experienced them. But, in a scientific work, it is not a question of displaying his inward sentiments. Here the intelligence must be differentiated from the sentiment, in order that the critical rôle which has devolved upon it may be exercised with the necessary serenity and detachment.

And now let us say that a primary condition for profiting by the study of a treatise on Reformed dogmatics or on the introduction to such dogmatics, is a preliminary knowledge of Reformed doctrine, as it is formulated in one of its three classic catechisms: the catechism of Calvin, that of Heidelberg, and that of Westminster; and in one at least of the four great confessions of faith: the Helvetic, the confession of La Rochelle, the Belgic, and the Westminster confession. It would be inexcusable for a French Reformed pastor not to be familiar with the text of the catechism and of the confession of faith which have fashioned the Church of his fathers. Reformed dogmatics, which is the science of the Reformed faith, necessarily presupposes a knowledge of the essential elements of this faith.

We shall see, later, that the Reformed dogmatician cannot hope to be fully understood except by those in whom there exists, at least in a virtual state, the *fides qua creditur*. It is impossible to display with full success a theory of knowledge except for those who have at least the organ of that knowledge. A physician cannot show light to a person born blind. He can explain the theory of optics to him; but in order to put anything behind the formulæ other than the mere words themselves, he must appeal to vague analogies borrowed from the sense of touch. But the smallest infant in the primary school born seeing will always be more sure about the light than a doctor of science born blind.

And so it is with the science of the faith. The definition and theory of faith may be declared to an unregenerate man, he may be told of the certainty of divine faith and of the spiritual light that it brings, and thus be able to form a vague idea of what it is by considering the power of this strong but undemonstrable opinion. The simplest believer will always be more sure about divine realities than a doctor of theology deprived—alas, from birth—of that optical organ which is faith (*fides qua creditur*). If therefore any one does not believe, we should exhort him to do so, or rather we should transmit to him, on behalf of God Himself, the divine commandment to believe. In fact, to the faith by which we understand now the faith which is believed, the doctrine of the faith presents itself, not like a philosophical thesis in the humble posture of a suppliant, but with authority like a queen: it has an absolutely obligatory character. We are referring, of course, to the faith confessed by Reformed Christians.

And, on the other hand, these same Reformed Christians teach a fact which is confirmed by experience, namely, that of ourselves we cannot believe and that justifying faith is a gift which God confers on the elect alone.

We are here confronted, they tell us, with something which

strongly resembles a paradox and a contradiction. Either maintain the natural inaptitude for faith and renounce the obligatory character of faith; or maintain this character but renounce the dogma of inaptitude. In either case, you must reform your Reformed doctrine.

The objection is specious. It rests on a confusion between the physical inaptitude for believing, implying the abolition of formal liberty, and spiritual inaptitude. This native inaptitude to be willing to do what is necessary in order to believe is qualitative.

It signifies no more than this: the moral quality of an unregenerate free agent being evil, in so far as he is not transformed spiritually and conquered by efficacious grace, he will never desire to be converted or assume the dispositions necessary for conversion, since his judgment of values in the contingent matter, whereby the will is enlightened, registers what he is in reality and invariably decides against God. And if this is so, it is not because he is moved by a force of nature by some constraint external or internal; on the contrary, he acts most spontaneously. It is not that he is impelled by a blind, irresistible instinct; on the contrary, he acts deliberately, from motives to which he himself attributes the value which in fact attracts him. His act is determined by that which constitutes the essence of his being. If he invariably decides against God, no other reason can be assigned than that which a free agent must give in the final analysis, namely: *Sic volo, sic jubeo, sit pro ratione voluntas.*

The necessity of the refusal of the unregenerate man resides in the stubbornness of his own fundamental will. The latter is not immutably bound to its refusal except in so far as this is preferred. The sinner's refusal of salvation is made as freely as God's decision to save, as freely as He decides the destiny of the sinner.

There is a sense indeed in which it may be said that God cannot do evil. This means that we know that He will always do that which is good because He is good and because He always registers in reality His quality of being good.

But there is also a sense in which He can do evil, if by this we understand that He has the power and the knowledge necessary to do it. The necessity in which God is of being good does not prevent Him from being free. The purely qualitative and voluntary necessity of the sinner, to refuse to do that which he should do in the concrete case under discussion, does not hinder him from being in like manner formally free. And if this liberty is called servitude and if one speaks of a slave-will, it is because there is no worse nor more unhappy liberty than that which consists in being so freed from the divine law that one never desires to conform oneself to it.

But the unregenerate sinner, when he has been called outwardly by the presentation of divine truth, can physically desire to employ the means whereby it is received, in a sense analogous to that in which it may be said that God can do evil and in a sense similar to that in which it may be said that an elect soul can utterly deny God.

In the offer which is made to him and in the resistible grace which accompanies this offer, the unregenerate sinner receives the physical and efficient power to ask for saving faith: a power parallel to that of the paralytic whom Christ asked if he wished to be cured. If the sinner repels this offer because he cannot accept it, in the first sense of the expression, that is to say, in the final analysis because he refuses flatly to will it, he must acknowledge that the immediate cause of his refusal is simply his own perfectly responsible will.

There are men who cannot believe. It is their misery, which they often deplore themselves. But when these men do not wish to have recourse to the means of grace which are offered to them, it is their sin. They are no longer men of good will.

Whether they are, or are not, links in a spiritual chain, matters little: conscience condemns the evil set in the presence of the good alternative, whether it be an absolute commencement or, as we maintain, the continuation of an absolute commencement.

In the second case, it qualifies as evil and worthy of the qualitative reprobation which attaches to sin, the entire chain as well as the first link and each of the links which compose it. And if the sinner draws upon himself, by his free obstinacy, the sanction which sin requires, his own conscience will repeat to him the word of the prophet to the rebellious people, the word which Calvin recalled so often: *Perditio tua est, o Israel.*

The sinner who wishes to persevere in his refusal *can* not will it: *qui vult potest nolle*, says Calvin, adding: "This is true if we consider the will itself (*velle*) then its effective power (*effectus*)".[1] Now to be responsible it is sufficient to be able, effectively and physically, to do the contrary to what one wishes.

Thus the Synod of Dort says with good reason: "If many who are called by the evangelical ministry do not respond to the appeal and are not converted, the fault lies not in the appeal

---

[1] *Praelect. in Lament. Jer.*, iii, 37, 38.

nor in the Gospel, nor in Christ offered by the Gospel, nor in God who invites by the Gospel and who bestows on them various gifts; but in those who are called, some not accepting the Word of life through negligence, others accepting it, as to its truth, but not receiving it into their hearts, in such a way, that, after the joy of a temporary and evanescent faith, they turn away; others at length choking the seed of the Word under the thorns of the cares and pleasures of the world, remain unfruitful". [1]

It will be said that this is a determinism of nature, which conceals and reveals itself at the same time, in this doctrine of the external call. We ask, in turn, what is understood by the term nature. Is it an impress in created things of eternal ideas residing in the divine essence? For Calvinsim, there can be no question of this sort of nature. Calvin, Beza and the Confession of La Rochelle unite in rejecting neo-Platonism. [2]

Or is it rather the more modern idea of invariable disposition to a phase of evolution, having its reason in an anterior state equally determined, and the whole proceeding from a primitive state containing in itself the reasons for its successive developments?

If this is the notion behind the criticism made of Calvinistic teaching on the loss of free will, such criticism is obviously ill-founded.

Since we teach that man has lost his free will and that he has become unable to accomplish the divine law perfectly, it is implied by these very terms which we employ that he had this free will in a former and different state and that he was able to realize the ideal to which he is bound.

The fixed disposition, which turns him away from obedience to God, is not primitive; it is acquired, and acquired by an act abusive of his free will. If man is now insolvent, it is because at a former time he rendered himself such.

If there is determinism, it is not a determinism of nature but a determinism of liberty, liberating itself from the Law and posing as autonomous: in a word, a determinism against nature, originating with man.

To explain the existence of the native tendency to evil that we find in every man, it will be seen that, whether we like it or not,

---

[1] C. iii and iv, art. 9.
[2] Calvin, *Com. on John*, i, 3: "Augustine according to his custom showing himself to be far too much of a Platonist, is enraptured with I know not what *ideas*, namely, that God before he made the world had the *form* of the entire work projected in his mind and that in this manner things lived in Christ which as yet had no existence"; Beza, *Nov. Test.*, ed. 1598; *Joh.*, i, 4, etc.; *Conf. Gal.*, art. xiv.

we must face the mystery without which, as Pascal says, nothing can be explained, namely, the dogma of the Fall and of original sin.

We saw in the previous Part that the radical evil in man admits of only two explanations: the sociological and the theological; and we gave reasons for deciding in favour of the second. According to this, the humanity, whole and entire, which multiplies itself by generation is essentially a moral organism.

Whole and entire, it has submitted itself to sin, and turned in the direction of sin, with and in the person of its head.

True, the individuals which actually compose humanity have not committed personally this abuse of liberty which constitutes them slaves of themselves and which was the act of the first sinner. But neither is the fault of the first sinner a purely individual act. The head of the race was virtually the humanity of to-day and the men of to-day are the men who sinned, multiplied and propagated (Genesis 1: 28). In the man of to-day, we rediscover still the same moral entity, diversified in consequence of the appearance of new elements which serve to constitute distinct persons in a unique organism: humanity.

It is this which sinned in the beginning and now that the root has become a tree, the tree and its branches and each of the cellules which constitute it are what the tree has made itself. Each one of us is the first sinner who reproduced himself, plus this new creation, a personality irreducible in the rest of us. We are not choosing between creationism and traducianism.

We are simply stating the fact that man is one in the sense that he reproduces himself. Actually, essentially, it is the head and root of the race who reproduces himself in each one of us. In the abuse which he made of his liberty, each of us has thus sinned in him and with him, inasmuch as each of us is his reproduction and his propagation.

On the other hand, inasmuch as we are distinct persons we retain that liberty which renders us responsible for our individual faults. But as it is the liberty of a being who has become radically a sinner, nothing that he does is pleasing to God, in so far as this being has not been regenerated.

A bad tree cannot bring forth good fruit, says the Lord; and the Apostle Paul infers from the state of servitude to sin the liberation in regard to the law of justice (Matthew 7: 18; Romans 6: 21). And we conclude that the objection according to which we must choose between the duty of believing and inability to choose the means which lead to faith is a false dilemma.

We choose a third position, native inability but efficient power, as soon as the truth has been presented and, in consequence, real responsibility. [1]

Nothing is commanded us in the spiritual order that we are not obliged to do; and theological science, in order that it may constitute itself as universal in the normal order, requires no more than this.

---

[1] Calvin treats the question in his sermons on the Book of Job: sermon cxxxiii (Job 34: 27).

CHAPTER 2

THE CALVINISTIC CONCEPT OF APOLOGETICS
AND POLEMICS

The discussion on which we have just embarked raises a problem of a more general nature. Have we indeed the right to develop arguments concerning the notion of liberty and responsibility in the presence of unbelievers? In doing so, are we not already impinging on the sphere of apologetics and polemics? To this question we must reply at once that we are.

And in this matter we are merely following in the footsteps of our most illustrious predecessors. The opening chapters of Calvin's *Institutio*, of Peter Martyr's *Loci*, of Zanchius' *De Deo* and *De Operibus Dei*; in brief, the works of the fathers of Reformed dogmatics all wear a distinctly apologetical colour.

They may even be said to constitute admirable sketches of religious philosophy, and moreover this character impregnates their entire work.

One of the ablest opponents of Calvinism in our time and country, Henri Bois, has felt this so strongly that he has entitled his critique of Reformed dogma, *La philosophie de Calvin*. Now, we are told, the doctrine of total corruption renders contradictory any attempt to construct an apology or a philsophy of religion, or even any philosophy whatever, from the Calvinistic viewpoint.

This objection comes to us from two sides. The eminent Catholic historian of medieval philosophy, Gilson, has paid us the honour of submitting it in person. On the other hand, that gifted restorer of Reformed theology, Karl Barth, remarks: "One cannot make a philosophy of religion without a bad conscience."

We understand the argument in this way. The dogma of total corruption regards the natural man as incapable of judging spiritual things. Such is the teaching of Paul, as well as that of the Reformation. Now, to construct a system of apologetics is to establish that natural reason which you recognize to be incompetent, as judge of divine things. It is impossible to imagine a more palpable contradiction. Let us engage in polemics; let us rush to attack the vain maxims of so-called autonomous reason; let us tear from the gnosis its false mask of Christian; let us

203

make human wisdom blush for its folly and human religion for its impiety. But, once for all, let us refrain from constituting reason the judge of revelation and thus the judge of God Himself.

Let us leave rationalism to make this vain attempt. Let Catholicism, authoritarianism built upon a rationalistic foundation, follow suit, if it is so disposed. But we, the sons of the Reformation, would commit a veritable suicide in taking even one step in this direction. We have no right to defend ourselves otherwise than by bringing forth fruit meet for repentance towards God.

Ragaz goes one better still when he says: "The conflict with atheism is itself an atheism".[1] Then away with theoretical apologetics. And Professor Gilson interjects: no philosophy, either, for a Calvinist. Philosophy is nature, that is to say paganism. It is natural reason. And on its own showing the entire effort of Calvinism is directed towards eliminating from theology every pagan element: it is condemnation of fallen nature, humiliation of independent reason. Naturally, it needs a theology, but it has no need for a philosophy. Even if it had the need, it would have no right to one.

Let us consider first of all the question of apologetics. We admit at once that the attitude of Karl Barth finds a ready explanation in the fact that it is a useful reaction against an error of method which has arisen in Christian theology and even in the bosom of Calvinism during its decadence. The Cartesian Calvinists took the wrong direction when they claimed to be able to justify the existence of a preparatory natural religion, founded on independent reason with the aid of methodical doubt. Remaining materially orthodox by the content of their *Credo*, they had ceased to be so formally. Without realizing it themselves, they had quitted the sphere of faith, like Roman Catholicism, to wander in the mists of gnosis.

They were able to do this only by postulating a principle utterly contrary to the primitive Reform, namely, that the affirmation of the existence of God and of the authority of Scripture is an object of science rather than an article of faith. They had forgotten that Calvin, for example, did not concede to human reason in the matter of natural religion any other power than that which consists in arriving at "an evanescent opinion fluttering in the understanding". He is speaking with regard to the existence and the nature of God.[2] They had forgotten a

---

[1] *Où sont les sans-Dieu?* in *Rev. du Christ. Soc.*, Sept.–Oct. 1934, p. 133.
[2] *Com. on Heb.*, xi, 3; cf. *Inst.* I, v. 11.

statement as decisive as this latter concerning the authority of Scripture: "They are rash who would prove to unbelievers by arguments that Scripture is of God, for this cannot be known except by faith."[1]

Contrary to the Reformers, Leibnitz conceived the apologetic method in the following manner: Revelation is an ambassador extraordinary bringing to reason certain religious verities which are above its comprehension. Revelation presents its credentials before the throne of the sovereign reason. The latter verifies their authenticity. When that has been admitted, but only then, it bows respectfully before the affirmations of God, sovereign like itself but more competent in these matters.[2]

It goes without saying that we cannot for a moment admit the idea of such an apologetic. The concept of a philosophy of religion, constructed by the autonomous reason, cannot be envisaged by us. We cannot and will not be rationalists. Nor can we confine ourselves to pure practice as Ragaz would seem to wish. His negation of formal duty and of the legitimacy of the theoretical conflict with unbelief is neither more nor less than a return to obscurantism. Now, if the dogma of total corruption excludes the rationalist method, the dogma of the state of integrity and the dogma of regeneration and progressive restoration to the state of integrity equally exclude the apologetic inaction and crude empiricism of Diogenes, who contented himself with opposing the fact of movement, to the captious arguments of Zeno of Elea.

Indeed, for Reformed theology, the *fides qua creditur*, aptitude to acknowledge divine truth and to believe in it, is not a faculty distinct from intelligent sensibility. It is not a supernatural faculty which God added to human nature considered in its state of integrity. The accidental disappearance of this aptitude has had the effect of modifying human nature profoundly. On the contrary, the *fides qua creditur* is a mode of intelligent sensibility in contact with God who reveals Himself to it.

The presence of this aptitude is the normal state of man. Its disappearance or its perversion is an accident as disastrous and as destructive as that of common sense itself. It affects the integrity of nature in the fallen man. Its restoration involves nothing less than the commencement of the renovation of fallen nature.

To believe, then, is not to renounce thought: it is to begin to

---

[1] *Inst.* I, viii. 12.
[2] Leibnitz, *Discours de la conformité de la foi et de la raison*, xxix.

think normally. As the Augustinian, Anselm of Aosta, observed, faith, far from arresting the play of thought, stimulates it. It tends naturally to transform the knowledge and the certainty which it possesses, because God has revealed Himself in it, and because He has revealed His eternal love in a certainty, deliberate, explicit and systematic.

It thus obeys the internal law of its being when it endeavours to define itself intellectually and to establish dialectically that, while supra-rational, it is not blind, but, on the contrary, scientifically legitimate. It always obeys its internal tendency in criticizing, from its own point of view, the systems which assail it from without.

Even if, *per impossibile*, there were no such systems, it would be compelled by its own internal logic to examine the theoretical difficulties which array themselves against it under the form of intellectual temptations, starting from the principles by which it is dominated and determined. Seeking intellection, it cannot but try to understand the possibility and the illegitimacy of such temptations.

Now, to do this is to construct a certain apologetic, the apologetic of faith seeking to understand, not that it may exist but that it may attain its *bene esse*. As Pascal says, it would not seek if it had not found already: but, precisely because it has found, it seeks.

Intelligent sensibility, even when it bows before religious mystery, as it is indeed obliged to bow before the mysteries of sensible nature, does not make a *sacrificium intellectus*, because it endeavours to understand why the human mind must expect to be surpassed in the sphere in which it encounters the mind of the infinite being.

The religious mind is not a renunciation of human intelligence for yet another sort of reason, because it is required to criticize this human counterfeit of mystery which is theological or philosophical contradiction. Such an apologetic is addressed essentially to him who seeks, but who would not seek if consciously or otherwise he had not already found. It is addressed to those in whom aptitude to acknowledge divine truth has been re-established.

We can visualize only two grave objections which might be urged against the Reformed conception of apologetics which we have just outlined.

In the first place, say certain scholastics, why cannot the reason which is supposed to be regenerate do what is impossible for fallen reason: namely, demonstrate religious truth *a simultaneo* or even simply *a posteriori* starting from facts physically or historically proved?

In the second place, it is objected, Calvinistic apologetics, if it could give satisfaction to the scientific instinct of the believer, has still neither religious motive nor apostolic impulse. Not being religious, it is no longer a theological science. Not being addressed to unbelievers, it merely draws attention to the fact already suspected, that Calvinism has no aptitude for evangelization.

It is scarcely necessary for us to add that we do not accept these conclusions. If reason cannot demonstrate the truth of objects of faith in a compelling manner, it is first of all because, even supposing it to be restored to the state of integrity which it held before the Fall, it could not find in itself the matter of objective knowledge. It never draws from its own resources. For knowledge as formal as logic and mathematics, it can only work on intuitions which have their origin in the senses and which are furnished by an essentially contingent experience. Starting with a notion of space other than that of which we have empirical intuition it constructs one or several geometrics which differ from that of Euclid. Reason cannot draw from its own resources even the directive principles of knowledge such as the laws of formal logic.

By their means it proves the fact of existence as a governing law and the mind and experience which come to it from without. This suggests the need for a guarantee by a legislator who is himself above all laws. But it goes without saying that the existence of the one who provides a guarantee for reason cannot be proved by it.

Not being capable of self-proof in the speculative sphere, and having to base itself on God in order to maintain the universal value of its own principles, reason would be ridiculous, indeed, if it were to demand a compelling logical demonstration of the existence of God, so apart from which it could not take the first step in speculation.

Faith is not the product of discursive reason. It arises when there has been revealed to a different faculty of reason, namely, intelligent sensibility, the fact that one must believe in something in order to accept life: that it would be folly to believe in something which was not essentially truth and the originating source of truth: in other words, in one who was not God.

That which is contrary to faith in principle is not necessarily absurd or contradictory. It is folly, says the Scripture. And this is comprehensible: the object of religious faith is not created things, subject to logical and mathematical law, but God, who is superior to all laws, and His promises which are free. Thus, it is not philosophy: it can only be wisdom.

Now, wisdom expressing itself in judgments of value belongs to the sphere of liberty. Faith is therefore, in principle, a free act. It no more depends on logical constraint than on physical necessity. On the other hand, if faith cannot be, by its origin, the result of logical constraint, reasoning, with its constraining necessities, can and must be introduced into it, by analogy with every practical action produced by a free agent.

Actions of this sort produce certain necessary consequences once they have occurred. Similarly, the propositions resulting from the initial act of faith, which is the act of a free agent, imply logical consequences which it is the rôle of reason to deduce from them. [1]

The Calvinistic apologist must, therefore, never try to produce the initial act of faith by the constraint of the syllogism. He knows that efficacious grace alone can bring it about infallibly, without destroying liberty in the process, since it persuades but does not prove. He will seek to be the instrument of this grace by presenting reasons of wisdom rather than proofs of reason.

Nevertheless, these considerations will not prevent a strictly Calvinistic apologetic from combining the methods of an apostle with motives of wisdom. Already in the sub-apostolic age we see spontaneous faith and catechetical instruction combining to promote the glory of God by combating the pagan and judaizing elements which had penetrated Christian doctrine. Faith, when it has become reflective and dogmatic, will also be concerned with eliminating these elements from religious science and even from philosophy. It is among such elements that the introduction to scientific and theological instruction recognizes heresy [2] and philosophical error.

Spontaneous faith is victorious. So also is reflective faith, for faith does not change its nature by becoming more profound. Apologetics does not endeavour to destroy the adversary's disposition to attack merely in order to comfort the believer; but, by the intellectual defence of religious truth which it presents, it seeks to become an instrument in God's hands, a means of grace, that shall produce in the opponent himself a deep and favourable impression of the truth of religious doctrine.

The natural man has no understanding of divine things. But

---

[1] *Westminster Confession*, cap. I, art. vi.
[2] It will be seen that we accept the basic definition of heresy given by Schleiermacher (*Foi chrétienne*, 22) and adopted by Auguste Sabatier.

Christ has sheep who are still provisionally outside His flock. More than one heretic or unbeliever is already, potentially, that is, through the power of God, a spiritual man. By virtue of the covenant of grace, among many of those born in one or the other sections of the *una sancta*, visible Christianity, He may have begun the process of regeneration even before their natural birth. On the other hand, by virtue of the liberty of divine election, many of those who are born outside the visible Church may be actually the subjects of grace.

In order that the divine work may be completed, it may suffice for certain intellectual misunderstandings to be dispelled. Preaching is not addressed to the elect or the reprobate, as such, but to sinners who seek and are called. Similarly, the apologetic labours of the theologian are not directed to carnal or spiritual men, as such, but to all who seek, whether they seek an intelligent understanding of their faith, because they believe already, or whether they seek the way of faith because they have been inclined to it already by grace.

The Calvinistic theologian knows that he who seeks shall find. Nothing can prevent him from wishing to act as director and guide to every sincere seeker. While the minister preaches and the theologian argues, the Spirit of God works in the hearts of those whom He has already turned towards the light. In His sovereign liberty He can, if He judges it to the purpose, use the preaching and also the apologetics to open the intelligent sensibility of the unbeliever or sceptic to the victorious action of grace. This action is not merely subliminal; it is also intellectual. "God does not work in us as in trunks of trees."

But in order to preserve a scientific value for his work, the defender of the faith will have to watch with scrupulous care lest his zeal should tempt him to garble the texts or the facts. He is trying to show, among other things, that respect for truth is always the sign of a more or less clear intuition of the presence of God, the guarantee of all truth, and he will not therefore feel authorized by the object which he has in view to substitute dialectical cleverness for a loyal statement of the facts. A passion for truth, controlling and regulating all others, is the *conditio sine qua non* of the scientific value of apologetics and of the respect to which it lays claim. Truth is God Himself. Or, more precisely, it is the agreement of the human mind with the originative and constitutive mind of God.

Finally, we do not accept the dilemma: either a logical demonstration of the faith or blind faith. There is a third possibility, but no more. We agree with the authors of the dilemma in recognizing that the solution according to which a truth could be simultaneously or successively an object of strict demonstration and an object of faith shows a misunderstanding of the nature of faith.

We have said that faith, in so far as it is a means of knowing, is a knowledge and a firm adhesion which rests on the authority of divine testimony. It is submission to God and complete confidence in His revelation. It has as its principle His authority, higher than which none can be conceived. It is an exclusive creation of grace but of grace enlightening the understanding.

Thus it excludes essentially the idea of control independent of God, such as that of the autonomous reason. God remains always the supreme guarantee of the value and authority of reason.

Faith excludes essentially the idea that the motives for accepting revelation can be at the same time the authority of God and that of autonomous reason. For, in that case, it would be the result of a synergy, of a co-operation between mutually exclusive divine and human elements, religious and anti-religious motives, the supreme authority of God, on the one hand, and the supreme authority of reason, on the other. The apologetics of a Reformed theology is strictly monergist, as Calvinism could not serve two masters whose authority cannot be shared. According to the precept of the Gospel, we must choose between them. It is impossible to serve both successively without denying one.

He who would begin with faith and finish with autonomous and independent demonstration, could only do so by substituting the latter for faith. And one cannot, at a given moment, do this except by recognizing the inefficacy of the rational motive and the sufficiency of the divine motive of credibility.

A rationalist apology is the theoretical negation of religion. There remains, however, a third possibility, namely, acceptance determined by a judgment of "discretion", as the theologians term it. [1] This is a judgment which results from the fact that contemplative intelligence, as distinct from discursive reason, perceives not only the determining character of the divine action, working on the will, but also the divine character of this action, and the folly of all revolt and resistance on the part of reason.

In this case, faith in the Word of God is not choked by autonomous science; but it is not blind, however, for the under-

---

[1] Calvin, *Com. on* I *John*, ii, 27; iv, 2; Pierre du Moulin, *Le bouclier de la foi*, Paris, 1846, sec. 6, p. 46 f.

standing has received eyes to see and ears to hear. This judgment of faith, at once enlightened and submissive, is thus described by Calvin: "We seek not for arguments or verisimilitudes on which to rest our judgment, but we submit our intellect and judgment to it as too transcendent for us to judge. This, however, we do, not in the manner in which some are wont to fasten on an unknown object which, as soon as it is known, displeases, but because we have a thorough conviction that, in holding it, we hold unassailable truth: not like miserable men, whose minds are enslaved by superstition, but because we feel a divine energy living and breathing in it—an energy by which we are drawn and animated to obey it, willingly indeed and knowingly, but more effectually than could be done by human will or knowledge. . . . This, then, is a persuasion such as requires no reasons: such a knowledge, in agreement with the highest reason, that the mind can rest in it more firmly and more securely than in any reasons: such a conviction, finally, as a revelation from heaven alone can engender. I am speaking of nothing more than every believer experiences in himself, although my words fall far short of the reality and are insufficient to explain it." [1]

The believer's acceptance of the content of revelation is not blind, since it is enlightened by motives of credibility; above all, by the consciousness that his understanding perceives something of the divine majesty of the sublime absolute with whom dogma is concerned. From this intelligent perception the believer draws highly probable judgments of value.

In the second place, when the mind reflects on the disproportion which exists between the simple probability of its judgments and the character of absolute certainty pertaining to faith, it becomes conscious immediately of the presence and action of a cause attesting itself to Him as a mode of the infinite mercy and power. To perceive this and to recognize as present Him whom one already knows as Creator, is not to be blind.

These considerations may be useful to the man who is still a stranger to theistic faith, if he will indeed admit that things must happen so, on the supposition—for such a one, it can be no more—that God is God and not a god like that of deism, which inevitably resolves itself into a form of dualism or unacknowledged polytheism. Thus they may have a preparatory apologetic value.

When we say "God is", we affirm a fact which is forced on us by the consciousness that we have of our own existence, of our

---

[1] *Inst.* I, vii. 5.

own mind, and in fact of the meaning which we attach to such expressions as "to be" and "to be true". The existence of God and the affirmation of this existence can only be in the nature of a principle, a principle supreme in all orders of truth. It would not be worthy of His majesty if one could approach Him like any other object. The existence of God is implied in all affirmation, all negation, all thought.

The objects of contingent knowledge, intrinsically problematical, may be compelled, in spite of their efforts, to betray their existence or their presence by the aid of a principle superior to them or independent of them: the reason drawing its inferences from the data of experience. But God, by definition, is not an intrinsically problematical and contingent object. The supremely real Being, the foundation of all necessity, ontological as well as noetic, He can only become a problem for certain minds as to His existence and the divinity of His revelation, as a result of a spiritual rupture of the moral nature, impairing the moral judgment.

Sometimes an unbeliever will admit that the inability of certain minds to know God and to perceive Him in His revelation may be the sign of an abnormal psychological state. In such a case, the power to cause this state to cease belongs solely to God, if and when it should please Him to re-establish in these minds a sense of the divine in a relative integrity.

If a correct use of the discursive faculties of reason were sufficient to find God and to decide that His revelation was authentic, there would be an end to the sovereignty and liberty of divine grace. God would be compelled to let Himself be attained and proved, as a passive object, not by the humble of heart but by the cleverest dialecticians. Such a god would not be independent; He would not be the independent being; he would not be God. Such a god would not be the God of Jesus Christ who conceals divine things from the wise and prudent and is pleased to reveal them unto babes (Matthew 11: 25).

Since the discernment of the marks of divinity which God has placed in nature and His positive revelation depends on spiritual conditions which the unregenerate man neither wishes to nor can fulfil, this discernment can only result from an act of God, restoring the religious receptivity of the subject, creating the spiritual conditions of this receptivity and effectively determining its acceptance by the subject.

The marks of divinity must therefore be evident to the intelligent sensibility as soon as the required spiritual conditions are present. This is necessary in order that faith may not be blind and that it may yet have a spiritual quality. These marks must not, however, be of a compelling or constraining nature, from the rational and sensorial point of view, but they must leave scope for those who do not wish to render to God His due, to continue in their state of inability to believe, as long as God has not enlightened their understanding and set in motion their will. What has been said is implied in the principles of the Reformed dogma of total corruption and sovereign grace.

This is why we do not hesitate to declare that apologetic arguments have no constraining force for the man who does not wish to place himself in the point of view of the faith. They have no persuasive value except from the moment when, at once vanquished and enlightened by grace, the natural man consents, as in his objective duty, to relinquish the autonomy of his reason and submit to the discriminating principle of religious truth. This principle consists in the affirmation of the absolute independence and exclusive sovereignty of God in the noetic order, as in all the orders of reality. It is the *soli Deo gloria*.

Subordinate motives of credibility rest on judgments of value. With Christ, we would say to their subject: *qui potest capere, capiat*; he who can appreciate them, let him do so. We address ourselves to those without competence in divine and spiritual matters, only in the hope that God will enable them to see marks of divinity in the doctrine which teaches that, from beginning to end, religious knowledge is the creation of His free revelation in men who, under the previous impulsion of grace, seek first His kingdom and His righteousness and not the preservation of the illusory rights of a reason claiming autonomy.

It will be seen that the dogma of election, the keystone of Calvinism, imposes on it an original apologetic method, equally removed from that of those who would substitute the authority of reason for the obedience of faith and from that of those who advocate a sort of practical obscurantism under pretext of preserving the religious character of the faith. The faith remains the faith. But it can assume a scientific form in dogmatics proper, and it contains the psychological and intellectual conditions for the elaboration of a specifically Christian philosophy. An attempt will be made to establish this latter proposition in the next chapter.

CHAPTER 3

CALVINISM AND PHILOSOPHY[1]

Can a philosophy be established side by side with dogmatics and with Christian and Reformed dogmatics in particular? By a philosophy we understand a discipline which is truly such, a discipline sovereign in its own domain, independent of dogmatics and nevertheless specifically Christian and Reformed,

To reply to this question, it is necessary to determine the sense which is attached to the term philosophy; also to understand the initial state of mind of a Calvinistic Christian, living in the light of his faith and who wishes to study philosophy.

Let us try, first of all, to give a definition of philosophy which will not prejudge the question proposed.

Probably one of the first points to be raised will be that man lives in a mysterious, and in many respects, hostile world. In order to dominate it intellectually and practically, he must know it well and, in the measure in which it is possible, understand it. The particular sciences endeavour to respond to these requirements. They are the products of vital necessity.

But the human mind is so constituted that it tends, as soon as it has the leisure, to draw its scattered fragments of knowledge into the synthetic unity of a first principle. We shall call that discipline philosophy, which, under the impulsion of this tendency, endeavours to give such completion to the particular natural sciences. It attempts this by examining freely the explanatory value of the principles put forward for its acceptance as keys to the synthetic understanding of the reality given by sensorial experience.

Starting from this experience, it examines the question of knowing whether the conclusions which it must draw from them lead or do not lead to the threshold of certain conclusions which may be precisely the affirmations of the faith.

We have offered a definition of philosophy which we believe to be broad enough to leave open the question under discussion and

[1] This chapter was complete when Etienne Gilson's *Christianisme et Philosophie*, J. Vrin, Paris, 1936, made its appearance. Believing that we have said what was essential, we have made no alteration apart from the addition of App. XIV, p. 403. A particular point, the Catholic notion of faith, demands, however, a somewhat detailed treatment which will be found in App. XV, p. 399.

at the same time precise enough to indicate what it is all about. If it is objected that such a definition seems to postulate the possibility of metaphysics, a possibility excluded by positivism; we reply that the problem consists in knowing whether a Calvinist is permitted by his principles to examine scientifically the reasons adduced by the positivist school, which entails an exercise in philosophy. Our right to philosophize is thus questioned by Catholic and rationalist alike. Rationalism refuses the right to Christians in general, while certain Catholics would restrict the prohibition to Calvinist.

Brunschvicg may be regarded as an authentic exponent of the rationalist attitude when he writes: "There is a point of view which is, properly speaking, philosophical, a point of view which presupposes itself to be without prejudice. Starting from it, once we have rid ourselves hypothetically of all prejudice, we return to the position of the consciousness of the Western mind. From this point of view, faith, in so far as it is faith, is merely the prefiguration, the sensible symbol, the approximation of that which human effort, properly speaking, is able to bring into the full light of day."

The learned professor proceeds to show that the Christian who wishes to be a Christian before he is a philosopher is obliged to accept the formula of Blaise Pascal: "Thou wouldst not have sought Me, if thou hadst not been already found by Me", a formula which he says, "implies a radical negation, indicative of philosophical unrest". And he concludes that Christianity from the moment that it takes possession of the whole man, does not allow him to be a philosopher "except by discovering to him a manner of philosophizing different from that of the philosophers". Let us consider the argument.

"There is a point of view which is, properly speaking, philosophical." We agree. There is, by general consent, a point of view which is religious, Christian and Reformed, and which considers theology, cosmology and anthropology only under the aspect of the glory of God and the salvation of men through Christ. This is the dogmatic point of view. And there is also the point of view which is "properly speaking, philosophical". After all, who is to tell us in what precisely this last point of view consists? Why should we be expected to accept the definition of it given by the rationalist system?

This is a question which a Protestant, even if he be a Calvinist, cannot but ask, and in asking it he is already philosophizing.

He will philosophize, for he will be free to try to fathom the mysterious reasons which are supposed to compel him to acknowledge *a priori* the sovereign rights of rationalistic philosophy. Ever since we renounced the *magisterium* of Rome, our dogmatic spirit has caused us to ask every human *magisterium* which claims to impose its dictation on us to state by what authority it does so. And we ask this even of the masters of the various and conflicting schools of philosophy.

We are told that, from the point of view "properly philosophical", the faith is a sort of provisional philosophy, of a poor quality, for the use of the ignorant, suitable at best as a symbol of that which human effort can bring to full light. But this somewhat obsolete Hegelian concept is a dogmatic point of view, pure and simple, like any other.

It may be a prejudice, it may also be the result of research, sincere and laborious enough, no doubt, but of which there is no *a priori* guarantee that it has been conducted under the required conditions and by minds exempt from those unconscious prejudices which may vitiate the whole work. The monopoly which a philosophical school thus arrogates to itself certainly does not rest on any evident law of thought imposing itself on all with the necessity of an axiom. In any case, if philosophy has anything to do with logic, it seems scarcely philosophical to debate with orthodox Christians on the question of whether they can philosophize and to expect them to accept as a basis of discussion a definition of faith which is that of symbolo-fideism. It would be difficult to find a better example of *petitio principii* than this.

And it is worse still when it is a question of defining the philosophical point of view. We are told that it is a point of view which presupposes itself to be without prejudice. It is as unphilosophical as it possibly could be to imagine that any point of view whatever could be exempt from prejudice, if by this term is understood the acceptance of undemonstrables before making use of them as a starting-point.

The philosopher who is content to exhaust his powers in the task of meditation, independent of all teaching, divine or human, is full of prejudices.

These prejudices may be highly respectable but they are none the less prejudices. Our philosopher believes in the validity of the efforts of the mind and of the reason, which is surely undemonstrable. Moreover, he believes in the authority of reason, but reason cannot demonstrate itself to itself except by enclosing itself in a vicious circle. He believes that autonomous reason is the only legitimate foundation on which to support his convictions relative to the first principle of reality, and, in so doing, fails to consider that reason itself forms part of the phenomena to be explained; that it is immanent to them.

It is by prejudice also that he believes a knowledge of the truth to have a value in itself, and that science is, of its very nature, beneficent.

And what shall we say of those prejudices, deeper and more unconscious still, which result from the formation of his mind, from the impression received through the dominant ideas of the civilization and culture to which he belongs? To presuppose oneself without prejudice is a sign of simplicity, not of philosophy.

Finally, we are told that Christians, since they believe themselves to be in possession of the ultimate universal truths and wish to see if these truths enable them to explain reality, cannot experience truly philosophical unrest. Is it not prejudice again which would confound philosophical with religious unrest? We are told that the Christian's manner of philosophizing is not that of the philosophers. And what if it is evident that the Christians have discovered the means of philosophizing with that calmness and liberty of mind which are so desirable to one who wishes to obtain objective results?

Christians do not philosophize like philosophers: Which philosophers? Unbelieving philosophers? Surely that is obvious; but who has decreed that the sole legitimate manner of philosophizing is that adopted by the immanentist philosophers? [1] The philosophers of the school of Alexandria did not philosophize in the manner of Bacon, while Descartes had yet another method. Must they all be omitted from the history of philosophy for this reason?

Bergson philosophizes otherwise than the author whose point of view we have criticized. He believes in the euristic value of mystic ecstasies. Shall we say that he is not a philosopher on the ground that he does not philosophize altogether in the manner of the "philosophers"? How then are we to define the truly philosophical point of view? We shall not seek a definition from the Calvinistic philosophers Vollenhoven and Dooyeweerd, nor shall we attempt to frame one ourselves, wording it so as to exclude, in advance, that of the rationalists. We shall not do this because the Reformed dogma, our dogmatic prejudice, if you will, forbids it at this stage of the discussion.

[1] With Prof. Dooyeweerd, we take this term in a more general sense than that usually attributed to it. By "immanentism" we understand every philosophy which has as its basis something immanent to the reality which it undertakes to explain, as would be reason, for example; cf. Dooyeweerd, *De Wijsbegeerte der Wetsidee*, Amsterdam, 1935, I, bl. 17.

We believe in the innate inability of the unregenerate to attain to God and divine things "by their intelligence or reason". And so long as they are not illuminated by the light of faith, we find it perfectly natural that they should philosophize as they do. They are logical with themselves.

This logic compels them to move in a vicious circle, and we fail to see how they could proceed otherwise. Actually they do what they must do from their point of view. This proves perhaps that it is illegitimate, intellectually, to start from this point of view; but that, of course, is another question.

For ourselves, we are conscious of having had the experience of a spiritual illumination by the intuition of faith, through the testimony and persuasion of the Holy Spirit in connexion with Scripture.

In the light of the doctrine which our Church has taught us— *fides ex auditu*: faith cometh by hearing—and which manifests itself to us irresistibly as divine, we have had a new vision of the world. Nature, although deformed by sin, manifests God to us. We cannot but recognize in all that lives and moves and exists the action and presence of God, of the God whom we confess in our creeds and confessions of faith. We have recognized Him because if we have consciousness of being effects, of not existing of ourselves, it follows that we are conscious effects, conscious of depending absolutely on a cause which is revealed to our intuition as being infinite in power and liberty in regard to all the laws which govern experimental reality. And it is outside this contingent reality that we find our foundation for philosophizing.

We should not, therefore, be logical with ourselves if we were to seek without declaring emphatically that we did so only because, in a certain sense we had found already. We have found something which guarantees to us the value of our efforts. Henceforth, in order to determine the properly philosophical point of view, we shall not assume ignorance of that which we know by the intuition of faith. Nor shall we expect others to admit that which they do not think they know, because they have not the same intuition as we have. We shall ask only what the metaphysician is attempting, whether he be a believer or not.

This is in fact the object pursued by a discipline which has to teach us what is the true character of this discipline. Now there exists a discipline which is called philosophy. This discipline, interrogating nature, asks it whether and to what extent human intelligence can understand and not merely recognize, how given facts can be traced back to their source.

It is clear that here liberty of thought is complete for the Christian. The intuition of his faith gives him indeed the solution of the problem. It causes him to know that it is God who is the Creator of the world and that it is the will of God which makes the necessity of all things.

But this intuition does not indicate the course to be followed in order that he may understand that this is so. Nor does it tell him if this understanding is possible. The Christian is thus in the position of a student who knows the solution of a problem in mathematics or physics, but still has to discover the reasons and the operations to be carried out in order to arrive at it. It is in this sense that he seeks, having already found.

Now, there is no *a priori* reason why he should not respect the rules of the game in his enquiry. Experience shows, by such examples as those of the Anglican Canon Mansel and the Calvinist Hamilton, that these rules can be scrupulously observed by Christians. These two philosophers, starting with concepts in our opinion erroneous, concluded that the absolute of their philosophy could not logically be harmonized with the notion which faith gives us of God. They were able to arrive at this conclusion in all loyalty precisely because their faith shielded them from the metaphysical unrest which it is desired at all costs to make an essential condition from the properly philosophical point of view.

In order to grasp the difference between the empirical and religious point of view, on the one hand, and the geometrical point of view, on the other, it must be borne in mind that, as Professor Brunschvicg has amply demonstrated, there are two species of judgments: the judgment of relation, which is that of the religious man and which must be that of the theologian when he investigates intellection; which is that of common sense and which must be that of scientific knowledge; and the predicative judgment which is that of the philosopher, it being understood that he is aiming at something other than the intellection of the theologian or of the physicist.

In ordinary usage, these two types of judgment give the verb "to understand" two very different senses. The judgment of relation results from experimental intuition. It proves that between two terms given by experience there exists a relation of dependence, of constant sequence, of difference, of equality. When this judgment makes itself explicit, it may take on the appearance of deductive argument. In reality, it is formed by the view of the relation. Descartes is not making a deduction when he says, following Augustine: *cogito, ergo sum*; he is seeing, or thinking he sees, immediately that there is an indissoluble relation between the act of thinking and the act of being.

When Calvin says: *si vita in nobis, ergo testimonium Deitatis*[1], he is verifying experimentally that the consciousness which one has of not existing of oneself is bound up with the consciousness of existing by another, by that which is by itself, which he finds present and acting in the depths of his being. He afterwards universalizes, by induction, the relation of absolute dependence expressed by his judgment.

The judgments to which the natural sciences lead, and which are called laws, are precisely judgments of relation, universalized by induction: in the first place, judgments of causal relations—causal in the sense of constant and sufficient succession; then, when the sciences have progressed sufficiently, of mathematical relations.

Now, for the theologian, as well as for the metaphysician, to understand is to see that the relations connect the facts. Facts are understood when relations of dependence, simultaneity, regular sequence or quantity, are proved to exist between them. Fundamentally, what we see is that observable realities have a certain behaviour, relatively to one another and relatively to ourselves. But, properly speaking, it is not understood in the sense of drawing the predicate from the subject. Neither theology nor physics can cause us to know these sciences as they are in themselves. These disciplines permit us to receive from them or to construct of them images, or rather concepts, analogical in theology, symbolical in physics.

Commenting on the statement of 1 John 4: 8: "God is love", Calvin writes: "In other words, it is His nature to love men. I know well that there are those who philosophize here more subtly, especially the ancient authors who have abused this passage, in order to prove the divinity of the Holy Spirit. But the sense of the Apostle is simple; namely, since God is the fountain of charity, let this affection flow forth and be shed abroad wherever He is known. He is not speaking here, of the essence of God, but is merely showing that we are affected by Him".[2] So much for Reformed theology.

Eddington writes: "Since we must cease to employ the familiar concepts, it remains only for us to use symbols. . . . Every time we establish the properties of a body under the form of physical quantities we give this information in the same way as we read a dial plate: that and nothing more".[3] So much for physics.

---

[1] *Praelect. in Jer.*, **x**, 10.   [2] *Com. in loco.*
[3] Quoted by Jacques Maritain, *Les degrès du savoir*, p. 313.

The world of physics is a world of symbols connected by mathematical relations. Dogmatics and physics, eminently practical sciences intended to forecast, provoke or prevent certain forms of behaviour in the real, subjective and objective, they can scarcely yield any information other than that which we have just indicated.

It is possible, of course, to conceive also a philosophy, and even a metaphysics, of the judgment of relation. But, in this case, we must realize what is being done and the ideal that is aimed at: it will not be a philosophy of rational comprehension, but one of intuitive intellection. The reasoning which will predominate in it will be inductive reasoning, which is a problem to reason itself. Its very foundation is still in dispute. From this point of view, what are called the proofs of the existence of God are merely the dialectic rendering, under the form of a hypothetical conclusion, of religious intuitions.

Besides, the judgment of relation is not the only one that is capable of forming the human mind: there exists another reasoning than induction. There is predicative judgment, as well as deduction and the syllogism.

Predicative judgment is that in which the attribute enters into the comprehension of the subject. Here, to understand is, indeed, still, if you will, to have the intuition of a relation; but this relation is that of conceptual container to the contained. To understand is to see that an idea which expresses, whether analogically or adequately, it matters not, the essence of a being, implies, excludes or tolerates another idea which is proposed as its predicate. Such understanding can only be obtained by deductive reasoning, which, given a form, becomes the syllogism. The knowledge at which it aims is that of beings in that which they have that is general, universal; that is to say, in their proper essence.

From this point of view, the cause is not considered as a true explanation as if it contained in itself the elements which are found in the effect. The concept, emptied of all explanatory content, the concept of the antecedent, recognized by experimental science as necessary and sufficient to predict a consequent phenomenon, itself demands an explanation for speculative reason when it aspires to understand ontologically. For speculative reason, the more cannot be explained by the less.

Is the establishment of such an ontological science possible? That is a question for discussion. There would seem to be no reason why a philosopher, even though a Christian, could not discuss it in complete liberty of mind and resolve it to the best of his ability. His religion does not compel him to affirm *a priori* that it can be established, nor does it forbid him to attempt to do so. But it must be acknowledged that, if this were possible, it would give, in a decisive manner, to reason, to the disinterested philosophical instinct, the satisfaction of understanding in the ontological sense of the term, as much as it is given to a limited being to understand,

In such metaphysics, whatever may be the opinion of our friends the scholastics—whom nevertheless gladly we salute with the title of philosophers—what are called the proofs of the existence of God (by movement, the existence and the order of the world) would not be proofs of His existence but explanatory propositions, conclusions to which the reason would be inexorably reduced. They would merely prove that the latter could not account for the world except by admitting a god, namely, pure act, necessary sovereignly intelligent—a god, not God, not the God of Jesus Christ.

As for Anselm's proof, in its authentic form, it is not, like Descartes' an attempt to pass from the ideal order to the real by a simple analysis of concepts, in order to prove a doubtful point. It starts with the intuition which faith has of possessing the truth and reality which is God—*veritas quam credit et amat cor meum*: the truth which my heart believes and loves—in order to understand the logical necessity of this existence. It arrives there by stating that it is impossible to conceive the being greater than all that one can think as having no more than an ideal existence.

The conclusion is certainly a predicative judgment, but this judgment rests on a previous existential judgment of relation: it is explanatory. Would a Christian philosopher also necessarily have to base his position on a previous existential judgment of relation: the negation of the philosophy of ontological comprehension? Or could he, on the other hand, consider the two methods as complementary? As we have already said, we believe he will do as the other philosophers to the best of his ability.

When he is developing a system of dogmatics, looking at the subject from the Calvinistic point of view, we suggest that he will have to start from the intuitions of the faith: to give his dogmatic construction a substructure of judgments of relation, faith in God, the creator and preserver of beings; to limit ourselves even to this, is acceptance of the intuition of the divine in the mind and of God in the soul and in the world.

Predicative judgment, nevertheless, has its place in dogmatics when it is a question of deducing the explanatory consequences of the principles laid down or of the truths acknowledged. In polemics, it can take part in the criticism of rejected opinions, in order to expose the internal contradiction.

Once more, when a Christian studies philosophy, nothing that we know in his religious principles obliges him to condemn, with the modern nominalists, the predicative judgment.

Nor does anything oblige him to think that it is the unique mode of philosophical reasoning. The faith leaves him free. There is no such thing as a specifically Christian mode of formal reasoning. The Christian knows, or should know, that, on the most favourable hypothesis, reason leads him to a god, not to God. But this must not hinder him from going as far as reason leads him, free to seek in the light of revelation the means of proceeding farther in knowledge.

As to the content of philosophy, is there a specifically Christian philosophy? If we concede to the editor of Pascal [1] that Christianity is essentially the historic apparition and incarnation of the only begotten Son of God, it seems evident to us that the conclusions of the study of the world, of the cosmos considered as such, cannot be specifically Christian. For this reason: we agree willingly that the incarnation is the essence of Christianity, on condition that the cause assigned to this great fact is the love which God bears to the cosmos; and that the end assigned to it is the salvation of sinners and the restoration of the world to its normal relation with its Creator.

This presupposes another fact, a formidable one this time, namely, sin. But sin is an accident, a contingent fact in its origin and of spiritual and moral nature. The Incarnation is the free response of God to this contingent fact. It has for its contingent end to turn the accident which is sin "to the praise of the glory of His grace". Now a fact as contingent, as free in its origin, as the introduction of sin into the world, and an equally free determination of God, like the gratuitous election of sinners to glory, the Incarnation of God, the Cross and the application of salvation to the predestinate, does not result from a metaphysical necessity.

These things cannot be deduced necessarily from either the nature of man as God has created him, nor the nature of God as it is revealed to us.

This justice of God which justifies the impious cannot be known except by a revelation, a Word of God. The essence of

[1] L. Brunschvicg.

Christianity is, by definition, the specific object of theology, the science of revelation: it is thus outside the sphere of philosophy, properly speaking. This latter, when it concerns itself with God, cannot take into account the free relations between God and His creatures fallen into sin. Its object will be the necessary relations between the supreme legislator and created beings, such as result from the general laws which govern the world in all degrees of reality.

In the nature of things, therefore, there cannot be a specifically Christian fundamental philosophy, in the sense that it can claim to demonstrate by independent means the sovereign God, Creator of heaven and earth *a nihilo*, the original liberty of man, his fall, total corruption and the *ordo salutis*, the dispensation of salvation.

But there can be, in principle, a philosophy of Christian dogma, as there can be a philosophy of any positive religion whatsoever. On the other hand, the Christian philosopher cannot avoid taking into account what he knows, even when he is dealing with natural philosophy.

It is a fact that Christianity has transplanted from the soil of Palestine into Graeco-Roman and modern philosophy a principle, an undemonstrable which is the reverse of the immanentist philosophies.

These philosophies are normalistic and autonomistic.

They presuppose the relative integrity of the organs of knowledge and the autonomy of the means of arriving at knowledge.

Christianity, on the other hand, at least in its Augustinian and anti-Pelagian form, is anormalistic and theonomistic. It realizes, with the Apostle, that the natural man understands nothing of the things concerning God. Its doctrines of redemption, regeneration and restoration presuppose the Fall and its ravages. It cannot forget, on the other hand, our Lord's warning: "Take heed that the light which is in you be not darkness". This warning necessitates a critique of knowledge when it would pass from the visible to Him who is invisible by essence. It is necessary even for the correct interpretation of sensible reality by judgments of value. It is necessary for simple existential judgments bearing on this sensible reality. The relative integrity of our organs of natural knowledge remains a problem for the believer in total corruption.

And this critique must be such that it has a basis transcendent to the world and to the intelligence which it essays to criticize and explain. The Christian needs it, for he has no wish to enclose himself in the vicious circle which Renouvier and

Gourd acknowledge as an ineluctable necessity from their immanentist point of view.[1]

The Christian, if he is faithful to the essence of Christianity, must be essentially theonomistic. He cannot neglect the theonomistic principle, even when he is philosophizing. No doubt, it is with his natural organs of knowledge that he will endeavour to understand the data of sensible reality and to relate them to a unique principle. But he cannot abstract from the fact that his faith makes him see this reality in a new light. All things, in fact, have become new for him from the moment when he became conscious of his union with Christ. Henceforth his judgments of value on reality are changed, and more than that, the entire situation has been reversed. The certitude from which Socrates started was that he knew nothing. From this state of total ignorance he hoped to rise to a knowledge of the supreme cause. The certitude from which the Christian starts, if he wishes to give his philosophy a specifically theistic tone, is that God alone is, in the strict sense of the term; that His will is the necessity of all things and that it is always good, acceptable and perfect. Here we have the condition of philosophical intellection of reality for a Christian conscious of the implications of his faith. *Credo ut intelligam*, said Augustine and Anselm.[2]

A philosophy, in order to be formally Christian, must start with this. The fear of the Lord—religion—is the principle of wisdom, according to Scripture. On the other hand, Christianity has not only introduced a new principle into philosophy, a basis transcendent to the world; it has provided an essential notion which, according to our exegesis, it owes to the canonical books of the Old Testament. This idea, however, finds its technical formula for the first time in an apocryphal book (2 Maccabees, 7 : 28).

It is the notion of creation *e nihilo*, the notion of total causality.

This is not the place to discuss the idea, but it may be said in passing that its philosophical importance cannot be denied. Every philosophy which accepts this notion as a principle of ontological explanation of the existence of contingent things is historically Christian by this fact alone.

But can there be a specifically Christian philosophy in the sense that it would bring the effort of its thought to bear upon sin and redemption by Christ, but would be distinct from

---

[1] Renouvier, *La critique philosophique*, etc., 10th year, April 30, 1881, n. 13; J. J. Gourd, *Le Phénomène*, p. 101; cf. Louis Trial, *Jean Jacques Gourd*, p. 118, n. 1.

[2] This point of view is strongly emphasized by Calvin in his 146th *Sermon on Job*, *Op. Calv.*, 35, p. 337 ff.

dogmatics? To this question we have already replied in the affirmative.

It can be shown that Christianity has opened a new and immense field for philosophical reflexion, properly so called, for that reflexion which seeks to understand by reason that which it has received on the authority of Scripture. We recall the names of Augustine, Anselm, Calvin, Pascal, Guélincx, Malebranche and Secrétan. Dogmatics authenticates, catalogues, interprets, formulates, and relates genetically the revealed data. Christian religious philosophy takes these revealed data as matter for the meditations of the reason or of the natural intelligence, but illuminated by faith. Christian reason does not aspire, in truth, to comprehend the mysteries of the faith. That would be a contradictory attempt.

But reason seeks, in complete independence, to understand why there are religious mysteries and to integrate them into the mass of mysteries of nature as conditions of a synthetic intellection of things.

It may be objected that in these circumstances the reasonings of Christian philosophers are of no importance for philosophers pure and simple. This agrees perfectly with the point of view of Christian philosophers if they are in the least degree Augustinian, Calvinian, or, shall we say, more directly, Pauline. If it could be otherwise, it would be a scandal for their faith and an insoluble enigma for their philosophy: is it not written that the natural man can understand nothing of divine things and that, in this sphere, little children can see more clearly than sages and the intelligentsia?

For the Christian and Calvinistic philosopher, the constructors of immanentist systems enter into arguments which have no psychological and historical importance, because they commence their work by enclosing themselves in a vicious circle.

On the Catholic side, it is denied that there can be Calvinistic philosophers, at least if they are consistent with their principles. For Calvinism, the primary philosophy, metaphysics, would be a useless luxury in any case, the need for it being fully supplied by dogmatics. Secondly, the end which it proposes for itself, the elimination of the pagan element from thought, would render philosophy impossible, even if it wished to offer itself this superfluous luxury.

In order to reply to these objections of principle, it is necessary to recall what attitude Calvinism takes in relation to the problem under consideration and to determine what sort of philosophy is possible for it.

Calvinism does not present itself as a new Church; it claims to be the ancient Church reformed according to the principle of the analogy of faith, which is the *soli Deo gloria*, that is to say, the sufficiency and sovereignty of God and His absolute independence in regard to every being other than Himself.

The external norm and source of its dogmas is given in the writings which the Church recognized already at the moment of its entry into the scene of history as canonical, that is to say, as a permanent divine rule of faith and life. These writings attest themselves as divine and canonical to the Calvinist by the mediate and immediate testimony of the Holy Spirit: mediate in the consent of the Church and the other characters of divinity: immediate in the act of personal faith.

Calvinism, being thus a form of theology and of the Church in the direction of the evangelical and Augustinian tradition, is strictly anormalist and monergistic. It believes that the result of the Fall is the total corruption of human nature. Here lies its anormalism. Its monergism consists in the fact that it teaches that it is the action of common grace alone which prevents the corruption of nature from becoming the annihilation of nature: and that it is the action of special grace alone which can restore it to its normal state by regeneration.

Calvinism thus aims at purifying the soul, the Church and the world from heresy under its Judaic, moralist, legalist form, in the first place. On this point its efforts may be confounded with those of Lutheranism, from which it took over the doctrine of justification *sola fide*. But it aims at a more extensive reformation than that system, and is distinguished from it by the intenseness of its effort against an aspect of heresy from which Lutheranism, of its own choice, reacts very imperfectly. This aspect is the pagan element which immerses God in the world since it does not separate Him from the world: which in every way menaces His sovereignty and confounds the signs of the divine with the *numen*, with God Himself, since it does not set these in opposition to Him.

Finally, Calvinism places itself on another plane than rationalism and historicism. Against rationalism, whether it be catholic, protestant or secular, it sees in faith the organ of religious certitude. Faith (*fides qua creditur*), the faith which grasps its object, is an integral element of normal or regenerate human nature. It is the intuition of the sublime majesty of God in Holy Scripture, in which He teaches, reveals, threatens and promises with authority. It is the intuition of the presence of God in us provoking and maintaining the activity by which we live and move and have our being. It is the intuition of the presence of an intelligent and free Being ruling the course of things.

In opposition to historicism, which would prove or deny the divine and the miraculous by the historical critique of human testimony, Calvinism declares the transhistorical character of miracle. Miracle cannot be established by human testimony until it has been, in some manner, made present to our mind, across the centuries by the testimony and authority of God.

"Faith", says Calvin, "cannot be content with the witness of men, whoever they may be, if it is not preceded by the authority of God. But when the Holy Spirit has testified to us internally that it is God who is speaking, then we give some place to the testimonies of men in order to assure ourselves as to the certainty of the history. By the certainty of the history I mean the knowledge that we possess of the things which have happened either through having seen them ourselves or through having heard others speak of them."[1] For Calvin, the authentication of the miracle must not commence with a critical examination by the independent reason. The "sign" is not perceived as divine by the consciousness until the latter has been illuminated by the Holy Spirit.[2] It is the analogy of faith which authenticates the miracle as such and not the miracle, proved rationally and historically, which establishes the dogma.[3]

Now, it is freely admitted on the Catholic side that such a faith can legitimately, and indeed must, attempt to erect itself into a dogmatic science, taking for its object God and man: God, or rather the glory of God: man, or rather the salvation of sinful man and of a lost world. But when we claim to philosophize, the following objections are raised:

[1] *Com. on the Harmony of the Gospels*, Luke, 1: 1, 2.

[2] *Com. on John*, iii, 2: "When the eyes are open and illuminated by the light of spiritual wisdom, miracles render a firm enough testimony to the presence of God."

[3] *Praef. ad reg. Gal. op.*, ii, 16 : *Proinde doctrinam, quae praecedere ab evangelista dictur, priore loco examinari explorarique par est. Quae si probata fuerit, tum demum a miraculis iure confirmationem sumere debet. Probae autem doctrinae, auctore Christo, isthaec nota est, si non in hominum sed Dei gloriam quaerendam vergit* (Ioann. vii, 18 ; viii, 50). *Hanc quum doctrinae probationem Christus asserat, perperam censentur miracula quae alio quam ad illustrandum unius Dei nomen trahuntur, et meminisse nos decet sua esse satanae miracula.* . . . The proper course is, in the first place, to examine and explore the doctrine which is said by the Evangelist to precede: then, after it has been proved, but not till then, it may receive confirmation from miracles. But the mark of sound doctrine given by Christ Himself is its tendency to promote the glory, not of men, but of God (John 7: 18; 8: 50). Christ having declared this to be the test of true doctrine, we are in error if we regard as miraculous works which are used for any other purpose than to magnify the name of God: and it behoves us to remember that Satan has his miracles also.

(a) The existence of God being, for the Calvinist, an object of faith and not of rational demonstration, metaphysics would seem to be useless.

We reply that metaphysics is, indeed, useless for the establishment of religion; but it is by no means useless for the purpose of endeavouring to make it understood that religion is the best key for opening the gate to the mystery of nature. Philosophy cannot provide a foundation for religion or theology. Fortunately this is the case, for all men have not the means of indulging in philosophical speculation, and all those who could and would like to do so are not called to such a task by God. But those in whom faith has stimulated an urge to understand, and who feel within themselves the philosophical vocation, will study metaphysics in a free and disinterested manner. They will give themselves up to this task not merely to satisfy their own deep inclination but above all to glorify God before men. They will endeavour to show them that faith can open the mind to the noblest ambitions of science, and it will be found, perhaps, that a task undertaken in scientific serenity and detachment, and with an absolute intellectual sincerity, may be used to criticize the systems impregnated with pagan elements. Moreover the desire to eliminate these elements is not antiphilosophical in itself.

The Christian philosopher knows by faith that there is a God. On the other hand, he is conscious that natural facts, in all degrees of the hierarchy of being, point like signals towards a supreme intelligent cause above all law.

What is contrary to the philosophical spirit in saying that one can arrive at a clearer understanding of these problems by exorcizing the phantom of a god identical with the world? Why should it be antiphilosophical to show that moral obligation cannot be properly understood apart from a supreme legislator from whose nature and will flows all law?

Even supposing that the philosopher cannot bring this demonstration to a successful conclusion, he can admit it honestly and revert to a discipline other than his own in order to establish the affirmations which his faith shows him to be truths. But when he reasons in his own sphere he will do so with the same independence as the unbelieving philosopher.

(b) But it is further objected that in attempting to eliminate the pagan element you must eliminate nature itself. Now nature is the text of philosophy. An Augustine and an Aquinas have been able to philosophize only by assimilating themselves to the thought of Plato, Plotinus and Aristotle, who were pagans,

AN INTRODUCTION TO REFORMED DOGMATICS

rectifying it according to their ability where necessary. It was Greek, and thus pagan, thought which taught Christians the sciences of nature and reflexion on the conclusions of these sciences. The Christian religion is essentially orientated towards the sacred and supernatural. Philosophy has for its sphere of investigations the natural and the profane, in which the pagans were pastmasters.

To which we reply that for Reformed Christians there is nothing profane but sin. For the antithesis sacred and profane, we would substitute special grace and common grace. This is why we cannot identify paganism with nature or confine the Christian religion to the supernatural. That which is pagan in ancient philosophy is not its enthusiasm for the study of nature: it is not the nature itself which this philosophy takes for its object: it is its pantheism, its deism: it is God denied or replaced by the cult of nature. But when a pagan thinker expresses and advocates something true, beautiful and noble, our faith teaches that he does so under the supernatural action of common grace.

It is well known that the early apologists saw in such cases the intervention of the Word of God. It is known that Zwingli said: "this is a word of God". It is less well known, and sometimes even unknown, that Calvin said the same thing: "Those who are afraid to borrow from the profane authors are too superstitious. For, since all truth is of God, if unbelievers have said something to the point and in accordance with truth, it must not be rejected, for it proceeds from God. Moreover, since all things are of Him, why should we not apply to His glory all that can be properly related to it?" [1]

For Calvin, the sciences cultivated by the pagans and the philosophical truths which they glimpsed are the magnificent result of the action of common grace. The pagan element which is to be found among them must not be confounded with them. It can and must be separated from them, and this is precisely one of the tasks of the Calvinistic philosopher.

(c) In assigning a religious object to philosophy, namely, God grasped by the intuition of faith, by the religious consciousness, Calvinism would substitute religion for philosophy.

We reply that it must not be assumed that rational demonstration is the sole legitimate process in philosophy. Somewhere both intuition and faith in this intuition must enter in. The positivist himself could not take one step in the way which his

---

[1] *Com. on Titus*, i, 12; apropos of a quotation by the Apostle Paul from Epimenides: cf. Justin, *Apol.* ii, 13; i, 5.

method lays down if he did not believe that this method was the necessary condition for attaining to the knowable. The rationalist can demonstrate nothing if he does not accept, by an act of faith, one or more undemonstrable principles.

Why may not the Calvinistic philosopher start with the intuition which his faith has concerning the sovereignty of God, above all law? This intuition gives him a transcendent basis to the reality which he is attempting to understand.

Besides, in assigning as a goal of philosophy God in so far as He reveals Himself to faith, a religious object is not thereby given to this discipline. A religious object would be God believed and acknowledged as the end of worship and the author of salvation. But, in order to approach God in this way, one must first of all believe that He exists. Now, the Calvinistic philosopher, starting from this primary intuition of faith, when he philosophizes, believes in and acknowledges God as first principle, supreme cause and ultimate reason of the universality of things, and in Him his own reason can rest. There is nothing specifically religious in this last consideration: it is, properly speaking, a philosophical point of view.

Actually, the end pursued by religion is worship and reconciliation with God. But the end here pursued is the repose of the intelligence in the contemplation of a principle beyond which it feels that there remains nothing to seek. Thus, Calvinism is not confronted by difficulties peculiar to itself. In comparison with other systems, it is as well, and indeed better, able to construct a philosophy of its own.

So the way is clear. We may now proceed to our discussion of the foundation and specification of religious knowledge by studying the true nature of Reformed dogma. In doing this, we shall be engaged in the study of philosophy, not of dogmatics.

CHAPTER 4

WHY CHRISTIAN DOGMATICS MUST BE THEISTIC

Calvinism is a form of Christian and Protestant theism. Furthermore, we maintain that it is the one strictly consistent form of Christian and Protestant theism.[1]

To show that dogmatics must be theistic, Christian and Protestant, and that Calvinism is such, is to give Reformed dogmatics the philosophical introduction which it requires as a scientific discipline.

Let us show in the first place that Calvinism is a consistent theism and that theism is the sole legitimate form of religious thought.

Apart from theism, we can conceive only two forms of religious thought: deism and pantheism. Now the divine, $\tau\grave{o}$ $\theta\epsilon\hat{\iota}ov$, is always perceived by piety as an infinite. By this we mean that it always reveals itself as realizing a certain ideal, without a limiting negation, except it be the idea of the unlimited faculty of perfecting itself.

This is true even of those religious philosophies, like that of Renouvier, which claim to deny the infinite as actually existing. In reality, these philosophies intend to deny only the mathematical infinite of number, time and space. But, whether they accept the word or not, the object of worship of the neo-critics, their divinity is necessarily an infinite in the sense that it realizes their religious ideal. Otherwise, they would not worship it at all.

The real distinction between religious deism and pantheism is not that the former denies absolutely the infinite being, while the latter affirms him. It is that deism instead of acknowledging the infinity of the being and of all the attributes of God retains the infinite in God only as regards one or several attributes. The infinity of thought: God is the thought of thought: the infinity of will: God is pure liberty, pure will, unlimited power: the infinity of love: God is essentially, uniquely, love.

If other attributes than those which we have just named are admitted to the *numen*, the divine, these attributes are generally limited by them, are subordinate to them, or are regarded as derived from them.

[1] Warfield, *Calvin and Calvinism*, p. 355 f.

Whether the *numen* is thought, having no other object than itself, or a tyrannical absolute, or love, without discrimination, it is infinite only in depth and in one direction.

It is in this sense that the god of deism is limited: limited in his being. Other beings can well be conceived, and indeed have been conceived as existing of themselves, independent of him or springing from nothing by an absolute beginning. Even if the creative act is reserved for a sort of divine monarch, such beings once created, will subsist of themselves.

This divinity will be a first cause, no doubt, but he will not be *the* first cause, efficient and materially total, of all being and of all that is positive and good in the acts of creatures.

All action that is accorded to him will be transferred to causes other than himself, every action of other causes will limit him in his action of himself. In finding or in creating free first causes, this god discovers his limitations. It is in this sense that one can say that the god of deism is limited and that his worshippers deny that he can be infinite.

Pantheism, on the other hand, openly confesses the infinity of the divine, but this infinite is conceived as the totality of being and of reality. God is all that can be seen and all that cannot be seen: all that has been, is, and will be. God does everything, for the simple reason that nothing exists except God (*acosmism*). [1]

The multiple is nothing more than a view of the human mind. The pretended free causes, so far from being first causes, are not even, properly speaking, secondary causes: they are moments of the first cause. In the final analysis, there is only one cause, God, who communicates to the sum total, that is to say, to His own substance, the movement of universal evolution.

This evolution is nothing less than the actual history of God Himself. If indeed one wishes to admit that in this infinite *magma* there are one or several nuclei or conscious *foci* analogous to man, one can, if religiously disposed, invoke it or them as one invokes the help of men. If preferred, the religious consciousness latent in every man can be nourished by the devout contemplation of the infinite *magma* to which we give the name of God, in which death will immerse us one day or another. Calvinism also, being a religion, can have no other object of worship than the infinite, but this infinite differs totally from the infinite of one or more dimensions of deism, and from the infinite (=totality) of pantheism. He is the infinite absolute, without any restriction whatever. The ineffable *numen* that we worship is not only τὸ

---

[1] [*Acosmism* (Greek α + κόσμος, world) the theory of the non-existence of the external physical world.]

θεῖον, the divine; he is ὁ θεός, God: God in the infinite, absolute, perfect, incommunicable sense of the term. God, the living and the true, totally different from creatures and yet related to them by analogy. Totally different because He alone is and is of an infinite essence; related by analogy to intelligent and free creatures because this essence is spiritual and because this spirit, sovereignly free in an eminent degree, is the ultimate support of the things of which He is the first cause.

He is adorable, because He is an infinite essence; able to succour, because He is spirit and the Father of spirits.

God reveals Himself by creation and redemption as the Sovereign all powerful and the Saviour all good. He thus answers to the preconception and the instinct of the theistic piety which He creates when He wishes to establish a receptive organ in man.

Our God, it will be observed, is neither the god of deism nor the god of pantheism. He is not the god of deism, confined within a unilateral infinity. That which is infinite in Him is Himself, His essence, in the absolute unity, the perfect simplicity of His being. He is, in an eminent degree, the most real of all beings: he is not the abstract and empty concept (the *ens generalissimum*) of being in the most general sense, but the ocean of being; immense, eternal, immutable in the majesty of the perfections by which He reveals to intelligent spirits what He is for them. And what He is for them He is in reality, for He is truth, but in a manner which surpasses all thought.

He is not the god of deism, for when we say, with certain deists, that God is the Creator "this expression may not signify any more than that He has called His creatures into existence, afterwards abandoning them, without taking the least care of them. But it must be understood that, as the world was made by Him in the beginning, so now He maintains it in the same state, in such manner that heaven, earth and all creatures subsist in their being only by virtue of His power. Moreover, God thus holding all things in His hand, it follows that their government pertains to Him and that He is their master."[1]

In this last affirmation, properly understood, lies our fundamental difference with deism. For deism, there are as many first causes as there are free causes. For us, there is one unique first cause, God; and there are also free beings who are real secondary causes. He is the unique first cause of all that is and of everything positive that is made or done, in the sense that by Him all that is created possesses life, movement and existence.

[1] *Geneva Catechism*, IV.

Materially, therefore, He is the sole first cause. But there are real secondary causes. The liberty of these causes, under the control and providence of God, impresses on the acts of which it is the subject the form which they assume. We act also, on our part, said Calvin to the libertines.[1] And the more intense the action of God, the more real is our subsistence, our formal action. For God does not destroy what He created, and He has created free subjects.

Nor is this God the god of pantheism. He is indeed, as pantheism affirms, the unique first cause. But this cause is never to be confounded with the creatures which He has established in their liberty; nor is He ever separated from them, since they cannot exist for an instant without Him.

He is the total material cause, not the unique formal cause; there are real secondary causes. Created beings are, if you will, accidents which subsist only in God by virtue of His continuous creative activity. But whereas in us the accidents are merely modes of our own substance, in God the creator these accidents are real substances, because created and distinct, infinitely, immensely distinct from God, because created *e nihilo*.

He *is*, and he alone, immutably; they do no more than subsist, that is to say, they are born, continue and pass away in Him. The essence of God can neither sink into matter nor be confounded with the finite spirits which it raises out of nothingness.

For Calvinistic piety, pantheism is an outrage on the incommunicable majesty, the awful purity, of God; while deism affronts the unity and unicity of His infinite essence. We cannot admit that God should be regarded as a simple *primus inter pares*, a chief among equals. He is God, the holy and unique.

Calvinism is thus definite theism. And since it distinguishes the *hypostasis*[2] of the Father and that of the Holy Spirit from the *hypostasis* of the Son; since nevertheless it does not distinguish God the Creator and life-giver from God the Saviour; since it could not even attempt to separate or divide these three hypostatic aspects of God, for three infinites in essence and in qualities cannot even be conceived as coexistent without coinciding so totally in their being that they cannot be three existences but must be identically and numerically the same—

---

[1] *Corp. Ref.*, 35, 188.

[2] *Hypostasis*, in theological language, when this term is applied to the Trinity, signifies a permanent and irreducible mode of personal subsistence in the being of God; a person, but not an individual, as are created persons, in the species which comprises them.

this being the case, Calvinism is not only consistent theism; it is a Christian theism.

That it is a consistent form of theism cannot be seriously contested. It makes the sovereignty and independence of God, the *soli Deo gloria*, the touchstone of its doctrine and worship, of its morals and sociology. Its teachings on preordination, the government of the world, predestination and grace, the mode of the Incarnation and the sacraments, are there to attest that it does not recoil from any of the consequences which flow from the principle of the sovereignty of God, the final arbiter of the destinies of creatures, whom the finite cannot contain.

And now, how does a Calvinist normally arrive at the knowledge of God? On what criterion can he depend in order to form the existential judgment which affirms God as the supreme transubjective reality?

We have already remarked that, in the ordinary course of events, he derives his knowledge of God from the Church, which communicates to him the revelation that she has received. The first representatives of the Church, for him, are ordinarily his parents or teachers. The Church is the mother of the faithful, says Calvin,[1] it is she who brings them forth as believers. The isolated individual—except for a miracle of the sovereign liberty of God—is nothing, no more in the sphere of the spiritual life than in that of terrestrial and merely human existence. "Faith cometh through hearing", says the Apostle, "and hearing through the Word of God". The Church claims indeed to draw from the Word of God written that which she teaches to her children. It is the province of exegesis and dogmatics proper to justify this affirmation of the Reformed Church. But it is always this Word of God, the contents of which are sealed in the heart of the child by the testimony of the Holy Spirit, that she teaches in her official catechisms and confessions. This incontestable fact may suffice for the present.

It remains only to add that by the Reformed Church in this connexion we do not understand any body which plumes itself on this title, but only one which has continued faithful or returned to the faith of its Reformer, its Fathers and its Martyrs.

How can a Calvinist know that this teaching concerning God is true? How can he know, not that there is a god—for this the light of nature will suffice—but that there is God, the spirit infinite, immutable, eternal in His essence, His wisdom, His justice, His goodness and His truth? He cannot know it by the

[1] *Inst.* IV, i. 4.

evidence of the senses: God is spirit, that is to say, invisible, transcendent to sensorial evidence. He cannot know it by the mediate evidence of discursive reason. The classical "proofs" of the existence of God are in reality not demonstrations but testimonies of inestimable value for the believer. But these testimonies are not, properly speaking, demonstrations. Considered as suggestions, they may be of use to unbelievers also in making them realize that the affirmation of the existence of God is not arbitrary; that in its support facts may be invoked such as the constitution of the human mind, the nature of physical realities, as well as moral, sociological and historical data.

But there is a third kind of evidence, one which belongs neither to the sensorial nor the rational order. It is addressed to the intelligent sensibility. It is that which is derived from the intuition of the divinity of the revelation: objective revelation in doctrine, when this doctrine is a word that has proceeded from God: subjective revelation, in the absoluteness of its acceptance by faith, as well as in the act of religion which is the prayer of the heart.

Objective revelation in doctrine, we said. "The eternal God is truth", writes Calvin, quoting and commenting on an utterance of the prophet Jeremiah. "That is to say, God does not borrow anything elsewhere, but He is sufficient in Himself and possesses by Himself sufficient power and authority. From His essence there shines a true and steadfast glory".[1]

The Word of God which the Church teaches carries with it the seal of its divine origin. It is aureoled with the glory of the sublime. This sublimity is not always literary, but it consists in the intrinsic sublimity of its thought. In the aesthetic order, its sublimity and majesty lie in the revelation of the infinite; in the religious order, the revelation of this infinity provides for the person to whom it is manifested a religious evidence, the sense of a presence which shows him that he must believe and worship.

In the religious order, "the truth is exempt from all doubt, since, without other aid, it is of itself sufficient to sustain itself".[2] It is only too certain that this evidence of the divine authority of the doctrine concerning God which attests its truth *suo pondere*, by its own weight, is not perceptible to all, "for all men have not faith", says the Apostle (2 Thessalonians 3: 2).

In order to be moved by the beautiful and the sublime, it is necessary that the intelligent sensibility, blunted by sin, should

[1] *Praelect. in Jer.*, x, 10.   [2] *Inst.* I, viii. 1.

237

recover its acuteness and its vigour. In order that it may distinguish between the perfection of the beautiful, which is the proportion and the harmony of the finite, and therefore the ornament of the finite creature; and the sublime, which is the revelation of the infinite manifesting itself as present and transubjective, the mind must recover an illumination which it has lost and which it cannot acquire for itself.

Here, discursive reason is powerless. This impotence is already certain in the artistic sphere. One may be superlatively well endowed for critical, mathematical and philosophical reasoning and be quite insensible to the beauty of a melody; one may prefer a daub to a masterpiece by Rembrandt.

Similarly, in religion, the natural man may find himself in the presence of God and feel nothing, perceive nothing but words and, behind the words, mere abstractions devoid of meaning. But let the idea fall into a prepared soil, into a sensibility all expectation, into an intelligence endowed with spiritual discernment and it will become a living word productive of thought and emotion. In order that it may not remain an empty formula, it will impose itself by its own authority as the manifestation of a presence.

Divine revelation, the manifestation of God by Himself being, by definition, the supreme example, one cannot imagine a criterion external and superior to it. It is an evidence of another order than that of the senses and the reason, since it is addressed to another organ of knowledge. But let that organ be created and this evidence will be perceived with the irresistibility proper to all evidence.

The sin against the Holy Ghost, the unpardonable sin, consists in seeing it and refusing to it the adherence of the will, by deliberately attributing a diabolical origin to that which one knows to be divine.

Now, a Calvinist is one who has experienced this irresistibility of the testimony and interior persuasion of the Spirit of God, and who, by grace, has determined in his will to respond to the affirmation of God. He believes in the truth of the word by which God affirms that He is, because he perceives it to be invested with the splendour of the divine majesty. On the other hand, this efficacy of the action of the truth on the soul detracts nothing from the spontaneity of the acceptance that it is given in the case of conversion.

By grace, the object revealed to the intelligence as true can be revealed as lovable in so sovereign a manner that it provokes love. Now, to love is to give oneself voluntarily, and that which is voluntary is free: in Anselm's phrase, *veritas quam credit et amat cor meum*. Moreover, when it is merely a question of faith in God as the transcendent creator and immanent preserver of all things, it is not necessary to be an orthodox Christian in the ecclesiastical sense of the word to perceive the authority which attaches to the simple affirmation that God is.

We could wish for nothing better by way of proof than this moving extract from Boutroux: "Authority cannot be eliminated from the religious life for the general reason that it is implied in the relation between God and man. God by definition excels man infinitely. How, then, can we affirm His existence otherwise than by a sort of induction founded on the authority which we attribute to the perfect Being represented to us by our mind? The divine reality surpasses our conception as well as our experience, but we cannot have an idea of it without feeling at the same time the duty of affirming its existence. God, in revealing Himself to us, does not speak as a phantom of the imagination, as an abstract ideal, but as having authority. . . . To say that God exists is equivalent to saying that goodness, love, mind, considered as real and possible, command the will of the reasonable being and are not merely objects of aesthetic contemplation".[1] So much for the objective aspect of revelation.

But revelation has its subjective side: the nature of the consent of faith and of faith itself, in so far as it is intuition of religious truth, constitutes a revelation of the actual presence and activity of God. "Faith is the substance of things hoped for, the evidence of things not seen" (Hebrews 11: 1). Notice that it is not said that faith is the starting-point of a demonstration, but that it is itself that demonstration or evidence.

In order to understand how this can be so, it is necessary to see clearly what is meant by the term "faith" in this connection. It is not yet justifying faith in the Reformers' sense, the firm certainty of the love of God manifested in Jesus Christ through the promises of the Gospel; nor is it faith in God as Saviour, the soul of which is love and which "worketh by charity". It is so much less than this that Calvin declares that in comparison with justifying faith, this faith is improperly so called.[2] On many occasions, however, he employs the term to designate this act of the mind.[3] It is what he calls faith in God as Creator. It consists in believing that God is (Hebrews 11: 6).

This belief can be called living faith because, while it is true that its content differs from justifying faith, its form is the

---

[1] *Esprit et autorité* in *Revue Chrétienne*, 1904, p. 103.
[2] *Inst.* III, ii. 5.   [3] *Ibid.*, I, ii. 1, 2; I, vi. 1, 2.

same. It is a firm and certain assurance—which does not rest on the evidence of the senses, nor on that of reason, but on the evidence of a word whose character bears in itself a mark of divinity.

In passing, we may add that in religious language, the terms faith, belief, to believe, designate the highest degree of certitude. This is just the opposite to what they signify in ordinary speech and in philosophical language, where they have as equivalents opinion, probability, to think probable.

Let us see now how faith, thus understood, can be by itself a revelation and a demonstration of the transubjectivity of God. If this existential judgment is a proof of existence it is because faith in God, a being totally infinite, participates by its object in the infinite, and because it must necessarily be an infinite act or not be faith in God. It is a proof of the present action of the infinite cause because it is an act which is an infinite effect.

"Faith", says Calvin, "must not . . . be enclosed in what we perceive, inasmuch as it is founded on the power of God. Now this power is infinite . . . and since it is so, it behoves our faith to increase . . . since our God does not possess merely a certain measure of power which can be enclosed by, or subjected to, human or natural powers, it behoves our faith also to extend high and low that it may become infinite".[1]

Through its object, faith thus participates in the infinite being. In spite of the appearance furnished by the senses or by rational credibility, as the case may be, it spontaneously declares itself to be certain of victory in the midst of destruction and ruin, even in the presence of this ἔσχατον, this end, which is death.

It takes success as a visible gift of God and from apparent failure it draws matter to prophesy imperturbably the final triumph of righteous causes for the moment defeated and crushed. When the shaft of immanent justice strikes the ungodly, it bows trembling before the judgment of God. Finding mystery everywhere in the course of events, it reverently accepts that profoundest of all mysteries, the dispensation of grace. Faith adores an unexpected mercy when God casts Saul of Tarsus in the dust, all bruised and wounded, and draws him behind His car of victory.

However it may happen, and in whatever way God may act, whether He be God manifest or hidden, faith bows in the presence of the infinite, of the divine abyss which lies uncovered before it. The more it is oppressed or pressed by adversity the more

---

[1] *Calvini opera*, xxxiv, 603 f.

spontaneously and vigorously does it expend its energies and display its powers.

Faith thus manifests itself to the consciousness of the believer as an effect which enables him, so to speak, to touch with his finger an infinite cause. Prone to believe without reserve that which is unworthy of absolute confidence, he realizes his natural inability to produce for himself the act which he performs.

The sublime paradox of faith disturbs and troubles its very adversaries, and those among them who are honest confess that it is sublime.[1] Being the masterpiece of the Holy Spirit, His signature imprinted in the human mind, it is to such a degree the proof and demonstration of what it affirms that through mere expression it frequently becomes contagious. "This is the victory that overcometh the world, even our faith" (1 John 5:4).

Prayer is an act of faith. We are not, of course, referring to mechanical prayers but to prayer which considers the meaning of the words when, for example, the Lord's Prayer is repeated. This prayer is essentially an act in the origin, cause and end of which God is manifested as the non-ego to whom it is addressed. Produced by a sense of need, prayer receives from it faith reflecting the divine sublimity which is its very soul.

Prayer is a superhuman challenge thrown in the face of adversity and autonomous reason. It is the cry of a nonentity lost in the immensity of the universe on this speck of dust which we call the earth,[2] sent up to the sovereign Being, trusting in His promise, believing that nothing can be too great for His power and nothing too small for His pity, since both the one and the other are infinite. Prayer calls down the presence of God, and since it is in itself a sublime act, he who prays receives the subjective certainty of the divine transubjectivity.

It is also, for this very reason, a mode of revelation, a mode of spiritual evidence of the reality of God. It is the echo within of the act of God which gives faith and draws those who believe to His embrace. When one believes and prays, one becomes immediately conscious of being efficaciously determined and

---

[1] Wilfred Monod, *Le Problème du Bien, essai de théodicée et journal d'un pasteur*, vol. III, p. 362: "The attitude is sublime . . . there is here something heroic, by means of which the orthodox soul resembles very closely the soul of the agnostic or of the fideist believer"; p. 363: "We know the secret of Calvinistic piety . . . an essential and metaphysical attitude of the soul, rooted in a moral attitude which is a form of radical heroism"; p. 813: ". . . conclusions which may be, in certain respects, qualified as sublime".

[2] Many moderns naïvely imagine that prayer could only be so regarded since the discovery of cosmic infinity by the aid of the telescope in 1610. This view is contradicted by history, *vide* Part II, chapter 14 of the present work.

caused by a power which cannot but be divine since it is capable of making the glory of the infinite majesty to pass through the act of a contemptible and finite creature.

Certainly, the will of the believer enters into the act of faith which dictates the prayer, but it is in order that it may surrender, because it feels itself to be dominated and vanquished. I should not believe if my will were not efficaciously inclined to desire it by the invincible attraction of divine truth which my intelligence perceives in a divine promise. One cannot imagine a freer, more spontaneous act than the act of faith: it knows neither logical nor physical constraint: it is voluntary in the most complete sense of the term and free because all that is voluntary is free.[1]

But it is in the very exercise of liberty that one becomes conscious of the infallible efficacy of a revelation transcendent to oneself. Now this act of supra-dialectical allegiance in the part of the finite intellect in regard to the infinite spirit, originative and constitutive of all reality, is not a *sacrificium intellectus*, a renunciation of the intelligence. On the contrary, it is the sole means of preserving the value of mental processes. It follows from the immediate intuition of the intelligence that it cannot find elsewhere a resting-place more certain and assured. The mind which refuses to found its faith in itself on faith in the absolute mind is condemned to a radical scepticism. And if it consents to assign to its unconditional faith a place lower than the absolute mind, then it will complete its own immolation.

Positive revelation permits the man who has received faith, and prays, to call by His name the absolute Being knowledge of whom is implied in our consciousness that we only exist relatively.

"Whoever examines himself, will find God within, 'for in Him we live and move and have our being'. . . . Certainly life is in us, and if so, it is a witness to the divinity. Who indeed would be so foolish as to claim that he had life of himself (*a se*)? As, therefore, men do not live of themselves but receive life from another, by a precarious title, it follows that God dwells in them. . . . This indeed is the true knowledge of God which manifests itself when one does not speculate on the airy questions debated by philosophers,[2] but realizes in his inner experience that God alone is. Why? Because we are. Now, properly speaking we are not, but we merely subsist. If we subsist, we must

[1] Bernard, *Sermo super Cant.*, II, *apud* Calvin, *Inst.* II, iii. 5.
[2] By these words our Reformer means that he disowns the "proofs" of the existence of God offered by the philosophers.

necessarily consider on what foundation (hypostasis). Thus, being will be found in the possession of God alone, properly speaking. Whence it follows that human life is a striking mark of the unique divinity".[1]

We must not misunderstand these *ergo's* with which Calvin adorns his discourse in order to express, articulate and explain the intuition (*experientia*), the immediate impression which the presence of God reveals to him in the pulsations of life beyond the discussions of the philosophers. There are no syllogisms, no predicative judgments in this passage. There are judgments of relation. Calvin feels that he lives, and, in the consciousness which he possesses of this fact, he reaches the absolute basis of his being, the immanent cause of his life: One who is of Himself. Then, by a species of induction, as Boutroux calls it in the passage quoted above, the Reformer extends his affirmation to all creatures.

He can give the name "God" to this absolute basis, because positive revelation has previously made it known to him in the majesty of the revelation of his infinite essence and because prayer has put him into living relationship with the living One.

Having received the illumination of faith through contact with the Word of God, the believer can perceive and interpret in a theistic sense the revelation of the divine in the universe and in the destiny which governs the course of his life and the course of events.

Whether it is a question of the progress of the universe or of history, its order reveals the controlling will of a supreme intelligence. The exceptional, the unexpected, the improbable event, reveal at the same time that this intelligence is free.[2]

The usual succession of probabilities permits man to organize his life in accordance with the rules of prudence. The irruption of the unexpected makes him realize that he has to reckon with the liberty of a wisdom whose designs baffle all human foresight. In fact, the realization of the unexpected, the paradoxical irruption of the improbable, invincibly awakens among most men a sense that they are in the presence of a planned event, of a mysterious will whose decrees infallibly come to pass, whether it is a question of necessary occurrences or of free acts. It is then that the philosophical "proofs" of the existence of God, restored to their true rôle of evidences, manifest their real value.

The cosmological proof from the contingency of the world suggests a cause adequate to the explanation of the existence of

---

[1] Calvin, *Praelect. in Jer.*, x, 1: cf. *Inst.* I, i. 1; *Com. on Acts* xvii, 27.
[2] Calvin, *Praelect. in Jer., loc. laud., Inst.* I, v.

the world and of cosmic facts in general. Reason is incapable of demonstrating that this eternal and immutable cause is God in the sense of the first chapter of Genesis. Faith, enlightened by the revelation of the dogma of creation, sees, in the existence and preservation of the world, a manifestation of the infinite power of which it is written: "He spake and it was done; He commanded and it stood fast" (Psalm 33: 9). Thus faith may be described as the consciousness of a destiny realized by a sovereign will. A consideration of the physical universe testifies to faith that we ourselves are included in that will.

The teleological proof leaves undecided the question whether "the Great Architect" is transcendent to the world or whether He is merely the "life force" groping its way tentatively in order to produce more and more perfect forms (Bergson), or "life" manifesting itself when and as it can, at random, under conditions which enable it to organize itself and the general similarity of which gives the impression of a single plan (Paul Raboud).

Faith, considered as such, does not have to take sides in the various scientific explanations of the origin of life, nor even of the organization of the world. It knows that "the counsel of God standeth firm". Even if it were proved scientifically that the dominant forms of living species are due to the laborious and often clumsy efforts of the "life force", faith would not confound this latter with God. It would know that the impulsions and directions taken, then abandoned, by this more or less blind ὁρμή were governed by divine providence. It would ascribe to this secondary, but none the less real, cause the gropings and checks that we encounter in the universe. The result of the study of living forms would compel us to recognize the preponderant action of a concourse of fortuitous circumstances, but it would not disturb our faith.

In the very existence of indispensable conditions for the organization of life, leading to the establishment of organisms, systems and an ordered cosmos, faith would acknowledge the authority of the Lawgiver who had submitted all reality to the laws which govern intelligence and bring physical reality under their sway.

In partial dislocations, faith sees the intervention and the deviations of created forces, free or blind, of the "life force" if you will, whose spontaneous play God has been pleased to permit, while controlling and bridling it at the same time by His providence, in order to integrate it into a cosmos.

To look for dialectical proofs of the existence of God by the contingency of the world, final causes, etc., in the beautiful fifth chapter of the first book of the *Institutes,* would be to mis-understand it altogether. For Calvin, neither the world nor history prove God by way of apodictic demonstration; they reflect as in a mirror the rays which burst forth from the mystery of the divine essence and thus reveal to us in varying degrees the names and attributes which enable us to know analogically what God is in regard to us, when we have been given eyes to see it.

Now, a revelation is a demonstration, if you will, but an immediate demonstration; an evidence certainly, but a supra-rational evidence; in point of fact, there can be no evidence or demonstration superior to that of a divine revelation. Since the irruption of sin into the world, the language of creation and the successive events which are therein unfolded have ceased to be clearly intelligible to fallen man.

The universality of religions and the elaboration of "proofs" of the existence of God indicate that, in spite of the Fall, man has not lost his sense of the divinity. On the other hand, the superstition and degradation of historical religions which always tend spontaneously towards polytheism; the perpetual oscillation of religious philosophies, between acosmic pantheism and dualist deism, prove that natural revelation is insufficient to lead man, left to himself, towards the living and the true God. *A fortiori,* it can teach him nothing concerning the merciful will of God towards him, which we shall discuss later.

In order that he may understand the teaching of nature con-cerning God as creator and preserver, man must first of all experience that partial or total restoration of the divine image which is regeneration. But even this is not enough. Many spiritually regenerate Christians understand the book of nature scarcely better than the unbelievers. To recover the forgotten meaning of its language, two things are required: a grammar and a teacher: the Bible and the Spirit of God. Without the teaching of the Spirit, the Bible itself is no more than a collection of documents of importance only for their psychological, historical and archaeological information. And if Holy Scripture is not received as the supreme rule of faith, the internal teacher speaks only with those "groanings which cannot be uttered" mentioned by the Apostle.

"In order to be enlightened by, and built up in, the true religion, we must begin with heavenly teaching, and it is im-possible for anyone to obtain even the rudiments of right and sound doctrine without learning in the school of Holy Scrip-ture".[1]

---

[1] *Inst.* I, vi. 2.

CHAPTER 5

AGNOSTIC AND ATHEISTIC CRITICISMS OF FAITH

We have shown that the foundation of faith is an internal evidence *sui generis* and that by its very nature the object of faith, God, and the revelation of God, is accompanied by a sense of obligation.

In his *Esquisse d'une morale sans obligation ni sanction*, M. Guyau has presented in a forceful manner some criticisms of the validity of this evidence and the legitimacy of this obligation. His critique is an apology for doubt. It is directed chiefly against moralism, against the theory which would base morals on faith in duty and which lays down as a principle that the first of duties is to believe in duty. *Mutatis mutandis*, it can be applied and applies itself, in the mind of the author, to religious faith.

How does our philosopher proceed in order to disprove an evidence which seems strange to him? We say advisedly which "seems" strange to him, for his definition of faith suggests that he has never possessed it, or that if he has possessed it, he has lost it for such a long time that he no longer remembers what it is. In any case, it proves that this positive and experimental philosopher has not devoted much attention to this phenomenon, among others, nor made use of his ordinary psychological acuteness in studying it.

"To believe", he says, "is to affirm as real for me that which I conceive simply as possible in itself, or sometimes even as impossible. Attempting to establish an artificial verity, an apparent truth, in this way means that all the while the mind is closed to objective truth which is thus rejected in advance without one knowing it". [1]

There are almost as many errors as words in this description of faith: we mean errors of psychological observation. It is clear that we are very far from the definition given by the writer of the Epistle to the Hebrews or by Calvin when one takes a view of faith such as we have just quoted; it is surely then "the mind is closed to objective truth, which is thus rejected in advance without one knowing it". But let us pass on.

At any rate, the author knows that faith invokes a "species of evidence", a particular sort which is neither that of the

[1] *Op. cit.*, p. 73.

senses not of discursive reason. He also knows quite well that "historically all faith—to whatever object it may be applied— has always appeared obligatory to its possessor". [1]

This is sufficient to show that his critique is directed against faith as we understand it. Among believers there are scarcely any, we imagine, except certain ethical Protestants of the school of Gourd, who would dispute his statement concerning the obligatory character of faith. But the blows which he deals to Kantian and neo-Kantian moralism are sufficiently strong to render it unnecessary for us to notice this exception here.

Here is his critique of the evidence of faith. According to him, it is the most superficial minds (representatives of Scottish philosophy and of the eclectic school) who invoke this "sort of evidence"; to base philosophy on common sense is to base it on a prejudice; such phrases as "the evidence proves" and "common sense demands" provoke a smile nowadays.

"Evidence is a subjective state of which one can often give an account by subjective reasons also. Truth is not only that which one feels and sees; it is that which one explains and connects. It derives its evidence and proof not from a simple state of consciousness but from the whole mass of phenomena which persist and support one another; one stone does not make an arch, nor do two or three; all are needed and they must support one another. Even when the arch is complete, if certain stones are removed, the entire structure will collapse. Truth is even so; it consists in a solidarity of all things. It is not enough that one thing should be evident; it must be capable of explanation if it is to acquire a truly scientific character". [2]

We need not waste time on the type of unfavourable prejudice which, in accordance with a process recommended by certain controversialists, has to be stirred up in the minds of hearers and readers by treating those who maintain the evidence of faith as of superficial intelligence. We are not called upon to decide whether Thomas Reid and Victor Cousin were men of superficial mentality or whether we must class ourselves in the same category.

These psychological questions are of no real relevance to the discussion. Even a superficial mind may have the good fortune to be right once in a while.

We might, in our turn, suggest that Guyau himself has judged the Scottish school very superficially and that he can scarcely be said to have taken much trouble to understand what Reid meant by "common sense".

[1] *Op cit.*, p. 68. [2] *Ibid.*, p. 66 f.

In a debate, what matters most is to discover the heart of the argument and to strike at the right spot in order to arrive at a conclusion.

We are told that "evidence is a subjective state of which one can often give an account by subjective reasons also." This is to consider things as a whole, in a confused manner and without taking account of the correctness of terms. Evidence is a quality of the object which has the property of introducing itself into the subject, in his sensibility and intelligence, in order to create certainty. It is an objective fact. The facts which have this objective quality produce in the subject perceiving it a mixed condition called certainty. This is the certainty which is a state of the subject and which, in this respect, is a subjective state.

But certainty can be explained in various ways. Sometimes it results from the constraint, the irresistible pressure exercised by the object on the subject's organs of knowledge, which are presumed to be functioning in good order. Sometimes it results from a physiological or psychological state unfavourable to the discovery of truth, because it is either abnormal or warped by prejudices which militate against the desire to know the truth. Everybody knows that wishes and imaginations are often mistaken for realities.

It is essential to avoid confusion between evidence and certainty. We have had to criticize not the evidence which produces legitimate and objective certainty but the certainty itself and the motives for this certainty: to see if these motives are objective, founded on the evidence, or purely subjective.

Now, when one examines the testimony of a subject who declares himself to be in possession of a certainty derived from evidence by means of an organ of knowledge the function and even the existence of which cannot be verified, it is important to guard against deciding *a priori* that his evidence does not exist and that this certainty is merely an illusion. A sweeping and dogmatic assurance of this sort is nothing better than a prejudice.

A man born blind cannot directly and by himself verify the existence and function of the sense which permits us to see objects at a distance. He cannot even imagine the meaning of light and colour. What would a sighted person think if a blind man made use of his admission that there are optical illusions and hallucinations to dispute and deny the validity of the testimony furnished by the sense of sight? [1]

---

[1] *Vide* Bergson, *Les deux sources de la morale et de la religion*, Alcan, Paris, 1932, pp. 244 ff; 263 ff.

There are certainly suggestions, autosuggestions, and hallucinations in the religious sphere, as elsewhere. But to claim on
this account that all mystical or religious intuition is caused by
autosuggestion, and that all vision is necessarily the result of
pathological hallucination, is merely to exhibit a rather crude
form of antireligious, or perhaps anticlerical, prejudice. It
should be remembered that persons suffering from religious
autosuggestion, on the unrefuted hypothesis that the religious
dogma is true, have also a *sensus divinitatis*, an intuition, a
more or less vivid sense of the divinity. Hence it follows that the
autosuggestion which they practise, whether unconsciously or
not, testifies, by its determining action on a diseased and per-
verted mind and on an abnormal will, to the transubjective
reality of the object of faith. The very hallucinations which the
subject interprets in a religious sense indicate the existence in
him of this *sensus divinitatis* which Calvin declares to be
indestructible in man.

As for the fact that a pathological condition accompanies or
even favours ecstasy in certain mystics who are regarded by
believers as veritable explorers of the invisible: since this condition sometimes accompanies also the ordinary simple religious
intuition common to all the faithful, the illusory character of
their inward certainty cannot be concluded from it.

A pathological state may, indeed, give the physical senses an
astonishing hypersensibility. Why should it not be the same in
regard to the secret sense of God? [1] We know, of course, that
irreligious prejudice will dismiss this remark as worthless. But a
prejudice, however violent, cannot dispose of evidence, nor of
the certainty which results from it, nor even of a mediate
demonstration. Still less can it disturb the certainty of those
who are conscious of being in immediate contact with the
object of their faith and under the influence of its efficacious
action.

Moreover, the universality of religious sentiment proves that
the religious instinct is normal in man, as even an atheist of Le
Dantec's type has to admit. Hence, the criterion of this instinct
is not the physiological process which may or may not accompany it. The criterion is, in the first place, the necessary rôle
which it plays as the guarantee of logical thought and as the
bond of union and coherence for that thought. In the next place,
it is its moral quality, its relative spiritual elevation, and finally
its religious value.

[1] It is a commonplace that the pioneers of the human race in all spheres
frequently exhibit certain pathological elements in their character.

If the testimony which produces religious certainty is not received, if God is not believed, then the final distinction between true and false disappears and one cannot tell whether intuition of the external world is not, after all, a great hallucination. It follows that, contrary to Guyau's view, an apologist will not have wasted his time if he has succeeded in demonstrating that his religion is the best of all religions because it is the most religious.

Guyau is right in saying that, in the final analysis, he is concerned with a question of verity rather than of validity. But he is wrong in assuming that phrases like "it is religious to believe in religion", "it is moral to believe in morality", are nothing more than tautologies, vicious circles. They signify quite simply that, for one who possesses the religious and the moral sense, the irreligious man and the amoral man represent abnormality. Only they say this politely.

But let us continue our consideration of the criticisms which this author levels at religious evidence. "Truth is not only what one feels and sees; it is what one explains and connects." We agree; what one explains and connects may be also truth: but there are illusory connections and false explanations not only in popular belief but also in scientific opinion—which fractionally educated people and the popularizers of science who write for them are apt to confound, always and everywhere, with a certainty which can never be overthrown.

On the other hand there may be isolated facts, well authenticated, capable of serving as materials for science, which may be integrated one day into a system, but which meanwhile remain truths and evident truths. Such facts abound both in the physical and the moral sciences.

"Truth is a synthesis: it is this which distinguishes it from sensation, from brute fact; it is a bundle of facts." Certainly there are syntheses of truth. Every science worthy of the name aspires to be one, but that stage is only reached slowly and after many trials and attempts. All truth is not synthesis: the humble brute fact, the most obscure sensation when rightly perceived and interpreted is truth.

There are also truths which, while not syntheses, form the conditions of every synthesis, which is by no means the same thing. This is the case with necessary truths concerning God, divine sovereignty and veracity, the principle of identity, the principle of contradiction and of sufficient reason.

"Truth does not derive its evidence and proof from a simple state of consciousness." Very true: the object derives its evidence from itself. Its proof is based on it. But the perception of this proof and evidence, the certainty which results from it, are necessarily, by definition, states of consciousness. The difficulty is due to a confusion between evidence and certainty, resulting probably from the so-called axiom of idealism: we know only ourselves and our states of consciousness.[1] He calls the reply realist, and such it may be in so far as it is affected by the object. " . . . But from the whole mass of phenomena which exist and support one another". This is so when it is a case of contingent things, problematic in themselves. In such cases, the logical or experimental bond is extremely useful in producing conviction and certainty which are states of consciousness. Moreover the perception of this bond is a simple state of consciousness which the mind does not introduce but which it discovers either immediately or, more usually, by a process of reasoning.

It is impossible to frame the simplest argument if one has no idea of the evidence which connects its terms. The evidence is indeed objective, but one's intuition of this evidence is always a state of consciousness. It is the consciousness of something objective, ideally present in ourselves, which we seek but which after all is a state of consciousness.

"One stone does not make an arch, . . . all are needed and they must support one another. Even when the arch is complete, if certain stones are removed the entire structure will collapse". We will not cavil by pointing out that there are such things as monolithic arches. It is perfectly true that all the stones of an arch balance one another, and it is equally true that there are systems of ideas and facts which in this respect resemble arches. Thus, the historians of dogma are in practical agreement that the doctrine of predestination is the keystone of Calvinism. But our author has omitted to mention the keystone. Now, we maintain that God is the objective condition and that belief in God is the subjective condition of the coherence of our thoughts. The arch of coherent thought has God for its pillars and faith in Him is its keystone. An arch cannot be built on empty space, its structure cannot be poised on nothing.

"Truth consists in a solidarity of all things". Surely, truth consists rather in the resemblance between the subjective representation and the objective reality. If it is found objectively

---

[1] Eugène Ménégoz, *Publications diverses sur le Fidéisme*, vol. V, p. 158: "As a matter of certain science we have no more knowledge of what our brains imagine and elaborate than we have of what takes place within ourselves. All modern philosophers are in agreement on this point." The leader of the symbolo-fideist school evidently regards this thesis of idealism as a universally acknowledged fact.

that there are lacunae between certain things or series of things, as modern microphysics teaches in agreement with Calvin,[1] truth consists in knowing this and in denying the (causal) solidarity of all things.

"It is not enough that one thing should be evident; it is necessary that it should be capable of explanation in order that it may acquire a truly scientific character." On the contrary, a thing is scientifically known when the evidence for it is obtained by scientific methods. Its nature indicates the scientific discipline to which it belongs.

In order that science may achieve its object and become the synthesis which it sets out to be—this science which is a state of collective consciousness—it is necessary that the thing of which it treats should be explained, unless indeed that thing be the reason underlying all things, the principle beyond which the human mind feels that it has neither the right nor the need to proceed, because it can rest upon it as a foundation. Objectively this principle is God; subjectively it is belief in Him. All words, all coherent thoughts, are conscious or unconscious acts of faith in God.

Apart from God, for minds which do not allow themselves to be influenced by practical prejudices, there remains nothing but scepticism, which is the suicide of reason. God is not indeed the explanation of anything. That is the reason why the effort which leads to the establishment of science is necessary. But He is the reason of all things, and this fact renders religious affirmation indispensable to science as a guarantee of the reality of its objective. How otherwise could we know that this vision of a palpable and ponderable world is not a gigantic hallucination, the creation of an ego more unreal still?

If this evidence must be called in question on the plea that the vision of an evidence is a subjective state, it is not easy to see in what way a connected system can be more certain than an isolated brute fact. A sea which makes its appearance in the middle of the desert cannot be other than a mirage, but the *fata morgana* is also an illusion; the shore which it shows the traveller with its towns and ramparts is as unsubstantial as the sea in the desert.

The practical and active Occidental is little inclined to doubt the substantial nature of the sun which gives rise to this phenomenon or the utility of the effort which it thus displays. The atheistic Buddhist of the Orient, contemplative and indolent, at any rate has not recoiled from the theoretical and

[1] *Inst.* I, xvi. 8.

practical consequences of his fundamental nihilism, the annihilation of desire, the spring of action, and the annihilation of the conscious ego, the unconscious magician, creator of the great illusion of the world as it appears to his subjectivity.

If the mere psychological existence of doubt creates the right to doubt, it is not easy to see how those who maintain a morality without obligation or sanction could revive the springs of action in a civilization like ours which has come to doubt the value of its own culture.

But this, they tell us, is an argument of social utility. We have not appealed to it in the preceding chapters and might therefore proceed without discussing it. However, we will stay for a moment and examine it in passing. It is urged that the argument implies a degree of scepticism which logically demands something more thoroughgoing and complete; that such reasoning is equivalent to the common saying: a religion is a necessity for the common people.

It seems to us that Guyau considers the question in a very superficial manner. When the advocates of faith in duty, which he has in view, and those of faith in God, which he regards as beneath notice, invoke the social utility of faith, they take it for granted that human society is a natural fact; that man is essentially a social animal. In endeavouring to show that amoralism or atheism are anti-social beliefs, they try to make it plain that such views are unnatural; that they fail to recognize a natural objective reality: in a word that they are pathological.

When objectors reply that truth has higher claims than mere utility and that we must look it in the face, they are saying something with which we fully concur. They do not, however, mention the fact that such a position commits them to more than one act of faith: first, the act of faith in duty, which they deny to be a matter of obligation, while by a happy inconsistency they take for granted the duty of intellectual sincerity; then the act of faith in the value of truth. Guyau well says: "The truth is not always equal to the illusion, but it has this to be said for it: it is true and in the sphere of thought there is nothing more moral than truth." [1]

He means, no doubt: "than the sincerity which loyally accepts the truth", but his act of faith in the dignity of reason acknowledging the truth, and in some sort of moral value of anything whatever, is absurd. In effect, he thinks that reason plunges by its original roots into the deep soil of the accidentally stable sequence of simple physical facts, which of their very

[1] *Op. cit.*, p. 73.

nature are purely irrational. He believes reason, and the morality based upon it, to be no more than a by-product of the blind evolution of matter.

Evolution is a magic word, the name of the dream which enchanted the 19th century. Religion, God, duty, may have their usefulness during a given phase of evolution, but this usefulness can be no more than provisional. It disappears with further progress.

But when the defenders of faith in God and those of faith in duty invoke social utility they have no intention of favouring the Machiavellian maxim that religion is a necessity for the common people. Such a maxim represents the lowest depth of immorality. It means, in effect, that rulers and leaders require a means of deceiving the masses.

What the defenders of belief in God are endeavouring to prove is its social value, that it is an essential condition of all human society, whatever may be its form, useful to rulers and leaders alike. What they are trying to demonstrate is that there can be no stable human society apart from some sort of spiritual sense, even though it be based on the poor humanitarian abstractions which atheistic demagogues put forward.

To recall this fact is not to close one's eyes to the truth, but to bow before palpable evidence, to invite opponents to draw from it the theoretical consequences which they do not wish to admit because they are enslaved by the social conformism of the anticlerical ideal to whose pressure they have submitted.

But we must pass on. Objection is made to the fact that faith in God is presented with authority; that it claims to be a command implying a duty[1]; that it involves what Paul calls "the obedience of faith" (2 Thessalonians 1: 8; 3: 14). In order to destroy the obligatory character of faith it is explained as "denoting an habitual attitude of mind" and that "an attempt to change this attitude abruptly will provoke resistance." According to this view "faith is an acquired habit, a sort of intellectual instinct which presses upon us, constrains us and in a certain sense may be said to produce a feeling of obligation."[2]

The doctrine concerning God is indeed an acquired notion. The actual acquisition may date from the age of infancy or it may, on the other hand, be quite recent. But the sense of the

[1] "The first commandment requireth us to know and acknowledge God to be the only true God and our God; and to worship and glorify Him accordingly"— *Westminster Shorter Catechism*, xlvi.

[2] *Op. cit.*, p. 68.

divine, the religious consciousness, is not an acquired habit. It is a universal disposition. It is implied in the very admission which our author makes that faith is "an intellectual instinct."

When he speaks of the *fides insita*, the faith inherent in man, Calvin says no more, and he says it no better.[1] Faith—faith in God—results from a sense of presence, presence manifesting itself at certain times with such power that the man who perceives it feels that he must yield to it and cease to deny what is taking place in his mind. The religious instinct, like all instincts, is an instigation almost synonymous with inspiration, but an instigation habitual and inherent in the human mind. When a man attempts to resist God revealing Himself within (Romans 1: 18-28), it is not surprising if he is brought to an abrupt halt.

But Guyau mixes with this sound view, the proper bearing of which he does not appreciate, an assertion in which true and false are mingled, because it proceeds from an observation founded on a faulty analysis of the facts. He tells us that faith indicates an habitual attitude of mind; that it is an acquired habit, and that the abrupt halt of which we have spoken is the result of the resistance offered by the habit to an activity which opposes it. It is this which produces the feeling that an obligation has been violated.

But, in the first place, even if we supposed that the idea was based on a well ascertained fact, the explanation would be inadequate. It is quite possible to have an habitual attitude deeply impressed on the mind without feeling that a sacrilege has been committed if anyone doubts its existence. For example, the habitual attitude of mind of the majority of the members of the white race is the dogma of the intellectual superiority of that race. We know, on the other hand, that a number of thinkers belonging to the white race have submitted this belief to a searching critical examination and have arrived at the conclusion that it is nothing but a prejudice devoid of scientific foundation. To our knowledge, the only feeling of obligation which these men of science have experienced has been that of their duty to scientific objectivity.

Moreover, the same observation may be made with regard to ignorant people. A farmer may be made to change his mind concerning the inconveniences supposed to result from a red moon without necessarily provoking a crisis in his consciousness, even if his prejudice is inveterate.

It is not enough, then, that the mind should have adopted a

[1] *Inst.* I, iii.

certain attitude for a long time in order that that opinion may appear to it to be of perpetual obligation. Something else is needed, namely, that the belief in question should be connected either by sentiment or by reason, or by both, with an element which imposes itself in the respect and veneration. And even this by itself is not sufficient. A belief respectable in itself will not necessarily appear obligatory to the man who entertains it if the motives for which he accepts it are of a purely speculative and traditional order.

An individual who has received certain religious beliefs by tradition, who has sincerely practised and been moved by them, basing them all the while solely on philosophical arguments, may lose them suddenly on being confronted with an equally philosophical and apparently triumphant refutation. It is possible that he may experience poignant regret but he will not necessarily feel that he has had to resist an obligation. He will feel, rather, as in the case of the biologist Romanes, that he has fulfilled the duty of intellectual probity. [1]

On the other hand, it is perfectly true that if a sufficiently developed natural sentiment, an hereditary instinct, is defied, especially if it is generally respected in the society in which one lives, an uneasy feeling may be produced, in extreme cases amounting to sheer self-loathing. It is also true that a very widespread custom, or even a mere fashion, can produce an analogous effect. This is generally feebler and resolves itself into a sort of shame or dislike of being thought ridiculous. In this last case, it is the gregarious instinct which is expressing itself. This instinct may, however, like all the others, become atrophied in certain people in whom the contrary individualistic instinct predominates.

But when it is a question of instincts which are not only normal but which have reference to the matter of the moral law decreed by God, whether it be acknowledged or not, and if these instincts are not atrophied, the effort to free oneself from them produces a sense of disquiet and often of despair.

Is this sentiment one of obligation? Not necessarily. It is a sort of instinctive warning of the moral order. What dominates it can only be a reaffirmation of the gregarious instinct previously repressed. It would seem that our author reduces the sentiment of obligation to this.

The evidence which it gives of the existence of this subconscious disquiet constitutes the truth underlying Dürkheim's theory, according to which a sense of obligation is reduced to a

[1] G. J. Romanes, *Thoughts on Religion*, ed. C. Gore, p. 27 f.

social instinct. This instinct is of an hereditary character and originates in the laws of the ancestral clan. Those who thus reduce the sentiment of obligation to the gregarious instinct do not always seem clear as to what constitutes obligation. They are often strangers to the very sentiment which they evoke.

The specific character of the moral fact is duty. The idea of duty implies that what is prescribed is due, that is to say, that it constitutes a debt which obliges the debtor in regard to his creditor. There is no such thing as duty, as Guyau admits, except in regard to persons. Practical reason sees immediately that if I belong altogether to God, from whose nature the moral law proceeds, that if I belong to Him by right of creation, I owe Him all that I am and do.

It is an objective evidence which produces the subjective state called certainty. The evidence receives further support from such sentiments as love, gratitude, reverence and fear, but its chief foundation is a sense of equity; fundamentally, the sentiment of obligation may be reduced to this sense. The sinner has the feeling that he has committed an injustice. He is conscious of not having paid what he owes to the Lawgiver who is also his Creator: in a word, of not having done his duty.

If he deifies his reason and forgets that it is God who guarantees it, he still retains enough of the religious instinct to transfer to this imaginary divinity, which he transforms into an absolute, the sentiment of respect and confidence due objectively to God alone. In perceiving that the moral fault is contrary to reason, to his "reasonable service", as Paul calls it, he perceives that it is not only absurd but sinful.

So specifically moral and distinct from tribal sentiment is this that the man who conforms to the exigencies of obligation, in so doing may have to defy convention and resist the dominant traditional opinion. Contrary to what ordinarily happens when a man resists custom, the fact of being an exception will give him a feeling of being a witness to the majesty of the moral law before those who do not know, or misunderstand, the meaning of duty. What Guyau takes for the sentiment of obligation is the precise opposite of this, namely, the spirit of conformism.

One may nevertheless attempt to maintain the gregarious and ancestral origin of the matter of the moral law, of the faith which it excites and of the authority which it attaches to itself, by claiming that humanitarian, democratic, co-operative, Christian sensibility should be able to efface the distinctions between the egos . . . The Christian says: "Do unto others as ye would that they should do unto you." To which the playwright moralist,

G. Bernard Shaw, replies: "Do not do unto others as ye would that they should do to you; your tastes may differ."[1]

We would reply that Christian sensibility has nothing in common with humanitarian sensibility. The former loves the "neighbour", the concrete individual; while humanitarianism enthuses over a remote collective abstraction called humanity. Christian sensibility, at least in its Calvinistic form, is opposed to the levelling passion of democratic sensibility. In proclaiming that God alone is Lord of the conscience, it safeguards the legitimate rights and religious liberty of the individual. In laying down that there is a social order of intangible creation, it gives to natural social and political liberties their charter. Precisely because it acknowledges Scripture to be this supreme charter, it is opposed to all dictatorship lacking counterbalance, including the dictatorship of the sovereign people. Thus it cannot be confounded with what is called democratic sensibility. Finally, Christian sensibility is characterized by solidarity, but this solidarity is that of an organism: it implies the irreducible diversity of the organs and the functions.

The formula: do unto others as ye would that they should do to you, far from effacing distinctions between the egos, assures to them permanence and bases this permanence of distinctions on divine authority.

That lugubrious jester, Shaw, mentally alert as he is, must know quite well that the very first thing a Christian wishes to be done to him is to have his legitimate tastes respected. This being the case, he is bound by his religion to consider the tastes of other people and not annoy them by tendentious observations which offend against good taste.

In regard to this matter the "golden rule" of Christian morality is so sublime in its simplicity that it comes with power to those whose minds have not been blinded by systematic prejudice, and may bring with it faith as soon as it has been properly understood. And this new-found faith will be imperative, claiming obedience to the precepts, revealing itself as invested with the radiance of truth. Thus the faith which claims obligation is not necessarily an inveterate habit.

Even when of quite recent origin, in a convert, for example, it is often very aggressive and of an absolutely imperative character in the mind of the man who professes it, both for himself and for others. This is a common case of religious psychology, on account of which two well-known converts,

---

[1] G. Palante, *Mercure de France*, June 16, 1908, quoted by E. Borel, *Le Hasard*, p. 235.

CRITICISMS OF FAITH

Paul and Calvin, have been sufficiently reproached for their absolutism.

What is needed, then, in order that religious faith may be a categorical imperative? It is that the object of worship, perceived by the mind of the believer as real, revealed to him as transubjective, should appear to his intelligence and affections as invested with an objective right to demand the unconditional obedience and surrender of every free being. Calvin regarded this as even a right of creation and preservation. "Ye are not your own. . . ." Being God's creatures we owe Him our entire being.

The right is objective and so is the obligation: it is a debt, something due, a duty. It may be objected that "faith cannot have any obligatory action on him who does not yet possess it." [1] No doubt this is true; a thing which does not exist cannot have any action at all. It has never been suggested that non-existent faith had any obligatory action. Faith can have an efficacious action only on condition that it is present and living. But efficacious and obligatory are not synonymous. This improper use of terms suggests that there is no very clear idea of what constitutes obligation, even under its psychological aspect.

It is not a question of whether non-existent faith can be operative. The question is whether faith in God as creator, with which alone we are concerned at the moment, ought to exist, should be present where we find it to be absent.

The agnostic replies that "one cannot be obliged to affirm that which, as a whole, one does not know and believe." [2] We reply that one is obliged to affirm that which he ought to know and believe. Ignorance is morally inexcusable when it is the result of culpable negligence, when it has its roots in wilful blindness or an implacable hostility of the heart.

We are told that, in so far as faith does not exist, there cannot be such a thing as a "feeling of obligation". But in the first place we would point out that the feeling of obligation is not here in question. We are discussing the obligation itself as an objective fact, whether felt or not. Now, duty is absolute: whether acknowledged or ignored, it binds, for it cannot be ignored where God is concerned except by the fault of the person who does so.

Secondly, it may be true from the point of view of formal logic, "rationally speaking", that the feeling of obligation must be preceded by faith. Psychologically, however, this order does not always conform to reality. God can make Himself felt as present and transubjective, and in fact frequently does so, by

[1] *Op. cit.*, p. 68.   [2] *Ibid.*

one who refuses to submit his will to the proposition: God is. In this case, the obligation to believe is more or less indistinctly perceived and the refusal often provokes remorse. Thus, despite formal logic, the feeling of obligation to believe may in fact precede faith.

Finally, the following argument is urged: "On the other hand, a simple doubt would suffice to release from an obligation which had its origin only in faith. And this doubt, once conscious, itself would create a duty, that of being consistent with itself, that of not blindly dabbling with an uncertain problem. . . . If it can be said that faith obliges, doubt obliges also."

The man who doubts has certainly no right to dabble with an uncertain problem; he must be consistent and sincere in his doubt. But what he is asked to do, in the first place, is to open his eyes and consider that, if there is no debtor, there can be no debt; that, if there is no lawgiver, there can be no law; that, if there is no Lord to whom is due one's all, there can be no such thing as duty. Would it not, therefore, be wise to ask oneself whether a doubt implying negation of duty, in general, involves the affirmation of the duty of consistency with itself?

In actual fact, Guyau doubts not only duty in relation to God, but duty as prescribed by independent reason. He doubts duty in general. How can a doubt which thus affects all duty create the duty of intellectual sincerity? Here, surely, is a palpable contradiction.

Since he admits that he is blind, we would ask the doubter who has learnt to doubt the value and legitimacy of a doubt which engenders contradiction to turn his eyes towards the spot whence light comes, according to the testimony of those who profess to see. We would ask him to sit at the roadside while the thoughts of men pass by and await the manifestation of that presence which, Pascal tells us, "may be felt in the heart". It is never lacking to those who are willing to accept objective evidence, which is, after all, the mother of subjective certainty.

All that is needed is to cease resistance and leave God to work in His own way. To the blind man who knocks, however hesitantly, the door is always opened. But it is not only agnostics who resist the Word of God, as declared by the Reformed Church. There are some believers who do so, too; believers who have come to faith in God by way of faith preliminary to the duty imposed by autonomous reason. To the study of their objections we must devote the chapters that immediately follow.

CHAPTER 6

REVELATION IN SPACE

The characters inscribed in this book of nature enable us to understand the invisible qualities of its author, "his eternal power and godhead" (Romans 1: 20). But, in order that they may become intelligible, the Spirit who proceeds from the first cause and from His wisdom must teach the seeker in the school of Scripture. Such is the conclusion at which we have now arrived.

Guided by Scripture, we have seen that every object in the world, and the world itself, throughout its entire duration and extent, is subject to a variety of laws—the law of formal logic, of number, of extent, of duration, of life, of the mind in its predominant functions, social laws, etc., which are like so many indicating arrows pointing towards the supreme cause of reality, from whom they all flow and who is Himself not, as Gourd represents Him, outside law, but, as Calvin teaches, above law.

Scripture declares that this supreme cause is autonomous; that He is a law to Himself and that this law is holiness, of which all holiness here below is but a pale reflexion, a distant analogy. In short, this cause is as free, as autonomous, as Kant imagines the human "moral person" to be.

The profound repulsion which Calvin felt for the god of pure will or capricious liberty, postulated by the sophists who succeeded the scholastics of the decadence, is, or rather ought to be, well known. [1] The God of Calvinism is indeed the sovereign God of universal preordination. But it must be clearly understood that this preordination does not destroy the liberty of creatures; that, on the contrary, it causes it to enter into the web of the sovereign decree, and that providence, in inclining free wills to conformity with it, maintains the reality and the laws of liberty conceived by the decree.

[1] "We do not approve of the fiction of absolute power which, as it is pagan, so it should rightly be held in detestation by us. We do not imagine God to be lawless. He is a law to himself; because, as Plato says, men labouring under the influence of concupiscence require law; but the will of God is not only free from all defect, but it is the supreme standard of perfection, the law of all laws"—*Inst.* III, xxiii. 2. We observe, in passing, that our Reformer, referring to another matter, makes a sharp distinction between the relative purity of "the sounder of the scholastics" and the sophists who were his contemporaries (*Inst.* II, ii. 6).

The beings which appear and pass away in their time, appear and become actual beings in reality, each one in accordance with his own nature, under the sovereign control of God. He it is who, according to His will, sometimes ratifies the destinies which they forge spontaneously and voluntarily, sometimes snatches them from this destiny by His power but always in such a way that the rights of His justice or the riches of His glory shine forth.

It will be evident that this revelation of the supreme sovereignty of God and of the total dependence of His creatures cannot be made to harmonize with the humanism of ethicalist theology, inherited from Erasmus, Castellion, Arminius and the 18th century in general.

Ethicalism sees a grave menace to itself in the Calvinist and Barthian reactions among Protestants, and in the Thomist reaction among Roman Catholics. And it is right in doing so. It is menaced in its vital principle at the point where the absolute independence, the autonomy of man, is replaced by the sovereignty of God. It is inclined also to attribute the Calvinistic revival among youth to the desire to reaffirm authority in all spheres, including that of politics.

It is certainly true that the need for restoring order and authority in the intellectual, moral, religious and social spheres is making itself felt. But this need arises from a sense of the duty of delivering minds from the tyranny of blind and fatal forces, in order to restore stability to thought and discipline to action. Submission to God is the means and condition of liberation from enslavement to human opinion. If we wish to restore legitimate authority it is only the better to assure true liberty.

But how is the attempt made to establish a connection between the Calvinistic revival and the claims of the totalitarian state in politics? In this way. There was, in the remote past, a sociological bond between the doctrine of divine sovereignty in religion and the theory of absolute monarchy in politics.[1] Therefore it must be the dictatorial and totalitarian tendencies of the present day in the political domain which favour the return to the God of Augustine, Aquinas and Calvin.

A detailed discussion of this point would take us far from our subject. Let it suffice first of all to repeat that Calvin refuses to attribute to God the *dominium absolutum* of Scotus and Occam; and that, on the other hand, it is precisely the Arminians, in agreement on this point with the Jesuits, and, in general, with the apostles of the liberty of indifference (such as Descartes and

[1] Victor Monod, *Le problème de Dieu*, concluding part.

Secrétan), who have been the most zealous defenders of this view. [1]

In the second place, let us take notice that the sovereignty which Calvinism ascribes to God belongs to Him only. Calvinism does not exclude *a priori* the eventuality of an absolute monarchy, if the social condition and culture of a people render it necessary. It is God who rules historical conditions and the forms of government which are adapted to them. But even an earthly absolute sovereign is required, in the presence of God, to respect the inalienable liberties of the "ordinances of creation", primitive and anterior to the Fall. Above the omnipotent sovereign, whether it be an hereditary monarch, a dictator, or the sovereign people, there is a charter of liberties granted to the subjects by God: Scripture and that inviolable asylum created by God, the human conscience. Calvinism, by its principle of divine sovereignty, also limits and restrains the arbitrary will of the human sovereign.

From all these considerations, it follows clearly that the desire to establish any absolute political power whatever cannot logically be held to explain the movement for a return to Calvinism. On the other hand, it seems to us that the realist philosophical reaction from humanist subjectivism is closely bound up with the Calvinist reaction. In spite of the affinities that we have noticed between Arminianism and a despotic conception of the sovereignty of God, we think nevertheless that the Protestant ethicalism of the present day is not itself essentially despotic in politics. If this is so, we have here a formidable argument against the contention that there is a necessary link between the idea of God and the form of political government.

The radical individualism of ethicalism would tend rather to lead the latter towards a sort of libertarian theory in ecclesiastical law, but in ecclesiastical law only. There, the caprice of the "moral person" would find no counterpoise apart from his own wisdom. But what matters above all to this form of religious thought is that man should be a first cause, ontologically independent of God in his volitions, and autonomous in the principles which it prescribes for the said volitions.

In order to ensure this result, it is indispensable to lay down the total independence of the futurition of free acts in regard to God. The future must be incapable of being foreseen even by

---

[1] *Apol. conf. Rem.*, cap. xxiv; Episcopius, *Inst. theol.*, 5, v. 3; Bellarmine, *De Grat. et Lib. Arb.*, CXI, 15; Cartesius, *Medit. Resp. sext.*, Amstel., 1654, p. 16 f. Secrétan, *Philosophie de la Liberté*, 1894, vol. I, p. 305 f.

God. He may be free perhaps not to create free beings like Himself, but, once they are created, He loses all decisive control over them.

If, on the other hand, it were laid down that God Himself had a successive existence; that He saw opening before His own vision the mysterious unknown of unrealized time, the same result would be equally well assured. Thus we see that the most daring and consistent exponents of ethicalism have not recoiled before conclusions that are so disastrous to religion.

It would seem that this anxiety to assure the independence and autonomy of free beings in regard to God was inspired, in the first place, among many, by preoccupations of an apologetic order. It was caused by a desire to discharge God from responsibility for the existence of evil under all its forms and to ensure the moral responsibility of creatures. [1]

These considerations, worthy as they may be, have proved inefficacious; in fact, through the desire to regard human autonomy as an end in itself, the pass has been sold and the defence abandoned altogether.

It is evident that, with Gourd, for example, the independence of the ego ends by becoming a kind of Moloch to whom everything must be sacrificed: for him, religious and moral considerations alike retire into the background. Moral obligation, he tells us, does not begin until it is established as such by the sovereign will of the subject, which remains independent from all points of view. [2]

The influence of "the philosopher of the inco-ordinate" has been felt in unexpected quarters. Bergson's view that matter is nothing more than spirit, dead or moribund, has been hailed as an astonishing discovery. Space, the sphere of matter, is now discredited to the profit of time, the sphere of the evolution of spirit, the essence of liberty, or rather of what constitutes liberty. The error underlying theological and philosophical systems prior to the philosophy of the *élan vital* and the generalized relativity of modern physics, consisted in seeking God in space, a false scent which vitiated Greek philosophy generally and Aristotle in particular. If it is difficult for "certain of our contemporaries" to exorcise the ghosts of Thomism and Calvinism, it is because they have "remained faithful to the viewpoint of the 19th century." [3] These awkward individuals continue to

---

[1] For some observations on the pseudo–problem of evil, see App. XI, p. 394.

[2] *Les trois dialectiques*, p. 269: "Whatever may be said about it, there is no such thing as an obligation . . . which obliges morally. One is obliged, because one desires to be so, at one's own risk and peril."

[3] Victor Monod, *Dieu dans l'Univers*, p. 326.

seek God in space. Their divinity must therefore be the God of Aristotle or of Newton; the unmovable prime mover, the mechanician, the engineering genius, all spatial images too favourable "to the God of Augustinian and Calvinian predestination". We must profit by the great lesson of the teacher of creative evolution and seek God in time.

In this way, since time is liberty in act, we should be able to get rid of the God who has ordained once for all "the theorem of the history of the centuries, and give our attention to the God who is a moral person".[1] On these lines, one might go beyond the new physics, and try to arrive at a synthesis of this God who is a "moral person" with the God who is a mathematician as postulated by the new reformers of science.

"Once we get rid of the purely abstract notion of a transcendent intelligence which has arranged the immutable destiny of the world in an eternal book, innumerable concrete facts compel us to postulate a cosmic will, more immanent and more supple, penetrated with contingency, more practical than logical, but untiring in initiative, seeking to excel itself every day."[2]

We fail to see in what respect a transcendent intelligence, with a book at hand in which it had arranged any destiny whatever, would be more abstract than one that was immanent, supple, somewhat lacking in logic but struggling untiringly to repair its own blunders. The former, surrounded by images of material signification, is perhaps too concrete. But as the nominalists consider that the more one rises into abstraction, the farther one retreats from reality, we may note that transcendent intelligence is itself an abstract notion.

The essential thought of the author seems to be this: henceforth it is no longer man but God who must excel himself. Frankly, we see here a degradation of the very idea of deity. As Prof. Burgelin trenchantly remarks: "We are not left even with the god of Voltaire, a good enough clockmaker to manufacture the world of Newton,"[3] but instead we have to be content with "a mediocre worker whose progress is never more than passably satisfactory."

We are assured that "a religious consciousness can understand and even love" this groping, fumbling will, which some would like to equate with the God of the Christians. Thus, all the history of modern theology, which "shows us the Chrisian soul turning aside from the sovereign God of Calvinian predestination", ends in offering the religious consciousness something

---

[1] Victor Monod, *op. cit.*, p. 333.
[2] *Ibid.*   [3] *Foi et vie*, Feb. 1935, p. 160.

which is below it, since it can be comprehended by it, something which, by overcoming a very natural reluctance, it can "even" learn to love.[1] The word "even" says much for the religious quality of this object of piety. Clearly, it is not God, but simply "nature" endowed with a not too clear-seeing will. So far as we are concerned, what we can comprehend, and "even" learn to love, we certainly cannot worship.

Fortunately, the author of those well-documented works *Le problème de Dieu* and *Dieu dans l'Univers* does not know everything when he claims that all modern theology is antipredestinarian, whether the epithet "modern" be taken to mean modernist or is merely used in the chronological sense.

In the former sense, Scholten in Holland, Schweitzer and Troeltsch in Germany, Auguste Sabatier and Jean Frédéric Astié in France, have attempted to harmonize Calvinian predestination with their "modern" systems.

In the second sense, we would point out that the activity of Calvinist theologians was very great throughout the 19th century, while to-day it has become so intense as to cause serious concern to the protagonists of Protestant ethicalism. We need only cite at random a few names of theologians who certainly cannot be numbered among the ancients, such as Abraham Kuyper, Hermann Bavinck and, in our own day, V. Hepp, in Holland. The Americans, Dabney, Charles and A. A. Hodge, Breckinridge, Thornwell, Shedd, flourished in the last century. B. B. Warfield lived in our own century, while Berkhof and Heyns are with us still. We recall again the names of Cunningham, Macpherson and Orr in Scotland, of Kohlbrügge and Wichelhaus in Germany, of E. Böhl and our distinguished contemporaries C. Bohatec in Austria, and E. Sebestyén in Hungary. All these men belong chronologically to the history of modern Calvinistic theology. Or are we indeed to understand that a modern historian, in the sense of Modernist, has to delete from the history of modern theology, in the chronological sense, the names of the Calvinistic divines of the 19th and 20th centuries?

It is only too true that many Christians have turned away from the God of predestination, but it remains to be seen whether this is due to the fact that they are Christians or to the fact that their Christianity has been coloured by the humanism of the Renaissance and the Aufklärung. On the other hand, we would ask whether those people, daily becoming more numerous, particularly among the younger generation, who are returning to the God of Calvin, Aquinas and Augustine, cease to be

[1] Victor Monod, *op. cit.*, p. 333.

Christians when they worship the God of Pauline theology, the Lord of heaven and earth, who is greater than all?

We are convinced that this is not Victor Monod's view, though he probably regards the return to the sovereign God of the Synoptists, of John, Paul, Augustine and Calvin as a purely accidental but regrettable fact; or, not to mince matters, as a passing fashion favoured by the consequences of the war. He thinks the movement is bound to meet with a check, since it is contrary to the spirit of Biblical prophetism, to the concepts of the new physics and to the religious philosophy advocated by Bergsonism. Prophetism, he thinks, like modern thought, will end sooner or later by turning men's minds from seeking God in space. On the other hand, they will be guided to seek in time a God who will be a perpetual source of ever fresh but never satisfying beginnings.

Let us note in the first place what we are told concerning prophetism. If we understand our author correctly, it was only the Greeks who taught men to contemplate God in the expanse of the cosmos. The prophets showed Him to us only in time. "How could a God as profoundly ethical as the God of the prophets express His personality by means of the phenomena of physical nature, which can arouse no response in the human heart?" This question will surprise the reader who is familiar with his Bible but a stranger to the fluctuations of textual criticism. The thesis in question can only be sustained by effacing, with a stroke of the pen, each time we meet them, the doxologies of Jeremiah, of the deutero-Isaiah and of Amos.[1]

Marti is almost alone in deleting them altogether. Wellhausen, Nowack and others admit their authenticity in the deutero-Isaiah. Von Orelli, Cripps, Van Hoonacker, G. Aalders, Van Gelderen whose fine commentary on Amos appeared in 1933, maintain the general authenticity of these doxologies.

No dogmatic principle is at stake here. We readily admit that an inspired prophet may have inserted these magnificent jewels into the works of his predecessors. But, since there is no general agreement on the subject among the critics, we have no right to regard this as a matter of established fact.

[1] The author of *Dieu dans l'Univers* recognizes two texts of Amos, since he quotes them, as prophetic. He similarly admits certain texts of the second Isaiah and of Psalm 19 (p. 26). But he tells us that, while celebrating the sovereignty of the God of nature, the Hebrews "more often show a feeling of terror in the presence of the power of the God of nature rather than a feeling of admiration in the presence of His providential wisdom." The texts to which we have referred reduce this affirmation to its true proportions. The real question is whether, for the prophets, God reveals Himself in nature as a person, wise or terrible. Here, again, the texts supply the answer.

Moreover, even if the relatively late composition of these doxologies could be taken for granted, the problem would remain equally difficult for Monod. He would still be confronted with the fact that at a given moment the religion of Israel, the religion of the psalmists and of one who is unquestionably a prophet, call him if you will deutero-Isaiah, found it possible to blend in a harmonious whole both moral preoccupation and the contemplation of God in nature. It would also remain true that this result was not achieved through reading the works of Aristotle.

The texts are abundant and decisive. They are saturated with the prophetic spirit. The prophets teach an ethical religion, no doubt, but they are not to the slightest extent ethicalists. Everywhere they base their moral demands and their hopes in the triumph of right on the exclusive sovereignty and the law of Yahweh. The doxologies establish and confirm this sentiment.

Let us cite, at random, some which we find most convincing. "He (God) hath made the earth by His power, He hath established the world by His wisdom, and hath stretched out the heaven by His understanding. When He uttereth His voice, there is a multitude of waters in the heavens. . . . He maketh lightnings with rain and bringeth forth the wind out of His treasures. . . . He is the former of all things and Israel is the rod of His inheritance: the Lord of hosts is His name" (Jeremiah 51: 15–19).

"Wisdom" and "understanding" are surely words which "arouse a response in the human heart". If the God of Jeremiah fills heaven and earth (23: 24), it cannot be "absurd" to seek and acknowledge Him in the spatial universe.

Listen again to these words of another who must be reckoned among the prophets: "Thus saith the Lord that created the heavens; God Himself that formed the earth and made it; He hath established it, He created it not in vain, He formed it to be inhabited: I am the Lord and there is none else" (Isaiah 45: 18). After this we are told that monotheism in Israel was not given to the teleological contemplation of the universe; and we are further informed that the God of Israel has no concern for the sun or the stars, and that He reveals Himself only by history and in time of which it is the content.[1] He never manifests Himself in sidereal space.

But listen again to the same inspired writer: "Have ye not understood from the foundations of the earth? It is He that sitteth upon the circle of the earth and the inhabitants thereof

[1] Victor Monod, *op. cit.*, p. 16.

are as grasshoppers; that stretcheth out the heavens as a curtain and spreadeth them out as a tent to dwell in. . . . Lift up your eyes on high, and behold who hath created these things, that bringeth out their host by number: He calleth them all by names by the greatness of His might, for that He is strong in power, not one faileth. . . . I, even My hands, have stretched out the heavens and all their host have I commanded" (Isaiah 40: 21, 22, 26; 45: 12).

If the God of the prophet of the consolations of Israel assigns to the stars the place which they must occupy in space, if He gives to each one its name, then He must be concerned with them to a very considerable extent. If the prophet invites his hearers to reflect on the foundation of the world and to lift up their eyes towards the starry skies, it is because, like the psalmist—himself surely a prophet also—he believes that "the heavens declare the glory of God and the firmament showeth His handywork" (Psalm 19: 1). In contrast with those who demand a system of radical ethicalism, he believes that God affirms His personality "by the phenomena of physical nature".

Again, Amos exhorts Israel to turn away from the sanctuaries of Bethel, Gilgal and Beersheba; to "seek Him that maketh the Pleiades and Orion and turneth the shadow of death into the morning and maketh the day dark with night: that calleth for the waters of the sea and poureth them out upon the face of the earth: the Lord is His name" (5: 8). Thus God manifests His power in the arrangement of the constellations and His ethical personality as administrator of justice in eclipses, tidal waves, floods and earthquakes. "The Lord God of hosts is He that toucheth the land and it shall melt, and all that dwell therein shall mourn: and it shall rise up wholly like a flood and shall be drowned, as by the flood of Egypt. It is He that buildeth his stories in the heaven and hath founded his troop in the earth" (9: 5, 6).

We think the reader will agree that the case is proved: it is evident that the religion of Israel has no such aversion to space as the ethicalists attribute to it. On the contrary, space is, for it, a source of divine revelation. It is the seat of the vast presence of God. Ethicalism, then, cannot look for any serious support from this quarter.

It can expect even less in view of the idea, so familiar to the prophets, of a future time and of events to come, which will be brought to pass by means of human wills, but the course of which is nevertheless irrevocably and infallibly fixed by the counsel (*'etsâh*, Isaiah 14: 24–27; 46: 9–11; Psalm 33: 11; or *sod*,

AN INTRODUCTION TO REFORMED DOGMATICS

Jeremiah 23: 18) of the sovereign deity and by His purpose (*zammâh*, Jeremiah 4: 28).

And, by a curious contrast, it happens that it is precisely the Greek Aristotle, advocate of the theory of God revealed by the physical universe, in space, who, for avowed moral considerations, dismisses the idea that the principle of the excluded middle can be legitimately applied to judgments bearing on contingent futures.[1] It is certainly not the God of this philosopher who conceives the decrees ruling the course of events which take place in the world, since he is ignorant of them until the moment when they occur.

But the radical indeterminism of Aristotle has not prevented Aquinas from using the materials of his system in order to reconcile faith in the predestinating sovereignty of the God of Augustine with the science of his time. From the very beginning, Calvinistic theology has worked well with the doctrine of the Stagyrite. There would seem to be no reason, then, why the indeterminism of this system of philosophy, or the principle of indetermination of the new scientific theories, should constitute an insurmountable obstacle to the Calvinist revival.

The sovereignty of God, on the one hand, and the total independence of the futurition of contingent events, on the other, mark a dividing line among minds which is not likely to be effaced. We can reckon on the durable character of this revival. The new physics, it is true, presents an idealist tendency among some of its most eminent representatives,[2] but that does not prevent one of them, Jeans, from finding his "mathematician" deity by the aid of a calculation applied to the spatial character of the universe.[3]

This proves that there is something artificial in a history of the idea of God, divided into spatial and temporal periods, the latter commencing with the philosophy of Creative Evolution and the new theories of physics.

Remember that, according to Minkowski, reality is four-dimensional, and space-time, in the concrete, constitutes an indissoluble unity. From this point of view, space, so far from being abolished, constitutes an element of reality as solid as time. Thus we see that, on this point, the new science agrees with common sense. Time and space are not entities but measures bearing on the duration and extent of finite concrete

[1] Περὶ ἑρμηνείας, IX, 19, a. 6 ff.
[2] A. S. Eddington, *The Nature of the Physical World*, xiii; J. Jeans, *The Mysterious Universe*, pp. 125–128.
[3] *Op. cit.*, p. 134.

beings. These abstractions are as inseparable as the extent and duration of these concrete beings.

We do not seek God in the spatial universe only, because if this universe had not duration, or time, which is an abstraction for concrete duration, it would be impossible to realize its existence.

Moreover, the cosmological argument is derived from the contingency of the world which, under one of its current forms, traces the supposed finite succession of temporal causes until it arrives at an eternal first cause, largely making use of the notion of time. The argument was employed long before the advent of the new philosophy and the new science. Jeans uses it in this form in order to postulate a creator, knowing quite well that Plato and Augustine were not ignorant of the fact that abstract time must be finite in the past; that it implies a beginning. [1] It is certain, therefore, that even the Greeks did not have to await the advent of the new theories in order to seek and find God.

Actually, He has been sought everywhere. For, overflowing all reality He is present everywhere, in all His works, as well in their extent as in their duration.

Let God be conceived by the man of science as an attractive motor, as an engineer-mechanician, or as a mathematical genius, according to the conception which the said scientist forms of the physical constitution of the world, it matters not in the least to the believer, as such, whether he be a theologian or not. Lord Kelvin, as a scientist, conceived the cosmic activity of God under the symbol of an engineer-mechanician. As a Christian, he knew Him to be "God the Father almighty, creator of heaven and earth". This knowledge of God as creator and preserver of the world was what mattered for his faith. The mode of creative activity may be studied from the viewpoint of physical science, but it is a matter of indifference to religious faith. If Kelvin had been led to conceive God, in his scientific theory, as a mathematician rather than as an engineer, nothing in the religious dogma which he had embraced would have been changed.

So far from having reason to fear the new physics, Calvinism among Protestants, and Thomism among Roman Catholics, bring to it an indispensable philosophical support. Both admit the existence of indeterminate realities, contingent in themselves and some of them free. Their futurition, however, is determined, that is to say, rendered objectively certain, by the

[1] *Op. cit.*, p. 134.

271

decree of the sovereign God whose efficacious will realizes what it wishes without destroying what it establishes. [1]

Calvin expressly acknowledges the validity of this distinction of the scholastics between absolute and hypothetical necessity. [2] He thus satisfies the observation which proves the existence of free and contingent realities and the reason which, no more than faith, can conceive of the liberty of independence.

"Actually, what science affirms and what we affirm with her, is that all things are determined. This, too, is the postulate of reason for which nothing happens without cause and without reason, not even what we call chance. It is very evident that, for an omniscient and onmipotent Spirit, the universe as a whole and in each of its parts is determined. But it cannot on this account be maintained that it is determined mechanically. Determinism is not a simple notion." [3]

On the other hand, as a result of these new observations, physical science finds itself implicated in an unexpected crisis. In the 19th century a particular kind of determinism, not that which is required by reason but a universal mechanical determinism, was regarded as a necessary postulate of science. Meanwhile, under the influence of positivism, it was laid down as axiomatic that "there is no sense in supposing the existence of things that are theoretically unobservable". Such things were considered to be outside the sphere of science, which had no other object than to verify phenomena and to integrate them into mechanical causal relations. Now, a thing theoretically unobservable is, by definition, not a phenomenon. This unobservable in itself was relegated to the sphere of the unknowable. There, on condition that they renounced the scientific spirit, faith and imagination could give themselves free scope. From this point of view, psychology can be regarded as a science only on condition that its content is reduced to this radical determinism. Materialism has high hopes of arriving at this position.

But the views which result from the quantum theory have introduced into physics a revolution much more perceptible and

---

[1] *Westminster Confession*, iii. i; v. 2.

[2] *Inst.* I, xvi. 9.

[3] Jacques Chevalier, *La vie de l'esprit*, p. 21. In connexion with what this author says concerning chance, it is interesting to note that the Calvinist theologian, Jean de la Placette, in his *Traité des Jeux de hasard, défendu contre les objections*, etc., La Haye, 1714, had already given what we believe to be the first scientific definition of chance, as follows: "For myself, I am persuaded that chance comprises something real and positive, namely, a conjunction of two or more contingent events, both of which have their causes but in such a way that in this conjunction nothing is known of them. I am much mistaken if this is not what men mean when they speak of chance."

profound than Einstein's theory of relativity and they have led to a principle capable of very wide application, which has been denominated "the principle of indetermination"—a term perhaps not altogether suitable since it is less a matter of things indeterminate than indeterminable.

What exactly is this principle? The learned professor of Bordeaux from whom we have borrowed the preceding quotation shall tell us: "Formulated by Heisenberg in 1927, this principle explains itself by the impossibility of defining simultaneously the position and speed of a particle, or of knowing, at a given moment, the energy of this particle, because our instrument of penetration, which is light, reacts on the object and because the meeting of a proton with an electron confuses the movement of the latter: it is as though, in order to observe the sun, we had to project a sun upon it".[1]

Thus, one of two characteristic qualities can be defined but not both at the same time. Now, the principles of mechanical determinism presuppose that the elements of the physical systems have, at each instant, a definite position and movement. The advocates of the new theory conclude from this that "it is necessary to consider this principle (these principles, respectively) not only as practically inapplicable to microscopic phenomena but as without any meaning in the world of atoms".[2] In other words, mechanistic determinism is theoretically without significance and totally unobservable in microphysics. It is important to note, however, that microphysics serves as a basis for macrophysics. At the root of things, indetermination reigns.

It follows that those who wish to maintain mechanistic determinism at all costs must question the positivist ideal and say that "it is not proved that positivist assumptions suffice to render science possible."[3] In that case the survivors of the period during which, both in the political and scientific spheres, men thought they had "extinguished the stars", are in a quandary. They find themselves on the horns of a dilemma: either they must maintain mechanistic determinism and renounce the positivist axiom that all that is not observable is chimerical, or they must renounce determinism in order to maintain the positivist axiom and adopt the principle which will indeed be for them a principle of indetermination and not only of indeterminability. Of the

---

[1] J. Chevalier, *op. cit.*, p. 23.
[2] Summarized from J. Joergensen *Sur les implications de la physique*, etc., i.. *Revue de métaphysique et de morale*, July–Sept., 1932, p. 341.
[3] *Ibid.*, p. 349.

two alternatives, the latter cannot lead far along the Damascus road.

In any case, one fact remains secure: science can survive a more or less definite rejection of universal mechanistic determinism. The proof is that it does survive. For us Calvinists, it is a matter of indifference to know whether things will continue thus for a long time or not. Our theologians did not find it difficult to come to terms with the dominant scientific determinism of the 19th century,[1] and the opening years of the present century. Moreover, Eddington is mistaken in thinking that predestination has received a fatal blow from the new theories of microphysics, through the so-called principle of indetermination.[2] Calvin, as we have seen, was strongly opposed to the physical determinism of the human mind (judicial astrology). He refused also to eliminate contingency from nature (stoicism). We have also noticed how the *Westminster Confession*, faithful to this point of view, reserves a place for contingency and liberty, both of which it sees as comprised in the divine decrees.

The difficulty which presents itself is not one for those who are acquainted with the so-called principle of indetermination. The theories on the constitution of matter and on the radical indeterminism of the Brownian movements,[3] brought forward by microphysics on the one hand, and the notion of law founded on the idea of statistics and on the calculation of probabilities, on the other hand, seem to contradict a law of the human mind which postulates that everything has its *raison d'être* and that, in this sense, everything is determined.

Now it is just here that the theistic intuition of a God whose sovereign will directs events comes to the aid of modern physics, showing it a way out of an initial contradiction that is apparently insoluble. The new theories, far from leading us to the "diligent student" god of the ethical school, industrious but a little clumsy, compel us to turn again to the God of Augustine and Calvin.

What is this initial contradiction and how does the idea of divine sovereignty help us in regard to it? In this way. Bachelard tells us that in the strictly scientific sphere, the first theses that demand consideration are those which form the basis of the kinetic theory of gases.[4] This theory, he says, brings a profound

[1] A. Kuyper, *Het. Calvinisme*, IV: *Het Calvinisme en de Wetenschap*.
[2] *Op. cit.*, 14, 292.
[3] [The irregular oscillatory movement of microscopic particles suspended in a limpid fluid, first described by a Dr. Robert Brown.]
[4] *Le nouvel esprit scientifique*, p. 113.

modification to the scientific spirit; he should have said, a veritable revolution. In his opinion: "the most important metaphysical characteristic of the kinetic theory of gases is that it realizes a transcendence of quality, in this sense that a quality not belonging to the components ,belongs nevertheless to the compound." The compound is determined; the components are indeterminate.

And here is the contradiction formulated by P. A. Carmichael: "The individual object is indeterminate; the class, determined; a property affirmed of one class of determinate objects is denied to the objects taken separately".[1] The fundamental defect of all statistical physical laws is precisely this, which serves as a principle to the kinetic theory of gases.

Now, unless we invoke the aid of a higher principle, we have here an evident violation of the principle *de omni et nullo*, a contradiction in terms. To subscribe to the doctrine of scientific indeterminism would be to agree to speak in contradictory terms.

How are we to extricate ourselves from the difficulty? One suggestion is that the contradiction should be transcended with the aid of the idea of probability. Unfortunately, the logic of probability is admittedly incomplete and, moreover, it is almost impossible to define probability itself. According to Poirier, there is no concrete objective idea of probability, apart from statistics.[2] It would seem, then, that we are in a vicious circle.

Theism, however, as we have defined it, enables us to overcome this contradiction, thanks to the distinction between the necessity of the consequent and the necessity of the consequence, indicated above.

"Although, in relation to the foreknowledge and decree of God, the first cause, all things come to pass immutably and infallibly; yet by the same providence, He ordereth them to fall out, according to the nature of second causes, either necessarily, freely or contingently.[3]

By virtue of this principle, the position of the electrons, entirely independent of each other by their very nature, may be indeterminate and uncaused in itself and yet governed by the immediate and efficacious action of the first cause, on whose will "the least" of creatures depends[4] for its movement and for its very existence.

---

[1] *Logic and Scientific Law*, in *The Monist*, April, 1932.
[2] René Poirier, *Remarques sur la logique des inductions*, Vrin, Paris, 1931, p. 14: cf. the article by J. Joergensen indicated above, relating Planck's unsuccessful attempt.
[3] *Westminster Confession*, V, 2.   [4] *Ibid.*, 1.

But is not this merely to replace a contradiction by a mystery? Where, then, is the gain for science? We reply that there is a margin, we were going to say an infinite margin, between a contradiction and a mystery. A contradiction is a suicide of the human mind when it is laid down as a principle. It is the negation of all science, of all knowledge. A mystery, on the contrary, is the normal result of the effort of the human mind when it returns, or attempts to return, to first principles. Scientific reason may endow it with hope, and religious faith will then find its normal atmosphere.

It is clear that there is no difficulty in admitting that the disposition of elements, unimportant in itself, depends on the efficacy of the will of an almighty cause. This efficacy is indeed a mystery, since God is, by definition, infinite and transcendent to all comprehension, but the acceptance of a mystery is not contrary to the dignity of the scientific mind.

The disposition of the pieces on a chess-board is contingent to the eyes of those who are ignorant of the complicated rules of the game of chess. It seems to defy all law and all calculation. It is not contradictory, however, to admit that the movement and disposition of the pieces depends on the will of an intelligent cause. The intelligence and the will of the player, the mutual relation between these two faculties, the relations which exist between the determination of the will and the muscular movement of the organism, the transmission of the movements of the organism to the pieces on the chess-board, are very mysterious things. This does not prevent us from finding a quite natural explanation of the movement of the pieces and of their disposition at the will of the player. Why may it not be the same with the will of God in its relations to the disposition of electrons? There is no contradiction in saying: "it is the will of God which makes the necessity of all things", whether of the components or of the compound.

Their necessity is always borrowed from elsewhere. In itself, everything created is contingent. The sole difference is that there are contingents which obey a constant and general order (the compounds) and that there are others the behaviour of which cannot be foreseen individually by the human mind (the components).

But, to God, whose originative and constitutive knowledge of reality is independent of the object, "nothing is contingent or uncertain".[1] Here we have the best explanation that can

---

[1] *Westminster Confession*, II, 2.

possibly be conceived of the laws of chance and of the very fact that chance has laws.

Calvin's religious determinism being the consequence of the free will of God, it is not affected by the theories of microphysics, provisional or not, as is the case with mechanistic determinism, in spite of Eddington's view,[1] and it allows the latter to surmount the preliminary contradiction which formal logic opposes to it.

Faith discovers in the order which reigns even in chance the manifestation of the supreme intelligence, and, in the variety and indetermination of individual cases, the manifestation of the liberty of this intelligence.

The frequent occurrence of the probable is a premium granted to the precautions of human wisdom. The impossibility of excluding from our previsions the eventuality of the occurrence of the improbable is a recall to the sense of our dependence upon God in regard to our destiny.

We have said that the sovereignty of God and of His efficacious will is the best possible explanation of the fact that chance has its laws, of the possibility of the calculation of hazards and of the fact that there is harmony between the probability *a priori*, affirmed by the calculation of the mind and of empirical probability, inscribed in the facts.

"Between *a priori* probability and *a posteriori* probability there is the same gulf as between *a priori* logical geometry and an *a posteriori* geometrical description of the real. If, therefore, there is concurrence between calculated probability and measured probability, it is perhaps the most delicate, subtle and convincing proof of the permeability of nature by reason."[2]

The calculation of probabilities is founded on the principle of sufficient reason. The universe of the new science, with its principle of indetermination, is a determinate universe all the same, since it is subject to the principle of sufficient reason. It is a universe which reveals itself as thinkable in the sense that the fortuitous phenomena themselves obey the law of reason. From this position, to infer that it is the expression of a thought, is only one step—a step that has been taken by many eminent exponents of the new theories in physics. For Jeans, science "is reduced to a simple contact between the mind and the creation of the mind —as when one reads a book or listens to music. . . . We discover that the universe renders patent the existence of a power which conceives and controls, a power which has something

---

[1] *The Nature of the Physical World*, loc. cit.
[2] M. Bachelard, *op. cit.*, p. 118.

in common with our individual minds."[1] The author, whose standpoint is not that of Reformed Christianity, does not admit "for ought he knows" that this intelligence can have anything in common with our emotions, our morality or our tastes.

It cannot be otherwise. Only the faith which proceeds from the Word of God can give to the God who reveals it to the world by the aid of the natural light of common grace, the names which acknowledge Him to be the God of the prophets and of our Lord Jesus Christ.

This is so true that Borel concedes only a minuscule initial to the god that he discovers in nature: "The true source of the conquest of the globe by man is faith in human reason, the conviction that the world is not ruled by blind divinities or by chance but by rational laws: ἀεὶ θεὸς γεωμετρεῖ: this Platonic motto signifies that the god who governs the universe has a reason similar to that of the geometers. In other words, that these can penetrate the divine and immutable laws of the world: from the day when man understood that he could set himself such a goal, he has never turned back from it."[2]

Natural science, while it has many eminent representatives who recognize the supreme intelligence at the root of things, is far from being in a position to replace religion for the Christian soul. It cannot enable us to contemplate the majesty of God in the grand vision which Calvin has shown to the Church, and which has been obscured later by anthropocentric theologians. Our Reformer was right when he said: "If the building is to be solidly constructed, it must be founded on a sincere and true faith. For the confession which ascribes glory to God is comparable to the surface of things, but faith hidden in the heart is the foundation."[3]

Monod sees clearly this convergence between the God of science and the God of faith, which has been very evident since the new theories have discredited mechanistic determinism. What he says on the subject is impressive, but unfortunately he dissociates time from space in the work of God on the plea that time has qualities which prevent it from being confounded with space and that, in co-ordinating it with the three spatial dimensions, these qualities are not eliminated.

This view does not seem tenable to us. The impossibility of eliminating the qualities proper to time does not prevent it from being equally impossible, not only to imagine but to

---

[1] J. Jeans, *The Mysterious Universe*, pp. 160, 162.
[2] E. Borel, *Le Hasard*, p. 3 f.
[3] Calvin, *Praelect. in Jer.*, x. 12.

conceive a finite being who could have any duration whatever, without being somewhere, in some place. If God is present not only in me, who am spatial because finite, but in all the finite beings coexistent with me, this means that He is everywhere in space, both near and far. "Am I a God at hand, saith the Lord, and not a God afar off? Do not I fill heaven and earth? saith the Lord" (Jeremiah 23: 23, 24). Here, surely, we have a spatial sense of God.

We have insisted on the reality of the revelation of God in space. With the inspired singer of Israel, we listen to the language of the heavens which declare loudly the glory of God: while space "sheweth His handiwork" (Psalm 19: 1). The reason why we have pleaded the cause of space as one of the sources of divine revelation does not lie in the fact that we, the "ghosts" of Calvinism, are attached to "the purely abstract notion of a transcendent intelligence which has arranged the immutable destiny of the world in an eternal book." The God of Augustine and Calvin is no abstract notion: at this moment He is preserving the universe by continuous creation: by His power all things are developing in the variety of the vast and apparently interminable series presented by nature and history. In the theology of Calvin and his disciples, that which God has decided in the transcendence of His decree, He accomplishes actually by the immanence of His providential act. Readers of the *Institutes*, whose author has been accused of pantheism (*inter alia!*), do not need to be reminded of the concrete reality of the energy always in act of the creative power of God.

For our Reformer, this concrete reality of God, the eternal worker who sustains the world is no meaningless by-product of dogmatic speculation. The idea forms such an important part of vital religion that he teaches it to the little children of the catechism: "the power of God is not therefore idle in Him, but it implies something more than this: namely, that He is always at work and that nothing is done without Him with His permission or by His command." [1]

We are here as far as possible from an abstraction like that of Spinoza. Deism knows only divine transcendence: pantheism only divine immanence. Augustinian and Calvinian theism sacrifices neither the one nor the other. No one can say, however, that his God has arranged, once for all, the theorem of history: for history, as the Calvinist sees it, cannot be reduced to the mere logical unfolding of a theorem.

Objective reality, with its lacunae, its inconsistencies and its

[1] *Geneva Catechism*, III.

unexpected successes in which the blind forces of passion, the deliberate initiatives of liberty (intelligent spontaneity) play their part, is the same for Calvinism as for the most decided humanism. The Calvinist believes, however, that an act can be free in the mode of its execution and yet pre-ordained with certainty, and that an infallible certainty, in the futurition of its occurrence.

To believe in the sovereignty of God is to believe that His almighty will chooses the concrete world to be real, with the qualities that we see in it, which means that, side by side with an absolute natural necessity, there exists also physical contingency and moral liberty.

History, past, present and future, as it unfolds itself in reality is, for Calvinism, a complex of concrete facts the occurrence of which has been divinely decreed. Among these facts are some which are necessary in themselves, others which are only necessary hypothetically as a matter of objective certainty. These latter, when they are free and when they are contrary to the law of God, happen only by His permission, which is never a naked and purely idle one. This permission implies the certainty of the occurrence of the contingent future and of the future free as to the mode of its execution. To believe this is to believe that man is a responsible agent dependent upon and governed by a sovereign God.

In the humanist camp, it is claimed that the sovereign God has been replaced by the God who is a moral person. But it is obvious that the latter is no God at all. If we understand by a moral person, a being whose intelligence is limited and who is subject to a law or even to a simple ideal emanating from a higher power, and hence heteronomous and dependent: then God is not a moral person.

If, on the other hand, we understand by a moral person an autonomous being, a being who is, in Calvin's phrase, "a law unto himself", a being whose law is his very essence, God is that Being. He is indeed the only Being who is autonomous. But then He is not a moral person, for a moral person is one who is responsible to another person who is a legislator superior to Him, the supreme lawgiver. But there can be no legislator higher than God.

Definitions are free, however, and we may understand by a moral person the being who is perfect and immutable holiness. In this sense, God, the God of Augustine and Calvin, is a moral person: nor does He cease to be such at the point where His justice becomes for us a mysterious and unfathomable abyss.

It must be clearly understood that God is not a moral person in the sense that He is responsible before the reason of an evolved simian, such as man is according to transformism, the conclusions of which are accepted by modern humanism.

In the final analysis, we would say that the term "moral" is really suitable only to describe the relations of finite beings among themselves. In regard to God, we have duties, but these duties are much more than duties of morality. They are duties of piety, for God is far superior to a moral person; he is the all-holy. The dogmatic theology of a religion which adores cannot therefore be other than theistic in the manner of Augustine, Aquinas and Calvin.

CHAPTER 7

WHY DOGMATICS MUST BE CHRISTIAN AND ORTHODOX

This is a revelation of God to which we have not yet made reference, as we desired to confine our preliminary studies to belief in Him as creator, comprised under the term theism.

Theism is the affirmation of the Being identical with Himself, all powerful and all wise, who reveals Himself to us as such in the existence and preservation of the world, in the direction which He impresses upon it, as well as in the consciousness which we possess of our own subjective existence. To us, namely, to those who have learnt to read the book of nature with the aid of that key which is the positive revelation of Scripture, communicated and explained in the first place by the Church, the mother of the faithful.

The revelation to which we have not yet referred is that of God in the moral consciousness or conscience. This is also a fact of nature, one of the works of creation, for the same reason as the instinct of self-preservation, the intelligence and the reason. According to Calvin, it is a *semen justitiae*, a "germ" which contributes to the manifestation of religion,[1] distinguishing between good and evil, between the just and the unjust, between the permissible and the forbidden, between all things which pertain to the order of moral categories.

Conscience affirms the sanction. It begins to realize it immediately in a case of violation which appears subjectively to the individual conscience, rightly or wrongly, as particularly grave. This beginning of sanctions is the strange phenomenon of remorse, which occurs unexpectedly even among those who regard themselves as "emancipated".

That men differ enormously among themselves in regard to the *matter* of the moral law is a fact too well known to require demonstration. Moreover, the moral sense can be atrophied, under the influence of various circumstances, as profoundly as the religious instinct and the other instincts of the spiritual life. But if that which appears good to one person wears an evil aspect in the eyes of another, the *form* of the moral sentiment,

---

[1] *Com. on Rom.*, ii, 15. By *semen* Calvin understands seed, germ, a natural or, n any case; innate aptitude (*Inst.* II, iii. 2).

282

which constitutes its obligation, remains as a universal characteristic of human nature. All men know themselves to be
restrained by something, and this because man is a rational
animal. He knows that he is obliged by the demands of practical
reason. The diversity of his moral judgments is due to the fact
that reason, influenced by the prepossessions of different
cultures, does not form the same judgments of value everywhere.

The sociological school explains the sense of guilt and remorse
by the offender's consciousness of the conflict between the
collective will of society and his own individual will. The sense
of obligation itself is held to result from the hereditary transmission of the collective will to the individual, under the form of
social instinct. It is fortified by the gregarious instinct of social
conformism. Man, in fact, is not only an individual; he is also
a social animal.

This theory is open to grave objection. In the first place, it is
an attempt at rational explanation on the part of an empirical
system. It is therefore suicidal: it supposes reality to be subject
to the exigencies of a reason whose business it is to understand
the decrees inscribed in the necessity of the facts. On the other
hand, this reason would have no other origin than the habitual
sequences, were it not for reason.

That man is a social animal will not be questioned. But
neither the individual nor the community create arbitrarily the
essential and elementary conditions of existence in human
societies. These conditions, among which certain moral obli-
gations hold the first place, must be taken for granted in the
nature of things. They are perceived as such immediately, by
emotive and rational intuition.

Intelligence and sensibility are innate in the individual. The
intelligence perceives the absolute necessity of complying with
certain demands in order that life may be possible. That is why
these demands produce an echo in the conscience as at any
rate hypothetical commandments; if you wish to live in society,
you must do such and such a thing. Now it would be unreasonable not to wish to live or to modify the conditions of life; thus
the commandment becomes absolute.

It is natural that what reason decrees should appear as a
commandment. It is natural also that, if this commandment is
disregarded, reason should take its revenge by disturbing the
sensibility with remorse.

This is all that heredity transmits. The unwritten laws of
which Sophocles speaks are of a purely moral order, human

because they are rational. But the sense of obligation does not transmit by heredity the matter of the classical, traditional prescriptions, which are frequently arbitrary. These prescriptions are known only through initiation. In societies which are called "primitive", they bind the initiate inwardly only by reason of their supposedly magical or religious origin. Thus, magic is, for him, both religion and the order of nature: it is divine. He believes it to be the height of folly to resist the higher powers which threaten him. The tradition of the elders binds him because he thinks it to be founded on force. The man who profanes a taboo may die of sheer fright due to the idea that he has unreasonably risen up against the expression of the will of his ancestors who are gods, that is to say, the small change of the absolute: at heart, he is conscious of having defied that which we call God.

Moreover, the conflict supposed by the theory between the will of the clan and that of the individual places us already within the sphere of formal moral liberty and thus within the sphere of ethics.

When the offender feels himself to be justified in pleading that he has been pushed irresistibly towards the violation of the traditional order by some divinity, he never fails to avail himself of this excuse in order to attempt to escape from social reprobation. This is what Œdipus did when he tried to justify himself.[1] We do not see how it is possible to deny that the attempt to excuse oneself implies the recognition of personal duty and, in case of violation, justifies the condemnation. The mere fact of the excuse removes us far from any "morality without obligation or sanction".

Finally, the proof that the imperative of moral consciousness is not identical with the collective will, whether ancestral or present, lies in the circumstance that it sometimes sets the individual in opposition to tradition or public opinion. It is not identical with the gregarious instinct, since it may lead a man to defy public opinion, or awaken remorse in him because he has conformed himself to it through cowardice. The history of missions furnishes many remarkable examples of this.

All these reasons seem to us pertinent. It is none the less true, however, that they make very little impression on the minds of the advocates of sociologism .Further, it will be realized that the existence of this school constitutes a serious challenge to the Kantian and neo-Kantian ethicalism of theological tendency which would base faith in God on faith in duty.

[1] *Œdipus Rex*, verses 956–998.

Among Protestants, the strict theism of Calvinism is the only solid foundation for the authority of conscience. Without it, sooner or later, morality loses its obligatory character and descends to the lower stage of a simple "science of manners".

When the conscience is not the intuition of the presence of the inward witness, of the judge and lawgiver, Lord of our life and master of our acts, by right of creation[1], it loses all absolute authority.

The weakness of ethicalism consists in the fact that it forgets that man is nothing by himself; that an authority which does not rest upon God must inevitably collapse.

Consider, for example, the Ritschlian approach to Christ. The historic person whose life is made known to us directly through the primitive documents which have been transmitted by the Church produces on the soul an impression of reality, provokes a judgment of unique value. He becomes the supreme object, the centre, the foundation of the Christian religion. He plays the part of God for that religion, without it being necessary for us to ask whether he is God ontologically.

Henceforth, according to Ritschl, Christianity is not so much a creed as a life, whose flame is kindled by contact with the person of Jesus through the medium of history.

We are, of course, ready to admit that the impression produced by the Christ of the canonical gospels is a mode of divine revelation. But, since it behoves one to be straightforward in a matter of such moment, we would say quite frankly, at the risk of appearing brutal, that the visionary with apocalyptic hopes who is frequently presented as the historic Christ inspires in us sentiments of commiseration rather than of adoration. Must it be said? The apotheosis of a man, be he the most sublime among the sons of woman, produces in us the effect of a return to paganism. The Protestantism that is itself a mere system of Jesuolatry is scarcely in a position to reproach Rome for Mariolatry.

If Christ is not the eternal and unique Son of God, consubstantial with the Father, the place which He occupies in Christian piety and the worship which He receives are usurped. A mere creature cannot legitimately be made the centre of religious devotion. By what right, we insist, can Roman Catholicism be reproached for its virtual deification of the mother of Christ, if we fall into the same error in regard to the man whom she bore in her womb?

God alone is God. He is, in a unique sense, "He who is". We

[1] *Inst.* III, xix. 15; cf. I, ii. 2.

know it because we have heard His word, proceeding from the burning bush that is Scripture. The divine majesty of the content of this revelation has bowed us in the dust, while it has created in us the faith that we have in the living and true God, the only One in whom we can and ought to place our entire confidence.

Knowing God, we have known our own insignificance and unworthiness: our insignificance as creatures, our unworthiness as transgressors of His revealed will.

At this precise point, the Reformed religion awaits us in order to indicate the absolute, unique and divine character of Christianity to those who, having known God as God, have received the grace to know themselves for what they are and what they are worth. To know oneself is to recognize one's place in relation to reality. Now, God is the supreme moral reality. The knowledge that we can have of ourselves in regard to our moral character is thus a function of the knowledge that we have of God and of what we are in relation to Him. And this is the principal and the sum of our practical wisdom.[1]

In the systems in which God is no more than a *primus inter pares*, a chief among equals, the fact that He is "a rewarder of them that diligently seek Him" (Hebrews 11: 6) goes without saying. Great stress is laid on "the infinite value of the moral person", on "the infinitely respectable character" of free will in the presence of whose decisions God Himself must bow with the respect which is due to autonomous reason on our "natural rights" in relation to God.

It is altogether otherwise with the idea which is given us by the Reformed doctrine of the formation of the religious bond which makes man, in the creative mind and under condition of obedience, a citizen of heaven.

Calvinism does not allow man for one moment to lose sight of the infinite distance which separates qualitatively the sole autonomous being from creatures who are themselves under the law [2] and thus heteronomous. It knows, as well as its opponents, that men are "the offspring of God" (Acts 17: 29),[3] but it conceives this relationship as one of analogy, founded on the spiritual character of the human soul created in the image of God.

It makes use of this notion in the spirit of the text from which it is drawn, not to put man on a level with God but to turn man

1 *Inst.* I, i.
2 *Com. in Mos. lib., corp. ref.*, 52, 49, 131.
3 *Vide* Calvin's commentary on this text.

from the thought of putting God below his own level by immersing Him in matter. It affirms to the utmost of its power the responsibility of man, while declaring with equal energy his entire dependence in regard to God, on his continuous creation and on the sovereign liberty of his grace.[1] It does not lose sight of the general teaching of the Scriptures concerning the contingent character of the divine dispensation which has made man a candidate for life eternal. (Isaiah 40:13-17; Job 9: 32, 33; 1 Samuel 2: 25; Psalms 113: 5, 6; 100: 2, 3; Job 22: 2, 3; 35: 7, 8; Luke 17: 10; Acts 17: 24, 25.)

"The distance between God and the creature is so great", says the *Westminster Confession,* "that, although reasonable creatures do owe obedience unto Him as their Creator, yet they could never have any fruition of Him as their blessedness and reward, but by some voluntary condescension on God's part, which He hath been pleased to express by way of covenant".[2]

This knowledge of God, transmitted to its children by the Calvinistic Reformation, is quite a different thing from a philosophical notion arrived at through the theoretical study of speculative reason.

"The knowledge of God is never without effect. . . Plato, although a poor pagan groping in darkness, denies that one could know this sovereign beauty which he imagines, without being ravished with admiration for it. How then is it possible to know God and nevertheless not be touched with any affection for Him? To love God as soon as we have known Him does not proceed solely from His nature, but the same Spirit who enlightens our understandings inspires also in our hearts an affection in conformity with knowledge . . . for God is not known at all by mere imagination, but as He manifests Himself within our hearts by the Holy Spirit".[3]

Now, by right of creation, the preceptive will of God, as it is revealed in the law expounded by Christ, appears to the conscience of the believer as the supreme rule of his thoughts and deeds. At the same time, his unworthiness as a sinner is revealed. He knows himself as signifying a moment of the will of the human race which, in the person of its head, has rebelled against the law and turned in a direction opposed to this law; as not being able to accomplish this law perfectly, which is humiliating to him, and as not wishing to accomplish it, which constitutes his guilt.

Not being able to: the determined orientation of his will to sin enslaves him to himself, a sinner, and liberates it in regard

---

[1] *Conf. Gal.,* viii.   [2] vii, 1.
[3] *Com. on* 1 *John,* ii, 3, 4.

to the law of God. It is in this sense that it is said to be impossible for the sinner to accomplish perfectly the divine law; that he is materially a slave of sin.

Not wishing to: the knowledge of the will of God, the offer which God makes to receive him as a child, the commands which He gives him, emancipate the sinner from all fatality, physical or moral. Through his knowledge of the law he is constituted formally free and therefore responsible.

It will be observed that the experience of the enslaved will, far from connoting the philosophical negation of moral liberty, implies it. There is nothing so strong, so formally free, as a deliberately evil will. On the other hand, there is nothing so tragic as the conflict, experienced by the sinner, between the stubborn "no" of his whole being and the "thou shalt" of the will of the Creator.

The consciousness of this conflict, which comes with knowledge of the will of God, awakened by common grace, a means which is resistible, produces irresistibly an aspiration towards deliverance, simultaneously with a feeling of guilt. This work of the moral consciousness must not, of course, be confounded with the conviction of sin produced by efficacious grace. But, while awaiting the latter, it puts the sinner in a practically intolerable situation, from which he can find no escape except by the prayer of the inspired elegiac: "Turn thou us unto Thee, O Lord, and we shall be turned" (Lamentations 5: 21).

As Calvin sees it,[1] this confession of the power of God is not enough by itself to establish a firm confidence; but it is already the principle of a good hope: God has promised to give His Spirit to those who ask Him. Through knowledge we can henceforth wish to ask Him. Our responsibility is thus engaged, no longer as descendants of the first sinner but in a personal manner.

Whence shall we seek help? To this question, the Christianity of Athanasius, Augustine, and the Reformers, makes a stupendous reply, divinely incredible to independent reason: "God is altogether given to us in His Son".[2] This brief proposition of Calvin summarizes the entire *evangelium de Christo*; all the message of the Church concerning Christ. This message reveals to the sinner that since God, in His grace, wills to love him to the point of taking his place in order to bear his penalty and expiate his sin, He loves perfectly, totally, even to the complete gift of Himself.

God, the absolute and independent being, who has nothing to expect, nothing to receive, from the creature; the sovereign

---

[1] *Com. in loco.*   [2] *Com. on John*, xv, 15.

being who has a right to all and who owes nothing to anyone; God is one of the modalities of the eternal relationship of His being, "God is altogether given to us. . . ." No other conception of God, in no other religion or philosophy, rises to the heights of the revelation brought by the Gospel. Let no one mention the pretended incarnations of Brahminism. India knows neither God, nor the Trinity, nor the Incarnation. It can offer us no more than a one-all, triads and avatars. The orthodox Christianity of the great councils calls for no sonorous epithets; it moves us only to mediate and adore.

If ever the sublime has assumed the form of a mark of divinity, it is indeed in this unique doctrine of the Incarnation of the sovereign God, transcendent, impassible in Himself, who takes, in the person of His Son, the very organs of suffering, a soul, a body, a human nature, in order to enter into humanity, to descend to its hell and, through expiation, to reconcile to Himself those who shall believe in Him.

The God of Arius and Socinus puts the cross on the shoulders of a creature, in order to reveal to the others the law of sacrifice and a benevolence which can abide its time.

The God of the Church alone loves even to the gift of Himself. "Now indeed," says Calvin, "the hearts which cannot be softened by such inestimable sweetness of the love of God must surely be harder than iron and stone".[1]

What can the quibbles of a science founded on the *a priori* arguments of naturalism weigh with those who have found their Damascus road in the presence of this supreme spectacle of love divine?

We are told that it was Athanasius who invented the dogma of the Incarnation. In this case, we must acknowledge the champion of the ὁμοούσιος to have been the greatest religious genius of all ages. Certainly his Gospel bears the seal of divinity, for it brings to the sinner the revelation of a divine love truly worthy of God and, at the same time, the answer to his agonized cry: "What must I do to be saved?"

In Christ, the sole-begotten and eternal Son of God, essence of His essence who is God, we contemplate God Himself, the living image of the Father, with the immediate vision of faith, and in His most profound relationship with the soul: the Father who is absolute love, the love which saves and succours the sinner, revealed in the gift of His Son. This is the supreme word of the Word which is announced to us and which thus attests itself as the Word of God.

[1] *Com. on John*, xv, 13.

This Word is again sealed in the heart of the sinner by the sacrament of baptism. Conferred from infancy, it brings to the sinner who has become an adult the assurance that it is God who has made the first advance towards him by introducing him to the covenant of grace.

The same Word shows that, in the august sacrament of the Eucharist, at the same time that we receive the offer of pardon through vicarious expiation and sacrifice, we obtain the certainty of the existence and of the real presence of the divine Being who communicates Himself to us.

Calvin has admirably expressed the nature of the certainty which attaches itself to the doctrine of the divinity of the Son of God. "This knowledge which consists in practice is doubtless surer and more solid than any idle speculation. For the pious soul[1] has the clearest view of God and may almost be said to touch Him with the hand, when it feels that by Him it is quickened, illuminated, saved, justified and sanctified."[2]

Thus it is by the strait gate of humiliation born of the consciousness of sin, by faith in the gift of God, who manifests Himself as the guarantor of the moral order; it is by this strait and narrow gate that one enters into the kingdom of which Christ is king.

True Reformed apologetic knows no other way of access to the Father. "In vain is Jesus Christ spoken of except to those who, being truly humbled, feel what need they have of a Redeemer by whose grace they may be delivered from eternal death. Therefore whoever does not wish to be deceived and to perish in his error, let him learn to begin at this end, namely, to reflect carefully that it is God with whom he will have to do, to whom he will one day have to render an account. Let him have before his eyes this judgment throne, which causes even the angels to tremble. . . . If any are offended by the fact that the divinity of Jesus Christ is united in one person with his human nature; if there are those who find it unreasonable that we should seek life in one who died, that we should regard the Cross which of itself is cursed as the source of our salvation: such are scandalized only in so far as, being without any fear of God, they cannot appreciate spiritual doctrine."[3]

Calvin's method is not to begin with an apology supported by

---

[1] Notice that, for our Reformer, it is a question of the pious, or believing, soul only; the soul of him who would regard it as a defection from faith to seek his salvation anywhere but in God.

[2] *Inst.* I, xiii. 13.

[3] Calvin, *Traité des scandales*, cf. A. Marie Schmidt, *Trois traités*, Paris, 1934, p. 172 f.

logical arguments or historical proofs: "to dispute with them according to the capacity of the human mind would be to act unwisely".[1] His discussions—and ours likewise—are addressed only to those who are genuinely troubled by problems arising from the Incarnation and the Cross, which cry out for a solution. To these he shows "that we cannot come to the wisdom of God by any other way than by becoming fools in the eyes of the world; but the foundation of such humility, as of all Christian religion, is the consciousness and the fear of God. If this be removed, it is in vain that one attempts to build".[2]

In other words, the Incarnation of Christ, the unique and eternal Son of God, is the foundation stone, the internal principle, on which all our Christianity must be based. Let others begin with reason, with religious consciousness or, in effect, with themselves; we are not concerned, for we "know whom we have believed".

The physical world has a meaning: it signifies that the totality of contingent beings which constitute it depends absolutely on a principle which is power and wisdom. The fact of moral consciousness has a meaning: it signifies that this necessary Being on whom all depend is justice and holiness. The fact of Christ has a meaning: He reveals to the believer that he is loved by one who is the Alpha and the Omega, the beginning and the end of all creation.

In this way, the world, conscience, and the Cross, combine to reveal the God of the Christians. Now, according to Scripture: "nò man can say that Jesus is the Lord, but by the Holy Ghost" (1 Corinthians 12: 3). This affirmation is also a fact of experimental intuition. God places the seal of His internal testimony on the external witness which announces to us sin and redemption by the Son made man. He who believes knows himself to be conquered effectually by such condescension on the part of a divine power whose presence he recognizes in the depths of his being.

Henceforth, for him, God is not only the Father, the principle of his being; He is not only the Son, logical cement of the universe and principle of its return to unity; He is the immanent principle of life, of physical life and of the spiritual life of faith: He is the Holy Spirit.

Thus the one God, unique in His essence, manifests Himself in His dispensations under a triple aspect. And since God is true,

[1] Calvin, *Traité des scandales*, cf. A. Marie Schmidt, *Trois traités*, Paris, 1934, p. 169.
[2] *Ibid.*, p. 171.

since He is truth itself, we believe that He is in His being that which He manifests Himself to be in His operations, and we confess the Trinity of divine persons in the unity and absolute simplicity of the essence of our God: "we know all these things as much by the testimony of Holy Scripture as by the effects, and principally by those which we feel in ourselves", as the Belgic Confession admirably expresses it.[1]

Orthodox Christianity is often reproached with being dry and abstract in its formulas. The Trinitarian formula, in particular, is represented as the petrified residue of the speculations of neo-Platonism. In reality it expresses, in scientific form, the most vital statements of the faith of those who brought together the writings of the New Testament. It proceeds from the intellectual necessity for harmonizing the religious faith of a conscious monotheism with the specific experiences which give birth to the Christian life.

Monotheism forbids believers to place their absolute confidence in any one other than God: entire reliance is His exclusive right. On the other hand, Christian experience shows the believer that he finds effectively his refuge in Christ, and his specifically Christian piety obliges him to place his entire confidence in Christ. This is why our fundamentally theistic dogmatics will be a dogmatics of the Trinity and the Incarnation, an orthodox Christian dogmatics, orthodox in the sense of oecumenical.

Orthodox our dogmatics will be because it will lay down certain existential affirmations concerning God and His creative, redemptive, and sanctifying acts, in contradistinction to dogmatic systems which formulate only "economic" affirmations and then judgments of value. But it will be truly dogmatic theology; it will not content itself with being a religious philosophy, because its existential judgments will not be the result of speculation but will be based on the positive revelation of God in His Word.

Now, it is not sufficient to connect the term dogmatics with the epithets Christian and orthodox in order to determine its nature scientifically. In the course of history, orthodoxy has become divided into two principal branches, each of which subdivides itself into two branches. There is a Catholic orthodoxy, Oriental and Roman, and there is a Protestant orthodoxy, Lutheran and Reformed. In what follows we shall endeavour to establish that Protestantism, and in particular Reformed Protestantism, is the scientifically legitimate form of orthodox Christianity.

[1] *Confessio Belgica*, 1561, art. ix.

In view of the method that we have adopted, it may seem strange that no chapter has yet been devoted to the subject of neo-Protestantism. Actually, we have had several occasions to criticize it in the course of our studies, under one or other of its manifestations, and we hope we have not failed to deal with it as it deserves. We shall continue to honour it with the critical study which is its due.

It so happens, however, that *hic et nunc,* at this precise point in our work, we have demonstrated that dogmatics must be materially, in its content, Christian and orthodox. It is not our fault if we have already drawn this conclusion.

Presuming it to be established that dogmatics must be materially Protestant and Reformed it may still be asked whether neo-Protestantism, although excluded fundamentally, cannot be commended to the acceptance of theologians on account of its form and method. The examination of this question will come in its turn; meanwhile, we shall endeavour to show that orthodox Christian dogmatics must be Protestant.

CHAPTER 8

CHRISTIAN DOGMATICS MUST BE PROTESTANT

We propose to establish that if dogmatics must be Christian it cannot be regarded as a scientifically legitimate discipline unless it accepts the formal as well as the material principle of the Protestant Reformation. That is to say, it will have to recognize, first of all, as supreme judge of controversies in all matters of faith and life, God speaking in and through Holy Scripture; it will have to lay down that the essential content of the evangelical message is the justification of the sinner solely by means of faith in Jesus Christ, the unique Son of God.

Just as the Incarnation and the Trinity are the principles which materially distinguish orthodox Christianity from other monotheistic types (Arian and Unitarian Christianity, Judaism and Mohammedanism); so, in the same way, the supreme authority of Scripture and the gratuitous character of salvation *sola fide*, by faith alone, are the principles which in the sphere of oecumenical Christian theism distinguish the Protestantism of the Reformers from Catholicism, oriental or occidental.

For the Reformers, there was no question as to whether the Church, the visible institution, was of divine origin; nor even whether, under certain conditions, it was infallible and indefectible. On these two points Calvin gives as categorical an affirmative as Luther. Neither the one nor the other had the least doubt as to the divine institution of the ministry of the Word and of the sacraments.

They did not deny that the Church had authority in matters of faith and discipline. Normally, the Christian cannot be conceived to the life of faith except in the bosom of the mother of the faithful, which is the Church. On her teaching and authority he depends all the days of his life.

It has been falsely asserted that, for Calvin, the visible Church was no more than the body of the invisible Church, which, by itself, would be the immortal soul and which could live on the earth deprived of its body.

What, according to him, can and does often happen is that "the order of the Church", its external regime, may be so corrupted that the Church no longer has a visible appearance, that is to say, that it may be deprived of the "marks" by the aid of which one can say with full certainty: the Church is here or she is there. These marks are the faithful administration of the Word of God and of the sacraments, and they may be defaced to such a point that the visible Church no longer means the visible appearance of a Church at all. By the grace of God, however, there survive in it "the vestiges of a Church", a minimum that Satan can never destroy.[1]

A human body may be ravaged by sickness to such an extent that it no longer seems to be a human form. It is visible all the same even though it does not retain the appearance that it should have and that one might expect if one had indeed before him a human organism.

For the Reformers, there never was any question of creating a new Church; their task was to restore the order of the Church which, according to them, was "in ruin and desolation".[2] The question was and still remains this: ought we to believe, with the certainty of divine faith, that the leaders of the Church, taken as a body, are infallible merely by virtue of their function; that they acquit themselves so faithfully of the office which has been divinely confided to them, that we should accept, without any examination, their decisions in matters of faith and life as irreformable, infallibly conformable to the Word of God and binding the consciences of the faithful. In other words, does the function legitimately conferred guarantee the infallibility of the functionaries or their chief—supposing that there must be one who is vicar of Christ—and that independently of their exclusive, interior and real submission to the Word of God?

The Protestantism of the Reformers teaches that the pastors of the Church have the right and the duty to proclaim to Christian people and to the world such understanding of God's Word as He has bestowed upon them at a given time and place. It recognizes, however, that through their own fault pastors may be unequal to their task or unfaithful to their mission and that the Holy Spirit is not necessarily always on the side of the party in power or tied to the majority—which may betray its trust— at a synod or council.

In a well-ordered state it is the mission of the supreme court of justice to interpret the law, to declare the right and to determine the procedure of jurisprudence. But it is not a law of nature that the judges of this tribunal are infallible, that their decisions must always be inspired by justice; that their interpretation of custom or of legal texts can never be reformed ultimately by the same court of justice, establishing a new

[1] *Inst.* IV, ii. 11, 12.   [2] *Conf. gal.*, art. xxxi.

jurisprudence. Magistrates are sometimes unintelligent, partial or servile. Why, then, should ecclesiastical courts be exempt from such defects?

The reason usually given is that here the eternal salvation of souls is at stake, while in the case of human tribunals it is merely a question of temporal interests. It is urged that God must have provided adequate means for the eternal salvation of those whom He has predestined to glory. To this end, it is necessary that they should be able to arrive at certain knowledge of saving truth. Thus we see the risen Lord, when commanding His Church to teach all nations, promising that He will be with her ministers until the consummation of the ages (Matthew 28: 19, 20). It is certain that God has always made provision that His elect should arrive at eternal life, which consists in knowing Him, the only true God and Jesus Christ, whom He has sent (John 17: 3).

In referring to churches subject to the yoke of error and superstition, Calvin declares that they are still churches, for this reason, among others, that "the Lord wondrously preserves in them a remnant of His people, however scattered they may be." [1] By this very circumstance the efficacy of Christ's promises is assured. He is with His ministers when they teach, even if their teaching is tainted with ignorance or error. He is even with an unfaithful preacher, when he prevents any but the elements of truth contained in his defective preaching from entering into the souls of the faithful. The example of the conversion of Mère Angélique of Port Royal furnishes a striking proof of this.

When evil grows in the Church to such an extent that it becomes unfit as an institution to fulfil its function, God can if it please Him, raise up by an extraordinary vocation such men as Calvin calls evangelists and we call Reformers. He thus re-establishes, in sufficient clarity and purity, the proclamation of the evangelical message and the administration of the sacraments.

The credentials of this extraordinary ministry consist in its fidelity to the Gospel and in the spiritual power of which it gives evidence in leading or restoring souls to faith in Christ, the unique and eternal Son of God, by preaching the remission of sins, obtained only through faith in His Blood.

We have here a proof that the material principle of the Reformation, the *sola fide*, is not only capable of ranging souls under the yoke of Christ, but even that this principle is truth itself. Those who accept it find it clearly taught in the Gospel

[1] *Inst.* IV, ii. 12.

of which it is the substance, and, in communion with their Redeemer, they experience not only the reality of their free pardon through Him but also that of the sanctifying power of His Spirit, apprehended by faith in the Word which is preached to them.

As to the formal principle of Protestantism, Scripture as the unique source and rule of faith and life, it is justified scientifically by a verification which is based on historical evidence.

It is evident that Christianity, confronted by the Synagogue, could only make good its claim to be the succession Church of ancient Israel by basing itself on the very principle which became the formal principle of the Reformation when confronted by the Church of Rome. In relation to the Synagogue and the Sanhedrin, the primitive Church was in exactly the same position as the Reformed Church in relation to the Papacy and the Council.

Christianity is formally a Protestantism opposing legitimist and traditionalist Judaism. Because Judaism has been vanquished and the centuries have rolled away, Christians of the sacerdotalist type have forgotten all this. But they would not be here to oppose Protestants with their legitimist prepossessions, that is to say, the preliminary legitimist question, under pretext that the Protestants have broken with legitimate authority; they would not be here, we say, if our Lord and His disciples had not adopted the same attitude toward the priesthood of Jerusalem as Luther and Calvin later adopted toward the priesthood of Rome.

What is the precise point which formally distinguishes historic Protestantism from Rome and Constantinople? It has already been said that there is no question of denying to ecclesiastical authority the right of declaring its sentiments and of judging in matters of religious controversy, provided it takes for its supreme rule the Word of God. Still less is it a question of encouraging the pride of private individuals by giving them the right to base themselves on their autonomous reason or sensibility, in order to reject that which is confessed by the representative Church.

The question is just this: when the representative Church—which is not necessarily to be identified with the Church pure and simple—claims in an arbitrary fashion to place her authority or her "tradition of the elders" on the same footing as the Word of God, does her decision bind before God the consciences of the members of the Church?

In other words, if a believer refuses to accept the instruction of an ecclesiastical tribunal, out of respect for the Word of God, is he necessarily and *a priori* a proud man? The Roman Church says "Yes"; the Reformed, "No".

In support of her affirmation, Rome cites certain well-known passages of Scripture: the famous *Tu es Petrus* (Matthew 16: 18) and the not less celebrated *Dic Ecclesiae* (Matthew 18: 17). But in so doing she encloses herself in a vicious circle. For, on the one hand, it is claimed that the private individual can only judge of the sense of Holy Scripture by basing himself on the infallible authority of the Church; while, on the other hand, texts of Scripture are quoted to him in order to prove this assertion. Thus an appeal is made to the judgment of the individual to decide, in his independence, the sense of Scripture which it is claimed that the representative Church alone has the right and power to judge.

But we need not insist on this point. Let us notice simply what has happened historically since the foundation of Christianity (of the Christian Church, we grant, despite the denials of certain neo-Protestants). At the time when our Lord exercised His "irregular" ministry, there existed a Church by divine right: the Synagogue. Rome will not dispute this. The regular authorities of this Church were able to base their authority on a passage of the Old Testament as clear as those texts of the New Testament invoked by Rome, namely, Deuteronomy (17: 8-13).

In this passage we read that, should difficult questions arise, the priest and the judge must decide, and that if anyone, through pride, refuses to submit to his sentence, he must be cut off, that thus the people may be preserved from presumption.

Now, He whom we recognize as the Christ was condemned in the place which the Lord had chosen, as the text of the Law prescribes (Deuteronomy 17: 8), by the priest and the judge, for having followed the example of the most faithful prophets of the Old Testament, who had judged that theirs was not a case of resistance through pride.

Unless we condemn the infant Church, which no Christian could think of doing, it must be acknowledged that there are, in fact, cases in which resistance to the regular ecclesiastical authority does not imply a revolt through pride; that there are some cases in which private individuals, like the fishers of Galilee, were obliged in conscience to make appeal from the sentence of the priests to that which impressed their minds as the faithful interpretation of the prophecies of Scripture.

How Rome would exult if this text of Deuteronomy could be found in the New Testament! But, since it is not to be found there, she must content herself with the *Dic Ecclesiae*. *Ecclesiae* is written with a capital as if it were a question of the universal representative Church, whereas the context proves conclusively that it is a question of the sentence by arbitration of a local church concerning a dispute between private individuals (Matthew 18: 15, 16).

As to the *Tu es Petrus*, it is well known that according to some of the Fathers, whose judgment is worthy of respect, the Church is founded, in virtue of this text, not on Peter himself but on the faith in Christ which he had just confessed[1]; or that, in any case, Peter here represents the apostolic college[2]. Whatever may be the case, it must be conceded that the Scriptural evidence is rather meagre.

Our Lord indeed declares that He has not come to destroy the Law but to fulfil it. Thus He does not dream of disputing the authority of the legitimate interpreters of this Law. Do they sit in the chair of Moses, that is to say, do they teach in conformity with the Law and in its spirit? He recommends the people to conform their life to this teaching, without taking notice of inconsistencies in the conduct of the teachers. But when it is a question of their actual doctrine, as opposed to that of Scripture, of "the leaven of the pharisees", the attitude of Christ becomes altogether different. There were in fact "traditions of the elders", "commandments of men" directly subversive of the commandments of God: rabbinical interpretations of the sacred text concerning the Sabbath, oaths, corban and many other matters.

Jesus puts his disciples on their guard against all this, appealing to their personal judgment, to their inner light (Luke 11: 35). He warns them to take heed that the light which is in them does not become darkness, for He knows well that if the blind lead the blind both are destined to fall into the ditch. The regular religious authority, we learn from the Fourth Gospel, had brought against Jesus the sentence of minor excommunication. It had decided that whoever should follow Him and acknowledge Him as a prophet, in opposition to the opinions of the religious chiefs of the people, should be excommunicated and cast out of the Synagogue (John 9: 22). Nevertheless Jesus persisted in His religious activity. He wished men to follow Him, to come to Him and remain faithful to Him. He promised that those who followed Him should not walk in darkness but should have the light of life.

---

[1] Chrysostom, *Hom. LV. in Matt.*, xvi; Jerome, *In Matt.*, vii; Augustine, *De Verbo Domini*, in *Matt. Serm.*, xiii; *In 1 Johann. Tract*, x; Ambrose. *In Eph.*, ii.
[2] Ambrose, *In Psalm* xxxviii; Augustine, *In Johann. Tract*, cxviii.

Moreover, when the sovereign pontiff or high priest, the authorized guardian of the Law, at the head of a religious tribunal, condemned Him as *min*, that is to say, a deceiver and an heretic, He broke his silence and threatened the priest in the name of His extraordinary vocation and of His messianic consciousness.

We are aware that Bossuet objected against Jean Claude, minister of Charenton, that Jesus Christ had been divinely authorized by His miracles, while the Reformers had performed none. But in making this point, three things were forgotten.

The first was that, in this respect, the Reformers resembled John the Baptist who "did no miracle" (John 10: 41) and whose mission nevertheless our Lord recognized; the second was that Jesus announced that false christs and false prophets should perform striking miracles in order to deceive the very elect; the third, that the Roman Church claims that she alone is in a position to distinguish prodigies of divine origin from those which proceed out of the pit. From this point of view, it is evident that Jesus, in order to be assured of His own mission or to assure others, would have had to submit His miraculous powers for the approbation of His adversaries, the religious chiefs of His people.

Actually, these men claimed that the miracles performed by the Nazarene did not surpass the limits of the power which they recognized in the magicians. They had fixed a higher standard, which they termed "a sign from heaven". When they sought such a sign from Him, Jesus asked them why those who used their judgment to discern the meaning of meteorological indications could not by themselves judge that which was right (Luke 12: 57). Thus He willed that, in regard to the appearance of Christianity, we should know how to discern the signs of the times.

We apply precisely the same rule in regard to the appearance of the Reformation. We do exactly what Jesus willed that individuals of His time should do, and what the New Testament approves concerning the believers at Berea who searched the Scriptures to see whether the things which they had been taught agreed with their doctrines (Acts 17: 11).

In taking the authority of God speaking in the Scripture as the formal principle of Protestantism, the Reformers merely restored the criterion which served as a formal principle for primitive Christianity.

We conclude that historic Protestantism is the historically authentic form of the Christianity of Jesus and of the apostolic

Church; that, scientifically, the method of dogmatics must be Protestant if it would be Christian in the historic sense of the term. We recognize also in this matter the truly divine majesty of this principle, when it ranges the religious consciousness of the fish merchants of the Lake of Tiberias, of Mary Magdalen, the perfumer of the Talmud, of the wool-carders of Meaux and of the old women of the tower of Constance, against sanhedrins and episcopal assemblies.

At the time of his celebrated conference with Claude, Bossuet having drawn the former to admit that an old woman might be right in opposition to a whole council of bishops, Bossuet declared that that was sufficient. He was surely right, though not in the sense that he intended.

The formal principle of the Reformation, the supreme authority of Scripture in matters of faith and life, has encountered a lively resistance from the beginning, coming from two parties radically opposed to one another: from Catholicism, in the name of the rights of the religious community; from neo-Protestant radicalism, in the name of the rights of the individual. We will examine successively the Catholic and the neo-Protestant criteria.

CHAPTER 9

THE FORMAL AND EXTERNAL PRINCIPLE
OF THE REFORMED FAITH

Normally, it is the Church which brings forth the souls of the catechumens to the Christian faith. In the supernatural sense of the term, she is the mother of the faithful.

By the term "Church", we do not understand exclusively the representative Church, synods, councils, and other ecclesiastical courts, but that divinely instituted society of the faithful with their pastors who dispense her teaching and sacraments under the authority of God, speaking in, by and with Holy Scripture, the supreme rule of faith and life. The representative Church participates in the supernatural character of the Church only because and inasmuch as (*quia et quatenus*) its disciplinary decisions are taken in a real spirit of submission to Scripture.

It is the Church, by means of her members acting in their respective vocations of parents, teachers and ministers, which places the soul of the child in contact with the verities of the faith and it is from her that he receives the supreme rule of faith and practice which is the canon of Holy Scripture. In the absence of the testimony of the Church, the catechumen would not even know that this canon existed as an established fact concerning which there can be no further dispute.

In acknowledging the Church's primary rôle in transmitting the canon of Holy Scripture and introducing the individual to the faith, we are not making a strategic retirement to new positions, the original ones having been rendered untenable owing to enemy pressure. We remain, on the contrary, firmly fixed in the positions which our Reformer occupied from the beginning. [1]

Calvin had nothing in common with the "fantastics" of his time whose radical individualism aimed at putting a sort of private inspiration above the authority of Scripture, confounding the promptings of their consciousness with the testimony of the Holy Spirit. [2]

For him, it is indeed from the Church, the guardian of the Scriptures, that the believer receives their text and contents. But the neo-Protestantism of to-day, like that of his time,

---

[1] *Inst.* I, vii. 3.   [2] *Ibid.*, 9.

objects to the identification of Scripture with the Word of God. It opposes to the religion of the letter "the religion of the spirit",[1] and it agrees with Rome in claiming that the canon of the New Testament is a creation of the Church. The limits of the canon of the New Testament having been determined, it is claimed, by the authority of the Church, orthodox Protestantism is held to be inconsistent in rejecting her infallible authority, on the one hand, and, on the other, in accepting the exclusive and closed list of the canonical books of the New Testament which rests equally and solely on the same authority.

Let us examine these two objections. In order to justify the former, it is suggested that the Bible abounds in palpable errors and contradictions. No doubt, we are told, Calvinist logic, denying human causality, would suppress the human element in the Bible. But unless we maintain that God inspires error, that He is the author of evil, we shall be convinced by the evidence that the Word of God in the Bible is mixed with a human element which must be separated from it if possible. The criteria for so doing differ with the various schools of theology, but in any case the "assured results" of Biblical criticism are held to have definitely destroyed the position of orthodox Protestantism.[2]

The question is vital for Calvinism for the following reason. The relation of absolute confidence between God and the believer is of prime religious importance. It depends for its existence on certain facts which serve as its foundation, namely, the facts confessed in the Apostles' Creed as objects of faith.[3] Among these facts are those which seem to be justifiable by historical criticism, whether directly, like the passion of Jesus Christ under Pontius Pilate, and the circumstances of His death and resurrection; or indirectly, like the virginal conception of the Son of Mary and His ascension into glory, in so far as they are attested by documents, the authenticity and antiquity of which can be disputed.

In binding the faith to the reality of facts which took place on the earth and in time, Calvinism cannot, it is said, avoid the critique of physical science, and for this reason cannot accommodate itself to that science which it finds indispensable.[4]

[1] *La religion d'autorité et la religion de l'esprit* is the title of a work by Auguste Sabatier which practically corresponds in scope with the second part of the present treatise.
[2] H. Bois, *La Philosophie de Calvin*, Paris, 1919, c. iii. *La Bible.*
[3] *Geneva Catechism*, xviii, 1.
[4] Höffding in his *Philosophie de la Religion* applies this idea, not to Calvinism in particular but to the Church in general.

In fact, by very reason of the vital importance of the questions at stake, defence undertaken by orthodox scientists is suspected of lacking in scientific objectivity; and their criticism can, with good reason, be discounted as a piece of partisan apologetics.

In the first place, we dispute the legitimacy of a tendentious process which lumps together vaguely all the believing critics under a sort of preliminary charge of legal suspicion, following the method of "prescription" dear to Tertullian and the Catholic controversialists of the 17th century.

In matters of science, what counts is far less the sentiments and general subjectivity of the scientist than the intrinsic value of the reason that he gives. If the reasons are valid, it matters little that his ingenuity in finding them has been stimulated by the inclinations of his inner being. It is the argument in itself which calls for examination; but, in proceeding with this examination, care must be taken not to be oneself also dominated by the indemonstrables which are the determining motives of all judgments of value in every normal person. Here we see the irremediably subjective character of all criticism bearing on fundamental questions in relation to the principles of the spiritual life. This is the reason why ancient history, and particularly the history of the origins of religion, is the most conjectural of the sciences.

We are not foolish enough to condemn modern criticism as a whole. The works of the best of its representatives have contributed and still contribute to a better understanding and a greater love of the sacred text. It would be absurd as well as unjust to accuse all modern critics of a spirit of systematic hostility to divine realities. It is undeniably the case with certain sectaries that an anticlerical passion drives them to a hypercritical attitude whose automatic extravagances are a sign of its origin. But it must be admitted that there are also "independent" critics who have no other passion than the desire to know and to understand, starting naturally from their own cultural point of view. And further it must also be stated clearly that there are modern believing critics, who sincerely desire to serve the cause of scientific truth, while preserving and securing that which constitutes for them the essence of Christianity.

So far from accusing these last of wishing to undermine the foundations of the faith, of being indifferent to all that is not pure science, of wishing only to demolish with no thought of building up, we should be tempted to put them on their guard against an unconscious apologetic tendency which might lead them—this is a paradox only in appearance—in doubtful cases to choose almost invariably a negative solution.

This is what we would say on the subject: every intellectual worker worthy of the name has something which for convenience we will call "a mysticism". He may even have two: a religious mysticism, a profound devotion to the person of Christ, for example; and a cultural mysticism, such as adherence to the positivist principle in science, to subjectivist and evolutionary humanism, to the doctrine of universal mechanistic determinism; in brief, to scientific conformism. Sentimentally, intellectually and in every other respect, criticism has gained as a result of the humanist ideology of the 18th and 19th centuries, so that "modern" man—"modern" let it be understood in the already historical and traditional sense of the term—if he wishes to remain or become religious, can no longer give his religion the hyperphysical and transcendent foundation of the affirmations of the Apostles' Creed: prophecy and miracle, in the sense of a special divine intervention in the causal series of events, appear to him as radical impossibilities. He is compelled to distinguish carefully between the faith of confidence and the faith of belief in "sacred history", which reflects a manner of thinking that his ideology forces him to consider out-of-date. Thus it is in the believer's subjectivity that he must seek the foundations of his religious life. Neo-Protestant theology thus betrays its connection with the philosophical psychologism dominant in mid-19th century France. [1]

At this point, the temptation becomes great to demonstrate to himself and to others the independence of faith in regard to the facts which orthodoxy considers to be the necessary foundation. In consequence, the results at which he arrives may unfortunately be influenced by this subconscious apologetic preoccupation.

What is more, they are already dictated by his ideology. If it is understood, in principle, that God cannot unveil the future to a prophet, nor raise the dead, the texts which suppose such facts can only be *post eventum* predictions or legends. It is in accordance with this systematic *a priori* that they will be dated and their historic value decided. In this respect, the unbelieving critics are in no worse position than the subjectively religious critics.

Some of the most eminent among the latter have declared that, for them, the question at stake was fundamentally one of a natural or supernatural mode of revelation. With Cornill, for

---

[1] *Vide* App. XII, p. 398.

example, apropos of the Wellhausen theory of the formation of the Pentateuch, we have a *reum confitentem*.[1] Consequently some of the "assured results" are only such for those who accept the Kantian, Hegelian or Comtist ideology. They rest upon an essentially subjective foundation. This is so true that they are called in question afresh by critics as "independent" as those who think them to have been settled *in aeternum*, but who are no longer under the direct influence of Hegel's philosophy. This is particularly evident in Old Testament criticism. To-day it is no longer possible to speak of the "unanimous consent" of all competent scholars concerning the existence, number, or order of appearance of the sources of the Pentateuch:[2] Eerdmans denies the principles by which they are distinguished. Volz and Rudolf have exorcized the spectre of one of the authors supposed by Wellhausen's theory; while Löhr rejects the whole hypothesis.[3]

It is because a new ideology has replaced that which was in vogue before the Four Years' War that misunderstanding has arisen between the old generation which remains attached to the "modern" ideology and the new generation which has become realist in philosophy and transcendentalist in religion. The latter is accused by the former of lacking critical sense and scientific interest. May it not be, rather, that its principles are different and that subjective criticism no longer awakens the same hope and fears? The scientific dogmatism of the 19th century would seem to have had its day. It is no longer fashionable to attribute to those indispensable instruments of research, scientific hypotheses, the same certainty as to established facts, nor to confound the former with the latter.

---

[1] Carl Heinrich Cornill, *Einleitung in die kanonischen Bücher des Alten Testaments*, sec. 12, p. 72: *Und viel und Grösses steht auf dem Spiele. Denn es handelt sich dabei um nichts Geringeres, als darum, ob es überhaupt ein Verständniss der Israelitischen Religionsgeschichte möglich sein soll, ob Gott in der nämlichen Weise in welcher er sich immer und überall in der Geschichte offenbart und betätigt, sich auch in ihrer grössten und bedeutesten Erscheinung, eben der Israelitischen Religionsgeschichte, offenbart und betätigt habe.*—And many important things are at stake. For the question at issue is nothing less than whether Jewish religious history is intelligible at all, whether God manifested Himself and acted in what was the greatest and most significant part of history, namely, the religious history of Israel, in precisely the same way as He manifests Himself and acts continually in all history.

[2] *Vide* the rectoral discourse of A. Noordtzy, professor of Old Testament at the University of Utrecht, 1927, translated into German under the title *Das Rätsel des Alten Testaments*, H. Wollermann, Braunschweig, n.d.

[3] Paul Volz and Wilhelm Rudolf *Der Elohist als Erzähler ein Irrweg der Pentateuchkritik?* Töpelmann, Giessen, 1933. L. Dennefeld, *Introduction à l'Ancien Testament*, Bloud & Gay, Paris, n.d. (imprimatur, 1934), p. 31 ff. (*Etat actuel de la critique chez les protestants.*)

If the Reformed Christian believes with absolute certainty in the historic appearance of Jesus the Christ, in the reign of Tiberius, in His crucifixion under a Roman procurator named Pilate, it is not on the evidence of a Josephus, a Tacitus or a Suetonius. The discussion of the texts of these authors can give no more than a certitude of probability, contested by scholars as well-informed and as competent as those who maintain the thesis of their historical reliability.

The existence of Jesus is as certainly an article of faith as His birth in the womb of a Virgin or His resurrection. We must therefore believe *a priori* that God has provided that it should be no more rationally demonstrable than the other articles of faith. The facts of sacred history cannot become certain with a certainty of faith except on condition that, by His infinite power, through contact with the inspired texts or by the supernatural teaching of the Church, the Spirit of God renders present the past and puts on it the seal of His inner witness, the persuasive force of which is irresistible. It is only after the exercise of this divine pressure that the human reasons take on a convincing signification.

The neo-Protestants of the present day, cured at length of the rationalism of the 19th century, in large numbers are passing through the same experience as ourselves on this point. They realize the inconclusiveness of historicism in the matter of religious certainty and freely grant that certainty concerning the real existence of Jesus is vital for the faith. There is no conflict of principle between faith and critical science, for the simple reason that the facts which form the object of faith as creed and those which serve as a foundation for faith as confidence, can neither be proved nor disproved by historical criticism. The Church cannot dispense with science, because barbarism is a form of evil. But she has nothing to fear from a science freed from evolutionary and humanist ideology.

But, as we have seen, it is denied that this gives one the right to identify the Bible with the Word of God. The facts are there, they say: it is no longer a question of hypotheses but of palpable phenomena, evident to all. There are manifest errors in the Bible. We must come to a decision then concerning this matter and admit that the Bible is not the Word of God but merely its vehicle. Representatives of dialectical theology go much farther and tell us that Scripture is the only place in which God speaks to us and, such as it is, even in those parts which seem to be the farthest removed from any spiritual value, it is divinely prepared to receive the light which shines upon it vertically from on high and illuminates the understanding of him to whom God speaks in the place and at the time of his appointment.

These theological attempts to reconcile an invincible certitude of faith, bearing the seal of its divine origin, with the facts which a sense•of scientific loyalty obliges one to consider as incontestable, express more or less completely certain objective realities. It is perfectly true that, in a certain sense which we shall endeavour to determine, the inspired books contain a human element; it is true also that, in the ordinary course of events, the Christian soul cannot discern the voice of God intuitively and in a sensible manner in certain pages of Scripture; it is true also that, in extraordinary circumstances, pages which appear unimportant, or even shocking, may be suddenly illuminated by a divine effulgence; it is true, finally, that the instinct of faith teaches ministers and people that it is in Scripture and nowhere else that they must seek the source and rule of their beliefs.

On the other hand, it must be admitted that the impact of the mass of facts invoked and advanced by German criticism of the 19th century has made such an impression on the mind of certain believers, including some reactionaries and even theologians who are numbered among the restorers of the Reformed faith, that many among them have imagined that it was impossible to maintain the complete identification of Scripture with the Word of God.

In this circumstance we recognize the presence of a subjective element, a sort of invincible prejudice. These men were initiated into theology at a period when the force of the evolutionary current swept aside all the improvised barriers which had been hastily erected to stem its irresistible tide. It is remarkable indeed that they were able to stand as they did. More remarkable still, and a veritable psychological miracle, is the fact that a disciple of Scholten like Abraham Kuyper, and of Kuenen like Hermann Bavinck, should have been able, in the full tide of the 19th century, with the profound erudition of which they both gave such ample proof, to dare to unfurl the banner of the ancient faith and affirm the integral inspiration of Scripture.

Those who have been brought up in a strictly orthodox atmosphere can have no true idea of the effort which must have been necessary for these scholars to emancipate themselves from the yoke which the prevalent view imposed at that period. It is a fact that their opponents were so convinced that they alone were in possession of the keys of science that more than one of them found himself unable to take the motives for Kuyper's conversion seriously.[1]

Moreover the new Calvinist doctors themselves felt that the theological formulas of the orthodox doctors of the 17th century on the inspiration and integrity of the sacred text were not altogether satisfactory. As regards inspiration, they thought it necessary to substitute for the "mechanical" view which, rightly or wrongly, they attributed to the divines of the 17th century, a more flexible concept, giving large scope to the personality and liberty of the sacred writers, to their manner of thinking and feeling. In short, they claimed to replace automatism by the idea of organic inspiration.

Inspiration in the sphere of thought is thus conceived as analogous to the mode of action of individual grace in conversion. Conversion has a primary cause: God who enlightens and persuades the understanding and moves the will efficaciously. Nevertheless the man himself is its formal secondary cause. It is he who feels, believes and wills to come to God, all the more freely because God moves him in bestowing an enlightened understanding and a more energetic will. In inspiration, God is the primary Author (*auctor primarius*). It is He who causes the sacred author to speak and to write and to express the truths which He wishes to make known to men. But the sacred writer is in fact the real secondary author of what he says or writes, using the intellectual, literary and philological means at his disposal, employing his memory and, if necessary, his personal efforts in research (Luke 1: 3, 4).

Inerrancy in regard to inspiration corresponds to the indefectibility, the inamissibility of grace in conversion. So far as the integrity of the text is concerned, it is well known that some divines of the 17th century taught that the correct reading was always preserved in one at least of the variants which exist in manuscripts.[2] Certain Lutheran divines sharply reproached Calvin for not taking this view and for having admitted, in the case of Matthew (27: 10), for example, that no known manuscript contained the reading of the original autograph.[3] The contemporary Calvinist school sides with the Reformer, conceiving integrity in the sense that divine providence has provided for the substantial preservation of the sacred text, in such measure that the entire range of dogmatic truth may be received by the

[1] W. F. A. Winckel, *Leven von Dr. A. Kuyper*, Amsterdam, 1919, p. 7.

[2] J. A. Quenstedt, *Theologia didactico-polemica*, 1702, I, c. iv, sec. 2, qu. XVIII (p. 194).

[3] Quenstedt, e.g., *op. cit.*, reproaches Beza and Casaubon (p. 197), Calvin (p. 204) and Pareus (p. 205) with this.

Church, in virtue of the principle of faith that God never fails us in things necessary.

Textual criticism follows the scientific rules which are applied to the publication of all ancient texts. On this point, the modification of the exaggerations of certain 17th century theologians was all the more necessary in view of the fact that, even among the Reformed, for instance in the *Consensus Helveticus*, statements were made which could not be reconciled with the conclusions of that sane and objective criticism, examples of which had been given by the Reformers, and in particular by Calvin and Beza among the Reformed.

Calvinist theologians of the present day are equally justified, in our opinion, in placing more emphasis on the personal and organic character of inspiration than did their predecessors in the 17th century. They are right also in abandoning certain hazardous speculations of the 18th century, such as Benedict Pictet's theory which limited inspiration to the ideas of Scripture.

It is possible, however, to be too exclusive in condemning the automatic process *en bloc*. God is free, absolutely free, as regards the modes of inspiration which it may please Him to adopt. His wisdom is infinitely varied. We must take inspiration as it is given. It would be absurd to deny the intervention of the writer's personality in an epistle like that of Paul to the Galatians. But it is by no means certain that cases of automatism do not exist elsewhere (cf. Exodus 34: 27, 28).[1] Think again of certain passages in Ezekiel and in the Apocalypse.

There are certain things which jar in the authors of the 17th century, things which are out of date and not likely to be revived among believers of to-day. But this latent defect which manifests itself by an application of the principle of inerrancy under the form of an artificial and forced system of concordism, is not peculiar to the orthodox. It was largely shared by their rationalistic contemporaries. It consists, we think, in the presupposition, accepted by both camps as a common premise, that the Biblical writers conceived the task of chronicler according to the ideas and processes of exposition adopted by modern historians. This premise, however, we are not able to accept now that we have become familiar with the facts of pre-classical psychology and with the processes which the chroniclers, moulded by this psychology, disclose to us.

[1] Sir Charles Marston sees yet another case of automatic writing in 1 *Chron.* 28:19. What he says concerning this particular mode of inspiration in Chap. XVI of his book *The Bible is True*, Plon, Paris, 1936, is very interesting.

It is correct, no doubt, to translate the expression *tôledot* in the Pentateuch by *history*. But, in reading the facts and genealogies narrated by the ancient writers, it is important to remember that they represent history *stylized* in accordance with artificial conventions known to their contemporaries, which we must take into account to-day (cf. the genealogy of Matthew 1 with the parallel passages of the Old Testament).

So far as the above observations carry us, we are willing to accept an organic concept of inspiration. But in order that it may be possible in certain circumstances to reintroduce the case of automatism, we shall endeavour to give a formula for it at once more general and more precise. Following Pierre du Moulin (Molinaeus), one of the masters of orthodox theology of the 17th century, we distinguish the matter, the divinely communicated instruction, from its written form.[1] And we say that this matter is totally divine: here, as in all action, God is the total and unique cause. In this sense, Scripture is from God without any human admixture whatever, according to Calvin's expression.[2] It has proceeded from God and not from men.[3]

But, if we consider the written form, we notice a double action, that of the first cause and that of the second. These two actions stand in the relation of the mind which commands to the organ which executes the command, sometimes in the possession of its personal qualities as well as of its limitations and of its intelligent spontaneity; at other times reduced to the rôle of a passive instrument.

The Spirit of God causes the sacred writer to express himself, but the latter does so in his own tongue, using his own peculiar methods, in conformity with the literary style which he employs and with the special object which God has arranged that he shall set out to achieve.

Hence it will be understood that a narrative by a writer, who has been moved by inspiration to record his memories faithfully, as they become present to his mind at the moment of writing, may show divergences of detail, "diversities" as Calvin calls them, from a narrative by another writer who sets out to collect testimonies accessible to his researches from sure witnesses, but whose memory may have retained details which have escaped the other writer and who presents them in a different

[1] Pierre du Moulin, *Le Bouclier de la Foi*, folio v.: "By the Scripture we understand not the paper and the letters but the divine instruction which they contain." Calvin expresses the same thought in *Inst.* I, vii. 2.

[2] Du Moulin, *Com. on 2 Tim.*, iii, 16.

[3] *Conf. Gal.*, art. V.

chronological order.[1] Such "diversities" are willed by God, says Calvin. The essential thing is that the writers should agree on the main point which is the sole real object of their records.[2] One may thus admit a certain inexactness of detail both in the presentation of facts and in chronological order,[3] while maintaining that both writers have enjoyed the privilege of inerrancy for the purpose of reaching the goal which they set out to attain under the impulsion of a plenary inspiration. This inspiration implies inerrancy in relation to the object which it reveals to the one who is its instrument.

The Gospels were not given to enable us to construct a life of our Lord in conformity with the requirements of modern biographers, but in order to make present to faith that which they are intended to reveal. So Zwingli well says: "If Luke speaks of eight days and Matthew of six, there is no real difference between the two. . . . In such matters, we should be neither extremely curious nor anxious. The Holy Scriptures are to be approached with simplicity and a pure heart. The language of truth is simple."[4]

The point of view of him who seeks God in the Scripture is not that of a chronologist. What we have just said concerning the Gospels is applicable *mutatis mutandis* to other parts of Scripture and to the Pentateuch in particular. It is obvious that the definitive editor of this remarkable work had a conception of the presentation of past events which differed profoundly from that

---

[1] This solution has already been suggested by the Calvinist poet Da Costa in regard to Luke 18: 35 ff. and Matt. 20: 29 ff. We arrived at it ourselves before we became acquainted with his work. The same view is maintained by the learned Calvinistic exegete, Dr. P. A. C. van Leeuwen, *Het heilig evangelie naar de beschreving van Marcus uitgeleegd door*, H. A. van Bottenburg, Amsterdam, 1928. Commenting on Mark 14:69, according to which, in contradistinction to Matthew, it is another maid who recognizes Peter, he cites the following passage of the Catena, in which the point of view is identical with our own: οὐ γάρ ἐξηκρίβωται τοῦτο τῇ μνήμῃ τῶν γραψάντων ἐπεὶ μηδὲ συνέχον ἦν εἰς τήν σωτήριον πίστιν. After which he makes the following observation: "The matter is of small importance. The real point is the awful fall of Peter; the details at the circumference of the narrative have not been related with the exactness of a notary."

[2] *Harmony of the Gospels*, Argument *ad fin.*

[3] Calvin gives numerous examples in his *Commentaries*. We limit ourselves to the following quotation: "There is no reason why Luke should not narrate in the second place the temptation which Matthew recounts in the third place. For the Evangelists did not undertake to follow the course of history in such a way that the order of time should be scrupulously observed, but merely to compile a summary statement of the principal points, in order to bring to our attention . . . that which was most necessary for us to know concerning the acts and words of Christ. . . . To know which was the second or the third temptation is not a matter that need worry us unduly." (*Harmony on Matt.*, iv, 5).

[4] *Ad. Matt.* xvii, I; VI, 1, 3, 2, 7 in S. Berger, *La Bible au XVIe siècle*, p. 110.

of a European historian of the 20th century. He relates concerning the same fact traditions presenting certain divergences, without troubling too much to harmonize them and without suggesting that any discrimination is to be made between them. He does not intend any of the historical memories of the past to be lost, and he is a stranger to the meticulous preoccupations of the moderns with regard to strict sequence in the narration of events. He cites certain *tôledot*, history stylized in epic and pre-logical form, because, being inspired, they throw a light, sometimes veiled but always precious, on the ways of God in regard to humanity or to His people. Always keeping in mind the fact that the main point for him is to instruct—which is not necessarily the main point of the modern critic—the inspired writer sometimes cites implicitly certain traditions borrowed from various documents, and the quotations which he makes from them present "diversities" such as those whose presence we have noticed in the Gospels. But inspiration accommodates itself perfectly to all the literary processes in use at the period of its exercise. The hypothesis of "sources", therefore, has nothing in itself contrary to orthodoxy.[1]

It is the task of exegesis, at once spiritual and scientific, to attempt to determine the particular category to which a writing belongs: whether, for example, the Book of Esther should be understood as a *midrash* or as a page of history.

It will be seen that the dogma of inspiration, understood as we present it, goes far, in principle, towards the solution of the difficulties which are urged against it in the name of facts. Henceforth we can study, with great liberty of mind, the questions of pure erudition and textual criticism which arise in Biblical exegesis.

The doctrine of inspiration does not compel us to believe that Moses is the author of the Pentateuch in the sense that Augustine is the author of the *Confessions*. It does not force us to deny the evident editorial modifications introduced in the course of centuries in order to place the Law in harmony with the social exigencies of a given epoch. It does not exclude the hypothesis that, in certain cases, these modifications may, in some detail, have contradicted the original in the process of alteration. Such a possibility is admitted by an exegete as resolutely conservative as the erudite and conscientious Aalders. [2]

Every hypothesis which does not deny *a priori* the inspiration

---

[1] H. Bavinck, *op. laud.*, I, p. 469 (No. 117).
[2] G. C. Aalders, *De profeet Jeremia*; J. H. Kok, Kampen, 1925, II, pp. 117-120, especially p. 118 (commenting on Jer. xxxiii, 14-26).

of the original text, which does not systematically exclude miracle and prophecy, and presuppose the humanist ideology of the 18th or 19th centuries; in other words, which does not imply that Scripture is incapable of fulfilling the principal function assigned to it by its divine Author, every such hypothesis has a right to the impartial and attentive examination of the Reformed exegete. Scripture was not given to the Church in order to provide an assurance that such a person was present on a certain occasion and not another, or that a miracle took place at one end of a village and not another. It was given to be rule of faith and life, to tell us what we ought to believe concerning God, His will and purpose in regard to His people and the world.

It is our desire to reaffirm the faith of the Reformers in the light of present-day science. For this purpose we have no need to go beyond what they believed touching the fact of inspiration, and we must be prepared to accept loyally the facts as they present themselves and to practise scrupulously the methods of a conscientious critic in the spirit of the faith which has been bestowed upon us and in the liberty indispensable to any science which wishes to be taken seriously.

We do not claim that we hold in our hands a magic wand capable of causing all objections of detail to disappear. There are difficulties in Scripture which are at present insoluble and which will probably remain so till the last day.[1] We content ourselves with showing that no one has the right to claim henceforth that it is impossible for a Christian acquainted with the facts to believe in the truth of the formal principle of the Reformed faith, which is that Scripture in all its parts was given by the inspiration of God and that the word contained in the sacred books proceeds from God and not from men.

"Now", says Calvin, "this cannot be known except by faith".[2] Faith, therefore, must be prepared to find in Scripture the matter for objections such as are found in the world and in the course of life. She must expect that Scripture which, from the formal point of view, is the result of the collaboration of God and man, should contain simultaneously astonishing marks of divinity and undeniable testimonies to the infirmity and weakness of man. And this only serves to set in relief the glory of God: "all flesh is grass and all the goodliness thereof is as the flower of the field. The grass withereth, the flower fadeth, . . . but the Word of our God shall stand for ever" (Isaiah 40: 6–8).

[1] H. Bavinck, *Geref. Dog.*, I, 116 (p. 468).
[2] *Inst.* I, viii. 12.

It is necessary then, as Pascal remarks, that there should be sufficient light for those who are disposed to believe to arrive at the faith, and enough obscurity for the others to find matter to resist.

We have insisted, in the first place, on the essential solution of the difficulties which are raised concerning the "diversities" presented by parallel accounts of the same event, because we feel that it is these which men have in mind when they speak of "palpable contradictions which stare one in the face".

If the objection had in view moral or theological contradictions, it would be even more feeble. The *form* of morality is the same from one end of the Bible to the other; God is the unique and supreme legislator. The *matter* comprises, on the one hand, precepts whose immutability proceeds from the nature of the ordinances which the supreme legislator has imposed upon His creation; and, on the other hand, precepts whose obligatory character is merely temporary, since it springs from necessities incidental to circumstances themselves temporary and produced by the state of sin. The laws of marriage, the rights of people, the personal status, largely depend on the social and ethnic environment of the period. It is evident that the material precepts pertaining to various moral situations must differ under the old and new dispensations of the covenant of grace. It is the task of Christian ethics to distinguish the temporal and transient from the eternal and enduring, in accordance with the principle of the analogy of faith and in the light of the final and fuller revelation which Christ has brought by the agency of His Apostles and Prophets.[1]

Let us remark further that it is important to distinguish between the private opinions or sentiments of persons and even heroes of the Old Testament and the positive teaching of the Old Testament. Calvin does not hesitate to admit, in David's lament on the death of Saul and Jonathan, a deplorable lack of moderation.[2] And, in our day, the eminent Dutch expositor van Gelderen expresses a severe judgment concerning the superstitious ideas of the dying David and the measures of vengeance that he took against his enemies.[3]

---

[1] Charles Hodge, *Systematic Theology*, III, xix, 1.

[2] In Calvin's sermons, regrettably omitted by the publishers of *Opera omnia Calvini*, by Brunschvicg, as "unimportant" and whose publication has been undertaken in Germany by Hans Ruckert, *vide* vol. I, p. 14: *Calvin, Predigten, 2 Samuelis* and p. 17 (I, 18–20) *Buchhandlung des Erziehungsvereins Neukirchen Kreis Moers*, 1936. The contemporary Calvinist exegete, Aalders, expresses the same judgment concerning Jeremiah's lie (38:27, 28).

[3] Van Gelderen *De Boeken der Koningen, Eerste Deel, I Koningen,* 1–11, J. H. Kok, Kampen, 1926, pp. 50, 51, 53, 70.

The differences of theological points of view when they have a real existence are to be explained not by a progress in *inspiration* which is a fact that does not admit of degrees, but rather by a progress in *revelation* which is more or less extensive, even among inspired writers belonging to the same economy of the covenant of grace and which is always partial even among the most eminent of the inspired writers. "Now we see through a glass, darkly", says the Apostle, now we "know in part" (1 Corinthians 13: 12). Strangely enough, Jülicher[1] alleges this very passage to prove that Paul was not conscious that he had produced writings comparable in authority to those of the Old Testament.

In the 16th century, Reformed orthodoxy was well aware of the great difference in illumination which existed between the equally inspired writers whose writings constitute the Bible. Thus, Calvin, after noticing the "diversity" which separates the Psalms from the "books of Solomon" according to the profundity of the subjects treated, adds: "What is more, among the Evangelists themselves there is such a great difference in declaring the grace of Christ that, if John be compared with the three others, they will scarcely show any rays of that great brilliance which appears so evidently in John. And nevertheless we receive all four equally".[2]

If it is asked how, in doubtful cases, we are to distinguish between the private opinions and sentiments of men whose history is related in the Bible and which are in contradiction with the authorized teaching of this divine rule of faith and life, Zwingli appeals to the discriminative principle of Reformed theology: "When you see one person quote a word of God which is clear and plain in a certain sense, while another brings forward a second one equally clear, which openly contradicts the first,[3] observe which is the passage that honours God and that which glorifies man. Hold fast that which gives God the glory and which ascribes to Him all the work, all the glory and all the honour."[4]

Calvin agrees with his predecessor in recognizing that the principle is in conformity with the teaching of Christ and must

---

[1] Jülicher, *Einl. in das N. T.*, par. 34.

[2] *Com. on the Epistle of James*, argument; cf. *Harmony of the Gospels*, argument, for the same idea.

[3] In this passage, Zwingli affirms that all the words of Scripture are words of God in the sense that they are all reported by divine inspiration. It is certain that he does not admit that God can contradict Himself. We have here the distinction made by later theologians between historical and normative authority.

[4] Zwingli II, i, 293 f., in S. Berger, *op. cit.*, p. 111.

serve as a "touchstone" for theology,[1] while Bucanus appeals to it in the 17th century.[2]

In conclusion, let us say a word concerning what are claimed to be scientific errors of Scripture in the sphere of natural and physical knowledge. We have no difficulty at all in admitting with the Calvinist, Bavinck,[3] that, in these matters, the sacred writers shared the opinion of the men of their time. But we maintain that Scripture does not impose on us erroneous scientific beliefs, for the excellent reason that it does not set out to present systematic instruction in the sciences. "Let him who wishes to study astronomy and the secrets of nature, turn elsewhere", says Calvin, commenting on the first chapter of Genesis.[4]

No doubt, the sacred writers make poetic comparisons in which one of the terms is borrowed from popular opinions, to-day considered to be false. For example, the moral exhortation addressed to the lazy to take as a model the ant (Proverbs 6:6 ff.) loses nothing of its value from the fact that it has been ascertained that, apart from one particular American species, this insect does not amass provisions in view of the winter—a season which, moreover, is not mentioned in this passage. In a general way, we would observe that Scripture, when it alludes to facts in the natural order, always speaks the subjectively true language of sensorial appearance. This solution, proposed by Calvin[5] became traditional in the Reformed theology of the 17th century which was opposed on this point to the exaggerations of theologians of other confessions (for example, in the controversy concerning the supposed solidity of the celestial vault).[6]

We do not deny that the scientific opinions accepted at the time when such and such a sacred author wrote have been recorded under the impulsion of the Holy Spirit. For all that is expressed in Scripture is there because God inspired in the human and secondary author the thought to put it there. But we agree with the Calvinist theologian, McPherson, that revelation

---

[1] *Opera*, Bruns., I, xii, 16; *Com. on John*, vii: 18.

[2] Cf. Bucani, *Quaestiones theol.*, loc. IV, xiv, Bern, 1605: *Quaenam nota est . . . per quam omnes homines sani doctrinam acquiescant esse veri Dei doctrinam? Quod quae doctrina nos unius et solius Dei gloriam in solidum et ubique quaerere et illi adhaerere docet, illa procul dubio veri Dei doctrina est, sed tamen sobi renati in ea, ut salutari et Dei doctrina cordis sui πληροφορία acquiescant.*

[3] *Geref. Dogm.*, p. 473 (No. 117).

[4] *Com. on Genesis*, i, 6.

[5] *Com. on Genesis*, i, 6: *Hoc mihi certum principium est, hic nonnisi de visibili mundi forma tractari.*

[6] *Com. on Psalm* cxlviii, 3; cf. Zöckler, *Geschichte, der Beziehungen zwischen Theologie und Naturwissenschaft*, Gütersloh, 1877, vol. I, pp. 690–716.

does not concern facts of this order, because Scripture was not given to teach us geology or astronomy, but in order to tell us infallibly what we ought to believe in divine things and what we ought to do to obey God. Augustine writes: "We do not read in the Gospels that the Lord said: I will send you the Paraclete, who shall instruct you concerning the course of the sun and the moon. He wished to make Christians rather than astronomers".[1]

We conclude that the Reformed faith which confesses that Scripture is the Word of God, and that it is there and there only that we must seek this Word, can and must be affirmed in all its scientific strictness. *Verbum Dei manet in aeternum.*

We do not deny that God inspired other writings than those which constitute the canon. Some have been lost,[2] and obviously we need not concern ourselves with them now. If they were rediscovered, we should not know for certain that they had been intended to serve as a rule of faith for us and we could only receive their doctrine by measuring it against the authority of the canonical books. There may be some which survive to this day. It is possible that the Epistle of Clement of Rome may be among the number, or some other writing of the Apostolic Fathers which has figured in the canon of the New Testament and of certain particular Churches. But the fact that these writings have been eliminated from the canon of the Church universal under the pressure of historical circumstances which are under divine control shows us that it was not the intention of providence to give these documents the rôle of faith and life for all the centuries but only for the time during which they were imposed on the acceptance of certain Churches.[3]

They are no longer protocanonical, in any case, since we must judge them by the rule of the canon received by the faith of the Church universal. But, here, Rome brings forward her objection, taken up by a great number of neo-Protestants: How can you know that the present canon is precisely this Word of God which you need and who guarantees to you its authority? The study of this question must occupy the next chapter.

[1] *De actis cum Felice Manich.* i, 10: *Non legitur in evangelio Dominum dixisse: mitto vobis Paracletum, qui vos doceat de cursu solis et lunae. Christianos enim facere volebat, non mathematicos.*

[2] Calvin, *Predigten 2 Sam.*, i, 18 (p. 12); *Com. on Ephesians*, iii, 3.

[3] Grosheide, *Algemeene Canoniek van het Nieuwe Testament*, Amsterdam, 1935, p. 17, note 5; p. 72; p. 85, note 6.

CHAPTER 10

THE TESTIMONY OF THE HOLY SPIRIT AND THE AUTHORITY OF SCRIPTURE

To the question which concludes the preceding chapter, Calvin, followed by the confessions of La Rochelle, the Netherlands and the Waldensians, replies: "Without doubt, by the unanimous voice of the Church, but especially, in the final and supreme analysis, by the testimony and inner persuasion of the Holy Ghost."

It is the unanimous consent of the Church which informs us of the fact that there is a canon of Scripture to which she submits, and it is the Holy Spirit who seals this affirmation of the Church in the hearts of the faithful by His creative testimony of faith.

"This is the principle which distinguishes our religion from all others, namely, that we know that God has spoken to us and are certainly assured that the prophets have not spoken of themselves but as organs and instruments of the Holy Spirit; that they have merely declared what they received from on high. Whoever therefore would profit by the Holy Scriptures, let him decide in the first place that the Law and the Prophets have no doctrine at all which has been given by the will or desire of men but only that which has been dictated by the Holy Spirit. If it is asked how we can know this, I reply that to doctors as well as to disciples God declares and manifests that he is their author by the revelation of the same Spirit".[1]

This reply has been criticized. We are told that Calvin must have confused the religious fact of Christian experience, which hears the voice of God here and there in Scripture, with purely scientific questions arising from history and criticism, such as the integrity of the texts and the conditions under which the canon was decided.

This criticism is only possible if one loses sight of the double signification of the term "canon". Empirically, and abstracting from all question of principle, by the term "canon of the Bible" is understood the list of books of which it is composed. It is thus that there are two canons of the Old Testament: the Hebrew canon received by Protestants and the canon called

[1] *Com. on 2 Tim.*, iii, 16.

Alexandrian received by Catholics. This means that certain writings of the Old Testament which figure in the Alexandrian list are absent from the Hebrew list. Thus, if we ignore the canons of certain heretical Oriental Churches of no importance and lacking any spiritual insight, it may be said that there is one canon of the New Testament for Christendom.

On the other hand, the term "canon" may be invested with a dogmatic significance. If the Bible be regarded as divinely inspired, its canon will possess a normative authority. From this it follows that the term canonical is susceptible of two different meanings. It may signify divine and normative, as in the Confession of La Rochelle, and it may signify transmitted by the Church and recognized by her as forming part of the list of the authentic writings of the Bible.

In the second acceptation, it is perfectly evident that the testimony of the Holy Spirit does not inform us what constitutes this list, nor the number, title, authenticity and extent of the works which compose it. In this sense Bavinck admits that the Holy Spirit does not pronounce on the canonicity of such and such a document.[1]

Here we have a purely historical question which must be resolved according to the methods of critical science. In order to ascertain what books a Church recognizes as canonical, we must ask, in the first place, not the Holy Spirit but the Church.

Theologians of the 17th century like Quenstedt[2] and du Moulin[3] willingly admit that the catalogue of canonical books—the canon in the second acceptation of the term—is not "an article of faith superadded to the others which are contained in Scripture". One may have saving faith while not knowing distinctly the number of the canonical books, or not accepting them in their entirety. It would be absurd to suggest that the Nestorians will all be damned for this reason.

When, therefore, it is a question of determining canonicity in the scientific sense, there is no other way except by experimental enquiry and the internal and external critique, in the literary sense. This is the process which Calvin employs in his commentaries on the antilegomena of the New Testament (the writings whose authenticity identified with canonicity was disputed in the churches and by the doctors of the first centuries of our era). In this matter he makes use of critical liberty, apart

---

[1] *Geref. Dog.*, I, p. 642 (s. 154).
[2] *Vide* the extracts from this theologian in B. B. Warfield, *Calvin and Calvinism*, p. 98.
[3] Pierre du Moulin, *Bouclier de la Foi*, IV, Concerning the Apocryphal Books.

from which there can be no scientific knowledge, and he is obliged to observe that the writing of these books cannot always be attributed to the authors which tradition assigns to them, or at least that this attribution may be uncertain.[1]

But it is none the less true that Calvin and the Reformers accepted the canon of the New Testament as the Councils of Hippo Regius and of Carthage had received it and as the medieval Church which they were engaged in reforming had transmitted it to them. Did they thus show themselves to be slaves of a tradition which might be rightly regarded as merely some wretched product of the human mind?[2] It is here that, in Reformed dogmatics, the function of the testimony of the Holy Spirit makes its appearance, being applied to the canonicity of the sacred books in the purely religious sense. The subject of the present chapter and of the two following is the testimony of the Holy Spirit.

This inspired Scripture which orthodox Protestantism makes the external principle of its theology is divided into two parts called the Old and New Testaments. Each of these parts consists of a body of writings composed by different secondary authors at different times and originally independent of each other. Not until long after they were written were they included in a single list called the canon. It was thus that the Jewish canon first made its appearance; then the canon of the books of the New Testament.

We will now discuss these two canons separately, because their authority is not established in the same way, for the Christian; the testimony of the Holy Spirit reaching us more immediately in the one case than in the other.

Among Protestants, the apologetico-historical school, even when orthodox, seeks to establish the canon by the historical critique. This method leads to a *cul-de-sac*. It can only produce a conjectural knowledge, reserved for an intellectual *élite*, for whom faith is not enough.

Le Clerc's line of argument in the 18th century,[3] resumed independently by Ritschl in the following century, possesses an undeniable value from a human point of view. It is certain that, in order to rediscover original and authentic Christianity, we must trace it to its source, or at least to an epoch in which the tradition concerning Christ was still living; certain too that, to say the least, the undisputed writings of the New Testament

---

[1] *Vide* Calvin's prefaces to the antilegomena on which he comments.
[2] Jülicher, *Einleitung in das Neue Testament*, 1906, p. 504.
[3] *Nouveau Testament*, translation, Amsterdam, 1703, Preface.

which form the core of the Christian canon, satisfy this need in a large measure.

But, for fidelity in the transmission of original texts, we are almost entirely dependent on the witness of the Church of the 2nd century; and, as our Lord left us no writings, speculative criticism must attempt to disentangle His authentic teaching from the modifications which may have been made in it by the thought of the men of the first Christian generations. The true Protestant canon, according to Eugène Ménégoz, must be the word of Christ, "our only Master". The trouble is that this canon is historically impossible to determine in any strict sense. History, by itself, without a religious axiom, can give the Protestant no authority distinct from his own "private opinion". Finally, the simple will have to be content with the *Professoren Christus* among many and various personifications.

As to the canon of the New Testament, properly speaking, it is represented as a late creation of the episcopate in response to the initiative of the heresiarch Marcion who was the first to entertain the idea of one. In actual fact, there is only one primitive Christian literature, which has been constituted a closed canon by the Church, with the intention of forming a pendant to the Jewish canon of the Old Testament and giving ancient catholicism a firmer base on which to build its tradition and its *regula fidei* than the allegorical exegesis of the sacred books of the Jews.

In order to establish this rôle of the episcopate in the creation of the canon, use is made of a text of Origen[1] according to which "the money-changers expert in the testing of currency" (οἱ δόκιμοι τραπέζιται) have not admitted (ἐνέκρικαν)—according to an alternative reading, have not examined minutely (ἀνέκριναν)—all the numerous gospels extant, but have received only (ἐπελέξαντο) "the four" that we possess. "The Church of God", he concludes, "prefers these four to the exclusion of all the others" (τάδε τέταρτα μόνα προκρίνει). It is generally admitted that the criterion employed was the supposed mediate or immediate apostilicity of the document.

We will not discuss the question whether Origen's "money-changer assayers" are intended to represent the bishops, as Jülicher would have it. This seems doubtful in view of a text of his Commentary on Matthew (25 : 27); also from the fact that, in his *Proœmium Lucae*, he attributes to the ancient people "the gift of discernment of spirits"; and, finally, because he believed that in his own time there survived certain rare Christians

[1] *Proœmium Lucae.*

endowed with this gift. Now, he could not have been ignorant
that the number of bishops was considerable at the time when
he wrote. We do not deny that at a given moment the criterion
of apostolicity was applied to the disputed writings. We would
merely observe that there are texts and facts which go to show
that these writings were often received for religious motives and
regarded as canonical, even though it was recognized that they
were not of apostolic origin.[1] Finally, a leading critic has confessed that it is impossible to do more than make conjectures
concerning the factors which concurred in the formation of the
canon. [2]

How much more solid, at first sight, appears the thesis proposed by Rome. The Roman Catholic knows no hesitation concerning the list of canonical writings. The contours of his New
Testament are delimited precisely by the infallible authority of
the Church, in accordance with the decisions of the oecumenical
councils of Florence and Trent. Unfortunately, the infallible
authority of the Church is, as we have seen, a colossus with feet
of clay. An authority decides nothing unless it has previously
been received. If the canon of the Word of God rests on the
decision of the Church, upon what then does the authority and
infallibility of the latter rest? The *Tu es Petrus* is in the Gospel
by Matthew. Let us propose for a moment that it proves what
Rome would have it prove. How am I to know that the Gospel
by Matthew is inspired, canonical, and a rule of faith?

Even if we abstract from this preliminary objection, how
strange it is to suppose, with the Roman system, that there can
be an authority superior to the Word of God, necessary to
legitimize that Word in the minds of believers. It is extremely
improbable that a text immediately and totally inspired by God
could not be received unless it had previously been authenticated by certain men, supposed indeed to be infallible but
admitted to be uninspired.

If we are to have a canon other than our own subjectivity, we
must put ourselves in the position of the Reformers, and indicate as the means of recognizing it, not the hesitant authority
of the critic, or the juridical authority of the Church, but the
unanimity realized practically at the end of the 4th century of

---

[1] *Vide* App. XIII, p. 398.
[2] Adolf Harnack, *Lehrb. d. Dogmengeschichte*, p. 343: *Nur im kürze kann
hier eingedeutet werden unter welchen Bedingungen—nur um vermuthungen
handelt es sich—der N. Tliche Kanon in der Kirche entstanden ist*—Here it
is only possible to indicate briefly in what circumstances—and it is only a
question of conjecture, after all—the New Testament canon originated in the
Church.

the Christian era and confirmed by the testimony of the Holy
Ghost in the hearts of the faithful.

Roman controversialists exult and imagine us to be very em-
barrassed when they object that the Reformers and the first
Protestants could not have known that the canon of the New
Testament was correct and complete by any other means than
the infallible authority of the Roman Church from whom they
received its sacred pages. But this triumph would be of brief
duration if these polemists agreed to regard these things as they
happened in reality, instead of remaining in the clouds of
speculation.

The Reformers and the first Protestants were certainly
Christians, and Christians living under the Roman obedience,
more or less defined, in imperial Germany, Gallican France and
an England in which the ties with Rome had been loosening
even before the reign of Henry VIII. Properly speaking, it was
from their respective national Churches, more strictly from the
local Churches in which they had grown up, that they received
the principles and elements of Christianity, including the teaching on the existence of Holy Scripture and of a Biblical canon.

Although the state of these Churches was unsatisfactory in
the extreme, they were still "Churches", diseased branches,
indeed, but still in some sense branches of the tree which in another figure is called the mystical body of Christ. When they
taught, among desolating errors, some point of divine truth,
they were able by its means to bring forth souls to the life of
faith. Their teaching, in the measure in which it was subject to
the Word of God, showed Christ and His Word; conformed itself to that Word, could be, and was, effectively sealed in the
hearts of true believers by the testimony of the Holy Spirit.

But it is important to render to the Church that which belongs to the Church, and to the Holy Spirit that which belongs
to the Holy Spirit. To the Church, it belongs to teach.

It is through her that the Reformers learnt the existence of
Holy Scripture, the New Testament, the Redeemer, the Incarnation, the Holy Trinity, the heavenly Father. These men were
not, therefore, *tabulae rasae*, nor did they wish to make a *tabula
rasa* of the past. They based their teaching upon the Catholic
Christianity in which they were born, and were content to abide
in it.

To the Holy Spirit it belongs to teach with the certainty of
faith those who understand the teaching of their particular
Church, which latter remains, in spite of all, a supernatural fact,
and certain of whose teachings, for example, the articles of the

Creed, the inspiration of Scripture, the canon of the New Testament, are the affirmation of divine facts and teachings. These spiritual realities, being transcendent to reason and the senses, can only be known in this sense by means of faith which is a supernatural organ, and the faith which believes on the authority of God is the testimony of the Holy Spirit whose mark of origin it bears.

What gave, and gives, in the eyes of orthodox Protestants an importance of the first order to the unanimous testimony of the Church concerning the canon of the New Testament, is the fact that God produces in their religious consciousness the certainty that the existence of the Church is a divine fact. And He produces this certainty by the very preaching of the truth which is already a word of God, as such, susceptible of being sealed in the hearts of the faithful before they have read the Scriptures.[1] This Scripture of the New Testament is given to them by their particular Church, the only one that they know directly, basing itself on the consensus of Christian antiquity which, triumphing over previous hesitations, settled its contents at the councils of Hippo Regius and Carthage in the 4th century. The slight deviations of certain heretical communities (Monophysites), or of particular teachings, on these points of detail, are insignificant in the presence of such impressive agreement. By the consent of the Church, our Reformers and their immediate disciples and successors were brought to feel a profound respect for the venerable documents which constitute the New Testament.

But they could not, legitimately, even before their separation from Rome, establish a certitude of divine faith relative to the canon of the New Testament derived from the tradition of the universal Church, in the sense in which the Tridentine Fathers willed that it should be received, namely, with a respect equal to the word of God, because this tradition does not respond to the required criterion: *quod semper, quod ubique, quod ab omnibus creditum*. [2]

This tradition in their eyes had been "believed" practically "everywhere" and "by all", but they knew very well that it could not command the epithet "always". Calvin, as an exegete, was not ignorant, for example, of the difficulties which had been experienced by the Epistle to the Hebrews or 2 Peter in gaining admission to the canon, and he was familiar with most of the reasons which can be urged against the attribution of these

---

[1] *Com. on Acts*, xvii., 11.
[2] [The Vincentian canon, so called because of its origin or association with Vincent of Lerins, *ob. circa* A.D. 450.]

epistles to the authors assigned to them by tradition. And Luther knew as much about this matter as his brilliant successor.

They could not legitimately base this faith on the decision of an infallible oecumenical council, for the excellent reason that, to their knowledge at least, no oecumenical council had sanctioned the canon in detail. The Council of Trent did so, indeed, but this was either after the death of the Reformers or several years after they had consummated their rupture with Rome. And when the Council of Trent assembled, there were reasons which, in their eyes, as in ours, disqualified it from meriting the title oecumenical.

Finally, they could not have based their faith on the decision of a pope speaking *ex cathedra*, even supposing one to have existed. The Vatican Council had not yet assembled, and it was not until 1870 that Roman Catholics knew that it was *de fide* that such decisions must be considered articles of faith.

Is this equivalent to saying that Roman Catholics at the time of Luther and Calvin were unaware of the existence of the New Testament? Certainly not. Those who were sufficiently instructed knew this fact perfectly well and indeed it was in the New Testament that Luther found the word which delivered him from the terrors which assailed his conscience. He had been told that God spoke through this book. He heard and believed, he knew henceforth by a direct experience that his teachers had not deceived him in this matter. It was in this way that the testimony of the Holy Spirit was engraven on his soul.

When the distress and misery of the Church became evident to Zwingli's eyes under the form of an irruption of pagan superstitions at Einsiedeln, as to Luther's under the aspect of a judaizing commercialism, it was to the New Testament that our first Reformers turned, even as Peter had previously turned to Jésus, because the Spirit of God showed them that this book contained the words of eternal life.

But one difficulty presented itself to which, under the pressure of the moment, they had to find a reply. It was in the reforming book itself that their adversaries sought for weapons with which to defend the errors from which the Reformers were delivering the Church. To the *sola fide* of Luther was opposed the Epistle of James. Zwingli, condemning the invocation of angels, was shown the angel in the Apocalypse causing the prayers of the faithful to ascend to heaven in the smoke of incense.

From such difficulties, the importance of which was exaggerated, the first two Reformers saw no other way of escape than to distinguish in the teaching of Scripture between that which is, and that which is not, canonical. Zwingli's criterion was the glory of God; Luther's, the plan of salvation. Without wishing it, as their subsequent attitude to the *illuminati* showed, this was to introduce subjectivism into the heart of the formal principle of the Reformation. Great honour has been paid to them on this account, but, for our part, we deplore this stupid error of the pioneers of the Reformation. We would not throw a stone at such men, however, for they have rendered too great services to peace of conscience and purity of worship for us to do aught but honour their memory.

They were not able, however, to see clearly the testimony of the Holy Spirit in all its fullness. It was given to the courageous and balanced genius of Geneva to visualize the situation as a whole. He had, of course, the immense advantage of succeeding Zwingli and Luther and of being able to gauge the extent of the danger with which "fantastic spirits" menaced the future of the Reformation.

Following the example of our Reformer, we start with these two immediately verifiable facts: there exists a New Testament, recognized by the Roman Church, in whose bosom the Reformers were born, as given by divine inspiration; which, moreover, must be received, on the confession of that Church, as instruction proceeding from God and not from men. This testimony of the Occident is corroborated by that of the Oriental Churches, abstracting as to points of detail from certain heretical communions.

We are aware, of course, that in the case of the deutero-canonical books of the New Testament this agreement was not established at first glance. The formation of the canon, as we know it, was the result of a slow and gradual process, the practical conclusion of which was demonstrated at the synods of Hippo and Carthage.

This process may be represented in the following manner. First, the Churches read in public the writings which their leaders and people acknowledged as prophetic or charismatic by reason of their apostolic origin or, in default, of their antiquity and utility; in other words, of their intrinsic value as historic witnesses or as instruments of edification. Several of these writings no longer figure in the present canon: those alone remaining in the first class whose apostolic origin has been firmly established by a constant tradition. In the second class were those which could not be rejected without offending the piety of which they were the objects on the part of brethren whose feelings in the matter had a right to be respected. Presumed apostolic authority, mediate or immediate, was doubtless an important factor, but not until after A.D. 265 did it become a *conditio sine qua non*. The proof of this is to be seen in the fact that Dionysius, bishop of Alexandria, who died in that year, simply to humour the sentiments of men whom he respected, sought to safeguard the canonicity of the Apocalypse by attributing it to another John than the Apostle.[1]

The consensus in question is thus the conclusion of an historic process, but henceforth nothing can prevent it from being what it is. The individual scholar may indeed ascertain that in this canon there are secondary parts less firmly attested by the external critique than the others. But he must acknowledge that the mass is cemented and that it has been proposed finally for the acceptance of the Church, which has recognized, and recognizes, that God has spoken to her in and through this Holy Scripture.

In regard to this social fact, nothing can be changed: the Church has received the canon of the New Testament as it is to-day, in the same way as the Synagogue had bequeathed to it the Hebrew canon. The canon cannot be remade for the simple reason that history cannot be remade. The Council of Trent had an humiliating experience in regard to this question when it wanted to add the Apocrypha to the Hebrew canon.

The existence of the New Testament is thus the first fact. But it may be asked, especially by those who do not believe that the Church has any right to impose its authority on the Word of God: whence does this canon derive its sanction? To this question we reply with another fact, one in the spiritual order, which is attested immediately by our knowledge. When the Church tells us that God speaks in the New Testament as He spoke formerly to His elect people in the Law and the Prophets, she has no difficulty at all in making us feel the reality of her assertion. In order to convince us of this, she can send us with confidence to meditate on the teaching which it contains: no Christian can fail to be touched by the divine character impressed upon it and reflected by it.

This immediate sense of the presence of a divine revelation, of a message which awakens confidence in the heart of the believer, is surely a manifestation of the testimony of the Holy Spirit. "My sheep hear My voice, and I know them and they follow Me" (John 10: 27). But among this number are some who still remain outside the faith of Protestantism, or who fancy themselves to be "progressive thinkers", when they are merely

---

[1] Eusebius, *Hist. Eccl.*, vii, 25; *vide* App. XIII, p. 398.

reverting to the proto-history of Protestant dogmatics, to the primitive stage of Luther and Zwingli. Calvin, who had himself experienced this sentiment, declares that the divinity of Scripture may be recognized as one distinguishes the sweet from the bitter, the white from the black.[1] But the gifted exponent of the doctrine of the witness of the Holy Spirit, by his more penetrating analysis, distinguished another fact to which he was, we believe, the first to give theological expression because he was the first to see that in that way alone the Christian consciousness could be guaranteed a truly formal rule which would deliver it alike from the tyranny of clerks and from the aberrations of individualist subjectivism.

In the form of an immediate impression of the divinity of the Christian message in its general sense, the testimony of the Holy Spirit is not sufficient to safeguard us against the aberrations of individualist subjectivism by giving us a divine external rule. The reason for this is that the weakness of our intelligence does not allow us to understand it all exactly and that what exists of the corruption of the heart renders certain parts of the message distasteful, offensive or at least inefficacious, while others experience in it a divine savour.

Hence the Christian runs the risk of seeking a remedy for these defects in illuminism—in which case, the evil will certainly become worse—or in a blind submission to an ecclesiastical authority claiming to be infallible. He thus becomes a stranger to the liberty which Christ purchased at the price of His blood, and submits either to the inclination of his subjective tendencies or to the hazards of his birth, to Rome or Byzantium or to something less still, as the case may be.

Those to whom God gives a clear view of these two perils and who know, by the immediate experience of which we have spoken, that God speaks to them in the Church's New Testament, are thenceforth the recipients of a new grace. They are able to verify in their own experience the promise of Christ: "Whosoever hath, to him shall be given" (Matthew 13: 12).

By the teaching of the Church, in the first instance, and afterwards by personal experience, they have learnt that God speaks in the New Testament. They know by faith that here is a word of God; that the historical process which gave existence to this unique jewel of ancient Christian literature is merely the human means whereby God has made over to His Church this priceless treasure.

Now, their faith in the material authority of a more or less

---

[1] *Inst.* I, vii. 2.

extensive content of the Scripture of the New Testament is metamorphosed into a more complete faith. They have recognized that the authors of the books of the New Testament present themselves as the depositaries, the witnesses and the interpreters of teaching given by and concerning Christ, which they themselves have a right to transmit to their readers.

How should we know this teaching apart from them? And, having them at our disposal, how can we ascertain whether they are competent and faithful? The method of oral ecclesiastical tradition across the centuries as a means of leading us to the knowledge of Christ is excluded, excluded through the experience that we have been made to realize of its deformations and excrescences, excluded by Christ Himself according to the testimony of the evangelists, who show Him to us condemning the traditions of the fathers when they are in opposition to the written Word of God, of which alone it is said, when it is a question of the past, that it "cannot be broken" (John 10: 35).

The way of interior illumination independent of the Word is also excluded. We cannot trust to it, for its light is deceptive. It is not necessary to be very well versed in the history of sects and heresies to know that. Moreover, according to the testimony of the evangelists, Christ himself has put us on our guard against the possible illusions of our natural senses (Matthew 6: 23) and he has taught us that knowledge of Himself is possible only to him to whom He communicates it (Luke 10: 22).

But, once more, how can we be assured of the fidelity and authority of the witnesses who render Christ present to our intelligence and to our heart? By critical and historical science? At best, such science could give us no more than probabilities, and faith cannot live on probabilities. "If we wish to satisfy our consciences", says Calvin, "so that they may not be tormented incessantly by doubts and questionings, that they may not stumble or waver at every scruple, it is necessary that the persuasion of which we have spoken should be derived from a higher source than mere human reasons or judgments or conjectures, namely, from the secret testimony of the Holy Ghost"[1] God alone can give authority to His Word.

Now, this is what He does for those who have renounced all human support to rely solely on Him who is never wanting in time of need. Through contact with the New Testament, God creates in those whom He has thus disposed, faith in the formal authority of this body of writings which the Holy Ghost has given to the Church. "Being thus enlightened by His power, we

[1] *Inst.* I, vii. 4.

do not now believe by our own judgment or that of others, that Scripture is of God; but above all human judgment, we conclude indubitably that it is given from His mouth through the ministry of men, as if we saw in it with our very eyes the very essence of God." [1]

Such faith is the proof of that which the eye of flesh cannot see. It is the foundation of the infinite experience, the seal and earnest of the Holy Spirit in the noetic sphere. He who possesses it, while he does so, cannot, strictly speaking, doubt. Let anyone come to him and ask: "Who can persuade us that one book is to be received without contradiction while another is to be rejected, if the Church does not give an infallible ruling concerning the matter?" and it will seem to him that a question of this sort cannot be asked "without great mockery of the Holy Spirit". [2] The canon of the New Testament in the light of faith appears to him as a creation of God through the anonymous ministry of men whose hands have long centuries ago fallen into dust. One does not correct a masterpiece of the past; one does not profane a sanctuary from which there ascends the *credo* of worshippers.

Before Scripture the believer must bow as if he contemplated with his own eyes God in His majesty and heard Him speak. God knows well that He is asking of the ignorant and the wise something which entirely surpasses their powers. The former do not even know their lack of knowledge while the latter imagine that they know more than they need. But the believer, seeing the impossible realized with a supernatural ardour, and under the influence of a power "which cannot but be divine", and that in him and in those who, like himself, have their eyes open to the dangers on the right hand and the left, perceive immediately that "it is God that worketh in us in this manner by His Spirit".

It is therefore the power of His action who works producing faith in Scripture, which constitutes the testimony of the Holy Spirit in relation to the canon. And it is, in particular, on this testimony that the New Testament is founded, while the latter also abounds throughout in "notes" of its divinity.

This purely religious method of establishing the authority of Scripture enables us to go beyond that of the historicism represented in Calvin's time by Carlstadt. But it is available only after certain historic experiences which show that there was something inadequate and delusive about the original attitude of Luther and Zwingli. To perceive the testimony of the

---

[1] *Inst.* I, vii. 35.   [2] *Ibid.*, 1.

Holy Spirit in the sense in which Calvin understood it and all the faithful in all time have perceived it, a certain psychological preparation was needed. It was lacking in the first Reformers.

The moment faith receives this preparation, it knows by the testimony and inner persuasion of the Holy Spirit that the canon of Scripture has been given by God to the Church to lead her into truth and to enable her to reform herself according to this divine rule. In other words, the truth whose divine radiance shines in her eyes and which by its intrinsic virtue quells her doubts, is the rule; the body of Scriptures of which the Church is the guardian is the Word of God; a statement of Scripture, even if it shocks the reason or the subjective sensibility, must be received solely on the authority of God teaching through His written Word.

For example, if a Reformed Christian were to doubt whether the doctrines of election and reprobation rested on a sound foundation, or to ask himself whether the Synod of Dort was right in its condemnation of Arminianism, he would not take refuge in a dogmatic conformism which would exalt the findings of a council, however venerable, into a supreme rule. He would seek light from Holy Scripture; and when, like Reuss, he had satisfied himself that "the canons of Dort can never be refuted on exegetical grounds", he would accept them, whatever the cost to his sentiments or his reason.

The testimony of the Holy Spirit which witnesses to him, which establishes and seals the authority of Scripture and which guides him as he studies it, is thus primarily a cause and not a reason. But it becomes the supreme reason when the believer realizes that this is the work of the Almighty, in obedience to whom he finds perfect rest of mind and heart.

Faith, therefore, is never blind, for it is preceded by a reasonable adherence to, and a sensible experience of, the majesty of the Word of God. Faith knows its object and appreciates its divinity, so long as it is not a mere opinion founded on experience.[1] On the other hand, when it becomes faith in divine authority, it does not cease to know what it believes. But it embraces the object known and loved, with a power of acceptance which the subject recognizes as surpassing his own powers and as divine.

To summarize: the believer is not confronted with the alternative of the objective authority of God, speaking through Scrip-

---

[1] This is why Calvin declares that faith consists in certainty rather than apprehension. The latter term signifies precisely an opinion conceived on the strength of sensible data.

ture, or the subjective authority of a religious experience causing him to recognize here and now that God is speaking. There is very certainly a subjective experience; but this subjective experience sends us back to the objective reality, which is God speaking in Scripture and which is the source of this subjective experience. And when the latter has caused its subject thus to renounce himself, to come out of himself, and to forget even his experience, in order to attach himself to the sole objective authority worthy of the name—then it is that faith is born. The latter has no foundation whatever, apart from the authority of God; concretely that of Scripture, the Word of God. Faith in the formal authority of Scripture is still, indeed, an act of the subject, the act of believing, of committing oneself on trust; but an act which implies the consciousness that it is, *qua* act, a perfect gift, an eminent and divine grace, the grace of believing that Scripture is the supreme necessary and sufficient judge of controversies in matters of faith, because it is God who speaks therein.

The Confession of La Rochelle invokes the same experimental fact in the sense in which the acknowledged leader of the Reformed had put it to the test. This explains how it can, without inconsistency, draw up the list of canonical books and appeal from them to the testimony of the Holy Spirit in order to distinguish them from the other ecclesiastical books (the Apocrypha). The canon is considered as a whole comprising Holy Scripture in its integrity.[1]

From this point of view, the contingent factors of the history of the New Testament canon, to which teachers of the modern school attach so much importance, lose the dogmatic importance that they would give it: whatever may have been the circumstances which have concurred in the formation of the canon, one thing is certain, namely, that men with their hesitations, their errors, their intentions, good or otherwise, their faithfulness also and the heroism of their faith, have merely been the instruments which God has been pleased to use, anonymous and without known authority. It is by their hands that He has bestowed the gift of the New Testament on the Church. Never has she been without a canonical Scripture: she has always had the Old Testament. Never has she existed for a moment without professing the doctrine taught in the New Testament, of which the *regula fidei* is no more than the faithful summary. Then, at

---

[1] *Conf. gal.*, art. iii, *ad init.* Concerning the erroneous idea entertained by Reuss, Berger and others apropos of Calvin's attitude to the Apocalypse and the last two epistles of John, *vide* B. B. Warfield, *Calvin and Calvinism.*

the moment marked by divine providence, at the hour when the doctrinal tradition was becoming hesitant and corrupt, the Church recognized the divinity of the Christian canon. She did not promulgate it at oecumenical councils.[1] Simple provincial synods, important indeed, such as those of Hippo and Carthage, registered and confessed the common faith. The Reformed Churches of France, Holland and England, did no more. No council, synod or Church can confer authority on a Word which establishes all authority because it emanates from God and because it attests itself by the seal of the Spirit of God as His Word.

Common sense is sufficient to tell us that the oral tradition relative to the person and teaching of Christ could not, without a perpetual miracle, preserve itself in sufficient purity except on condition of being committed to writing: *verba volant, scripta manent*. Christian instinct presupposes axiomatically that as truly as Christ is the revelation of God to the Church, so truly has God provided that the tradition of the revelation committed to writing should preserve for us, in the measure in which such a thing is necessary, a documentation transmitting to us in their purity the essential characteristics of this revelation.

Thus it is that a New Testament is seen to be necessary. The Church, the guardian of Scripture, has for its function to show us where is this New Testament, of which books it consists, and how we are to recognize the marks of its divinity. The Holy Spirit alone can raise to the level of the certainty of faith these data of common sense and of the testimony of the Church.

[1] Jülicher, after having admitted that it would be a false view to consider that the writings of the New Testament had been raised from the rank of ordinary books to the dignity of divine documents by the vote of a majority at a council (*Einleit.* 6, p. 432), speaks nevertheless of "canonization". But when this is in question in the Church of Rome, he can only point to assemblies such as the "synod" held under the presidency of Damascus in 382. The canon of the New Testament at this synod is the same as ours. But the said synod was so little a council of the universal Church having authority over all the churches, that the author in the same page of his book (p. 432) tells us that Philostratus, bishop of Brescia, great presecutor of heretics, in the year 385 passes in silence in his catalogue the epistle to the Hebrews and the Apocalypse. This is all the more significant seeing that he held the former to be Pauline and the latter apostolic. The history of the pretended epistle of Paul to the Laodiceans (*ibid.*, p. 494) is even more significant.

CHAPTER II

THE TESTIMONY OF THE HOLY SPIRIT AND THE CANON OF THE OLD TESTAMENT

All orthodox Christian Churches recognize that the Old Testament contains a divine revelation preparatory to the coming of Christ. They also acknowledge that, although destined especially for the people of Israel, the Church in gestation, it contains a divine message for the Church baptized by the Holy Spirit on the day of Pentecost. Like the New Testament, it contains pages from which the divine majesty shines with brilliance to the view of faith: to these pages Christian piety turns with the same devotion as to the choicest passages in the Gospels.

But the Old Testament was born in a civilization far different from ours, which has been subjected to Christian influences. The rudeness of manners and naïve liberty of expression which it reflects here and there shock the refined feeling and delicacy of spirit developed by the culture which dawned on the shores of the Lake of Gennesareth. With the result that some Christians are astonished that Calvin should have been able to say of the whole of Scripture that it "bears upon its face as clear evidence of its infallible truth, as white and black do of their colour, sweet and bitter of their taste".[1]

We shall not accuse them of reading Scripture with the eyes of a Voltaire because they fail to recognize the voice of God in certain pages of the Old Testament whose spirit does not appear to them to be reconcilable with the mildness of the evangelical law. Nevertheless, we subscribe to our Reformer's view, with the restriction which he himself has made: "if we consider Scripture with clear eyes and unbiased judgment, it will forthwith present itself with a divine majesty which shall subdue our presumptuous opposition and compel us to render it homage."[2]

Now we claim that this condition is not satisfied if we apply the spiritual principles of the perfect revelation brought to us by Jesus Christ, to a preparatory revelation adapted to the needs of the times in which it made its appearance and developed. Jesus taught the Pharisees that there are certain laws in the Old Testament whose presence there is explained by the hardness of

[1] *Inst.* I, vii. 2.   [2] *Ibid.*, 4.

heart of the men for whom they were made (Matthew 19: 8). This lack of historic sense smacks of the 18th century, and, if we are delivered from it, we shall see in the progressive character of revelation an analogy with the constant and general method of God in the order of nature and common grace which raises humanity from barbarism to culture.

Whatever one may say, the old dogmatics had a very clear vision of the progressive character of divine revelation. "When the first promise of salvation was given to Adam", says Calvin, "only a few feeble sparks beamed forth: additions being subsequently made, a greater degree of light began to be displayed and continued gradually to increase and shine with greater radiance, until at length all the clouds being dispersed, Christ the sun of justice arose and with full refulgence illumined all the earth." [1]

And this divine method was already explained by the pedagogic character of a revelation which addressed itself to a humanity yet in its infancy.[2] In accordance with this historic point of view, Calvin replies to the objection of the "ignorant" drawn from the rigour of the divine chastisements recorded in the Old Testament: "And for this reason, they can scarcely help imagining, like the Manichees, that the God of the Old Testament was different from that of the New. But we shall easily disencumber ourselves of such doubts if we attend to that mode of divine administration to which I have referred—that God was pleased to indicate and typify both the gift of future and eternal felicity by terrestrial blessings, as well as the terrible nature of spiritual death by corporal penalties, at that time when He delivered His covenant to the Israelites as under a kind of veil." [3]

This is not making any concession to Modernism, nor is it any more subjectivist than asking those who read Scripture not to forget that the nature of the law of peoples varies with the historical and psychological conditions of the particular community to which it is applied.

God speaks in the Old Testament, and the faithful who study it in the objective spirit which we advocate make the experience that, there also, His Word carries within itself its own authentication and that it generates faith.

This authority of God which makes itself evident to the believing soul by His own divine majesty is certainly a form of the testimony of the Holy Spirit, but it is not as yet that which witnesses in us that the Old Testament, taken as a whole and as

---

[1] *Inst.* II, x. 20.   [2] *Ibid.*, xi. 23.   [3] *Ibid.*, II, xi. 3.

the Christian Church has inherited it, is canonical in the religious sense of the term.

The divine witness which attests the canon of the Old Testament to us Christians, born beyond the influence of the ancient Synagogue, is an external testimony. It comes to us immediately from without, and not until we have been enabled to understand it does this witness become an inward persuasion of the Holy Ghost. It comes to us from the New Testament which we already know to be canonical and by whose inspired Word we are persuaded irresistibly. From the New Testament we learn that Israel had a "Scripture" which "cannot be broken" (John 10: 35), and that, for Jesus and for the apostolic Church, this Scripture was the Hebrew canon which the Synagogue receives to this day. All orthodox Christian communions hear the same external testimony of the Holy Spirit and submit to it in principle. If the canon of Trent differs from that of the Protestants, it is because the theologians at that council held the mistaken view that our Lord and His Apostles made use of the Alexandrian canon.

But everybody acknowledges the existence of a canon of the Old Testament, although this evident fact is disputed in a more or less confused fashion by modern critics. To listen to them, one might imagine that history had proved that no such canon existed. According to them, the canon of the Old Testament is the creation, not of Israel, nor of the Judaism of Ezra or of the Maccabees, but of the primitive Talmudist Judaism. Thus, it is not an authority acknowledged by Jesus Christ. It does not rest on His authority but on that of the rabbis.[1] Thus, confessional Protestants in receiving the Hebrew canon as a supreme authority, depend, in the final analysis, on the authority of the Talmud.

It is sufficient to read with a little attention works like those of Michel Nicolas, Cornill and George Moore, for example, to ascertain that one is not in the sphere of a serene and impartial science, but on the stormy sea of polemics. There can be no doubt that it is confessional Protestantism at which they aim, through a presentation of facts which attempts to be scientific but merely succeeds in being pedantic. To engage in controversy is in itself perfectly legitimate, but it loses its value when it leads, however unconsciously, to neglect of the decisive facts and exaggeration of unimportant matters of detail.

[1] Cornill, *Einleit. in den kanonisch. Büch. des Alt. Test.*, 5th ed., p. 300. Michel Nicolas, article *sub voc.* in Lichtenberger, *Encyclopédie des Sciences religieuses.*

Let the case be judged fairly. We shall endeavour to support our position only by patent facts whose verification is altogether independent of any dogmatic point of view.

The first of these facts is a formidable *ignoratio elenchi* on the part of the critics. Against Protestant dogmatics, it is sought to prove that, at the time of our Lord, there was no canon of the Old Testament in the sense in which it is now understood (*im Sinne der altprotestantischen Dogmatik*, Cornill says expressly).[1] And, to prove it, an attempt is made to show that there was no list of sacred books, firmly established once for all by a "canonization" (*Kanonisierung*) emanating from religious authority; in other words, that there was no canon of the Old Testament in the sense understood by the Church of Rome!

Moore makes the same mistake in regard to this subject as Cornill,[2] while Sember, according to the Calvinist theologian Gravenmeijer[3] was, at one time, a most zealous advocate of this idea. Strictly speaking, however, says Gravenmeijer, who may be regarded as an authentic representative of the viewpoint of the classical Reformed dogmatics, "canonical does not signify included in the register of ecclesiastical books, but a book having authority, divinely inspired and containing the doctrine which is the canon, that is to say, the rule of all that we must believe and do in order to salvation".[4]

For Rome, the canon derives its authority *quoad nos* from the authority of the teaching Church. The originality of the Reformers' view consisted in reversing these terms and basing the Church on canonical Scripture, whose authority is founded immediately on the testimony which God himself renders to it. The Roman definition of "canonical" may, of course, be preferred to ours, but it is absurd to argue that if the Lord did not accept the former the latter must have been unknown to Him.

This confusion of ideas leads Cornill to fall into another paralogism. He recognizes expressly that the Law had received its definitive "canonization" in the time of Ezra, well before the Christian era, and because some unknown Jew, "very independent in his beliefs",[5] must have written, according to him in the 1st century, a pseudepigraph, the Book of Jubilees, in which the Samaritan chronology is preferred to that of the Hebrew text,

[1] *Op. cit.*, 47, 8.
[2] George Foot Moore, *The Literature of the Old Testament*, chap. i, p. 10 f.
[3] *Leesbook over de Geref. Dogm. eerst stuck*, p. 111 n.
[4] *Ibid.*, p. 111 f; cf. Du Moulin, *Bouclier de la Foi*, sect. iv.
[5] E. Stapfer, *La Palestine au temps de Jésus-Christ*, p. 234, n. 3. This free lance of Jewish theology was heretic enough from the Pharisaical point of view; he did not believe in the resurrection of the body (iii, 24).

the German critic draws the unexpected conclusion that this latter text was not an authority for Jesus and that a declaration as formal as that of Matthew (5:18)[1] must not be interpreted too strictly. As if, in the presence of the words reported by the Evangelist, one could infer from the laxity of the author of the Book of Jubilees in regard to the Law, a laxity on the part of our Lord concerning the same subject.

Besides, how can it be seriously disputed that in the 1st century, the text not only of the Pentateuch but also of the books of the Bible, was considered sacred? The testimony of Flavius Josephus on this point is explicit: "No one has dared to add anything to it, to take anything from it, or to change it in any way."[2] The testimony, subject to correction for the past, is unexceptionable for the period at which the author lived. We know, moreover, that Rabbi Akiba—far more important for the history of the canon than the author of the Book of Jubilees, of whom it is not known whether he lived under the Asmonaeans, after Herod, or very much later—attached the greatest importance to the minutest details in regard to the orthography of the Biblical text, which proves that for him this text was sacred.

As they cannot find their notion of the canon in Josephus, or in the New Testament, the critics will have it that the idea of the canon, in the sense in which we understand it, must be foreign to the 1st century. Michel Nicolas consents to see in the idea of a Torah something approaching it, and he finds in the fact that this term is reserved for the Pentateuch the proof that there was not, properly speaking, any canon of the Old Testament other than the first five books of the Bible. Cornill is better informed; he knows that "the Old Testament, in its entirety, is sometimes called the Torah, after this essential part" and that this manner of expressing oneself is to be found in the New Testament itself. In several places, fragments drawn from the second and third parts of the present Jewish canon are quoted as being taken from the Torah, from the Law[3] (e.g., Psalm 82:6 in John 10:34; Psalm 32:19 and 69:5 in John 15:25; Isaiah 28:11, 12 in 1 Corinthians 14:21; cf. John 12:34).

These texts prove clearly that, for Paul and the author of the Fourth Gospel, certain words taken from the collection of prophets and hagiographs had the same evidential, canonical and normative value as the words taken from the Pentateuch. Torah

---

[1] Cornill, op. cit., 48, 3.
[2] Cont. Ap., i, 8.
[3] Michel Nicholas, article Canon de l'Ancien Testament in Lichtenberger, Encyclopédie des Sciences religieuses; Cornill, op. cit., 48, 3.

signifies divinely normative instruction, law; and this is precisely what the authentic Protestant dogmatic understands by canonical. It would appear that in some quarters the exact opposite is believed to be the case.[1]

Facts being what they are, one is obliged to recognize that a canon existed, in the sense in which we understand it, at the time of Josephus. But, as the question has been put badly, there is no doubt that all that we ask will be conceded.

It is admitted that, according to the only contemporary Jewish testimony, the famous half page of Josephus, our term "canonical" means that these books were "rightly believed to be divine dogmas"; that they formed the actual Jewish canon; that they constituted a practically closed collection owing to the impossibility of tracing the exact succession of the prophets beyond the period which follows the reign of Xerxes; that "a common opinion was held on this subject, a firm practice of the spiritual life of the godly in Israel" and that the criterion of canonicity was inspiration. In this matter the religious authority could do no more than recognize this general sentiment. [2]

The text of Josephus is so clear that less than this could not be conceded. But we repeat, no more is asked. Listen to Gravenmeijer who could not have had Cornill's admission in mind since he wrote several years before the latter: "The sacred collection of divine Scriptures grew little by little and the canon of the Old Testament was not made but became such. Under divine direction it was gradually formed by the addition of writings which were made manifest as divine by their very contents."[3]

But, it is insisted, this practically closed canon in fact "was not at all exclusive of other collections, of other books which might come from God. Thus the modern idea of a closed, completed, definitive canon did not exist in the 1st century".[4]

Certainly, and this is the thesis of the classical Protestant orthodoxy and of the Catholic Churches of East'and West. They agree in teaching that God had left the door open for the addition of a second collection of canonical books, namely, those of the New Testament, which He intended to give shortly to His Church. It is strange that neo-Protestants do not realize

---

[1] Cornill, *op. cit.*, p. 294 f. König himself makes the same mistake, vide *Kanon und Apocryphen*, Gütersloh, 1917, pp. 27–31, 37 ff.

[2] Cornill, *op. cit.*, 48, 7.

[3] *Op. cit., eerst. stuk*, p. 47.

[4] E. Stapfer, *La Palestine au temps de Jésus-Christ*, p. 344. On the contrary we notice that Oskar Holzmann (*Neutestamentzeitgeschichte*, p. 193) admits that Paul at least knew the Scripture as something complete (*Abgeschlossenes*), as a unique whole, and that it may be considered that at the beginning of our era the canon of the Old Testament existed in its entirety.

that if our Lord and His Apostles had entertained the notion of a closed canon in the absolute sense of the term, according to the "modern conception", they would have rendered impossible faith in the divine authority of the New Testament.

Prejudice sometimes leads critics of the new school to affirm hastily "facts" which are manifestly false and sometimes to present affirmations without a shred of serious proof as facts beyond all cavil. Thus, Stapfer can calmly declare: "Josephus says positively that the twenty-two sacred books were not all equally honoured".[1]

Now, if reference is made to the text of the Jewish historian, it will be seen at once that he is not speaking of the twenty-two sacred books at all; he had finished enumerating them with the simple statement: "But the four which remain contain hymns to God and examples of life for men." Then he adds that since the time of Artaxerxes all events have been put on record but that the writings which relate them are not worthy of the same confidence as those which preceded them, because the succession of the prophets is uncertain.

This is merely a lapse on the part of the learned author, but it is significant: for a brief instant the historian has effaced himself in order to give place to the controversialist. As an example of "facts" without proof presented as certain and admitted by everybody, we may mention the existence of the enlarged canon of the Septuagint and its admission by the Christian Church for which it was "in the earliest period her only Bible".[2]

Now we shall show later that there is literally no proof at all of the existence of the famous Alexandrian canon among the Jews of the 1st century or subsequently. We will return to this point. But when we are told without reserve that this was the sole Bible of the Church during the earliest centuries, we are indeed astonished. Certainly, the Septuagint version was the Bible of the apostolic Church outside Palestine, as it was that of Philo and Josephus. But the canon was something quite different. The

---

[1] *La Palestine au temps de Jésus-Christ*, p. 344, puts the inspiration of Moses above that of the other sacred authors. But we do not see that he can make a distinction between them. It was in the 18th century of the Christian era that Jewish theology formed a strict theory of the three decreasing degrees of inspiration corresponding to the three divisions of the canon. Stapfer appears to us to have confused the order of the times. Neither the New Testament, nor Josephus, nor even Philo, we believe, had any knowledge of these three degrees of inspiration. *Vide* W. J. Beecher, *The Alleged Triple Canon of the Old Testament*, in the *Journal of Biblical Literature*, 1896. The reasons alleged by König, *loc. cit.*, appear to us feeble in the extreme.

[2] Cornill, *op. cit.*, 48a, 2: We cite Cornill merely because we happen to have opened him at this page, but we could have quoted Moore or Stapfer to the same purpose. It is a view held by them all.

Apocrypha are never quoted by these authors and there is no reason to believe that these books formed part of the Bible of the Hellenistic Jews.

As for suggesting that the so-called Alexandrian canon was the universal Bible of the Christian Church immediately after the apostolic period, this is to take something for granted which has no support in fact. The Alexandrian canon was so far from being the Bible of the whole Church that Cyril of Jerusalem in his fourth catechesis not only forbids the reading of the Apocrypha and declares expressly that in so doing he is following the tradition of "the apostles and ancient bishops". Athanasius, who must be regarded as a competent witness, gives evidence to the same effect as Cyril.[1]

In brief, there was "Scripture", a canon of the Old Testament, in the sense of the classical Reformed dogmatics, in the time of our Lord and his apostles. This was the Palestinian canon. It was recognized as such by the New Testament, which is our authority on the subject. Consequently, in receiving it, we are not in the least degree showing our dependence on the Talmud.

The fact of the existence of the canon of the Old Testament is not denied by learned Catholics, but they draw from the indications in the New Testament concerning the canon of the Old Testament other conclusions than those drawn by Protestants, and they follow another tradition than theirs. The canon of the Old Testament accepted by Rome consequently contains the Apocrypha which pass for having formed part of the Alexandrian canon. Although the Council of Trent made no distinction between these writings and those of the Hebrew canon, the habit of calling them deutero-canonical is widespread among Roman Catholic exegetes.

Protestants, on the other hand, stand by the Hebrew canon which, moreover, is universally acknowledged to have been that of Jerome. Calvin was strictly consistent in the application of the principle that the Palestinian canon should be followed. Luther less so; for example, he disputed the canonicity of the Book of Esther.

Now, if Luther and the Reformers decided in favour of the Palestinian canon, it was by no arbitrary choice. They found themselves confronted by two contradictory traditions in the Catholic Church. The fathers and doctors who were ignorant of

[1] Beside these (namely, the books of the Hebrew canon, a list of which he has just given), there are still other non-canonical books of the Old Testament, which are not read except to the catechumens: the Wisdom of Solomon, Ecclesiasticus, Judith and Tobit—Athanasius *Synopsis* quoted by Du Moulin (Molinaeus), *op. laud.*, sect. VI.

the Hebrew language and of the customs of the synagogue—and these constituted the great majority—received the writings contained in Christian manuscripts from the Septuagint translation. Those who were better informed, who knew Hebrew or at least were conversant with the authorized tradition of the Jews, maintained the Hebrew canon. Melito of Sardis, Origen and Athanasius, in the East; Jerome, the learned Hebraist, who gave the Church his admirable translation known as the Vulgate, in the West—these, among others, were in the latter category. The Council of Laodicea also gives us a list agreeing with that of the Jews of the present day, but we will not insist on this, since the authenticity of canon 60 of this synod is disputed. Even if it is not authentic, however, the canon attests the existence of a powerful tradition.

Throughout the Middle Ages [1] and even after the decision of the Council of Trent in favour of the Apocrypha,[2] there were learned Catholic doctors who maintained the tradition of Jerome, of the "Ordinary Gloss" and of the decision attributed to the Council of Laodicea. Jerome and the Gloss consider that it was through ignorance and misunderstanding that the Alexandrian Apocrypha were introduced into the canon and that this excited ridicule among the Jews.[3]

It is this consideration which led Protestants in general, and Luther first of all, to opt for the learned tradition of the Catholic Church against its popular tradition. Obviously, in controversy with the Synagogue one can only appeal to the books which it recognizes as sacred. Luther and the Protestants did not forget that in relation to Judaism, the Christian Church is a reform movement,[4] which bases itself on the Law of the sacred books as against the "tradition of the elders".

Now, when Luther, influenced no doubt by his antisemitism, rejected the Book of Esther, he was conforming to the tradition of Melito of Sardis and Athanasius, who omit this book from their Hebrew canon,[5] probably because the lists which they had received emanated from Jews who did not admit it. It is known that it was disputed, together with two other books, by the rabbis late in the 1st century and that the Jewish Synod of Jamnia pronounced in its favour. After all, Luther's mistake in

[1] *Vide* J. Basnage, *Hist. de la Religion des Églises Réformées*, 1725, vol. II, p. 459 ff.; L. Dennefeld, *Introd. à l'A. T.*, p. 213 ff.
[2] *Ibid.*, p. 215.
[3] Jerome, *Praefat. in Danielem; Gloss. ordin. praefat. de lib. canon.*, vol. I, p. 1.
[4] Luther, *Von dem Missbrauch der Messe*, zte. *Theil.*, p. 276 ff., ed. Berlin 1905; Calvin, *Inst.* IV, ii. 7.
[5] Eusebius, *Hist. Eccl.*, IV, 26, 12–14; Athanasius, *Epist. Fest.*, 309, pp. 6, 26, 1176, 1436.

this matter seems to have been that he agreed too closely with one of the most respectable traditions of primitive Christianity.

It should be added that the absence of the Book of Esther from Luther's canon does not appear to have had any appreciable effect on the development of his theology. We cannot recollect a single occasion on which this book played any part whatever in theological discussions between confessional Protestants and Catholics. On other grounds, however, there is good cause for gratitude that it did eventually receive recognition from the Churches as canonical.

But we hasten to deal with the reproach which has been made against us of having preferred the canon of the rabbis to that of Christ and the apostolic Church. We consider that there is scarcely a question between us and Rome in which the historical evidence is clearer than it is here.

In order to prove that our Lord and His Apostles made use of the Alexandrian canon—which would thus have existed in the 1st century of our era—certain texts of the Gospels and Epistles are cited, which show that Jesus, and more particularly Paul, were familiar with certain of the writings which Protestants to-day qualify as apocryphal and which Catholics have raised to the rank of deutero-canonical.[1]

Let us suppose that all these texts contain allusions or even quotations expressly taken from the Apocrypha. This would signify nothing against us. We are not concerned to prove that all the Apocrypha were unknown, as devotional literature, by the Jews of the 1st century in Palestine. We do not dispute that on occasion the first Christians or the Lord Himself, in their discourses or hortatory epistles, may have used expressions borrowed from the Apocrypha, which their memory recalled because they were so familiar with them. The French Reformed Church in the Confession of La Rochelle declares that these books are "useful", although unsuitable as a foundation for any article of faith. The 39 Articles of the Anglican Church maintain the same dogmatic reserve, while admitting that the Church reads them in public "for example of life and manners". The Belgica takes the same position.[2]

---

[1] Here is a list of these texts taken from the *Introduction à l'Ancien Testament* of Dennefeld, professor at the Faculty of Catholic Theology, Strasbourg, p. 208: Allusions to Wisdom: Matt. 27: 39–42; Rom. 1: 20–34; 9:21; Eph. 6: 13–17; Heb. 1:3; 1 Peter 1:6–7; to Ecclus.; Matt. 6:14; to II Mac.; Heb. 2:26–35; to Judith; 1 Cor. 2:10. The writer claims that these texts prove the deutero-canonica to have been known in Palestine, which is doubtless true. He adds however, that he sees in this a proof that they were recognized as having authority. Utility, no doubt, but not authority. He says, besides, that the Palestinian Jews had already rejected them from their canon.

[2] *Conf. Gall.*, art. IV; *Conf. Angl.*, art. VI; *Conf. Belg.*, art. VI.

But all this is beside the point. It is a question of ascertaining whether Jesus and the writers of the New Testament considered these writings as canonical, that is to say, as furnishing authority for matters of faith. Now, none of these alleged quotations or allusions is preceded by the formula: "It is written" (=it is divinely prescribed). One cannot therefore argue from their presence to their canonicity. There are citations from pagan poets and from the Book of Enoch in the collection of books of the New Testament. This does not necessarily signify that the works from which they are drawn were regarded as inspired.

Actually we do not find in the New Testament any list of the canonical books of the Old Testament. The sacred books of the synagogue are generally designated as "the Scriptures" and often as "the Law and the Prophets". This latter expression seems to exclude the third part of the Hebrew canon, the *ketubim* or hagiographa. But this is explained if one takes into account the fact that the writers of this third section, although not exercising the prophetic charge, were nevertheless recognized as inspired by *ruah nebuâh* by the Prophetic Spirit and that they could be considered prophets in the broad sense of the term, as Cornill admits, according to the *Seder Olam*, the Talmud and Josephus.[1]

But we know positively that, at the moment when the Gospels were written, the Jewish Bible comprised other books besides Moses and the prophets, properly so-called. In fact, according to Luke, the risen Lord began His demonstration with Moses and the prophets, showing after this that His passion had been predicted by "all the Scriptures" (Luke 24: 27). These last "Scriptures", distinct from the first two sections, can only have been the hagiographa. This authorizes us to understand "Moses, . . . the Prophets and . . . the Psalms" (verse 44) as designating the three parts of the actual Jewish canon. The third part was termed "the Psalms", because the Psalter was placed then, as now, at the head of this section. It seems to have been the usual custom to designate a section by the book with which it commenced. This explains how Matthew presents as being found in Jeremiah a quotation which he takes from Zechariah (Matthew 27: 9), and why Jeremiah is named by the same evangelist, in preference to other prophetic writers, as being one of the personalities of whom our Lord was reputed to be a possible reincarnation (Matthew 16: 14).

It is well known, indeed, that, at a certain period, certain lists placed Jeremiah at the head of the collection called to-day

[1] *Einleitung in den kanonischen Bücher des Alten Testaments*, 5th ed., p. 300.

345

the minor prophets; while the arrangement which prevailed at a later date placed Isaiah at the head, in accordance with the chronological order.[1] The Jewish historian, Josephus, bears witness to the present Jewish canon and its triple division, but with a different distribution of books.[2]

What is the order known to Jesus and the New Testament? It seems clear that we can conclude from Matthew (23:75) and Luke (11:51), compared with 2 Chronicles (24:20), that the Bible of Jesus commenced with Genesis and closed with 2 Chronicles, as do the Jewish Bibles of the present day.[3] Jesus declares that the scribes and the pharisees will be among those guilty of shedding the blood of the martyrs, of whom we read from one end of the Bible to the other (Matthew 23:27–36).

But as it so happens that the Book of Esther is one of those books which are not quoted in the New Testament, for want of an occasion, and that Athanasius does not mention it in his list; while, on the other hand, we know that it was disputed by certain rabbis, Luther cannot be accused of having raised his judgment against the authority of the New Testament, nor against the authority of a unanimous tradition, by his rejection of it.

Such are the indications which furnish us with the most ancient and the most authentic sources in favour of the Hebrew canon. On the one hand, a Catholic exegete as eminent as Podechard admits that there is no proof whatever of the existence of an Alexandrian canon in the 1st century of the Christian era. Josephus knows no dispute among the Jews on this subject. Philo, who lived at Alexandria, never quotes in all his voluminous works a single one of the apocryphal books forming part of the supplementary canon admitted by the Council of Trent.[4]

The only manuscripts of the Septuagint which contain them, together with others not admitted by the Church of Rome herself, are Christian manuscripts of the 4th century.[5] This is insufficient to give us any information concerning a supposed canon of the Septuagint of the 1st century. It may be argued that

[1] *Vide* the *beraïtha* recorded in the treatise *Babhâbathrâ*, f. 14b.

[2] *Cont. Ap.*, i, 8.

[3] *Vide* for Matthew, F. W. Grosheide, *Het Heilig Evang. volg. Matth., in loco;* for Luke, Godet *Comm., in loco;* E. König, *op. cit.*, p. 12 f.

[4] It is retorted that neither does he quote certain books which belong to the undisputed canon. But this argument leads nowhere. No one doubts that Philo admitted the same books as the Palestinians. It is a question of proving the existence of an Alexandrian canon. This time his silence which coincides, in fact, with that of the New Testament and of Josephus deprives the advocates of the pretended Alexandrian canon of a positive proof, which is necessary to their case.

[5] *Vide* App. XIV, p. 398, for E. Podechard's judicious remarks in *Revue des Sciences Religieuses*, July 1930, p. 498 ff.

Greek-speaking Christians should have been in a good position to know what was the canon of the Hellenistic Jews. Actually nothing is less certain. They may have known in a general sense that these Jews, naturally enough, valued their own productions highly, and starting with the obvious principle that the Synagogue should be judged by its own sacred writings may have drawn a false conclusion from it. When one knows how often in our own days religious communities living side by side are completely ignorant of one another, the possibility of such a misunderstanding need not surprise us. Moreover, the Greek Fathers who lived at Alexandria, like Athanasius and Gregory Nazianzen, kept exclusively to the ancient Hebrew canon.

An argument in favour of the existence of the canon of the Septuagint among the Jews has been drawn from the fact that the Falashas admit it. But these people are degenerate Egyptian Jews abysmally ignorant, who received their Bible from an Abyssinian Christian monk[1] and moreover, they are a far cry from the 1st century of our era.[2]

We conclude that Protestants, who cannot admit the infallibility of one part of the Catholic tradition discordant with the other, without serious historical proofs, have no reason to admit any canon of the Old Testament other than the one whose existence is attested by the authoritative documents.

It is from the New Testament itself that they take the canon of the Old; it is from Christ that they have learnt to acknowledge its divine origin. Can our Catholic brethren deny that, in bowing before Christ's authority, we are following an impulse which comes from the Spirit of God?

In exhorting the faithful to accept as canonical in the Old Testament only those books and all those books admitted by the Synagogue, we are not engaging them in researches beyond the powers of the majority. The Palestinian canon is substantially well established and the New Testament teaches us that to the Jews have been committed "the oracles of God" (Romans 3 : 2). They are thus competent to show them to us, even as the Christian Church is competent to show us its own sacred writings.

Here again, let common sense speak. The Scriptures of the New Testament approve it and the Holy Spirit seals this approbation in our hearts and minds.

[1] A certain Qozmos, according to a document dated 1382–90, published recently, *vide* C. Conti Rossi, *Appunti di storia et litteratura falasola* in *Revista degli studi orientali*, VIII, p. 567 ff. and S. Feist. *Stammeskunde der Juden*, Hinrichs, Leipzig, 1925, p. 86 f.

[2] Moreover, the Falashas recognize only the Pentateuch as strictly canonical, *vide* E. König, *Kanon und Apocryphen*, p. 44.

CHAPTER 12

THE UNITY OF THE CHURCH AND THE FORMAL PRINCIPLE OF PROTESTANTISM

It is admitted by Catholics that the superiority of their principle which places the authority of the representative Church above that of Scripture does not consist in the fact that it prevents the appearance of sects. History records that condemnations pronounced by Rome or by oecumenical councils have often been followed by the birth of schisms and heresies. What the champions of Rome maintain, more modestly, is that their principle prevents ecclesiastical divisions in the body constituted by those who accept it. The Protestant principle, on the other hand, when it is applied, cannot fail to produce divisions between the Church which condemns in the name of Scripture, and those whom she condemns, who base themselves equally on the same authority of Scripture.

The fact is that whether we are Catholics or Protestants or Modernists, we are all confronted by a problem far more complicated than our Roman brethren would appear to think. The problem which calls for a solution is how to safeguard order in the Church under the authority of God, and at the same time the liberty of the individual Christian conscience, of which God alone is Master.

Catholicism, including less consistent forms of this Christian type than Rome, thinks only of the rights of the religious society. It desires, above all things, to maintain order in the Church. It has a very clear conscience concerning one side of the truth, and for this it deserves commendation. It does not intend that an arbitrary individual shall impose his tyranny on the faithful or that they shall be left to the mercy of his caprice.

Meanwhile, it altogether loses sight of the other element of the truth: the right of the individual conscience. Thus, it falls into the opposite extreme to that which attracts neo-Protestantism. The latter, in principle, though not always in practice, has scarcely any thought except for the rights of the individual, and, in its efforts to safeguard them, it loses sight of the essential conditions of religious social life.

When Catholicism makes the spiritual relations of the believer with Christ to depend on his submission to the prelates of the representative Church, in order to maintain the element of truth it desires to preserve, it applies a method fatal alike to the life of the Church and to the peace of the individual conscience.

As rupture with the ecclesiastical authority imperils the salvation of the soul of the refractory person, even if he is inwardly convinced of being faithful to the Word of God in resisting, it seems well, from the Catholic point of view, that the occasion of a refusal of obedience should be psychologically more difficult, because more dangerous, and, consequently, more rare. In actual fact, schisms are infrequent and sects comparatively few in Catholicism. They are there all the same, and their quality makes up in gravity for whatever satisfaction may be derived from a consideration of their quantity.

The most usual result of schism in Catholicism is that those who remain true to its formal principle make an exclusive claim to the title of Church, excommunicate the refractory individuals and hurl anathemas at all who profess opinions contrary to the received doctrine.

Decisions of the representative Church in matters of faith being irreformable, schism when it takes place can only be healed by the total and unconditional surrender of those who have been cut off from the society which believes itself alone to be the universal Church. This renders appeasement of doubtful value.

But the principle itself is such that it never allows one to know, with the certainty of divine faith excluding the free investigation of the individual, that it is indeed the Church which has spoken. The proof of this lies in the fact that Roman Catholics are not the only ones to make use of this principle. There are the Eastern Orthodox, to say nothing of other communions, oriental and African. There are the Anglo-Catholics, the Old Catholics, the Jansenists. Who can tell, in the name of a criterion. accepted by all "Catholics", whether the Vatican Council was a truly oecumenical council or not?

From this, it follows that those among the "Catholics" who recognize the infallibility of the pope, speaking *ex cathedra*, can only do so through prejudice of birth or of ecclesiastical affiliation unless they appeal to their own private judgment, which, we are assured, is always fallible. And when they have concluded in favour of the legitimacy of the council, at the cost of some strain on their principles, they are not even at the end of their difficulties. They still lack an infallible interpretation of the meaning of *ex cathedra* pronouncements "in matters of faith and morals".

349

Further, the Catholic system which has been conceived in order to maintain absolute doctrinal unity, cannot even realize that, except in an administrative and external manner, and by dint of a ruinous tolerance in favour of the *ecclesia discens*. This system of guaranteeing the faith has ended by itself taking precedence over the faith which it is a question of guaranteeing. There are scarcely any Catholics, apart from professional theologians, who are really interested in doctrine. For the great majority of the faithful, and for many of the clergy also, dogmas are hardly more than abstract formulas to be accepted with the eyes shut, without troubling about their spiritual import. There is little danger, to-day, that ordinary Catholics will divide on such questions as the Trinity, the circumincession and procession of the divine Persons, the hypostatic union and transubstantiation. But let them study questions truly vital for them, like the rights and limits of pontifical authority in political matters, and also, for the most cultured among them, matters of science and Biblical criticism, and you will hear on all sides of mental reservations, *distinguos*, even upon revolts to the point of schism, resistance claiming to be legal, and even such teratological cases as that of the theologian who, in his own name, professes the orthodox doctrines which in other works he attacks over a pseudonym. This is how the system affects private individuals.

With the teaching Church, *ecclesia docens*, the effect is quite different. Since his infallibility has been proclaimed, the pope has scarcely ventured, under *ex cathedra* conditions, to sally forth from a majestic silence, prudent and enigmatic. It is the commissions that speak, and, in case of necessity, they can always be disowned. Meanwhile, we witness an increase in condemnations, excommunications, arbitrary acts which are difficult to understand from a theological point of view, side by side with a strange toleration of scepticism in high places. In brief, we observe a general policy which tends to create the impression that the Church of Rome is a system of government rather than a religion.

The intransigence, the apparent immutability and external unity which Rome presents, may indeed impress many souls who are weary, with good reason, of the instability, the laxity, and the divisions of a certain type of Protestantism. But many of those who have been thus attracted, and who have then had a closer view of the system, seeing it no longer as a mirage created by imagination or ignorance, have been sadly disillusioned. The doubts which seize the minds of so many "born Catholics" cause them sometimes to give up all theological study, and sometimes to apostatize.

We are not condemning the men but the principle. We are well aware that, as a whole, the men are of a very different calibre spiritually from the majority of those with whom our first Reformers had to do. On the part of many Roman Catholic thinkers, firmly attached to their faith, we remark genuine efforts to understand the Protestant position. But the leaders, even when they are not concerned with policies, but with disquieted believers, are ill served by the fact that their principle leads them generally to see pride in the *non possumus* of the individual conscience.

The Church, that is to say, in actual fact, the "tradition of the elders", interpreted by authorized prelates, must always be right. Office, independently of interior submission to the Word of God and of spiritual life, provided always that the legal forms are observed, is held to guarantee the infallibility of the doctrinal decisions. From the evangelical point of view this is the heresy *par excellence*, the heresy of which Christ was a victim and which led the Jews to deicide.

In opposition to the tyranny of Rome, neo-Protestantism loudly vindicates the rights and the duties of the individual conscience. This vindication also constitutes an important, and even essential, element of evangelical truth. But, in the intoxication at the recovery of individual liberty, too often the rights and duties of the Church have been disregarded or denied. Some have gone so far as to demand that the Church should acknowledge the principle that each individual *et sentire quae velit et quae sentiat dicere*, should hold what opinion he pleased and say all that it pleased him to think.[1]

To-day, Protestantism, suffering as a result of its first excesses and their fatal consequences for the collective religious life, lacks the real vitality inherent in positive Christian faith, and has been profoundly modified, for the most part unconsciously, by the influence of the realist reaction in the theory of knowledge. In these circumstances, it is content to leave to theology the task of formulating in doctrine the results of religious experience, and to the Church the right and duty of declaring *hic et nunc* what constitutes her doctrine, which, for that matter, is always capable of improvement.

But, too often, it refuses to the Church the right of controlling the teaching of her ministers, whose individual convictions it seeks to safeguard. Regarding the idea of a confession of

---

[1] [Richard Watson (1737–1816), bishop of Llandaff, *Apology for the Bible ...
Letters . . . to Thomas Paine*, 1796, letter i, an answer to Paine's *Second Part*, 1795.]

faith, a rule of instruction, and an authoritative synod as "tyrannical", it imagines that the formation of sects may be avoided by total and uncontrolled liberty. It fails to realize, however, that to do this is tantamount to giving over the Church to complete doctrinal anarchy and abandoning the faithful to the tyranny of the pastoral will, more arbitrary and intolerable that that of the pope.

But the exigencies of reality have rendered the consistent application of the principle impossible. Deviations in a particular direction have sometimes gone so wide, either in doctrine or morals, or both, that moderate neo-Protestantism could not support them, and has had to resort to measures of repression, as instanced by the intervention of Adolf Harnack in the ecclesiastical case in which the German pastor, Jatho, was involved. Schisms and sects have thus become inevitable, and sometimes they find a certain justification in the arbitrary character of the decisions which condemned those who nevertheless well deserved censure. There is no longer, in fact, any objective rule to which one can refer. It has been suggested that the person of Christ might provide this rule, but this is impossible, seeing that the person of Christ, as understood by neo-Protestants, is no doctrinal authority, His words not being infallible. Moreover, have not some neo-Protestants even denied the historical existence of this Person, in the name of their hypercriticism?

A truly evangelical Protestantism can afford to show tolerance towards minorities which have returned to the faith of the Reformers. But such an attitude was rare in neo-Protestantism at the stage of juvenile intolerance which characterizes all movements that are growing in popularity. It was felt rather that the Church must be preserved at all costs from the contagion of obscurantism; that "science", theological and otherwise, must be defended vigorously against those who dared to dispute its "assured results." It was felt to be quite natural in those days that the "out-of-date" advocates of the supernatural, of the doctrines of grace and of the *sola fide*, should be excluded from academic chairs. If needs be, recourse could be had to the secular arm to effect this, as in the case of Adolphe Monod.

But as these "backward and obscurantist" individuals also had an individual conscience, it was inevitable that the chapel should be erected in opposition to the church and the conventicle to the temple. The sects are still with us and the reason is not difficult to understand. There were some who found it impossible to regard the system of Hegel as the last word in science, or to identify faith in indefinite progress with the

Christian eschatological hope of which it is the negation. History shows neo-Protestantism to be incapable of applying to the "backward" its principle of absolute liberty of teaching in the Church, except by ceasing to be itself and beginning to be in religious sympathy with the convictions of historical and confessional Protestantism.

Thus, it is seen that the search for a principle, the acceptance of which would assure in all cases the administrative unity of the Church, is the pursuit of a chimera. In this connection, the liberal principle is no more effective than any other. Strong convictions, from the moment that they are thought to be based on the positive results of an objective science, are probably less capable of toleration than those which regard faith and the profession of religious truth as a free gift of divine grace transcendent to reason and to scientific induction properly so-called. "There must be also heresies among you, says the Apostle" (I Corinthians 11: 19). They are bitter fruits of sin; too often, sin of the individual, obstinately attached to his own private opinion; sin also of ecclesiastical courts and tribunals, at least as often jealous of their own prerogatives.

However prejudiced one may be against Calvinism, we believe there is one reproach that can never be levelled against it: that of being chimerical. Because it is not chimerical, and because it is aware of human limitation, Calvinism confines itself to laying down a principle which renders the unity of the Church possible, provided that the Church, on the one hand, and individual Christians, on the other, confess from the heart both the distress of the Church and the misery of the Christian man.

Consider first the distress of the Church. The Church, messenger from beyond, lives in the present age which is evil, and, in the measure in which the regeneration of her members is imperfect, bears the evil within herself. Her sanctity is actual, in this sense, that the work of sanctification has even now commenced in the souls of the regenerate and that it already bears admirable fruit here and there.

But the sanctification of the Church is only virtual, eschatological, "in hope", in this sense, that not until the harvest, at the consummation of the age, will the growth of the new life achieve maturity and the tares be separated from the good grain.

The Church is saved; but, according to the Scriptures, this also is only "in hope", a hope which will not make ashamed, indeed, since it is founded on the promise of Him who is faithful and true. But it is a hope and a promise which always have reference to the age to come. While awaiting the time when she will know even as she is known, the Church neither knows nor prophesies except in a partial and fragmentary manner.

Because she has received a supernatural commission, a commission to proclaim the Gospel, she knows herself to be indefectible, infallible even, as Calvin expressly says,[1] when she proclaims the substance of that Gospel, on condition that she is unconditionally subject to the Word of God. She thus accepts and fulfils her duty of protecting the integrity of the Gospel against human falsifications, from whatever quarter they may come.

But she must be prudent in the condemnations that she pronounces, because, conscious of her own sin and misery, she confesses that the purest particular Church is never incapable of error in the disciplinary formulation of her theology.[2] If she is indeed that which she should be, the mother of the faithful, she will know how to distinguish, in the exercise of discipline, those who, though still far away, are turning towards Christ, from those who deliberately remain at a distance.

The power of the keys in the Reformed Church implies pedagogic tact and Christian love rather than juridical virtuosity.

Again, there is the misery of the Christian man. He realizes that the representative Church often represents quite another spirit than the true spirit of the Church and that she is fallible. Therefore, he has both a right and a duty to examine, by the aid of the light vouchsafed to him, whether what she teaches is in accordance with the Word of God, or not. It will not suffice to tell him that the Word is respected; he must see whether the affirmation corresponds with the reality. Cases may even occur in which he has to choose between the alternatives: Christ or the representative Church.

But, if the believer knows that even he himself is infallible as to the substance of the Gospel, in so far as he is absolutely subject to the Word of God, he must know also that he is fallible in his theology. In so far as his Church remains firmly established on the foundation which has been divinely laid, he will be aware that there is greater possibility of error in regard to secondary points on his part than on the part of men to whose faith he knows that he must render homage and who fulfil the office of their vocation in declaring that which has been given them to understand of the Word of God. As long as he is not compelled to say or to do something which his conscience, based upon the

[1] *Inst.* IV, viii. 13.
[2] *Westminster Confession*, XXV, v.

Word of God, would forbid, he ought to remain in the Church and obey her discipline.

Practice of the communion of saints by the individual implies, on Reformed principles, humility and filial love, rather than the servile sentiment of juridical obligation.

It follows that unity *in necessariis* will be less the result of the exercise of a blind discipline than the fruit of a Christian life renewed by faith, in the Church and in the individual. For Calvinism, the solution of the problem of reconciling the rights of the Church with the duties of the individual lies in the humility shown by both. As firm convictions are not invariably associated with a sufficient degree of humility and brotherly love, the empirical Church appears, even when she is faithful to Reformed principles, under the aspect of pluriformity. This is a result of sin and also of the limited character of our religious knowledge, especially when we have to pass from theory to practice.

Those who think, for example, that the Church cannot accept subsidies from the State without committing a sin, find it difficult to remain in the same administrative organization as those who hold the contrary opinion. Similarly, those who feel that only perfectly orthodox ministers should be allowed to hold ecclesiastical positions, cannot remain in the same synod as those who believe that the rôle of the orthodox in the Church is the same as that which Christ assigned to the leaven in the Gospel. No doubt we shall long have with us uneasy souls who will regard an unsociable isolation as a *sine qua non* for the preservation and purity of the faith. Others animated by a sense of the spiritual and scientific power of their cause, will seek by peaceful persuasion the conquest of positions occupied by brethren who do not yet share all their beliefs, but who, in their judgment, are moving towards the light and into a more complete comprehension of truth.

Thus, there will be separations; but, however regrettable and humiliating these may be, they will not have the gravity nor the final character of the schisms caused by the application of the Catholic principle. In empirical reality, the methods and the applications differ, but, the goal aimed at remaining the same, the spiritual unity of the Church is not irrevocably compromised.

Particular Churches, attached to the same fundamental articles of faith, preaching the same Gospel, having the same ministry, the same sacraments, and communicating in the memory of the same fathers, always leave the door open to possibilities of reconciliation, of federation, and of fruitful collaboration.

It may be asked how, according to Reformed principles, that which fallible tribunals bind and loose on earth can be bound and loosed in heaven, as our Lord intended, if it so happens that they should be mistaken and the condemned party right.

We have already replied, in principle, to this question. Decisions of ecclesiastical tribunals are sanctioned by divine authority in the sense that, so long as the honour of God is not derogated from, the discipline of the Church must be respected and attempts at revision must be pursued in accordance with regular procedure and with respect for the peace of the Churches. It should be remembered that the Roman Church herself does not claim infallibility in purely disciplinary questions submitted to her jurisdiction.

Even if the condemned party is persuaded in the internal forum of his own conscience that he has right on his side, he must nevertheless submit himself to all the censures pronounced against him, while leaving the justice of his cause in the hands of God. It will thus be seen that there is a sense in which an ecclesiastical sentence ill-founded in fact may be considered as provisionally executive, even from the invisible and heavenly point of view. Here, the sons of Rome and Calvin's children can communicate in respect of order and hope in the appeal to the infallible judge: *Domine Jesu, ad tuum tribunal appello*: Lord Jesu, to thy tribunal I appeal.

But the Reformers go further than this. They consider that a Church, even if she is faithful and, in this sense, fundamentally indefectible, may be mistaken in theological matters distinct from the basic principles and articles of faith common to the Church universal. But, as the individual knows that he is himself liable to this regrettable eventuality, he will esteem the order and unity of the Church of sufficient importance not to embitter the dispute, even if he thinks himself to be right in these secondary matters. In this way, he will show that he remains faithful to the spirit of the Reformers; that he is to be distinguished from the sectaries.

Bossuet asked how an appeal could be made from an ecclesiastical tribunal of the lowest rank to one of a higher order, and finally to the national synod, when, in regard to all these degrees, the matter had, all the time, been judged by the Word of God. It is astonishing that so able a theologian was not able to see that, all other things being equal, one may normally expect to find more light and less personal bias at a general synod than at a local council like a consistory or a colloquy.

In temporal tribunals, judging earthly matters, it is always the law of the land which is the supreme standard, as Scripture should be in ecclesiastical causes. This does not prevent there being tribunals of various degrees and a supreme court, judging in the last resort. It is not clear why this should not be so in a normally constituted Church.

The Calvinistic synthesis of the authority of the Church in matters of controversy and of individual liberty of conscience in these same matters supposes a mutual toleration in secondary articles of religion and even in the disciplinary formula of the fundamental articles. That is to say, this synthesis has for its theoretical basis the famous distinction, proposed by Calvin,[1] between the articles of faith which constitute the sum of Christianity and those which have not sufficient importance to justify a rupture of external communion.

This distinction, which common sense itself demands, is made already in Scripture, where the Apostle compares theological systems to constructions of gold, silver, precious stones, wood, hay and straw, erected on the foundation apart from which nothing can be built, namely, Jesus Christ (1 Corinthians 3: 10–15). He declares that even those who have erected structures made of fragile and perishable materials "shall be saved, yet so as by fire", providing that they have built upon a solid foundation. The same distinction is made in the Epistle to the Hebrews (6: 1).

According to these Scriptures, one may speak of fundamental articles of faith, meaning those which it is necessary to believe in order to be saved. Or, again, meaning those which must be professed explicitly by a religious community in order that it may have a right to be considered a living branch of the true Church. In this sense, we may say that the fundamental articles are those which rightly interpret the Gospel, as summarized in the words: "God so loved the world that He gave His only begotten Son, that whosoever believeth in Him should not perish, but have everlasting life" (John 3: 16). We may consider the Apostles' Creed, that of Nicaea—Constantinople and the Athanasian Symbol as the faithful expression of this Gospel. Every particular Church which preaches the Gospel forms part of Christianity and builds on the foundation which cannot be removed.

Finally, if one understands by fundamental articles the

[1] *Inst.* IV, i. 12.

articles of faith necessary not only. for the continuation of the life of the Church but also for its state of spiritual health, its normal state, we may say that these fundamental articles are contained in the Geneva catechism and the Reformed confessions in general.

We refuse the title of Christians only to those separated societies which exclude themselves from the *una sancta* by refusing to recognize in the symbols which we have mentioned the expression of the Gospel, and who commit schism through failing to acknowledge the continuity of faith of the Church through the ages. These societies, almost entirely secularized, are circles of moral and religious, sometimes even racial, culture, rather than Churches. Their theological syncretism has led them to deny the absolute character of the Christian religion and the unique sense in which Christ is the Son of God.

They are not Christian Churches in the simple and historical sense of the term. Nevertheless, we willingly acknowledge, with Jurieu,[1] whom no one will suspect of latitudinarianism, that these societies may contain true Christians, protected by their ignorance from the doctrines which are professed in them. We admit also that this ignorance may not necessarily be limited to simple believers. Invincible prejudice may be found among pastors and teachers too. The defects of their theological vocabulary may, by a miracle of grace, conceal the substance of a living and childlike faith in the most exalted sense of the word.

The definition of fundamental points that we have endeavoured to make enables us to determine, with a sufficiently scientific strictness, where is the visible Church. It does not permit us to delimit the frontiers of the invisible Church, of the mystical society composed of true Christians. Concerning this latter, one cannot say, indicating with the finger: the Church is not here, or the Church is not there. One cannot say this, because the Holy Spirit does not withhold His interior action, nor does Christ withdraw His real presence, at the precise point which a scientifically and logically fundamental formula might seem to suggest.

It may be objected that there are divergences between the Churches of the Reformation on the articles which they consider fundamental for the normal life of the Church. That is so. The formal principle of the authority of Scripture and the material principle of salvation by grace do not render impossible

---

[1] Pierre Jurieu says this positively of Arians and hypothetically of Socinians in the event of their sect becoming as widespread as the former, vide *Le vrai système de l'Église et la véritable analyse de la foi*, Dordrecht, 1786, pp. 102, 153.

the pluriformity of religious movement whose point of departure is authentically Reformed. These divergences among the daughter-churches of the Reformation are connected with the more or less logical manner in which they apply these principles and the spirit in which they are received.

Lutheranism regards as in conformity with the formal principle the right which the Church possesses of enjoining on her members all that is not absolutely contrary to the Word of God in tradition. It holds as in conformity with the material principle the co-ordination of the glory of God and the salvation of men. Dissenters and sects of Reformed type for the formal principle demand a Judaic adherence to that which is written, without tolerating any rational deduction whatsoever.

Between these extremes is the Calvinistic Reform which deduces from the formal principle that all tradition in conformity with Scripture by legitimate deduction must be preserved; that all tradition or rule of order in conformity with the spirit of Scripture may be sanctioned for practical reasons, but cannot be enjoined in the internal forum of the believer's conscience. As regards the material principle, the Calvinistic Reform deliberately subordinates the salvation of men to the *soli Deo gloria*.

Moreover, it is historically false to claim that the Churches of the Reformation have not dared to say what points were fundamentally necessary to a normal life of the Church. Their autonomous existence, their confessions of faith, and their official catechisms protest against such an accusation. The growth of sects and certain heresy trials prove that, in certain circumstances, Protestants have erred by excessive audacity rather than by prudent timidity.

In a later chapter we shall discuss the question whether the superiority of the Reformed system over the Lutheran can be established scientifically. In this case, the value of the Protestant principle, as strictly formulated, in comparison with certain exaggerations and attenuations, will be comparable to that of the Catholic principle, which must be defined scientifically by its advocates, in such a manner that the Orientals are distinguished from the Latins, and these in turn from the Old Catholics and others.

We frankly admit that sectarian Biblicism leads inevitably to endless divisions. Since its true name is Legion, like the spirit of the Gadarene demoniac, it is in direct opposition to the prayer of Christ for his disciples: "that they may be one even as we are" (John 17: 22). By this fact, it stands condemned on the very battlefield which it has chosen,-namely, Scripture. Sects, says the Apostle, are the fruit of a carnal spirit.

It is evident, however, that practical necessities impose on all religious societies, according to the time, place, and general circumstances, rules and customs that are necessarily variable. On the other hand, Scripture envisaged as a vigorous code, a fixed law, cannot be adapted to these changing needs. It is only living when the Church receives it as a principle of unlimited fruitfulness, as a spiritual rule whose applications, unceasingly modifiable in accordance with circumstances, are entrusted to the intelligent fidelity of the guardians of order in the Church.[1]

This is the condemnation of the narrow and legalistic Biblicism which characterized many of the Anglo-Saxon sects of the 18th and 19th centuries. The severe judgment that we have passed on sects must not be interpreted as implying their exclusion from the universal Church, nor even from historic Protestantism. That which is carnal, and even demoniac, in them, must not make us forget that, in other respects, however irregular their methods, they work for the conquest of souls by Jesus Christ. The majority of them firmly maintain the fundamental articles of the Christian faith, rejecting their formulation and ecclesiastical terminology only that they may cling to them with greater tenacity; moreover, as a rule, they are strongly attached to the essential doctrines of the Reformation. Even when they anathematize the Church, the latter must not cease to place the ideal unity of the mystical body of Christ above the narrowness and inconsistencies of certain of its living members.

And now how can the quality of fundamental be recognized in an article of Christian faith or practice? It is the very life of the Church which permits us to reply to this question. Since we are on the ground of confessional Protestantism, it must be understood that we take this term of faith in the sense in which the Reformers, and Calvin in particular, have acknowledged it.[1]

We do not understand by it the *fides informis* of Roman Catholic theologians, the simple intellectual assent to the teaching of the Church considered as divine revelation.[2]

We understand the term to signify the result of a hyperphysical operation of the Holy Spirit, not only enabling a sinner to receive efficaciously, without doubt, the verities revealed in Scripture, but consisting chiefly in a sure and certain knowledge of the love of God, as He has revealed it to us in Jesus Christ,

[1] *Inst.* III, ii. 557, 8, 30, 41, 42.
[2] *Vide* App. XV, p. 399.

and in the promise of the Gospel, a knowledge which is never separated from charity or hope.

This is justifying faith embracing the promise which God makes to us that He is willing to be for each one of us a Father and a Saviour. This distinction is essential if we wish to avoid disputes about words and fatal misunderstandings in speaking of faith and of justification by faith alone.

Now, in the most extended sense of the term, all that contributes immediately to favour this "confidence of the heart",[1] and to be its effective foundation, is truly fundamental.[2] Without the Word of God, without the facts affirmed in the Apostles' Creed as they are explained in the catechisms of the Reformed Churches, faith would lack that divine foundation which is intellectually necessary to it. On the other hand, if it were not actuated by charity, that sublime summary of the divine law; if it had no recourse to prayer in the spirit of the Lord, it would not be so founded that it could be recognized as living faith.

From what has been said, we conclude that the fundamental doctrines are contained in the explanations of the Creed, the Decalogue and the Lord's Prayer given by Luther's Little Catechism, the catechisms of Geneva, Heidelberg and Westminster.

The sacraments have been instituted to confirm and seal faith. Strictly speaking, faith may be living, even if it does not enjoy these aids. They are necessary, not for the *esse* but for the *bene esse* of faith. The doctrine of the sacraments is fundamental only in the restricted sense that it is necessary for the normal life of the Church. This is the reason why we do not consider that the Society of Friends must be excluded from visible catholicity.

The more a Church is conscious that its teaching provides faith, faith in the sense of the Reformers with a divinely certain foundation for the intellect and for the heart, the more it will be conscious of being built upon the true foundation. The more the believer proves in his soul that the teaching which his Church dispenses to him, furnishes his faith with an unshakable foundation and favours its exercise, the more he will venerate this Church as a spiritual mother and will be resolved to remain in her communion, notwithstanding the more or less evident imperfection of her teaching upon nice points of theology, which has no direct relation to that which forms the basis of his confidence in the love of God, and that which gives life to that confidence.

---

[1] *Inst.* III, ii. 7, 8, 30, 41, 42.   [2] *Geneva Catechism*, XVIII, i.

From what has been said it will be seen that we were right in maintaining that the Protestant sects and the ecclesiastical divisions of Reformed Christianity do not necessarily proceed from a faithful and intelligent application of the formal principle of the authority of Scripture. More often than not, they spring from lack of a sense of proportion, which leads men to raise to the rank of an *articulus stantis vel cadentis ecclesiae*, of a dogma necessary to the very existence of the Church, some exegetical interpretation having no vital quality at all.

In this way Protestant separatism links up with Catholic separatism. Both are united in denying, here in practice, there in theory, the legitimacy of the distinction laid down by Calvin, between the fundamental and secondary articles of the faith.

But the imperfect application of the formal principle of the authority of Scripture does not prevent this principle, in the expression given to it by Calvinism, from presenting an undeniable superiority to the Catholic and neo-Protestant principles. Catholicism and neo-Protestantism stand opposed one to another in a sterile and irreducible opposition. The one has no place except for the authority of the representative Church; the other takes into account only the liberty of the individual conscience. This superiority arises, therefore, from the fact that Calvinism integrates the elements of truth contained in the two others. As it is the most general expression and synthesis of these truths, it places us on a higher spiritual plane.

CHAPTER 13

THE FORMAL AUTHORITY OF SCRIPTURE A PRIMARY PRINCIPLE IN THEOLOGY

The formal principle of the divine authority of Scripture bears the same relation to theological thinking as the leading principles of understanding do to thinking in general. That is not the judgment of catholicism and positivism. According to both, Protestantism in setting up this principle, has plunged into a subjectivism so complete that henceforth it can seek the rule of its theology only in the individual conscience identified with divine revelation.

It is a fact that, at the extreme left of Protestant dogmatic thinking, this conclusion of the Catholic controversialist is readily accepted. Confessional Protestantism is taxed with inconsistency in this respect. One must choose, we are told, between the internal authority of the testimony of the Holy Spirit and the external and formal authority of the sacred text; between the religion of the Spirit and one religion of the letter among many others. Castellio was the true father of Protestantism, while Calvin remained a medieval thinker! The former realized that the seat of authority could not be other than the ego, and that authority itself could not be other than the religious consciousness of the individual.

"He relied only on the illumination of the Holy Spirit to reveal the true sense of that which had been previously dictated to the sacred writers. . . . But this inspiration of the Holy Spirit was confounded by him with that of the conscience; these revelations made to the lowly are nothing else but the intuitions of a moral and religious sense fortified by meditation".[1]

Thus, revelation becomes a subjective religious aspiration sharpened by the human activity of meditation: the voice of conscience and of the Holy Spirit together form one sole and identical modality of the moral sense. But one could not remain static on a pathway as slippery as this. It is only too evident that individual consciences do not reach the same conclusions in regard to what they agree to acknowledge as religious truth. Moreover, some of them are led by the relentless force of logic

---

[1] F. Buisson, *Sébastien Castellion*, I, 314; cf. 201.

to place religion on a plane in which the question of truth and error no longer corresponds to the reality which it is itself concerned with creating.

According to this view, Christianity is not a doctrine but a person: the Person of Jesus. Or, perhaps one ought to say, the experience of Jesus reproducing itself in those who place themselves in a religious attitude similar to His. Jesus is still the Christ in the sense that He has realized the ideal of the religious life and that He has also shown us the way. The theological ideas which He shared with the men of his time matter little. The essential thing is that He was the ideal religious man. Now, we have a religious nature, even as we have aesthetic, moral, and scientific instincts. If we do not wish to atrophy our nature but, on the contrary, wish to develop all our spiritual potentialities, we must cultivate our religious instinct; and how can we do this better than by imitating Jesus?

As for our theological ideas, we know that they are symbols, which it is probably impossible to discard altogether, if only for sociological reasons. Let us construe them, therefore, in such a manner that they may be harmonized with the culture of our time and environment, and that they may favour the development of our religious life, knowing well that they can teach us nothing concerning that unknowable and inco-ordinable which we call God.[1]

Thus, in order to preserve the value that is called religion, it is admitted that negative and irreligious philosophy was right in making a void in the heavens and silence in the intellect. It would seem that, in order to live, we must renounce the supreme reason for living, which is God, the living and the true. We do not deny the sincerity, often passionate sincerity, of this apologetic adventure, but we would ask what can be the meaning of the intensive culture of a personality destined soon to be dissolved in the unconsciousness of death. We would ask why one should believe in his religious instinct, as in all other instincts besides, if not for the motive of believing that it is a gift of the living God who promises victory over death and who can neither deceive nor be deceived. Why should one labour or make any effort at all for what, after all, is nothing?

If there is nothing, the last word of wisdom is not the painful culture of a vain desire and an unattainable ideal, but the total renunciation of all activity. Thus, in fact, the authentic Messiah would not be Jesus but the Buddha. In the final analysis, this

[1] We have tried to give a fair summary of the religious agnosticism of J. J. Gourd and his disciple Trial.

apologetic, which sets out to salvage what is of value in Christianity, arrives logically at Buddhism.

Religious psychologism is not only disastrous in its consequences; it is contradictory, in its inmost essence. It tells us that the religious question is not one of truth, and that a religious doctrine is neither true nor false, but a sentiment useful or otherwise. Meanwhile, it presents itself as true, but if that could be substantiated, it would be its only merit. We have shown that, actually, this theory is suicidal to Christianity. Moreover, it cannot be true, since it is itself a religious doctrine and we have been told that all religious doctrine is outside the plane in which one engages in combat between truth and error.

Perhaps it is not a religious doctrine. It must, then, be a philosophical doctrine concerning the fact of religion. It is just this, we believe, which is at the bottom of the thought of its advocates. And in this case they are right indeed, for it is scarcely possible to conceive one that could be more alien to the religion of the Prophet of Nazareth who is presented to us as the ideal type of the *homo religiosus*.

Nothing is gained, however, by taking refuge in this rather subtle distinction. We have shown that every immanentist philosophy is enclosed in a vicious circle and that its basis is chimerical. If the laws of thought are not established by God, whose veracity is originative and constitutive of reality and of its legitimate representation, there can be no distinction between truth and error. But if these laws are of divine origin we can distinguish between religious truth and irreligious error. In either case, the theory in question is beside the mark.

Like all immanentist philosophical doctrines, it can, of course, try to explain the religiosity of man from its own point of view: but it is incapable of giving an account of religion, the apperception of that transubjective reality which is God.

Itself an emanation from man, subjectivist agnosticism leaves man in the solitude of an effort which makes him fall back upon himself. If God is not the *principium essendi*, the principle of being in theology; if a Word proceeding from Him to tell us on what conditions we can be united to Him does not constitute its essence and its basis, then theology and the religion of which theology is the science are mere luxuries for the leisured, like art or high literary culture.

They are not even a form of wisdom, for it is contrary to practical reason—and, at the same time, supremely irreligious— to place one's entire reliance on a reality which is not the absolute being in the order of truth; which is not the God whose knowledge is originative and constitutive of reality.

The principle of radical subjectivism cannot be a principle of theology, for it would leave us only a choice between two impossibilities: either to maintain, with the moderates, that there is such a thing as a religious verity, while declaring that one cannot be certain of having ever encountered it; or to deny that there can be any question of truth in spiritual matters, and to attempt, as it were, to cultivate the spiritual life *in vacuo*.

At the opposite pole to radical subjectivism stands Catholicism, which would set up a not less absolute objectivism in the shape of the infallible Church or the Pope speaking *ex cathedra*, whose authority guarantees to us that God has spoken in the Scriptures,[1] that the list of writings which compose it is correct, and that the sense attached to the divine Word is the true interpretation. Every precaution is taken against the vagaries of a private judgment let loose by subjectivism.

The difficulty is that this objectivism is a *pium desiderium* rather than an accomplished fact. We must still take into account the subject who believes in the Church's teaching, because God has revealed it to this concrete entity which calls itself the Catholic Church. "An authority", says Claude, "can decide nothing until it is accepted". Now, it is the subject who accepts, and he can only do so by virtue of a decision of his own private judgment—unless, with the Reformers, we are prepared to deny that the subject who gives his assent on the faith of the divine authority is acting on his own private judgment.

Again, does the authority of God make itself understood outside the subject, in the Church, in the Scripture, or in the subject, by an inner light which persuades him to believe? In the first case, the subject cannot make his faith rest only on the motives of credibility, for then it would be a *fides humana*, and we should have to fall back on private judgment once more. Nor can he decide, without reason, to believe the Church on her mere word, for the question at issue is precisely how to know that it is God who is speaking, whether by the Church, or the Scripture, or by both, and on what grounds He is to be believed.

Suarez[2] admitted the difficulties of the situation, without being able to deal with them effectively: the subject believes

[1] A. Pighius, *Hierarchiae eccles. assert.*, Col. 1551, I, ii, fol. 11b: *Omnis ergo quae nunc apud nos est scripturarum auctoritas, ab ecclesiae auctoritate dependet necessario.*
[2] [Francisco Suarez (1548–1617), Jesuit theologian.]

the Scriptures, which teach him the infallibility of the Church, because it is revealed; and in like manner he believes that the Scriptures are revealed, because she says so.

Nor is De Lugo[1] in a happier position, for he returns by a circuitous route, to the view held by Canus which Suarez criticized because it savoured too much of the *testimonium Spiritus sancti* of Calvin. Lugo admits that the act by which the subject acknowledges that divine revelation has been given is not determined by divine attestation but by the immediate intuition of the divinity of this revelation. While this intuition is supernatural, it cannot properly be called faith, for the latter always implies that something is accepted as true through reliance on testimony. And thus we arrive at the *instinctus specialis*[2] of Canus, who, unlike Calvin, however, does not inform us on what he bases the faith in this divine testimony.

The Catholic principle cannot be the principle of theology, because it fails to attain what it seeks, namely, the complete dependence of the subject on the Church; and because, contrary to its aim, it ends in the "authority of the Holy Spirit", which cannot henceforth be denounced as fanatical illuminism when it is invoked by Calvinists.

As a consequence of having placed the Church above Scripture, Rome has ended by the practical apotheosis of the man of the Vatican. Considered under this aspect, the system tends to dechristianize itself, and Christian souls find it difficult to breathe the atmosphere of a sanctuary which rather resembles that of a tomb. On the one hand, Christian liberty is suppressed. On the other, there is something worse still. Neo-Protestantism bounds forth with the fervour of youth towards the broad open spaces, but in its progress the faith is overthrown. Neo-Protestantism, whose original intentions sounded so well, has had the painful experience of witnessing, in the name of a strict application of its principles, and from within its own ranks, the rise of desperate denials of the reality of God, the existence of Jesus Christ, the life beyond the tomb—denials which empty theology of its substance and the sanctuary of its worshippers. Happily, it is true that the majority of neo-Protestant theologians receive help from God which raises them above their false principles and which places them in communion with the Christ who speaks with authority in the New Testament. But we see where the principle may lead us and have no wish to

---

[1] [Juan de Lugo (1583–1603), cardinal, Jesuit theologian.]
[2] Canus in H. Bavinck, *Geref. Dog.*, I, p. 623 (Melchior Cano, 1520–60, Dominican theologian).

enter upon the hazards of a voyage of discovery with no other guide than the uncertainties of private judgment.

The acceptance, on divine authority, of the canonicity of the New Testament, as God presents it to us through the hand of the Church, is the only way in which the Holy Spirit directs us, after having enabled us to recognize His existence. This is the only solution that remains. Thus, our faith, freed from the servitude of men, feels itself to be free with the liberty promised to whoever shall follow Christ.

It cannot, therefore, be truly said that orthodox Protestantism is a first step towards subjectivist individualism, for its subjectivism is counterbalanced by the authority of Scripture.

In accepting the formal authority of this Holy Scripture, acknowledged by all orthodox Churches, the Reformed Christian starts with a fact as objective and social as possible, namely, the agreement of the Church with his consent. On the other hand, it cannot be claimed that this suppresses the individual by subjecting him to an external and mechanical conformity, for it is in the individual soul that God indwelling—*quid interius Deo?*—and not the religious society, makes the need for the canon to be felt, and gives due weight to the marks of divinity which manifest themselves in it.

Individualist subjectivism, however, is to be found in the will which presides over the affirmation that it is this Church, this council, this tradition, rather than the others, which is infallible. Social conformity is to be found in the authority attributed to the individual judgment (reason, sensibility, moral consciousness) which in the vast majority of average persons is no more than the unconscious echo of the imperatives dictated by the common public opinion and environment with which they are surrounded. He who receives the authority of the Word contained in the New Testament knows quite well that he is conforming himself to a public opinion, one which owes its origin to a protest against social authority, made near Golgotha, in the garden of Joseph of Arimathaea; which held sway in the catacombs, and, later, in the "Desert"; which fought in the arenas of Rome, and rowed in the galleys of France. He knows, too, that this opinion finds its adequate expression and its canonical rule in the New Testament; also that he is an integral part of a society called the Church, and that he would be nothing spiritually unless he had been brought forth by this mother of the faithful.

But he knows also that his opinion is something more than mere opinion; that it is faith, because it takes its stand on One who is above the Church and above himself; who judges both him and the Church. He does not place his confidence in the representative Church or in himself. He believes in the Word which God addresses both to him and to the Church and which manifests itself as divine by the fact that, when proclaimed, it opposes collective tyranny everywhere and at all points, and because it liberates from every authority, civil or religious, which would claim to bind the conscience or dominate the mind.

In this way, it seems that there are only two possibilities for individuals, as well as for religious societies: opinion or faith; the human autonomy of the representative Church or of the individual, together with, as a consequence, the reign of the human will or the sovereignty of God, Lord of the Church and of the individual conscience, exercising His royal authority by His Word and by His Spirit.

The canonical authority of Scripture is the condition of faith and liberty. A faith which does not base itself upon God is not faith; a liberty which does not find its charter in the Word of God is not more than an illusion of the mind, a dupe of social convention, masquerading under the cloak of pretended psychological spontaneity. "Where the Spirit of the Lord is, there is liberty" (2 Corinthians 3 : 17), and there only. "If ye continue in My word," says Christ, "ye shall know the truth and the truth shall make you free" (John 8 : 31, 32).

We see, then, that religious subjectivism and Catholic social authoritarianism, each in its own way, bears powerful testimony to the reality of the fact that God reveals His presence and His activity in the mind of the individual and in the social body of the Church. But each of these two opposing tendencies is concerned with a single aspect of the truth only, the one tending to anarchy, the other to tyranny; and when the disciple of Jesus Christ becomes aware of these two abysses he is directed by the Holy Spirit towards the Reformed principle of the authority of Scripture.

In the preceding pages, we have endeavoured to make it plain that the two exclusive tendencies in question, already condemned by experience, are scientifically disqualified as principles, since, far from being certain in themselves, they lead to certain impossible positions, contain internal contradictions, or else eventually arrive at the very Reformed principle which they set out to avoid.

We have not asked our opponents to prove their respective principles. Such a demand would have been unreasonable. The term "principle" connotes something incapable of demonstration, having in itself its title to credence, beyond which one cannot go and which may serve as a starting-point for every proof. But it was legitimate to attempt to show that what were proposed as principles, the autonomy of the individual or the sovereignty of the representative Church, cannot be raised to this rank except by an arbitrary decision and do not contain in themselves the qualities which one should expect to find in a principle.

For our part, we do not claim to be able to prove the external principle of the Reformation, which is the authority of Scripture, nor its internal principle, which is the testimony of the Holy Spirit, affirmed in and by faith. But we can try to show, as against our critics, that our principles have the same character of necessity and autopisty, of evidence *sui generis*, as sensorial evidence or the evidence of the principles of reason, although upon another plane. It is legitimate also that we should be asked to show that they do not terminate in the radical subjectivism with which Rome reproaches us, nor in the ecclesiastical authoritarianism imputed to us by the protagonists of the "free religion of the spirit".

With Calvin,[1] we admit two principles, one external, the other internal. The external and objective principle is the fact assured to and perceived by the soul that God reveals Himself and speaks in Scripture. The internal principle, interior to the subject, is the persuasion of the Holy Spirit which raises this knowledge to the height of a certainty of divine faith, a certainty distinct from sensorial and rational evidence, and entirely supernatural.

This duality of the principles of religious knowledge establishes between the latter and natural knowledge an analogy which results from the fact that both are forms of knowledge; that, independent of and outside the subject, there is an objective reality which is given to be known, and that the object is confronted with a subject whose function is to accomplish that transitive act which is the act of knowing, of interiorizing ideally in oneself the real knowable object, of assimilating oneself to it ideally.

This is true in the natural order. In vain, idealism would invite the subject to draw his knowledge of the world from his own resources. This can only result in a phantasmagoria having no connection with reality. On the other hand, exclusive empiricism is powerless to transform its sensible image into a mind thinking by concepts.

Similarly, in the order of religion, it is impossible to draw

---

[1] *Com. on 2 Tim.*, iii.

from the organ of knowledge the transcendent object which we seek to know. If God says nothing concerning the manner in which I must serve Him, and if there is no word from Him assuring me of His reality independently of mine, and of His benevolence towards me, I can know nothing about these things which are the very substance of religion.

On the other hand, if He speaks to me in Holy Scripture, or through a Church, and I am incapable of distinguishing by an inner light His Word from the voices of deceivers, this Word remains the same for me as if it had no existence.

Thus, there is a legitimate subjectivism considered from the point of view of religious realism, and in this respect the theology of Rome is not more objective than those of Calvin or his opponent Sébastien Castellion. The external principle of Protestantism, however, satisfies the condition required for all principles, so that it can serve as a starting-point for subsequent demonstrations and is indispensable for furnishing the elements of these demonstrations.

If God has spoken, it should be possible to deduce the consequences which result from the general facts, promises and warnings, which He declares. If He has not spoken and does not speak on these questions, there is nothing to demonstrate.

It is the same with the internal principle: if the spirit of discernment enabling us to acknowledge and understand the Word of God, so far as essential matters are concerned, is wanting, nothing can be known concerning the truths which the soul needs to know in order to glorify God and find in Him its supreme happiness.

These two principles have already the essential quality of every principle of autopisty: they carry within themselves their own "credentials to be received without contradiction".

It may be objected that, as regards the evidence *sui generis* of which we speak, and which we attribute to the two principles of the Reformation, namely, Scripture and faith, the character of universality is still required to make it objective: but this is to forget that neither have the principles of a rational evidence an absolute universality. Without speaking of pathological cases (blindness from birth, illusions, etc.), there are the questions of the value of sensible experience and of the reality of the external world. Since sceptics exist, there are no absolutely universal principles, but faith in principles is not a question of majorities: "Monks are not reasons", it used to be said; and, let us add, nor are subjectivists. He who believes knows that virtually and eschatologically faith has overcome the world.

These principles of faith play the same part, *mutatis mutandis*, as the leading principles in the sciences. Those who apply the principles are not certain of attaining truth, always and everywhere, without responsibility and automatically. But they know that they are following the legitimate method. Similarly, those who follow the Reformed principle sincerely and who desire only to be obedient to the voice of God, are not dispensed from making an effort to understand it. When they interpret Scripture by Scripture and according to the analogy of faith, however, they are not building on their own private judgment but on the most catholic judgment possible, namely, that faith in the need for a divine canonical authority is the point at which legitimate subjectivism draws the subject out of himself into contact with the transubjective: God and his Word.

It has been said that, between this written Word and the subject, there is always the fallible interpretation of the latter, and that therefore he must go further and presume the necessity for an infallible guide to interpretation. This is true, surely, for the Roman Catholic. Between the text of his catechism, of the canon of a council, of an encyclical or a sermon by his parish priest, there is always his fallible interpretation. And when these things become burning questions for him, all the world knows it only too well.

But, as we have seen, the real drawback is that he can never know with a certainty which is not wholly arbitrary that the infallible authority has actually spoken. Moreover, even if this were not so, fallible intermediaries would impose themselves between this authority and the subject who still remains fallible.

The Protestant believer is no more infallible than his Catholic brother, but, in order that he may understand Scripture, he places himself under the direction of two guides whose divine and infallible authority all Catholics acknowledge unconditionally, namely, Scripture and the Holy Spirit. The Scripture interpreted in its difficult passages by the parts whose meaning is obvious; the Holy Spirit, promised to all who ask for Him (Luke 11: 13), and declared by the Scripture to be an unction present in all those who follow the apostles (1 John 2: 19, 20, 27).

Calvin takes his stand on the true ground of the common experience of believers and of faith in the fidelity of God, when he writes, apropos of the apostolic precept concerning the examination of the spirits: "All doctrines must be proved by the Word of God; at all times, if the Spirit of wisdom is not there, it will profit us nothing to have the Word of God in our hands and not be able to interpret it. . . . Therefore, before we can be competent judges, it is necessary that the Spirit of wisdom should be given to us. . . . Now, since the Apostle might recommend this to us in vain if we had not the requisite knowledge for judging, he makes it clear that believers shall never be destitute of the Spirit of wisdom, as far as it shall be expedient for them, on condition that they ask him from the Lord." [1]

Here, then, is a principle: Scripture, the supreme rule; an exhortation: "try the spirits"; a promise: God will give His Spirit to him that asks; an assurance: Scripture will be understood by the believer, as far as it is necessary for him to do so. The Calvinist's freedom of thought is founded on the authority of God speaking in His Word, and on the faith that will not fail him in time of need. This excludes neither the aid nor the decision of the Church. On the same page of his Commentary, our Reformer co-ordinates with this personal or particular examination of Scripture, the public examination; and, in the substantial agreement of those who accept the principle laid down, he sees rightly the confirmation of its objective and supernatural value: "It is certain that this is a singular work of God, who, having subdued our stubbornness, causes us to feel the same thing and unites us in a true union of faith."

Those who desire further knowledge of this "singular work of God" cannot do better than study the impressive harmony of the symbolical books of the Reformed Churches, realized without the intervention of any central authority on earth, by the Spirit and the Word written, which proceed from Christ, the king and head of the Church.

In conclusion, the principle of the authority of Scripture, founded on the testimony of the Holy Spirit, as the basis of our preaching and dogmatic science, does not imply, as Bossuet suggests, that there is a point at which the catechumen must ask himself whether Jesus is the Christ or an impostor, and whether the Scripture brings to us the echo of the revelation of God or whether it is a tissue of fables.

The Church supposes that there is a point at which the catechumen does not know Jesus Christ, namely, before He has been presented to him in the Gospel, even as the fellow-citizens of the Samaritan woman did not know Him until she had spoken to them; also, that there is a point at which he does not know that there exists a Bible, which the Church believes to be divine, before she has spoken to him about it. And always, as in the case of the Samaritans, who at first believed on the testimony

[1] *Com. on* I *John*, iv, i, *ad fin.*

of a woman whom they did not recognize as infallible, but whom, nevertheless, they judged worthy of belief, the catechumen will be moved immediately by grace to believe in the human but very venerable testimony of the Church. And when he has known and tasted the Scripture, there is a point at which he will say to the Church, as did the Samaritans to the woman of Sychar: "Now we believe, not because of thy saying: for we have heard Him ourselves and know that this is indeed the Christ, the Saviour of the world" (John 4: 42).

But, even when this point has not yet been reached, one can believe legitimately, with a human faith, in the value of the human testimony of the Church, whose teachers themselves believe on the authority of God, perceived immediately in their mind as a testimony rendered to Scripture.

According to Reformed principles, the catechumen does not necessarily begin with doubt and end in confusion. He starts with ignorance, in order to arrive at certainty, in the communion of the faith of all those who receive the authority of Scripture on the testimony of the Holy Spirit and who interpret Scripture according to the principle of the analogy of faith.

CHAPTER 14

WHY CHRISTIAN DOGMATICS MUST BE CALVINISTIC AND REFORMED

The Churches and the various sects which adhere more or less faithfully to the evangelical Reformation may be considered as capable of being reduced scientifically to three distinct types: the Lutheran type; the Calvinist, or Reformed; and the Arminian.

This is not the place in which to make a detailed comparison of the particular doctrines of these three forms which evangelical Protestantism has received from history. Such detailed comparison belongs to the sphere of symbolics and of dogmatics proper. We would observe, however, that no one can make such comparison without being impressed by the spiritual unity of evangelical Protestantism.

In spite of doctrinal differences, the importance of which cannot be gainsaid, Christian theism, the oecumenical faith of the first councils, the formal principle of the authority of the Word of God, the material principle of salvation by faith, are maintained and formulated in the symbolical books of Lutherans, Calvinists and Wesleyans alike.

This being the case, why should we be concerned to reaffirm Calvinism in the sphere of theological science? Why claim for this particular type a sort of dogmatic monopoly, as the title of the present chapter would seem to suggest?

In replying to these questions, let us make clear, first of all, that we have no wish to deny Lutherans or Wesleyans the right to expound and defend scientifically the Christian faith as they understand it. All we say is that, for propaedeutic reasons, the dogmatic theologian is bound to indicate the motives of general order which impel him to teach Reformed dogmatics in preference to any other; to explain why he considers that, from the point of view of the internal structure, as well as from the relations with the general data of human sciences, something of importance would be lacking in any system of evangelical dogmatics if it were not of the Reformed type.

This is not to show a sectarian spirit, but rather to refuse to consider the accident of a personal conviction as sufficient to furnish a scientific explanation of his choice.

But will not a treatise on dogmatics proper contain precisely this scientific reply in regard to each particular doctrine established in accordance with a sound logical and exegetical method? We do not think so, for it would still be necessary to explain scientifically how it comes about that the advocates of different types of theology, all supposed to be equally well informed, do not succeed in assimilating the arguments presented.

In order to explain this fact, which some may find disturbing, we must go back to the principles which serve as criteria for the dogmatic exegesis of each of the types in question and try to understand why they are received as such. We shall disregard the criteria which cannot be made to agree with the fundamental dogmas of evangelical Protestantism.

Let us endeavour, in the first place, to characterize the three types whose existence we have assumed. In order to be as objective as possible, in the first place, we will enquire of the Lutherans how they regard the Reformed, whom they do not distinguish from evangelical Arminians (Wesleyans). We will address ourselves to a man immune from all sectarian bigotry, whose dogmatic genius we admire, namely, the Lutheran bishop Martensen. "The Swiss Reform"—this is his designation for what we call the Reformed type—"proceeds essentially from the formal principle of the authority of Holy Scripture; Lutheranism, on the contrary, finds its starting-point, its determinate cause, in the depths of the Christian consciousness. It is the experience of sin and of redemption. It is connected, by preference, with the material principle of gratuitous salvation. The difference consists in the Mosaic legalism from which the (Swiss) Reform was not able to free itself, while all the time vigorously waging war with the same thing as it existed in the Roman Church. . . . While the (Swiss) Reform has never been able to deliver itself from this inconsistency, Lutheranism has always affirmed the Gospel in all the plenitude of its grace." And, for Martensen, this difference blazes out at the point where "the conception of the Christian life reveals itself with most evidence, namely, in the doctrine of the sacraments."[1]

The lines we have quoted are characteristic of Lutheranism. The predominance of the soteriological criterion in order to explain Scripture canonically (the *sola fide* of Luther), the essence of Lutheranism defined by its psychologism ("it is the experience of sin and of redemption"), the doctrine of the sacraments: it is all here.

---

[1] *Dogmatique chrétienne*, trs. Ducros, Paris, 1879, pp. 84–85.

It need not surprise anyone to find the portrait of "the Swiss Reform" unflattering, but we understand Martensen's meaning quite well. It is perfectly true that the Reformed catechism affirms the authority of Scripture almost at the beginning of the exposition of Christian doctrine, and it is true also that Reformed dogma gives a definitely wider scope than Lutheranism to the *tertius usus legis*. According to it, not only degenerate but regenerate man is subject to the divine law. As to the reproach of legalism, we will not discuss it here. We need only remark that, in our view, it is applicable only to certain Puritan and Methodist conceptions of piety which we regard as deviations from the Calvinist type.[1]

Finally, it is exact to say that the doctrine of the sacraments marks a profound difference between Lutherans and the Reformed.

If we enquire of John Wesley, who claimed explicitly for himself the title of Arminian,[2] how he regarded Lutherans and Calvinists, we learn that he considered Luther's particular formula on justification as tending to antinomianism,[3] whence the subordination of the material principle to the formal principle in Methodism. As for the Calvinists, he considered their doctrine of predestination to be blasphemous and revolting to the heart.[4]

The formal principle predominates, but the criterion of the interpretation of Scripture is humanitarian sensibility and a rationalism impatient of mystery when the demands of humanitarianism are at stake.

It will be noticed that in attempting to describe how Methodists and Lutherans regard the Reformed, we have given some idea of how the latter regard them. Reformed Christians certainly form a type distinct from the two others. Methodists and Lutherans have not always shown much indulgence towards their Calvinistic brethren. One has only to recall Luther's curt behaviour towards the Swiss at Marbourg and the slight success which attended Calvin's advances towards the Lutherans. The friendship of the Wesleys for Whitefield did not prevent their

---

[1] The broadmindedness expressed by the catechism of Calvin on this point will surprise many readers. One of the first occupations of the Huguenot ministers affected by the revocation of the edict of Nantes, on landing in Puritan England, was to engage in a lively polemic regarding the English Sunday.

[2] In 1778, Wesley founded *The Arminian Magazine*, thus affirming his solidarity with Arminius in his denial of the Reformed doctrine of predestination.

[3] *Vide* Victor Monod, *Faut-il revenir à Wesley?* p. 7; reprint of an article in *Christianisme Social*, March, 1936.

[4] *Ibid.*, p. 10.

dissension with him on the question of Calvinism; while, on the other hand, the Calvinists were undoubtedly severe in their dealings with the rationalizing disciples of Arminius at Dordrecht.

These ecclesiastical ruptures and heated controversies make it evident that both sides realized that there was more at stake than the fate of particular points of theology. It was and is still felt to be a question of a distinguishing principle of dogma. Among the Reformed, this principle can easily be cleared from the objection which they make continually against Lutherans, Roman Catholics, and even evangelical Arminians, of not taking into account sufficiently the honour, glory, and authority of God.

It is important to notice exactly what they say about them. They do not dream of suggesting that non-Calvinists may not sing the praises of God with as much fervour as themselves; that Jesuits may not display a burning zeal for His glory, even though one criticizes some of their attempts to justify their motto: *ad majorem Dei gloriam*. The zeal of a Quenstedt or a John Wesley is not questioned by anyone amongst us.

By their *soli Deo gloria*, Reformed Christians understand the following axiom: the principle of the analogy of faith is that in no sense does God depend on His creatures, either in the order of reality or in the order of thought; but that, on the contrary, His decretive will has sovereign dominion over all things, while His preceptive will has supreme authority over all minds, so that He is the author, the first cause and the source of all good.

It is in accordance with this principle that the *auctoritas normae* must be distinguished from the *auctoritas historiae* in Scripture; that which forms the rule of faith and life from that which is communicated to us by way of historical information. In conformity with this analogy of faith, dogmas must always be formulated, and there is no other distinguishing principle of the orthodoxy of the canonical interpretation of Scripture. The principle of the analogy of faith as a rule of the spiritual interpretation of Scripture is identified by Calvin with the *soli Deo gloria* in his epistle to Francis I.[1]

But if the Calvinist has in view the exclusive glory of God, he

[1] *Calvini Opera*, I, 12 f; II, 12, 16; cf. *Com. on John*, viii, 50, and *Romans*, xii, 6; also G. Bucani, *Quaestiones theol.*, Berne, 1605, *loc.* iv, xiv: *Quaenam nota est per quam homines sani doctrinam agnoscunt esse veri Dei doctrinam? Quod, quae doctrina nos unius et solius Dei gloriam in solidum et ubique quaerere, et illi adhaerere docet, illa procul dubio veri Dei doctrina est*—How can doctrine be recognized as sound and true? Doctrine which seeks genuinely and entirely the glory of God and teaches us to cleave to Him, is without doubt the true doctrine of God.

thinks also of the salvation of man. Calvinism subordinates the anthropocentric preoccupation to the theocentric preoccupation in religion, but the latter by no means excludes the former: it merely relegates it to its rightful place.

Formerly, Neeser, in classifying Calvinism among the religions of sensibility or of mystical sensuality,[1] seems to have misunderstood the theocentric character of our Reform. It is certain, however, that Calvin consistently opposed religious eudemonism and that he condemned it as contrary to the theological spirit. In his letter to the Genevese, Sadolet displayed an exclusive enough preoccupation with salvation for which Calvin reproached him in the following terms: "It savours little of a true theologian to attempt to confine man to himself so much rather than to command and instruct him that the beginning of directing his life aright is to desire to increase and show forth the glory of the Lord. . . . It is for God before all things that we are born and not for ourselves."[2]

On the other hand, if Calvinism puts at the foundation of its doctrine the infinity of God, and at the corner-stone of the dogmatic edifice this infinite sovereignty manifesting itself as the principle of unconditional election to salvation, the affirmation of this divine omnipotence does not proceed solely from the principal religious preoccupation, which is zeal for the glory of God. It has also as an object the satisfaction of a legitimate preoccupation with salvation and of the desire to give the will the moral energy needed in order that it may triumph in the struggle in which it must take part.

This is misunderstood by Bois, who speaks of an exclusive preoccupation with the glory of God. But the fact that Neeser has been able to make a mistake in the opposite direction gives a presumption that Bois may have erred at the other extreme. Moreover, Calvin's own words place this beyond doubt. "When we say that God is omnipotent, it is not only that we may honour Him, but in order that we may be at rest and invincible in the face of all temptations, for, since the power of God is infinite, He is well able to preserve and guard us".[3]

The doctrine of predestination, which is, as we have seen, the keystone of the Calvinistic system, clearly places in evidence the double quality which it possesses of affirming the divine independence and at the same time assuring the soul of its salvation. This doctrine, indeed, has its logical foundation in

---

[1] *Le problème de Dieu*, p. 61 f.
[2] Epistle to Sadolet, *Calvini Opera*, V, p. 391 ff.
[3] Sermon xc on Job, *Calvini Opera*, XXXIV, p. 363.

the idea that God is independent of the creature to such an extent that he cannot depend on it even in connection with the knowledge that he has of contingent future events.

How does it come to pass that the analogy of faith is understood by Lutheranism as a precedence of the material principle (salvation by faith alone, distinguishing between the *auctoritas normae* and the *auctoritas historiae*)? Why is it essentially a psychological experience of sin and of pardon? Two names seem to us to summarize the reply to this double question, recalling the historical conditions in which Lutheranism originated and revealing the sources of its dominant tradition.

Luther and Melanchthon both contributed to the rise of Lutheranism. The powerful personality of the former, the decisive experience which he had of his sin and of the certainty of its pardon, have marked with a profound and indelible impression the learned theology, as well as the popular piety, of the Lutheran Church. It seems to us that, here, we have the explanation of the psychology of this communion. It has become unfaithful to the mind of the Master on the question of predestination and free will, under the influence of the humanism of Melanchthon who found favourable soil for his views in the sentimental tendencies of the German genius. To the extent to which he developed independently, when he was not under the immediate influence of Luther's presence, Melanchthon approximated to the Erasmian type.

We think we can explain the anthropocentrism of John Wesley by the fact that his work must be regarded as the miracle of a paradoxical revival of the evangelical plant growing in the soil of an England dechristianized and impregnated with humano-deist philosophy. In spite of his painful misunderstanding of Luther's thought, the case of Wesley is an astounding miracle of grace. It proves that the Anglican Reformation concealed unsuspected sources of spiritual rejuvenation. Voltaire imagines himself to be living in the twilight of Christianity, when, behold, the Methodist revival illuminates the scene.

As for Calvinism, it is remarkable that, after a brilliant period lasting about a century, it entered into decadence before the beginning of the 18th century, whose atmosphere almost proved fatal to it. It continued to drag out a languishing ecclesiastical existence here and there, but it had practically disappeared from "enlightened" centres, and almost everywhere its rare defenders were banished far from academical chairs and seats of learning. And, to-day, when the scientific and philosophical ideology of the 18th and 19th centuries is, in its turn, entering the obscurity of another twilight, we find ourselves assisting at a vigorous Calvinistic revival.

The synchronism seems to us significant. It connotes the existence of a conflict between two principles engaged in mortal combat: the principle of the absolute sovereignty of God, on the one hand; and, on the other hand, that of the autonomy of man in his reason, his sentiment and his will.

Why have the Reformed Churches, in contradistinction to the Lutherans and Arminians, grasped the analogy of faith under the aspect of the vindication of divine sovereignty? Surely, because they are the heirs of Zwingli, Calvin, and Beza. By their culture these men were humanists, deeply versed in knowledge of pagan antiquity. They realized its greatness, while they noted its permeation of the Church, her worship, and her popular devotions. The cradle of the "Swiss" Reformation, as Martensen describes it, was actually situated in a pilgrimage centre. The aversion of the pre-Calvinian Reformed for the mass and the "idols" expressed itself in terms of extreme virulence, as witness Marcourt and the affair of the placards. Calvin wrote the *Treatise on Relics*, while he expressly disapproved of the iconoclastic vandalism of the Huguenot soldiery.

The Reformed movement aimed, above all, at reasserting the sovereignty of God, in the sphere of thought (exclusive authority of the Word); in the sphere of salvation (justifying faith, the gift of divine predestination); in the sphere of worship (validity of the second Commandment of the Decalogue, condemning images); in all spheres of human activity (the Law as a rule of life for the regenerate); and in the cosmic order (efficacious providence and preordination). Why did the "Reformed" Reformers pass from an aversion from paganism to a lucid and consistent application of the *soli Deo gloria*? That is a secret of grace.

Divine grace prepared the way of the Lord by endowing exceptionally synthetic minds, like those of Zwingli, Calvin and Beza, with an extensive classical culture, which caused them to connect closely their dogmatic constructions with the premises laid down by divine revelation. The distinguishing principle of the *auctoritas normae* in Scripture is evidently one which does not lead us to deny that which has been previously acknowledged as true and that which one continues to acknowledge as true.

Now, Calvinism is purely and simply theism in cosmology; oecumenical Christianity in objective soteriology; evangelical Protestantism in criteriology and subjective soteriology, formulated with all the logical consequences demanded by these various stages of Christian thought.[1]

The Lutheranism of Melanchthon and the Arminianism of Wesley profess, as explicitly as Calvin, the infinite and immutable omnipotence of God; but they deny immediately what they have just affirmed, by laying down a philosophical concept of created liberty according to which the exercise of this liberty produces a change in God, limiting His omnipotence.

Lutheranism professes that the Son of God has assumed a humanity similar to ours, while denying what it has just affirmed, by its doctrine of the ubiquity of the body of Christ.

Arminianism professes that God is the sole author of salvation, while denying what it has just affirmed, by declaring that God cannot save man without the co-operation of his free will, which, in the final resort, decides his own salvation.

In the long run, these denials of the original thesis become so insistent that the party affirming the antithesis gains the upper hand, and, in the end, the thesis is denied; first, the sovereignty, power and omniscience of God; then the Incarnation, grace, and the rest. In brief, the dogmatic decomposition of Protestantism sets in, and we find ourselves confronted with a sentimental or rationalistic Christianism.

Calvinism is strictly consistent in the genetic development of its theism, its oecumenical Christianity and its evangelical witness, but this can only become really evident through the study of dogmatics proper. The Reformed dogmatic theologian is in a position to give reasons why he advocates a return to Calvinism, which are based on the internal structure of his theological system. Such a return is desirable if only to resolve the existing conflict between religious thought and scientific ideology.

It cannot escape an attentive observer of movements in thought that the intellectual climate of to-day is far less favourable to psychologism than that of the 14th century. This explains why Lutheranism which, Martensen assures us, is essentially a psychological experience,[2] exercises a less powerful attraction to-day than in the days when the subjectivist philosophies held sway.

In order to stem the tide of Calvinism, a return to Wesley has been suggested.[3] Wesleyan Arminianism is certainly nearer to the Gospel than Arminianism pure and simple, but the

---

[1] B. B. Warfield, *Calvin and Calvinism*, p. 354 ff.
[2] *Dogmatique chrétienne*, p. 84.
[3] Victor Monod, *Faut-il revenir à Wesley?* p. 22.

Arminianism in it is closely related to the ideology of the 18th century which it sought to Christianize by meeting it on its own anthropocentric plane. Its theodicy is strangely reminiscent of the deism of the period. Romantic sentiment and utilitarian reason it sets up as judges of the ways of God, who has scarcely any reason for existence other than the salvation of man.

Further, the Reformed view of the sacraments as pledges of the divine promises of salvation becomes, for many modern Methodists, in spite of Wesley, a useless excrescence. Why should the promises of salvation need visible seals? Surely they are sufficient in themselves, and, moreover, does not God by His very nature owe salvation to the sinner, who is, after all, the deciding factor in the case?

This obsolete theodicy does not corresponu to the hard experiences of generations that have known world war and have endured the consequences of such a catastrophe. More and more, believers are becoming conscious of the futility of humanitarian optimism and of the need for basing human efforts upon the free grace of the sovereign God.

It has been objected that science precludes any possibility of a lasting return of enlightened Christian thought to this sovereign of an earth that we know to-day to be nothing more than a minute atom lost in some region of an infinite universe.[1] It was all very well, perhaps, at a period when the world was conceived as a vast disc around which encircled a comparatively small sun and tiny stars.

This sort of argument ignores the fact that Calvinism in its popular preaching, as well as in its scientific manuals, taught what all informed people knew long before John Damascene in the 8th century,[2] namely, that the earth is a "speck",[3] a "point",[4] in a universe which, though vast, is finite,[5] since infinity belongs to God alone.

[1] Apropos of the discovery of the satellites of Jupiter by Galileo, Wifred Monod writes: "As a result of this blow, the Calvinist notion of the deity became untenable: those who talk of bringing theology back to it forget that they have no power to join together again the fragments of an infinitesimal universe, which to-day is in pieces. The neat little universe of Moses, of the Fathers, of the Schoolmen, the microscopic universe of Calvin, adapted to his absolute God as a box is to its lid, is in tiny fragments, or, rather, it has evaporated." (*Le Problème du Bien*, I, p. 687 f.)

[2] John Damascene, *De Fide Orthodoxa*, II, x: *Terra . . . multum certe coelo minor est, in ipsius centro instar puncti appensa* (Migne, 94, p. 910, col. 2).

[3] Calvin, 148th sermon on Job (38:4, 11), says that the earth is a mere "pilule" in comparison with the heavens.

[4] Zanchius, *De operibus Dei*, II, v: *. . . coeli comparatione, minus est quam punctum tota terra.*

[5] *Inst.* I, xiv. i, *ad fin.*; cf. B. B. Warfield, *Calvin and Calvinism*, p. 294.

383

This sort of argument is actually the result of a curious psychological transposition. To-day, since we are Copernicans, who locate the sun in the centre of the solar system, we are apt to consider the centre as the privileged place. We speak, moreover, of theocentrism, anthropocentrism, and of questions of central importance, and are tempted to attribute to the ancients our manner of viewing things. As it is certain that, with few exceptions, they thought the earth to be at the centre of the universe, we attribute this geocentrism to a disproportionate view which we suppose them to have entertained concerning the importance of man.

Nothing could be more false. For them, the spherical universe was divided into inner regions, those nearest to the circumference being the superior regions, in which were naturally to be found the lightest and most ethereal bodies. The grossest and heaviest fell, and the lowest and most humble place of all was precisely the centre occupied by the earth, which is, as Calvin says, "in this hollow abyss".[1] It is obvious that the proof of the immensity of the physical universe given by the telescope cannot exercise any influence whatever over Calvinistic dogmatics nor affect in the least the revival which is now taking place.

Calvinism was, however, in the 16th century, as it is to-day, more than ever, geocentric in the modern sense of believing Copernicans: the earth is sufficiently at the centre of the divine plan to have been the theatre of the Incarnation and Crucifixion of the Son of God. But it is precisely here that we see the superiority of Calvinism over the Wesleyan Arminianism towards which some are looking. If the earth is, in God's view, a privileged planet; if, for Him, man is the most excellent of creatures, it is not on account of the local situation of this globe in the universe, nor by reason of the intrinsic dignity of this "lord of creation". The importance and the value of these creatures are due solely to the gratuitous election of God, who chooses the vile and base things of the world to confound the mighty.

It is certain that anthropocentric psychology is disturbed, with Pascal, by the disproportion between the immensity of stellar space and the infinitesimal smallness of our earth, a disproportion disclosed by science. Every religious doctrine which justifies the importance of man in regard to God by the intrinsic dignity of a creature so minute comparatively, at some time or other must create tension between the religious hope which projects a prayer towards the sky and the science which

[1] *Com. on Ephesians*, iv, 8; cf. *Praelectiones in Jer.*, x, 12; 95th sermon on Job, *ad fin.*

demonstrates that the prayer will lose itself in a practically infinite void. (The universe of up-to-date science, however, unlike that of the 19th century, is no longer really infinite.)

We have never found a trace of this cosmic conflict among Calvinistic thinkers. Their leader, far from experiencing it, wished that all Christians could be astronomers,[1] and never tired, in his preaching, of dilating on the immensity of the works of God. This, because he who believes in the infinite God never feels himself to be alone, however vast the universe may be. He who believes in the liberty of divine election, gratuitous and unconditional, can only adore when he hears the Creator of the universe and of the Church, declare, by the mouth of the prophet, to this "dust of the earth" which has consciousness of being: "I have loved thee with an everlasting love" (Jeremiah 31: 3).

Reformed dogmatics, like other Christian systems of theology, claims to be an attempt to express and formulate the faith in a scientific manner. Its aim is even higher than that. It desires to become an act of adoration before the mystery of the divine ways in their unsearchable wisdom; renouncing every proud attempt of theodicy. [2] With head bowed in the dust, it would listen to the Word of God. It speaks when it believes that God has spoken, but remains silent in the presence of the silence of His Word. Here are its credentials. It has no others, but these should suffice to enable us, if it please God, to enter upon the field of dogmatic theology which our fathers so diligently cultivated.

[1] 34th *Sermon on Job*, ix, 4–15.
[2] 142nd *Sermon on Job*, xxxvi, 20–24.

APPENDIX

I. *Canonical* (*canonique*). Lalande in *Vocabulaire de philosophie*, supplement, tome II, p. 989, gives this word the following definition: "Term employed by Adrien Naville (*Nouvelle classification des Sciences*, 1901) and by J. J. Gourd (*Philos. de la Religion*, p. 30) to designate whether substantively, the regular sciences, or adjectivally that which is ordinarily understood by normative, on the one hand, and technological, on the other." It is in the first sense that we employ the adjective canonical.

Following Wundt (Goblot, *Traité de logique*, p. 3), we distinguish between the normative or canonical disciplines and those which are speculative. For Wundt, logic, aesthetics and ethics are normative sciences. Julius Kaftan and Hermann Bavinck, the former Lutheran, the second Reformed, claim the character of normative discipline (*Normwissenschaft, Normatieve Wetenschap*) for dogmatic theology, because this discipline determines what must be believed, on divine authority, instead of limiting itself to translating the subjective experiences of a religious individuality into intellectual formulae.

Goblot objects to Wundt's distinction that "all sciences are theoretical and speculative, since their immediate object is always to establish certain verities and if possible to give intelligible reasons for so doing." But it is not sufficient that a science should have as its object the establishment of certain verities and that it should invoke intelligible reasons in order that it may be entitled to be described as a speculative science. A science becomes canonical or normative when, as the philosophy of another science or of technical or aesthetic arts, the truths which it establishes by the aid of intelligible reasons employ rules in order to determine the direction of these disciplines and thus become the principles of methods and processes which must be applied. In this sense of formal logic, aesthetics and the introduction to Reformed dogmatics are canonical disciplines.

A science is canonical also when it associates authoritatively, in the name of its principles, certain propositions which must serve as absolute and universal rules of spiritual activity. It is in this sense that moral theology, which lays down principles of conduct, and dogmatic theology, which tells us what we must believe, are recognized, the first by Goblot, the second by Kaftan and Bavinck, as normative (i.e., canonical) sciences.

II. Here is Charnocke's thesis: "God in regard to His existence, is not only the object of discovery to faith but also to reason. . . . His existence is both an article of our faith and of our reason. Faith, in fact, properly concerns things which are above reason and which depend purely on revelation. That which can be demonstrated by natural light is not also properly an object of faith."

Disturbed by the passage of Scripture on which he is commenting: "He that cometh to God must believe that he is" (Hebrews 11: 6), the English divine is obliged to concede that, with regard to certainty obtained by means of revelation, the existence of God is an object of faith. Thus, for him, this object of faith was previously a rational certainty. This makes the fundamental dogma of religion a sort of mixed article and the result of a logical demonstration rather than of an authority, interior and exterior, imposing itself on the religious instinct. Charnocke wishes to be orthodox: but it must be admitted that he is far from the standpoint of Article IX of the Confession of La Rochelle. Calvin, on the contrary, considers that it is faith which discovers God, or rather that it is to faith endowed with a certitude *sui generis*, that God reveals Himself. For him, reasonings are efficacious only when they follow faith and deliver it from rational difficulties. By themselves, they can only produce opinions without certitude, consistency or duration. The God to whom they lead is never the true God.

But hear Calvin's own words: "It is impossible that the religious sentiment would always have been maintained among all peoples and nations, if the minds of men had not been seized by this persuasion that God is the Creator of the world. It would seem, then, that this knowledge which the Apostle comprises under faith can exist apart from faith. I reply that there has always been some opinion among all nations that the world was created by God: but there was no steadfastness in this. For, as soon as they imagined some god, they wandered away in their thoughts to such an extent that, like blind men, they perceived the shadow of some uncertain divinity rather than retained the true God in their minds. Moreover, seeing that it is only an evanescent opinion that flutters in their minds, it is very far from a true understanding."

That is to say, our Reformer regards natural revelation as capable of being understood only by a mind transformed by the grace of faith. No doubt God has written His name in the sky with the stars but still eyes are needed to see and intelligence to understand. To declare is not to deduce by syllogisms but to give a testimony to which the hearer either accords or refuses credence. "Thus the minds of men are blind to this light of nature, which shines in all creatures until, being illuminated by the Spirit of God, through faith, they begin to understand that, without this, they will never be able to understand. In this manner, the Apostle rightly attributes such understanding to faith."

A point which must be made plain is that this insufficiency on the part of the subject who receives the revelation of nature is only the result of a perversion of the will. It belongs also to a weakness of the understanding. "Having such a spectacle openly before our eyes, we do not cease to be blind, and this not merely because the revelation is obscure but because we are bereft of sense, and because in this respect not only the will but also the power is lacking" (cf. Stephen Charnocke, *Discourses upon the Existence and Attributes of God*, discourse 1; *Calvin Commentaries* on Hebrews 11: 3 and 1 Corinthians 1: 21).

III. *To come out from oneself and be raised above oneself* (p. 41). Speaking of the knowledge obtained by faith, Calvin says: "To such a degree does it surpass all human senses that it is necessary for the spirit to rise above itself to attain to it (*Adeo enim superior est ut mentem homines se ipsam excedere et superare opporteat (Inst. III, ii. 14))*". This image, unrealizable for the imagination, is in some way necessary for the intelligence. It is a question of making it understood that, in the knowledge of God, the act of knowing has for its goal the entering into a representative relation with the Being who is infinite and pure spirit. It is thus an act to the realization of which the faculties and organs capable of revealing definite material realities are inadequate.

Emile Boutroux uses the analogous image of "surpassing one's nature". This expression, justified as it doubtless is, requires some reservations. From the Calvinistic point of view, it could only be applied to our present nature, corrupted by sin. Faith forms part of normal human nature. That is why, all things considered, we prefer the expression employed by Calvin.

But we must protest against the contemptuous attitude which G. Matisse affects in regard to a great thinker like Boutroux. He speaks of his "lack of intellectual serenity" and his "general dissolution of thought". This because "he can calmly speak of surpassing one's nature, guiding one's intelligence in a different direction from the mechanical nature of things", thus assuming an intellectual attitude comparable to that of the man who wanted "a projectile to attempt to exceed its own speed" (*Les ruines de l'idée de Dieu*, p. 20). The author himself would seem to be comparable to the man in the Gospel who offered to take the mote out of his neighbour's eye, while quite oblivious of the beam that was in his own; for, on page 6 of his brochure, he employs an expression similiar to that with which he reproaches Boutroux. He does not hesitate, in fact, to declare his belief that humanity "will be able to surpass itself". Are we to regard this as a case of general dissolution of thought?

IV. Benjamin Breckinridge Warfield, one of the highest authorities in all that concerns Calvinistic thought, has underlined the characteristic trait of the Calvinian turn of mind which may be described as antipsychologism in dogmatics. "When Calvinism contemplates the religious life, it is interested less in the nature and psychological relations of the emotions which arise in the soul—with which the protagonists of the new science of religious psychology are occupied so unprofitably—than in the divine source whence these emotions spring and the divine object which they grasp" ("Present Day Attitude to Calvinism", in *Calvin as a Theologian and Calvinism Today*, Philadelphia 1909, p. 38).

V. It is interesting to compare Bacon's words on psychological introspection with the well-known thesis of G. Remacle in *Revue de metaphysique et de morale: la valeur positive de la psychologie*, 1894: and *Récherchés d'une methode en psychologie*, 1896–7. For Remacle, introspective psychology is illegitimate as a science, since, at the moment when the psychologist thinks he is observing himself, he is transforming his states of original consciousness into objects. He can only observe them by spatializing them. There is thus no efficacious introspection. In the process of introspection, pure appearances are inevitably substituted for real phenomena.

Bacon has a similiar observation: "When the human mind applies itself to the study of matter and of the work of God under our eyes, it draws from it a science real like the world itself: but when it turns in upon itself, it is like the spider spinning its web. It brings forth nothing but subtle doctrines: admirable for the delicacy of their work but without solidity and of no use" (*De augm. Scient.*, I, 31).

VI. The following passage from a letter written by Beza, then at the Colloquy of Poissy, to Calvin, makes one realize how much difficulty the artifices of the "sophists" (the nominalist representatives of a debased scholasticism) occasioned even the best Calvinist theologians, unprepared by scientific methods of Biblical exegesis for meeting the captious quibbles of their opponents. But this scholastic method enjoyed such prestige in the eyes of the contemporary public that it had to be employed by these men (among whom was Peter Martyr Vermigli) accustomed as they were to the solution of such kinds of *jeu d'esprit.*

"If our Martyr arrives in time, that is to say, if he makes great haste, his arrival will relieve us extremely, for we are confronted by veteran sophists, and although we are confident that the simple truth of the Word will triumph, nevertheless it is not given to all to resolve their sophisms instantly and to adduce relevant passages from the Fathers" (letter from Beza to Calvin, August 30, 1561, in Baum, *Bèze,* Vol. II, App., p. 59; cited by Benjamin F. Paist, junior, in the *Princeton Theological Review,* July 1922, p. 423).

VII. Le Roy gives a good idea of the difficulties in which the advocates of transformism find themselves as a result of the researches of contemporary biologists like Fleischmann in Germany and Vialleton in France. In the curious passage which follows, this eminent disciple of Bergson endeavours to extricate the system from the compromising consequences of its connexion with the hypothesis of man's animal descent. The double movement of his mind is evident in the way in which one position after another is abandoned and then resumed.

"The transformist doctrine, when reduced to essentials, occupies a truly impregnable position. But its real meaning needs to be clearly understood. Whether there has been continuity or not in the origin of species . . . matters little in one sense: what does matter is that no living form remains suspended in thin air. (We find it difficult to grasp the meaning of this metaphor.) A transformist is not one who professes such and such a theory of mechanism or of evolutionary vitalism, or regards the source of life as one rather than multiple: he is not even one who maintains that living things descend one from another by generation properly so called. Lamarck and Darwin charged evolution with parasitic hypotheses when they translated it into terms of heredity, adaption and descent. The essence of transformism consists simply in recognizing the existence of a physical connexion between living things, in the idea that living things function one for another, whatever may be the exact nature or modality of their connexion." (E. Le Roy, *L'exigence idealiste et la fait de l'evolution: le principe du transformisme,* in *Revue des cours et conferences,* 1st series, No. 6, Febuary 26, 1927.) It would seem, then, that even the most intransigent fixists are fundamentally transformists, for they all believe that there is a certain connexion between the life of plants and that of the animals which derive from them an important part of the oxygen that they breathe. Le Roy continues: "This solidarity may determine not only the structure of living things but also the historic order of their successive appearances. The fact is undeniable but it is susceptible of various explanations (including the fixist explanation?) . . . Until a new theory makes its appearance, however, the only connexion between living things which can be visualized with any degree of exactness is relationship by descent."

VIII. Durkheim seems at times to admit the innateness of the individual intelligence by itself. In regard to the concepts furnished by the collective consciousness, it would stand in the same relation "as Plato's, $\nu o \hat{v} s$ in regard to the world of ideas" (*Formes élémentaires*, p. 622). "This would be the content of knowledge and its accidental rather than its essential form, which would be due to the action of the collective consciousness. For it must be remembered that there is something impersonal (=universal) in us, because there is something social in us" (*ibid.*, p. 636). But in that case the doctrine of our sociologist appears to be limited to an affirmation of the existence of latent innate ideas, connected in the presence of an aptitude, with what amounts to a faculty for thinking universally by concepts. This would seem to arise clearly from the following passage: "To say that concepts betoken the manner in which society pictures to itself things, is to say that conceptual thought is coeval with humanity. We ourselves refuse to see in it the product of a more or less late culture. A man who could not think by concepts would not be a man: for he would not be a social being. Reduced to individual perception alone, he would be indistinguishable from the beasts" (*ibid.*, p. 626).

But, here, Durkheim reverts to the position of medieval and Calvinistic scholasticism, for both of which the mind is a *tabula rasa*. Apart from experience, for example, it has no idea of the part or the whole; but once the mind has acquired these, it sees immediately, in virtue of its innate aptitude, that the whole is greater than the part (H. Bavinck, *Geref. dog.*, I, p. 228). The small boy who offers his sister a bun in order that she may protect him from the big bully knows this well enough without anyone teaching him, for his mind obeys innate laws. The following passage from Bonaventure seems to us to explain the matter clearly: *Lumen illud sufficit ad illa cognoscenda (principia)—post receptionem specierum sine aliqua persuasione superaddita propter sui evidentiam. . . . Naturale enim habes lumen quod sufficit ad cognoscendum quod parentes sunt honorandi, et quod proximi non sunt laedendi, non tamen habeo naturaliter mihi impressam speciem patris vel speciam proximi* (Bonaventure, *Sent*, II, dist. 10, art. 1, qu. 1; dist. 23, art. 2, qu. 3; dist. 39, art. 1, qu. 2).

The principal difference that we discern between Durkheim's system and scholasticism consists in the fact that the latter, which cannot be accused of underestimating the essential importance of social action, insists more on what the individual mind owes to the knowledge which it soon acquires concerning a natural order and a certain compulsion in things.

But on this point, and precisely because of it, the scholastics seem to us to get the better of Durkheim. "What could be more arbitrary", says Parodi, "than to say that religious or metaphysical ideas originate solely through the contacts of the individual with his social environment, through these relations with collective forces alone and not, just as much, from his contact with the physical and terrestrial environment, with nature as a whole, and from the experience which he acquires of cosmic forces in general?" (*Philos. contemp. en France*, p. 155, note 1.)

IX. To the testimony of the two Woltjers, perhaps suspect because they are Calvinists, may be added that of another scientist, an atheist or at least a definite agnostic, George John Romanes: "We are thus, so to speak, driven to the theistic theory as furnishing the only explanation of this universal that can be named. In other words, we cannot by any logical artifice escape the conclusion that, so far as we are capable of judging, the universal order must be regarded as due to an integrating principle, and that the latter, so far as we can judge, is very probably of the nature of the mind. At any rate, we must admit that we cannot conceive it under any other aspect. In my opinion it is not possible to conceive or to name any other explanation of the natural order than that of intelligence as the supreme directive cause" (*Thoughts on Religion*, London, 1902, p. 71 f.). Force of habit alone prevents us from being conscious of the intellectually insurmountable character of the fact that science cannot exist unless it is founded on the fact that nature is a cosmos (p. 87).

The testimony of this scientist is all the more remarkable, since, at this period of his life, he refused to accept definitely the existence of a supreme mind, on the plea that the cruelties of nature prove that it must be entirely foreign to the moral order. He found it impossible to maintain this intellectually untenable position, and died confessing his faith in the God of the Scriptures.

Moreover, the imprint of the seal placed on nature by intelligence is, at this point, so evident that Kant constructed his system on the supposition that the order of phenomena is the creation of the human mind which introduces them into the forms of its sensibility. The Kantian explanation has been exploded, and its very remains have been swept away in the *débâcle* of idealism. But the fact which it attempted to explain remains: the cosmos is recognized by the intuition of the mind to be the product of intelligence, the expression of an originating and directing mind.

X. Calvin refers to the infinity of the divine essence in two passages in his *Praelectiones in Jeremiam*, 51: 18 and 23: 24. The first shows the religious importance which he attaches to the idea of the essential omnipresence of God in the world, a notion which he derives from that of the infinity of the divine essence as expressed in the second of these texts. The doctrine of the infinite and replenishing presence of God is of paramount importance, because it is essential to a true knowledge of Him: *Nam haec est vera Dei cognitio, dum illum existimamus solum esse* (infinity of essence) *dum tribuimus illi immensam essentiam quae coelum et terram impleat* (essential omnipresence or immensity) *cum agnoscimus esse spiritualis naturae: cum scimus illum denique esse solum, proprie loquendo, coelum et terram et quidquid in ipsis continetur, subsistere in eius virtute.*

The second passage shows: (a) that the infinity of the essential presence is implied in the idea of the infinite essence; (b) that this essential omnipresence is not explicitly taught in Scripture; (c) that, as a matter for subtle discussions, it would only be a vain speculation; (d) that what must be given prominence is the infinity of the divine providence and knowledge: *Hoc etiam non debet subtiliter exponi de immensa Dei essentia. Verum quidem est extendi essentiam Dei per coelum et terram, ut est infinita. Sed Scriptura non vult nos poscere frivolis illis et infructuosis cogitationibus: tantum docet quod prodesse nobis possit ad pietatem. Ergo quod hic pronunciat Deus se implere coelum et terram referri debet ad providentiam ejus et potentiam* (commenting on Psalm 139: 7 he says: "It would be doing violence to this passage to adduce it as a proof of the infinite essence of God").

XI. *The pseudo-problem of evil* (p. 264) is urged in some quarters as a decisive objection against faith in God's sovereignty, in the positive fact of His self-revelation in the conscience, in nature, in the specific act of religion which is prayer, and in Scripture.

In the first place, there is physical suffering, excruciating pain often inflicted not only on criminals but on little children and animals too. The very structure of the biosphere involves the employment of suffering. Species of animals are made to devour one another. Such a world cannot, it is contended, have a beneficent being for its author.

Then there is moral evil. That God, while able to prevent it, should have permitted its existence and development, is held to prove Him to be a stranger to our moral principles, His very omnipotence to render the objection insurmountable; hence we must substitute for it either the tentative and clumsy efforts of a sub-intelligent will or the notion of a divinity whose power is strictly limited, a stranger, external to creation.

Those who contend for a well-meaning but awkward god or one whose efforts are largely ineffective, may be scandalized to find that we relegate the consideration of their view to an appended note. Let us admit that, if the case should fail, we should not be very disturbed. There are salutary shocks which serve to awaken the lost sense of mystery, and mystery is as necessary to religion as air to the lungs. One can adore only that which passes all understanding. That which can be comprehended is no longer adored.

For the man who has been apprehended by the sovereign God, there is no such thing as a problem of evil; there is only the mystery of evil. He can no longer consider evil as an enigma propounded to human wisdom. He has learnt to regard it as a real enemy which must be vanquished around him and in him; an adversary which has already been conquered in principle, because God has promised victory.

Our Reformer brought to the "problem" of evil no other solution than the conclusion of the book of Job, namely, faith. Faith knows that if it cannot understand what God is doing or permitting now, it will understand later. There is no real problem in the exercise of God's sovereign dominion over all His creatures. He has a perfect right to call into existence the jungle, with its repulsive inmates, if it so pleases Him. He has no account to render to us and we have none to demand from Him. Faith tells us that His goodness has condescended to call out of nothing a strange world in which the law of conflict reigns and in which the living can only live by suppressing other living creatures, while His wisdom is guiding that same world towards light and peace.

If we had no other reason to adduce but the divine will, that would have to suffice, for we know that this will is that of the perfect Being; that it contains in itself its most just and wise reasons. But revelation gives us certain indications which we have no right to neglect and which, on the contrary, we have a duty to employ.

Scripture teaches us that this world of animal life "subject to vanity" but "not willingly" (Romans 8: 20), is predestined to arrive at such a state that present suffering will seem insignificant indeed in comparison with the glory of its future transfiguration. It likens existing nature, which sighs for deliverance, to a woman in travail.[1] Suffering thus assumes a preparatory significance which ennobles it and explains its educative rôle for the whole of animate nature.

The bounty of God, far from ignoring the ontological misery, inherent in the finite creature, makes use of it as a purifying element in view of the destiny which He has reserved for the world when it shall arrive at the end which He has proposed for it.

On the other hand, Scripture teaches that the domain of bestial ferocity stops at the limits of that which God assigned to unfallen man. Of this peaceable region, man must be the dreaded guardian. Outside it, hostile nature exists as a warning against sin—which was no surprise for God.

As regards sin itself, moral evil, if God has allowed an abuse of liberty to enter into the purview of His decrees, no doubt it is because He judges that a world in which sin gives their names to repentance, pardon, heroism and sacrifice, has greater value and brings to light better, in the sight of angels and men, His justice and His mercy: that it is aesthetically and morally superior to a world of amoral innocents or of just persons frozen in their impeccability. This judgment of value pronounced by God must suffice for us, if we believe in Him. For those who do not believe, the question has no significance.

It is this judgment of value which allows us to adore the holiness of God as conceiving the possibility of moral evil and resolving to let it appear in order to vanquish it. It is this hope, created by Scripture and nourished by the faith of the Reformers, which allows us to regard the physical pain of the amoral animal as a messenger of God, preparing the brute creation for the transfiguration which will make it eventually the ornament of the finally glorified creation.

But how was it possible for God to describe a world which included monsters like the "leviathan" and the "great serpent" as "very good" (Genesis 1: 31)? We reply that this judgment was perfectly justified as implying that His creative power had

[1] *Com. on Rom.*, 8: 21 and *II Pet.*, 3: 10; cf. *Inst.* III, xxv. 11.

made it so, germinally, by virtue of promises to be fulfilled in due season.

In turning aside from the divine purpose and the hope founded upon it, however dimly realized, sin and its conscious principle have indeed subjected creation to that vanity of which St. Paul speaks. It can no longer be a question of the natural result of an effort groping tentatively to its beginnings and meanwhile buoyed up by promises.

The "expectation" in which the whole animate creation is associated with the distress mixed with hope experienced by men demands a "redemption", a deliverance such as the Christian faith proclaims (Romans 8: 19–23). It is true that there are sinners who exclude themselves from this hope for ever by their final impenitence. This is the mystery of the secret justice of Him whom the Scripture calls "the Judge of all the earth" (Genesis 18: 25), but the same Scripture shows even these to be among the objects of His "tender mercies" which "are over all His works" (Psalm 145: 9). The human conscience ratifies a sentence consistent with justice. What it cannot understand is that an obstinate continuance in rebellion against God, yet unbroken, should not eventually be followed by irrevocable loss.

To believe in God, in a God who is all wisdom, all justice and all mercy, is to believe with an invincible certainty that there are reasons of justice unknown to us at present, which make it just that, among some, the rebellion should not be broken by efficacious grace. What we cannot understand now we know by faith that we shall understand later. For faith, there is no problem here; but a mystery which calls for the confidence of the believer.

Neither the expectations of faith, nor its trembling before justice, nor the judgments of value which it forms or predicts, are capable of demonstration. If they were, faith would be no longer faith; it would be rational knowledge. Religion would be useless and the time would have arrived for philosophy to take its place. But that can never be, for philosophy is incapable of refuting the prophecies of faith. He who believes the teaching of Jesus Christ, of the Apostles and Reformers, takes his stand on impregnable rock.

The idea of citing God before the tribunal of the reason of an evolved simian, in order to hear Marcion's speech for the prosecution and Leibnitz' for the defence, is surely one of the most fantastic concepts of which even rationalist and ethicalist theology is capable, fruitful as it is in paradoxes.

AN INTRODUCTION TO REFORMED DOGMATICS

XII. *Psychologism dominant in mid-19th century France* (p. 305). "Never, perhaps, since the Renaissance, has philosophy held itself so aloof from the sciences as during the middle of the 19th century in France. Still attached to the Scottish tradition on this point, the eclectic school persuaded itself that psychology, completed by the history of philosophy and by a general view of the moral sciences, furnishes a sufficient foundation for a philosophical doctrine. As to the sciences which are called positive, such as mathematics and physics, and the natural sciences, they are the exclusive province of those who cultivate them; and philosophy has no more reason to occupy itself with them than it has to be disturbed by them. It can do no more than salute them from a distance, defend their principles against the attacks of empiricism, and offer them good advice in the manner of Bacon and Descartes."—A. Cournot, *Traite de l'enchaînement des idées fondamentales dans les sciences et dans l'histoire*, ed., L. Lévy-Bruhl, Hachette, 1922, Preface, p. vii.

XIII. *The Epistle of Jude and 2 Peter triumphed in virtue of their intrinsic value.* Jerome (*de Vir. inlust.*) says of the former: *auctoritatem vetustate jam et usu meruit et inter sanctas scripturas computatur.* The criteria here are not the apostolicity but the acknowledged authority and utility of the writing. The latter criterion alone is put forward by Eusebius in his testimony to 2 Peter: It was placed with enthusiasm (ἐσπουδάσθη) among the Scriptures on account of its value (χρήσιμος φανεία).—H.E., vii, 25, 80.

Apostolic authorship was not considered by all to be an indispensable criterion of canonicity. Dionysius of Alexandria (+265), taking the grounds of faith and charity, endeavoured to maintain the canonicity of the Apocalypse, while attributing it to another John than the author of the Fourth Gospel. Later, Pope Gregory the Great continued to maintain the canonicity of the epistle to the Hebrews, while questioning its Pauline origin (Julicher, *op. cit.*, p. 513). A similar attitude was adopted by Calvin and by the confession of La Rochelle which reckoned only thirteen epistles as Pauline.

XIV. "More than one point, besides, remains obscure and doubtful; for example, the spread of the Alexandrian Jewish canon. Did the Jews of Egypt receive the deutero-canonical books, as Dennefeld thinks? It seems difficult to obtain any certain knowledge on this matter. The only argument which might dispose us to accept this view, namely, the presence of these books in the Greek Bible, appears scarcely conclusive, for the most ancient witnesses to the contents of this Bible are the Christian manuscripts of the 4th and 5th centuries. Do they teach us anything concerning the spread of this Bible among the Hellenic Jews? Dennefeld himself does not conceal the fact that Josephus, who made use of the Septuagint, received only the restricted Palestinian canon, and that Philo, who praises the same version, and sometimes also uses it, never quotes from the deutero-canonical books."—E. Podechard, *Revue des Sciences Religieuses*, July, 1930, p. 498 ff.

XV. We had not read Prof. Gilson's *Christianisme et philosophie* when we offered this definition of the Catholic notion of faith. In Part I we have described this notion in slightly different terms: "In a general sense, it may be said that, for the Church of Rome, faith is a pure and simple intellectual assent to the teaching of the infallible Church." The eminent interpreter of medieval thought criticizes this definition (pp. 76–79): according to him a Catholic does not believe less immediately in God by means of the Church of Rome than a Protestant by means of a synod "assembled anywhere, provided it is not held at Rome". In the second place, faith is not purely and simply an intellectual assent "since the intellect believes the divine word only because it is moved to do so by the will and . . . by love" (according to Augustine and Aquinas).

We said that faith was an assent to the teaching of the infallible Church because we had read in the catechism of Séez that "the faithful are obliged to believe all that the Church teaches, because the Church is infallible" (*Catéchisme de Séez*, approved by Mgr. Claude Bardel, Séez, 1904, p. 117).

Now, when a Catholic receives a dogma, or rather, "all that the Church teaches, because the Church is infallible", does his faith connect itself with God as immediately as that of a Reformed Christian who receives the same dogma from his Church after she has shown him that it is taught in the Word of God? By virtue of the infallibility of the Church, a Catholic is obliged to believe that the invocation of saints is lawful, even if he is attracted by the Reformed interpretation of Scripture on this point. The Reformed Christian is not obliged to reject it until after his Church has convinced him that such invocation is contrary to the Word of God. And if a council, even one assembled at Rome and presided over by the Pope, defines a doctrine that can be proved by the Word of God, the Reformed Christian is bound to accept it, even if his own Church has not yet discovered this truth.

It is true, then, to say that, between the faith of a Catholic and

God, there intervenes an infallible Church, and, concretely, the Pope speaking *ex cathedra*. The Church tries, indeed, to demonstrate to the faithful that in teaching her own infallibility she is founded on the word of Jesus to Peter, on the promises of Christ to the Church.

But even if, after all, the reasoning of Calvin or of Claude seems unassailable to him, the faithful Catholic is still bound to believe in this teaching on infallibility. No doubt, he will believe only because he believes the Church to be right in spite of what seems to him so obvious; but, here again, he does not believe in God except through the mediation of the Church.

In the present Part (II) we have added: "on the ground of divine revelation". This agrees with the definition of faith and the act of faith to be found in the catechism of Séez (p. 67), which reads: "Faith is a supernatural virtue by which we believe firmly all that God has revealed to His Church, because God has revealed it and the Church teaches it to us." To such an extent is faith an assent to the teaching of the Church that if a Catholic received every dogma, but abstracted from it the authority of the Church as the reason for his belief, basing himself directly and solely on the authority of God speaking in Scripture, he would not have faith!

That faith is, immediately, adherence to the teaching of the Church, and, mediately only, adherence to the authority of God, seems to follow from the act of faith in the catechism: "My God, I firmly believe all that the holy, catholic, apostolic Roman Church commands me to believe; I believe it because it is you, O infallible truth, who have revealed it to her." Faith is presented here as an assent ("I firmly believe") to the teaching of the Church, as a response to her immediate command ("all that the . . . Church commands me to believe"). Moreover, according to this same catechism, it is a sin in the first place against the Church, " when one refuses to believe any of the truths taught by the Church".

The doctrine of the catechism of Paris appears to be a little less "high church" than that of the Séez catechism. This is not absolutely certain; although, if it were, we should simply have to record a lack of unity which we have no right even to suppose. But, however this may be, is faith, according to Catholic teaching, "purely and simply an intellectual assent" (to the teaching of the Church)?

"No", answers our eminent critic, "for Augustine and Aquinas give as motives the will and love. Calvinistic faith also is addressed, in the first place, to the intellect".

We reply that the terms "pure and simple intellectual assent" do not exclude, according to our view, the will as a motive: it is supposed, on the contrary, by the very term "assent". It seems to us that one must always assent by an act of the will; the whole controversy concerning the servile will implies this. But assent, pure and simple, is intellectual, and we agree that it can be described as "purely and simply" so, when the supernatural theoretical reasons which justify it (God has revealed . . . the Church teaches) are not accompanied by emotional elements, and when the instruction received in the intellect is absent from the heart, where it provokes no burst of adoration, confidence or love. Is such faith still a supernatural virtue according to Roman theology? Yes, without the slightest doubt: it is the *fides informis,* a firm and certain assent to the truths revealed on the authority of God and of the Church (*Conc. Vat.,* sess. iii, *de fide,* c. 3; Thomas Aquinas, *S. Theol.,* II, 2, qu. 2, art. 1, qu. 4, art. 2; Bellarmine, *de justificatione* I, c. 4, 6; Becanus, *Theol. scol.,* II., 2, tract. I, c. I f.; Perrone, *Praelect. Theol.,* V, 1840, p. 251 ff.).

This *fides informis* corresponds to the *fides historica* of Protestant theologians, disputed by Catholic controversialists. With such a notion of the first of the theological virtues, it is easy to see why Catholics are scandalized when they are told that a man is justified (held and reputed to be just) *sola fide.*

Moreover, according to them, in order that faith may be justifying, if it be *fides informis,* it becomes *fides caritate formata,* the faith formed by love. But it must be understood that the *caritas,* the love which Augustine, Aquinas and others require, in order that the faith may become *formata,* is a virtue quite distinct from faith. One does not sin against faith, by sinning against love.

We have observed that the Reformers profoundly modified the concept of faith. It may be asked, then, what there is in "Calvinistic" faith which is absent from Catholic faith. The first modification to be noticed is that the *fides informis* is no longer regarded as a theological virtue, nor even, properly speaking, as faith at all, but as an act of the intelligence which is only called faith by an abuse of terms. This is the *fides historica.* Formally, a Catholic who has only the *fides informis,* and a Calvinist who has only the *fides historica,* do not differ appreciably: they resemble each other in this, that neither the one nor the other has faith.

The second modification bears on the distinction between *fides informis* and *fides caritate formata.* This distinction is rejected. One thing cannot receive its form from another essentially distinct, while retaining its own nature. It will become something else in the process.

The concept of faith is modified by its motives. We have seen that faith, according to Catholics, has for its reasons the divine revelation in Scripture and in the Church ("we believe . . . because God has revealed it and because the Church teaches it to us"). For the Reformed Christian, the sole reason for faith is the revelation of God in Scripture.

It is only because he sees the agreement between the teaching of the Church with Scripture that he accepts that teaching. If a Church claiming to be *the* Church teaches anything clearly contrary to Scripture, he must reject it. The sole authority is that of God speaking in and by Scripture, and Scripture is not only the unique rule but also the unique source of faith, This difference is not emphasized by Calvin in the chapter on faith in the *Institutes* because, in his time, Catholic theologians in general taught that the assent of faith rested upon the content of Scripture.[1] The Vatican Council had not yet met and entire agreement had not been reached concerning the seat of authority.

The concept of faith is modified in its very nature. It is not merely an assent of the intellect: it is also, and above all, an assent of the heart.[2]

Finally, it is modified in its principal act. It is understood that "if the Word of God flutters only in the brain, it is not in any way received by faith."[3] But it is not sufficient that one should receive the truth of the promises of grace and pardon even in the heart: the principal act of faith consists in applying them to oneself personally. This is so true that the certainty of final perseverance and of salvation may become a certainty of divine faith.

It will be seen that, in claiming that Reformed Christians have profoundly modified the concept of faith, we are guilty of no exaggeration. Moreover, in defining faith, in the Catholic sense, as we have done, we have not sought a definition which would allow us to reject it, as some may suggest. We have tried to understand the views of Catholic theologians, and, if we have not copied any of their definitions, it is because we have thought it preferable to show our brethren how we regard their theology, after having endeavoured sincerely to assimilate its deep meaning, which does not always appear in formulae drawn up with a special view to forestalling objections.

[1] *Inst.* III, ii. 8.   [2] *Ibid.*, 8, 36.   [3] *Ibid.*

We may be told that the definitions given are calculated by their inexactitude to injure the prospects of reconciliation among Christians. We believe, on the contrary, that they will contribute to hasten it, because the real faith of Catholic believers is so similar to ours, formally, and so different from the definition of their present theology that they will finish, perhaps, by feeling that, after all, there may be something that requires reforming and by approximating to the ideas concerning Scripture of Pierre d'Ailly, Nicolas de Clemanges, and so many other ancient doctors whom M. Gilson knows so well, and often recalls with such felicity.

SOLI DEO GLORIA

INDEX OF PROPER NAMES

INDEX OF PROPER NAMES